THE SCOTT AND LAURIE OKI SERIES IN ASIAN AMERICAN STUDIES

*From a Three-Cornered World: New and Selected Poems*
by James Masao Mitsui

*Imprisoned Apart: The World War II Correspondence of an Issei Couple*
by Louis Fiset

*Storied Lives: Japanese American Students and World War II*
by Gary Okihiro

*Phoenix Eyes and Other Stories* by Russell Charles Leong

*Paper Bullets: A Fictional Autobiography* by Kip Fulbeck

*Born in Seattle: The Campaign for Japanese American Redress*
by Robert Sadamu Shimabukuro

*Confinement and Ethnicity: An Overview of World War II Japanese American Relocation Sites* by Jeffery F. Burton, Mary M. Farrell, Florence B. Lord, and Richard W. Lord

*Judgment without Trial: Japanese American Imprisonment during World War II*
by Tetsuden Kashima

*Shopping at Giant Foods: Chinese American Supermarkets in Northern California*
by Alfred Yee

*Altered Lives, Enduring Community: Japanese Americans Remember Their World War II Incarceration* by Stephen S. Fugita and Marilyn Fernandez

*Eat Everything Before You Die: A Chinaman in the Counterculture*
by Jeffery Paul Chan

*Form and Transformation in Asian American Literature*
edited by Zhou Xiaojing and Samina Najmi

*Language of the Geckos and Other Stories* by Gary Pak

*Nisei Memories: My Parents Talk about the War Years*
by Paul Howard Takemoto

*Growing Up Brown: Memoirs of a Bridge Generation Filipino American*
by Peter Jamero

*Letters from the 442nd: The World War II Correspondence of a Japanese American Medic* by Minoru Masuda; edited by Hana Masuda and Dianne Bridgman

*Shadows of a Fleeting World: Pictorial Photography and the Seattle Camera Club*
by David F. Martin and Nicolette Bromberg

*Signs of Home: The Paintings and Wartime Diary of Kamekichi Tokita*
by Barbara Johns and Kamekichi Tokita

*Nisei Soldiers Break Their Silence: Coming Home to Hood River*
by Linda Tamura

# NISEI SOLDIERS BREAK THEIR SILENCE

## COMING HOME TO HOOD RIVER

*Linda Tamura*

UNIVERSITY OF WASHINGTON PRESS
*Seattle and London*

This book is published with the assistance of a grant from the Scott and Laurie Oki Endowed Fund for publications in Asian American Studies.

© 2012 by the University of Washington Press

Design by Thomas Eykemans
17 16 15 14 13 12    5 4 3 2 1

UNIVERSITY OF WASHINGTON PRESS
PO Box 50096, Seattle, WA  98145, USA
*www.washington.edu/uwpress*

LIBRARY OF CONGRESS CATALOGING-IN-PUBLICATION DATA
Tamura, Linda, 1949–
Nisei soldiers break their silence : coming home to Hood River / Linda Tamura.
    p. cm.
Includes bibliographical references and index.
ISBN 978-0-295-99209-9 (pbk. : alk. paper)
1. World War, 1939–1945—Participation, Japanese American. 2. World War, 1939–1945—
Japanese Americans. 3. Japanese American soldiers—Oregon—Hood River—History—
20th century. 4. Japanese American soldiers—Oregon—Hood River—Biography.
5. Hood River (Or.)—Ethnic relations—History—20th century. I. Title.
D753.8.T36 2012        940.54'8173089956079561—dc23        2012011201

To the memories of Dad and Uncle Mam, whose
military service prompted my many questions,
and Mom, for her abiding faith.

This was not a proud chapter in the history of the Hood River valley. I know it's an agonizing chapter that some would just as soon not reopen. But a wound as deep as this one cannot heal if it is not appropriately treated. Today we get about that healing process with the best of our ability.

Congressman Greg Walden
*Memorial Day, 2011, Hood River, Oregon*

# CONTENTS

# PREFACE

O N the evening of November 29, 1944, residents of a small, rural community defaced a downtown memorial board that listed the names of 1,600 men and women who had served in the armed forces. By the next morning, sixteen names had been blotted out, dashed with black paint:

George Akiyama
Masaaki Asai
Taro Asai
Noboru Hamada
Kenjiro Hayakawa
Shigenobu Imai
Fred Mitsuo Kinoshita
George Kinoshita
Sagie Nishioka
Mamoru Noji
Henry K. Norimatsu
Katsumi Sato
Harry Osamu Takagi
Eichi Wakamatsu
Johnny Y. Wakamatsu
Bill Shyuichi Yamaki

Those young men were all American citizens, but they had one commonality: their parents were of Japanese descent. (The names of Sho Endow, Sumio Fukui, Frank Hachiya, Setsu Shitara, Fred Sumoge, Nob Takasumi, and Harry Tamura were not on the memorial board because they had registered for the draft outside Hood River. Isao Namba's name, mistaken for a Finnish name, remained.)

That act—and an inflamed campaign to discourage the return of these men and their families—placed the community at the center of a nationwide debate about the meaning of citizenship in this country.

This is the story of those men, their exploits during World War II, and their relationships to their community—my hometown.

# ACKNOWLEDGMENTS

THEY were reluctant to share their stories with a Sansei (third generation) who might put their words in print. But eventually they indulged me, and that made all the difference. I am indebted to each of the veterans who so willingly spoke with me, especially Uncle Mam Noji, George Akiyama, and Dad, the first three to participate. Members of their families (including spouses, siblings, and children) also assisted by telling of their family experiences and by helping to locate photos.

I am grateful to two who assisted in carrying out this project. Joan Yasui Emerson ably conducted eight interviews with local community members, even taking an oral history class from my mentor, Charlie Morrissey. And Tim Rooney volunteered to tape-record veterans' interviews and did so with such good nature that the lights and mikes seemed little distraction.

The resourcefulness and openness of Keith Doroski and Bud Collins of the Hood River American Legion added immensely to this project. Other locals who provided important information include Dallas Fridley, regional economist; Connie Nice, The History Museum, Hood River County; Melanee Gillette, Chamber of Commerce; and the late Dave Burkhart, former agriculture extension agent. The late Harry Inukai and Bessie Asai and Marie Asai helped me to collect local data, and Hiro Nishimura assisted in gathering materials about the Military Intelligence Service.

Other skilled resource experts include Gary Klein, Ford Schmidt, and Rich Schmidt, at the Mark O. Hatfield Library, and Dick Breen and Tim

Kelly, at the J. W. Long Law Library, all at Willamette University; Alice LaViolette, Oregon State Library; Gary Halvorson, Oregon State Archives; Kenneth Schlessinger, National Archives and Records Administration; Marie Masumoto, Toshiko McCallum, and Jane Nakasako, Hirasaki National Resource Center at the Japanese American National Museum; Kevin Flanagan, National American Legion Library; Mike Wells, Office of Policy and Planning, National Center for Veterans Analysis and Statistics, U.S. Department of Veterans Affairs; and the staffs at the Franklin D. Roosevelt Library, Department of the Army, the Public Library of Anniston–Calhoun County, and the Tualatin Public Library.

I greatly appreciated the critiques of scholars who read portions of my manuscript, including Roger Daniels, Art Hansen, Eric Muller, Ralph Falconeri, and Paul Spickard. At Willamette University, the early support of my deans, the late Larry Cress, Ken Nolley, and Carol Long, paved the way for my work. My writing group colleagues in the Graduate School of Education—Karen Hamlin, Steve Rhine, Hank Weddington, and Neil Liss—gave me invaluable feedback and questions about early drafts.

Special thanks goes to Willamette University for the Atkinson grants that helped to support my research. Many thanks to editors at the University of Washington Press who guided my book through its stages and gave me such helpful feedback: Beth Fuget, Marianne Keddington-Lang, Mary Ribesky, and Laura Iwasaki.

Most of all, I thank colleagues, friends, and family who invited me to tell about the veterans and who continue to honor them, for their stories must not be lost.

# ORAL HISTORY METHODOLOGY

THEY were quiet, modest men who were more comfortable puttering in their gardens than speaking into microphones. From others, I knew they had overcome tremendous difficulties—but those stories seemed locked in their minds. Might they be willing to bare their souls and help someone from another generation examine the legacy of Nisei (second generation) veterans? I had a few advantages. The mothers of three of them were among the people I had interviewed for my book on the Hood River Issei (first generation)—and all had seemed exuberant about their participation. Two were relatives: my father and my uncle, who admitted that they would talk about their military past only because I was their daughter and niece. So my initial goal was to make it safe—even invigorating—for the men to reflect on their past.

We began at my parents' home in Hood River. Three Nisei (my dad, Harry Tamura; my uncle, Mam Noji; and George Akiyama) sat on the living room sofa and even agreed to let a friend, Tim Rooney, videotape our interviews. (I'd met with each independently and secured their written agreements and survey information.) We began with collective questions about their lives as retirees and then moved to their early schooling, their parents, and World War II. They answered spontaneously; a response from one generally prompted elaboration from the others. (We all lunched on Mom's delicious chow mein afterward.) Two days later, I interviewed the trio at other venues: Panorama Point overlooking the valley orchards, where they spoke of their Issei parents' early labor and influence in their lives; Frank Hachiya's gravesite at Idlewilde Cemetery, where they spoke of his sacrifice and saluted him; and a valley orchard, where they immediately examined the trees and reminisced about life as farmers. After that, they were each willing to be interviewed one-on-one in their homes.

Later on, I audiotaped interviews with other Nisei veterans and then expanded to their siblings and finally to members of the mainstream Hood River community, hoping to gain as many viewpoints as possible. Making contact with two Nisei discipline barrack boys (imprisoned for insubordination) added a new dimension. After several phone conversations, I met each in Los Angeles for more extensive, face-to-face interviews. One of them, who had been very open on the phone, was hesitant about being tape-recorded, confiding, "I'm not a public person." Eventually he agreed because, he said, "You asked" and "I just want the story out."

Interviewing non-Nikkei residents brought its own challenges. My friend Joan Yasui Emerson graciously joined me, interviewing eleven locals. It became clear, however, that some who spoke with us were reluctant to uncover the full story; a few became evasive about or "forgot" details of their own involvement. Similar to Hood River Nisei, I developed my own internal radar for sensing people's reluctance, even misgivings, about conveying their feelings or discussing actions of the past. A stranger once approached me with a simple "I know who you are." There were definitely stories that were inaccessible to me, but I am indebted to those who were willing to share theirs.

Obtaining a range of oral history testimonies gave me access to candid, personal stories that led to a fuller examination of issues contributing to Hood River's story. This process required that I prepare fully in order to ask open-ended, neutral, objective questions that respected the integrity of each person while also examining different viewpoints. Such interviews led to often surprising access to documents and photos but also required further investigation in order to answer other questions or verify details, the reason I often cited several sources in my notes. (This included examining and cataloging citations from various newspapers, including the *Hood River News* and other local publications.) Ultimately, my goal was to examine all sides of an issue so that I could present a more balanced picture. When inserting quotations in the text, I did sometimes make minor editorial changes intended to clarify an interviewee's point (for example, replacing pronouns or adding assumed words) or to reduce redundancy.

I did my best to follow the Oral History Association's principles and best practices, striving to "retain the integrity of the narrator's perspective."

My most gratifying moments occurred when Nisei accompanied me to my speaking engagements, for they always received resounding accolades. Once, four Nisei heard their own voices depicted when four friends joined me to tell their story. Another time, my Uncle Mam acknowledged a standing ovation by continuing to videotape the crowd and then asking his own questions (on tape) when participants came to shake his hand.

At one event, two Sansei approached me separately, wondering, "How did you get Uncle —— to talk so much?" The uncle they knew typically spoke no more than five to six words at a time, they confided. Those comments underscored the purpose of this project—and how far we had come. Nisei veterans did willingly share their stories. Now I am fortunate to continue their telling.

# INTRODUCTION

I T was the fall of 1945, and the GIs were finally headed home. War weary
and eager to rejoin their families, they were nonetheless anxious about
how their former neighbors would receive them. During the four years
since they had been inducted into the U.S. Army, their hometown community had become a national spectacle, featured in newspaper and magazine
editorials across the country. Now citizens throughout the nation were
closely observing the soldiers' return.

George Akiyama had barely survived point-blank Nazi gunfire in France
and Italy and wore a uniform decorated with both the Silver and the Bronze
Star. On the way to his family's farm, he decided to get a haircut at a downtown barbershop he had patronized before the war. "I went up there and sat
in the barber chair," he recalled. "The barber comes up to me with a razor in
his hand and says, 'I ought to slit your throat.' I looked at him and said, 'Boy,
you're worse than some of those Germans we fought.' I just walked out."

Following six months of language study at the Military Intelligence Language School in Minnesota, Mamoru (or Mam, as his family and friends
called him) Noji had served in the South Pacific, translating military documents and interrogating prisoners of war. Shortly after he returned home,
a neighbor asked to purchase the family's eighty-acre farm. When Mam
explained that the family would then have no income, the single-minded
neighbor countered, "Well, you could move." No, replied Mam, leaving
was out of the question.

Both native sons, George Akiyama and Mam Noji were Nisei, children of Japanese immigrants, who had been born, raised, and educated in Hood River, Oregon, a hamlet community nestled along the Columbia River Gorge at the foot of Mount Hood. Near the turn of the century, their fathers were among the Issei, the immigrant Japanese, lured by the demand for cheap labor in the valley's fertile, forested terrain. Working as section hands on the railroad, clearing land for property owners, and working as mill hands, they contributed to the area's burgeoning development. Eventually, they settled in the pristine valley. Laboring ten hours a day, they cleared acres of fir, pine, and shrubs, transforming the area into thriving farmland that eventually bore strawberries, asparagus, and a good share of the valley's famed pears and apples. As they began to prosper and as their numbers increased, attacks from nativist groups and other farmers became more frequent. In 1920, a state report on the sentiment of Oregon communities toward Japanese residents pinpointed the "Japanese Question" in Oregon as "more acute in Hood River than in any other place in Oregon."[1] By 1930 the valley's Japanese population had grown to 514, second only to that of Oregon's Multnomah County (home of Portland).[2]

War brought the ultimate paradox. Five months after World War II began, the Akiyama and Noji families, like 108,000 other Nikkei, or people of Japanese descent,[3] were forced to abandon their West Coast homes, properties, and businesses while their sons, including George and Mam, served in the U.S. armed services. After President Franklin D. Roosevelt signed Executive Order 9066 in 1942, *all* West Coast Nikkei, even those who were American citizens, were confined to government-run concentration camps in desolate parts of the country.[4] It was not until the spring of 1945, three years later, that their families were finally able to return home.

Yet the Hood River Nikkei were still unwelcome in their Pacific Northwest hometown. Full-page newspaper ads, signed by hundreds of community residents, warned "So Sorry Please! Japs Are Not Wanted in Hood River." Leaders of a local veterans' group proposed a constitutional amendment to deprive Akiyama, Noji, and other Nisei of their American citizenship. A year before they returned home, in a move that brought nationwide condemnation to their hometown, residents removed the names of sixteen servicemen from the community honor roll that listed locals serving in the military. The names of Akiyama and Noji were blotted out along with those of fourteen other Japanese Americans.[5] Newspaper editors and columnists across the country criticized the action as exclusionist: "Tops in blind hatred . . . an all-American low in intolerance and bigotry," *Colliers* commented; *The Defender*, an army newspaper, stated, "We cannot forgive them, because they indeed know what they do"; and the *New York PM* gave Hood River the "Award for Most Contemptible Deed of the Year."[6] U.S. military commanders, GIs, and even federal officials weighed in against the community of 11,500,[7] inflaming debate among citizens in the valley and across the country.

Still, despite the national furor and their own private fears about their hometown reception, Akiyama and Noji were among the 40 percent of Japanese Americans who chose to return to the valley. This was their home, where they had been raised and schooled. Here were their families' properties, where their parents had invested raw muscle power in transforming marshland and stump-covered hills into fledgling farms whose seedlings had finally borne fruit. Some felt they had no choice but to resettle, for their livelihood was rooted in this valley. Yet there were raw emotions and lingering doubts. "It hurts," mused Noji. "Your feelings for friends turn upside down. You could see it in their faces."

This is the story of those young men who served their country yet were unwelcome in their hometown. The story is difficult to tell, since many veterans' families still reside in the community. Some might ask: Why bring up the past? This modern-day mecca of windsurfing, winter sports, and upscale tourism is physically and culturally unlike the war-entangled farming community of the 1940s. Newcomers and younger residents are largely unaware of their valley's once sordid reputation. And most locals, both Nikkei and non-Nikkei old-timers, would prefer not to dredge up their community's tainted past. As one Nisei veteran observed, "You don't want to admit everything that's bad because otherwise it'd be all bad." For many of the now elderly (and few remaining) Nisei, reliving those memories would be an excursion into shame, peeling back the patches of self-respect and dignity they have worked hard to restore. Preferring to exorcise this historical blight from their memories and move on, they are understandably reluctant to disturb the fragile skin over those wounds and to stir up repressed memories of their postwar return. It's simpler to avoid reliving the past, the contradictions, the questions—even their World War II service. As one local Nikkei explained, "The silence here about the war years has been deafening."

Yet the past is irrefutable. Actions in the valley grew to symbolize an exclusionist and unpatriotic image of the place, becoming grist for debate among citizens across the country. After a local Nisei died during a precarious mission in the South Pacific, sentiments intensified, prompting local and national repercussions. Remnants of that blight still linger—yet little has been told. This book is about the men at the center of this controversy and their evolution from farm kids to young adults forced to rebuild their lives, economically and socially, and make peace with their hometown. One became the first to challenge the state's civil service system when he was denied a position because of race. Two spent forty years challenging courts-martial, convictions, and imprisonment. This book addresses festering questions: What led to eruptions of hostility in the community that bore life consequences for these Nisei? What memories and reflections illuminate those situations? What should we learn from the past that can enlighten our future?

The voices of these soldiers, their families, and members of the mainstream white community depicted in this book are based on more than one hundred oral history interviews as well as correspondence and family and archival documents. Sources include five hundred letters and documents uncovered from files of the local American Legion post, which led the anti-Japanese campaign during the pre- and postwar years. Also prominent is the little known case of dishonorably discharged GIs who had been sequestered under armed guard during President Roosevelt's visit to their base camp.

This study addresses a gap in scholarly research on the resettlement of Japanese Americans after World War II. Historian Arthur A. Hansen maintains that this period has been "relegated to the margins of scholarly literature and popular memory" and that this neglect promotes the false concept of a "model minority" who instantly metamorphosed after the war.[8] Brian Niiya has recognized the lack of a definitive study on resettlement.[9] Tetsuden Kashima has challenged Japanese Americans' collective "social amnesia" regarding this "crisis period," culminating in shame and suppression of the wartime experience.[10] Though Hood River is commonly referenced in the annals of Japanese American history as a disgraceful wartime example, resources are isolated and limited. And little is devoted to the returning GIs. If these stories are to be preserved, they must be told now.

Among those Hood River veterans (seventeen from the honor roll and seven who were unlisted), only four were alive in 2011. Sadly, this generation of now elderly citizens is slipping away. In 2012, with fewer than 1.5

million World War II veterans alive, the Department of Veteran Affairs noted that 680 were expected to pass away each day.[11]

This, then, is the untold journey of these largely unheralded veterans. Embedded in a past in which fear, mistrust, and sheer economics overtook a community's ethics and commitment to civil rights, it also raises questions about the parallel challenges we face today as well as the actions we should take to resolve them.

Local Nisei Bessie Asai reminisced about those difficult times: "We can forgive but it's hard to forget." It is in remembering that we can learn from—and act to correct—mistakes from the past.

# NISEI SOLDIERS
# BREAK THEIR SILENCE

PART I

# EARLY YEARS

ONE

## *"Growing Up in Two Worlds"*

# BALANCING JAPANESE AMERICA

**W**E hoed berries before we went to school. When we came back from school, we hoed berries 'til dark. . . . That was our life," explained Harry Tamura. As farm kids who were the children of immigrants, Japanese American veterans in Oregon's Hood River valley grew up immersed in the robust work ethic of settlement farmers surviving in a new land. Their parents, struggling to eke out livings and support their families on small parcels of farmland, depended on their children's extra hands to manage the burgeoning farm chores. For Japanese American sons and daughters of all ages, work was necessary and expected.

So fathers, mothers, sons, and daughters worked together on their family farms, scattered among fertile, volcanic bluffs along the eastern slope of the Cascade Range, sixty-six miles east of Portland. Their secluded valley, just ten miles wide and twenty-six miles long, nestled at the base of snowcapped Mount Hood to the south and extended northward to where rugged, basaltic columns one thousand to three thousand feet tall met the wind-whipped waters of the Columbia River. The stream called Hood River brought glacial water from the mountain, dividing the valley into what locals dubbed the East and West Sides.[1] A river town formed at the nexus of its namesake and the Columbia River, served by river steamers and the Oregon Railroad. By the 1920s, the town had become a thriving business center, with two banks, three hotels, a railroad depot, a Carnegie library, six churches, telephone and electric service, a paid fire department, and fruit warehouses for its three thousand residents and valley farmers. In rural areas where most Japanese families lived, travel was cumbersome, and residents relied on services in their own small settlements, each with its own store, church, school, and often post office.[2] From the 1920s, the lives of the future veterans were confined largely to farms in those separate locales: Oak Grove, Frankton, and Barrett to the west; Dee to the southwest; Odell, Mount Hood, and Parkdale to the south; and Pine Grove to the east.

"When we were small, we didn't do much [work]," recalled George Aki-yama, the eldest of five Nisei whose family lived on an Oak Grove bluff west of town. "But when we were going to high school, our parents were just *waiting* for spring vacation!" Springtime meant hoeing strawberry plants, thinning clusters of young Bartlett and Anjou pears, or spading rills in the soil, allowing irrigation water to reach plants at the ends of rows. Through summer, Nikkei family members cut and packed bundles of asparagus spears, picked strawberries, and continued to irrigate family crops. In the fall, as young seedlings bore fruit, the family picked, sorted, and packed apples and pears. During the winter, they pruned the limbs of overgrown fruit trees, then picked up and burned the excess "brush."

## ISSEI FAMILY FOUNDATIONS

Their immigrant parents, the Issei, were Japanese nationals who had arrived in the United States near the turn of the twentieth century. Most intended to work on the West Coast only until they could earn enough money to buy land in Japan and secure their lives in their native country. Lured by exaggerated "get rich quick" myths, Issei males were intent on earning money quickly, and most expected to return to Japan as wealthy men within three to five years. First solicited as laborers for jobs that locals avoided, young Issei men drove heavy steel spikes in railroad ties; they also felled trees and used dynamite to clear heavy stands of conifers for landowners. Sometimes they received plots of stumpland or brushland scattered around the Hood River valley in exchange for their labor. Often they saved their meager earnings to purchase marginal land covered with stumps, brush, or swamp. Intent on maximizing the use of their land, they grew strawberries, cane berries, and asparagus as quick cash crops between their newly planted apple and pear seedlings. During those early years, some also took on second jobs or leased property from others.[3]

Picturesque Hood River valley gained national attention for its award-winning apples and for a heated controversy involving its Japanese American World War II veterans. (The History Museum, Hood River, 1948)

Eventually Issei realized that, in order to achieve financial success, they would need to work longer in the United States. So the middle-aged men married, adhering to traditional Japanese values that emphasized family unit and lineage. Those who could afford the expense returned to Japan to seek wives. Most chose a more economical route: arranging picture bride marriages by exchanging letters and photos with young women in Japan.

Destitute Issei newlyweds lived in hovels and worked exhaustively each day. George Akiyama explained that his father "cleared land for the orchards, pulled out those trees with stump pullers with a team of horses, blew out the trunks with dynamite, picked up all the roots, plowed and got the land ready for planting trees. While the trees were young, he raised asparagus. They had to have some income to keep them going." His mother, as a new bride, worked alongside her husband on the farm. Every hand was needed to eke out a living.

## FARM KIDS AND FAMILY VALUES

Not surprisingly, the second generation, the Nisei, grew up with orchards, fields, and barns as their playgrounds, while their mothers and older siblings worked nearby. As toddlers, Nisei climbed apple trees, played tag in the fields, and roasted volunteer potatoes [unplanted potatoes from reseeded plants] in the hot embers of bonfires for burning brush. When they grew older, Nisei children joined the family workforce. Shig Imai, the eldest of five sons, whose family farmed in Dee, lived eleven miles southwest of town. "Every time we had a minute," he recalled, "we had to work on the farm, besides going to school."

For immigrant families of all ethnicities, survival in a foreign land demanded cooperation and selflessness from every member, young and old. John Bodnar's book on immigrant history describes the need for immigrant parents and children to work together, share scant resources, and mute personal needs and wants in order to help their families achieve even a modest standard of living. Simply put, the family's welfare took priority over individual interests. (Bodnar did note that, unlike Issei women, the wives of Irish, Italian, and Greek immigrants did not work outside the home.)[4]

For young Sagie Nishioka, the eldest of three Nisei raised in Dee, those family responsibilities were overwhelming. After his father died when he was fourteen years old, Nishioka became head of the family for his mother and two young siblings. "Those were the days we had to do hard work," he explained. "The hours were ten hours for a regular day. . . . We rented about ten acres for strawberries and seven acres just for pears and cherries. . . . I had to drive the horses to cultivate. We didn't have very much money, so we weren't able to buy a lot of machinery." Work and family survival took precedence over school. "A lot of times I couldn't do homework because I was either too tired or had other things to do. Too many hours I was working, plus going to school. Because of this overload, I got sick."

Shouldering such heavy family burdens, young Sagie rose at five in the morning to do his chores. After school, he returned to the family's strawberry fields until seven or eight at night. Only then did he manage to tackle his homework. He was thankful that an understanding teacher recognized the symptoms of overwork and often sent him home to rest.

As newcomers in an alien society, Issei raised their children according to the lifestyle they knew best: the customs, diet, values, and language of Japan. Nisei learned to manipulate grains of rice and pickled vegetables with their chopsticks; chant *gochiso-sama* (the food/drink was very tasty) after meals; mold rice cakes filled with sweet beans for New Year's Day; and chide one another using parental cautions such as *da-me* (don't). With Hood River's undulating terrain and poor country roads, Nikkei families, who lived far apart, rarely socialized during slack times on their farms. Bound by common language and customs, Nikkei families still gathered for New Year feasts at one another's homes and, after the 1920s, met for parties and games at Japanese community centers in downtown Hood River and in Dee.

Japanese families in the United States were influenced by Japan's Meiji era (1868–1912). After the arrival of Commodore Matthew Perry in 1853 forced Japan to open to the West and the Tokugawa shogunate was overthrown in 1868, Emperor Meiji's regime initiated a period of modernization. Japan began adapting Western models as it revamped its government, economy, legal system, communication and transportation networks, schooling, and military. By the early twentieth century, the small island country had emerged as the foremost Asian military power. It financed this rapid industrialization and military expansion, however, by levying heavy taxes on Japanese farmers, who were already burdened by poor harvests, low prices, and a strained economy. Most immigrants, including those from Hood River, came from southwestern Japan,[5] where the population was growing, farms were already smaller per capita, and residents (considered to be of pirate and warrior stock) were viewed as "venturesome and enterprising."[6]

Immigrants were buoyed by promising advertisements from emigration companies and encouraged by their own government. Many were younger sons whose elder brothers would inherit the family names and properties, others were elder sons determined to pay off family debts, and some were eager to avoid the military draft instituted in 1889. The majority of Hood River Nikkei families came from these farm families, beset by their country's economic and social pressures.[7] And it was due to Issei investment in farming and the growth of their American-born children that they would stay in this country.

Norms that were prominent in Meiji Japan had roots in the country's long-standing feudal system and included both Confucian and Buddhist influences. The "family" (*ie*) was central to Japanese society. Both the family and Japanese society in general were organized around a hierarchical structure. Status in society was based on a clear class system and prescribed roles imbued with a deep sense of duty to one's superiors; the husband and eldest son ranked at the top of the family hierarchy; family status was based on age and gender; and family members supported one another by emphasizing duty and obligation. Sociologist Harry Kitano observed that Issei were able to adapt more readily to their low status as immigrants in the United States because they had become accustomed to those roles in Japan. Therefore they easily transferred the deferential and compliant behaviors they had practiced in Japan to their relationships with America's "white man," or *hakujin*.[8]

From their Issei parents, Nisei also learned the value of *enryo*, or practicing deference, reserve, and restraint in everyday behavior. They demonstrated this quality by turning down second helpings, even when they were still hungry, or by accepting a less desirable item, knowing someone else preferred the one they wanted. It appeared when they turned down offers of help or hesitated to impose on others, speak out, or ask questions. Nisei recognized the impact of "obligation" (*on*), feeling a duty to repay favors and gifts from friends, acquaintances, and family members. Heeding their parents' admonitions that the group's welfare took precedence over their own, Nisei learned to subordinate their wishes to those of siblings or friends. They learned how to avoid confrontation by keeping a low profile, staying in the background, and avoiding eye contact. They also acknowledged the value of a strong work ethic, especially one involving physical effort. In their new "culture of everyday life," Nisei grew up learning typical Japanese behaviors by watching their parents, who modeled conformity, obedience, duty, reserve, and work.[9]

## STRADDLING TWO CULTURES

Yet, while becoming familiar with the culture of their parents, Nisei were also citizens of the United States of America. As they grew older, they found themselves in an awkward position, as if each straddled the Pacific Ocean, with one foot planted in Japan and the other entrenched in American soil. "We had to grow up more or less in two worlds," explained Shig Imai's younger brother Hit (Hitoshi). "Our parents had their ways and we had our ways." Affirming Nisei upbringing in two societies, sociologist Thomas D. Murphy noted that much of what the Nisei learned in one society they were expected to forget or disregard in the other.[10] These "ways" of the Nisei were not unique, for they could be likened to those of other second-generation Americans, according to Marcus Lee Hansen, the Norwegian American historian considered the father of immigration history. Acting on their standing as American citizens, the children of immigrants tended to reject their parents' heritage in favor of newly learned American traditions, in effect, becoming marginal in both societies.[11]

For Nisei, language became the most obvious challenge, apparent from the first day of school. "When I started first grade, I'm sure the only English words I knew were 'hello' and 'good-bye,'" recalled Mam Noji, the eldest of four siblings. His family and three others shared a cramped home in Parkdale, fourteen miles south of town, in the direction of Mount Hood, until the Nojis moved to the second floor of their new barn. Few working Issei parents, including the Nojis, had the time or opportunity to learn English. As a result, families spoke Japanese almost exclusively at home. Even as Nisei learned English at school and from white classmates, they were limited to speaking Japanese when conversing with their parents. As Hit Imai rationalized, "Anytime I spoke English to my parents, they figured I was talking something bad."

Younger Nisei, following in the footsteps of older siblings, often found that their transition to school was easier. Harry Tamura's older brother, George, explained, "My folks were pretty strict about speaking Japanese at home. Dad said, 'When you're at home, you speak Japanese. When you go outside, speak American because you're in America.' But when I went to school in the first grade, all I could speak was Japanese. I flunked because I couldn't speak. Dad and Mom were so embarrassed . . . but they understood why." Since Tamura's father had studied English in Portland, he tutored his son. "We started with ABCs and worked our way up. After that, I didn't have any trouble." Brother Harry and two younger siblings benefited from George's lessons.

Most Hood River Issei were literate, and many had completed more than the six years of education mandatory in Japan after 1908. They valued education and citizenship as ways of helping their children to succeed and overcome discrimination, encouraging Nisei to "listen to the instructors carefully," "do whatever the teacher [says]," and "study hard so [you will] not get behind."

At school, however, other cultural differences became apparent. During the early years, Santa ignored the homes of Nikkei children, who also received Valentines from classmates but did not give any themselves.[12] At school, Nisei noticed that their white peers were already familiar with nursery rhymes read by their teachers. Classmates talked animatedly about visiting their grandmothers and grandfathers, concepts unfamiliar to Nisei, for the o-baachan and o-jiichan their parents spoke of were merely strangers in distant Japan. Then, too, their parents, hampered by the language barrier, rarely attended school meetings and joined them only for special exhibits of their artwork or writing.

Yet, as Nisei began to notice differences between their families' ethnic traditions and those of their white peers, shame, embarrassment, and even defiance often emerged. For some, it was easy to blame those differences on not being white. "I think we were kind of ashamed of being Japanese," admitted George Akiyama's younger brother Sab (Saburo). "During Depression years, you know, we couldn't afford to buy bread, so my mother used to make rice balls for lunch. Kids teased us about eating fish eggs and rice. We used to tell them they would be poisoned, and we used to take rice balls and chase them! I'd think as a youngster, 'I wish I were white!' You know, so I could be like the other kids." Traditional American celebrations became illuminating lessons in American culture. "Neighbor kids had birthday parties. The first birthday party I was invited to when I was in about the sixth grade, I couldn't believe it. Ice cream! At home we used to have ice cream maybe once a year on the Fourth of July!"

Nisei spoke hesitantly about feeling shame. "We were kind of embarrassed because the parents couldn't understand English so they didn't participate in those school meetings," explained George Akiyama. "That made us feel bad. . . . It was kind of hard for them to mingle because they couldn't speak." In *Made in Japan and Settled in Oregon*, her book about growing up in Hood River, Mitzi Asai Loftus also recalled feeling shame because of her parents' lack of English skills. She whispered to her mother in stores, hoping her mother would whisper back rather than speak Japanese aloud. When her parents spoke their native language in public, her embarrassed sister hid.[13] Historian Paul Spickard theorized that, even more than wanting to be white, Nisei simply "wanted to be accepted by Whites as Americans."[14]

Issei, recognizing the widening cultural chasm between their children and themselves, viewed language as a way to bridge the gap. Characterized by a system of honorifics, Japanese language (*nihongo*) uses different forms based on the status and role of speakers, such as whether the speaker is a man or a woman, an adult or a child, of higher or lower status.[15] Issei insisted that their children attend Japanese language schools. Masuo Yasui, spokesman for the Issei, met with the county school superintendent to explain that learning Japanese would help children grow to "know and understand the two countries and work to bring two countries closer."[16] "Most of us attended some Japanese school," explained Mam Noji. "The parents didn't want us to lose Japanese tradition and knowledge and culture altogether. . . . After public school, we must've gone three days out of the regular school days. And maybe on Saturdays." But the youngsters did not attend of their own accord, Noji confessed. "Most of us Nisei went to Japanese school to please our parents."

Engaged in a gentle tug-of-war, Nisei complied with their parents' demands, though often unwillingly, and frequently found excuses to speak English behind their teachers' backs in Japanese school. They also noticed that the extra demands of language school and farmwork cut short their time for the play and social activities that many of their white classmates seemed to enjoy. "I had to go to damn Japanese school in evenings, Saturdays, then work from daylight to dark," recalled Shig Imai. "I came up the hard way, different than carefree kids who were Caucasians." For most immigrant families, in fact, the contributions of their working-age children (from about age fourteen) finally tipped the scale in their favor as they sought to achieve economic survival, according to Bodnar.[17]

Imai was also a Kibei, a Nisei who grew up in Japan, having been sent there to live with his parents' families and attend Japanese schools, eventually returning to the United States. Issei considered it a privilege for a child to be reared by the head of the family and educated in Japanese culture. The practice had an additional benefit: it freed young mothers to work alongside their husbands. (Some ten thousand Kibei resided in the United States by World War II.)[18] Imai had lived with his grandparents in Japan for three years and then, at almost ten years of age, returned to Oregon with a visiting uncle. "I had to learn English all over again," he remembered, "because I was about three years behind."

The Junkichi Hachiyas, another Hood River family, left the valley for Japan soon after they inherited property near Okayama. Sixteen-year-old Frank was a bold and independent Nisei who often got into scrapes with white neighbors and kept his grade-school classmates in stitches by crawling on the floor and clowning around. In his parents' homeland, he developed a renewed appreciation for his birthplace. "Now I don't mean I don't like Japan," he wrote to a former teacher, "but I will never get so that I like her as well as America." Admitting his emotional birthright as an American, he continued, "I read where some people stated that they did not fully appreciate their country until they traveled abroad. And I, too, after living across the sea, realize it now." Hachiya became discouraged when his English-language skills deteriorated while he was attending a private Japanese high school. "It was hard for me to keep up a conversation. The words just didn't seem to come out," After four years, Hachiya convinced his parents to let him come home to Hood River when his father returned to follow the fruit harvest as a migrant worker. He lived with a former neighbor and eventually graduated from Odell High School.[19] Born in the United States and educated in Japan, Kibei found themselves compromised in both countries, where their language and social habits set them apart.

Increasingly at odds with their parents, Nisei (including the returning Kibei) displayed a "disconnect between issei and nisei," as characterized by historian Franklin Odo, and by becoming "strangers" to their parents, according to scholar Eileen Tamura.[20] They revealed this clash by rebelling. Adolescent Nisei rejected everything (except food) that marked them as Japanese, observed minister and scholar Daisuke Kitagawa. In fact, he maintained, in order to be respected by their Nisei peers, they had to be rebellious.[21] Of his upbringing, Hit Imai remembered, "When we went to school, from grade school on, we were taught to be American citizens and do everything the American way. But the parents were born in Japan and they've got other values, Japan-style. So a lot of times, while parents are

Frank Hachiya was an independent and precocious child, pictured here (back row, second from left) with his classmates and teacher Miss Smith at Odell Grade School. Hachiya's actions during the war would bring him recognition across the country, including mention in a *New York Times* editorial. (Bessie Asai, c. 1931)

trying to teach you, if you were more American then, you aren't gonna follow their footsteps."

Japanese dependence and mutual responsibility within the family and group often went head-to-head with American ideals of independence and autonomy. In those cases, Issei commonly chastised their offspring for what they viewed as impolite or rude antics while Nisei rolled their eyes at their parents' restrictive and old-fashioned behavior. Issei who had stronger ties with their homeland taught more stringent Japanese customs. Others recognized that they were now rooted in this country, where their farms were beginning to flourish and their children were citizens. Those Issei promoted American life and values that would enable their children to succeed. Older Nisei family members tended to speak more fluent Japanese and were more familiar with Japanese traditions, while younger Nisei were more likely to adopt American middle-class norms.[22] Hit Imai, a younger son, reflected, "As you grew older and older, . . . you're gonna follow your own footsteps, being American."

By now, Issei had come to realize that returning to Japan to live was improbable. "They had sunk the roots in so deep here," explained Mam Noji, "especially when they brought the women over and had children and family." Recognizing barriers of race and poverty in the United States and the effects of shame on Nisei, Issei parents sacrificed their own needs "for the children's welfare" (*kodomo no tame ni*). They often denied themselves fashionable clothes or modern conveniences so that their children could be neatly attired and might be less vulnerable to discrimination.[23] "Every day they sacrificed," George Akiyama reminisced. "Work every Sunday, long hours every day. They didn't hardly go anyplace. My mom came home to cook after work, then she had to work afterward. She didn't even have time to relax." Harry Tamura recalled how his parents took smaller portions of food so that their three growing sons and daughter would have plenty to eat. In a realistic moment, Mam Noji admitted that though his parents willingly neglected satisfying their own personal needs, "they didn't have much to give us." Their altruism, however, contributed to an unspoken sense of *on*, the idea that children would repay their parents and contribute toward their happiness.[24] Achieving success, and thereby bringing honor to the family, was the ultimate goal.

Their parents' traditional lessons made an impact, according to Nisei veterans. "Our parents were good teachers," remarked Noji. "Their cultural background weighed heavily on us." George Akiyama conveyed this by explaining a Japanese norm. "One word they all went by was *gaman*, 'perseverance.' Just don't complain too much and just do it. . . . They want[ed] their kids to go to school, do their best. They always [said], 'Do your best and do what's good for your country.'" There were practical applications. "Like my dad used to say, 'If you're gonna be a ditch digger, be the best digger out there.' That's the attitude." His mother's and father's teachings impressed younger brother Sab. "The parents always used to instill the idea that you gotta excel, you gotta do a little better than your friends. . . . We were kind of underdogs, so to speak."

By the 1930s, Nikkei composed 6 percent (514), the highest proportion it would reach, of Hood River County's population of 8,938, with a total of 50 Indians, Mexicans, and Chinese rounding out the minority population.[25] Still, Nisei remembered being accepted by peers during their school years. "I think we were pretty much accepted as fellow students. Most Nisei were good kids on the whole. I think teachers appreciated that we were trying," reflected Noji. "We were good representatives of our people, I would say." Noji, in fact, was elected president of his student body at Parkdale High School.

Likewise, white peers recalled the camaraderie and academic records of their Nisei classmates. "In grade school there were only one or two Japanese in our school," recalled Athalie Lage, community volunteer and widow of a former state legislator. "But then when we went to junior high and high school, we met a lot of them. They were always the leaders in the class because they worked for their grades and they did well. . . . They fit in. They were just like the rest of us." By 1940 a higher percentage of Nisei men on the West Coast completed high school than did their white peers.[26]

"There was no animosity at all," recalled Bob Nunamaker, a retired fruit grower. "Basically, Japanese were well accepted. . . . We played baseball together." Local newspaper columnist and school cook Jane Franz Rice held a view about her peers that purged color and culture. "We were very loving people, even at a young age. We knew no difference in whether we were going to school with totally white kids or Japanese kids. They did not know that they were Japanese; they thought that they were part of us."

Nisei youth did recognize differences, however. Working on their family farms, attending Japanese school, and joining their families for ethnic get-togethers consumed their lives, leaving little time for socializing with white classmates. Nisei were straddling Japanese and American cultures, seeking their own balance. As they grew older, they also discovered that hard work and good intentions were not automatic tickets to acculturation in this country, where their race and prosperity would become obstacles.

# TWO

# "Nice People So Long as They Are in a Minority"

## THE JAPANESE AMERICAN COMMUNITY IN HOOD RIVER

ssei were welcomed on the West Coast when they first arrived in the late 1800s. The Chinese Exclusion Act of 1882, and later the Alaska gold rush, had drained the Pacific Northwest labor force. In 1884, after the Japanese government, plagued with economic problems, allowed its working class to seek jobs outside the country and emigrate to the United States, American employers viewed Issei as a source of cheap labor. Willing to accept less desirable jobs for lower wages than others received (because those salaries were twice their paltry earnings in Japan), Issei found jobs working on railroads and farms and in lumberyards, sawmills, and canneries. By 1910, more than seventy-two thousand Issei had arrived in the United States, with three-fifths residing in California, one-fifth in Washington, and one-twentieth in Oregon, which did not have a port city for Japanese ships.[1]

Issei, who first took jobs as section hands on railroads, made up 40 percent of Oregon's railroad laborers by 1907. They were drawn to agricultural work because of the higher wages, and by 1909 more than one-fourth were working as farm laborers. Seasonal migrants at first, some invested their earnings and advanced from laborers to sharecroppers, leaseholders, and farm owners. They established farming communities in the Montavilla and Gresham-Troutdale areas near Portland, at Lake Labish north of Salem, and at Hood River.[2]

Oregon's Hood River valley, an undeveloped area isolated by the basaltic bluffs and rough terrain of the Columbia River gorge, would become one of the state's largest settlements of Issei. Its river, called "Waucoma" for its cottonwood trees by the Upper Chinook tribe who lived on the area's plentiful fish, wildlife, herbs, and roots, acquired other names: Labeasche, from Lewis and Clark, and Dog River, after starving settlers survived on dog meat in the 1840s. The area became dependent on logging, cattle, hogs, and subsistence farming in the 1870s. Before the turn of the century, small sawmills began processing the stately yellow pines that covered the valley floor. Without logging roads or a river deep enough to float logs downstream, however, mills had to operate close to the felled logs. The Oregon Lumber Company's solution was to build a railway from Hood River to its mill and timberlands at Dee.[3]

When Issei laborers arrived shortly after 1900 to lay the Mount Hood Railroad's spur line, they were enchanted by the valley's scenic wonders. With snowcapped Mount Hood towering above them to the south and Mount Adams rising in the north, Hood River offered nostalgic reminders of rural Japan. The valley, fertile from volcanic ash, was also gaining a national reputation for its apples after winning sixteen awards at the 1893 World's Columbian Exposition and the 1900 World's Fair in Chicago and dominating the apple competition at Portland's 1905 Lewis and Clark Exposition.[4]

The Commercial Club of Hood River touted the valley's growing reputation, beckoning newcomers to "The University of Apple Culture," where three-fourths of the tillable land was undeveloped and natural conditions of soil, temperature, and climate were "well-nigh perfect" for growing fruit. A 1910 booklet calculated the average price of land at $150 per acre and estimated there would be profits in the sixth year, with owner costs of $400 per acre until then. It projected the value of orchards (which averaged sixteen acres) at $3,000 per acre by the tenth year and maintained that this picturesque and thriving resort town connected by rail and water should appeal to business investors, too, with its abundant pure water, light, heat, and power as well as telephone and mail service. The booklet promised a community of "people accustomed to culture, refinement and education," with schools, churches, and clubs, including a University Club of 135 members.[5]

Young Easterners, including Ivy League graduates, became enthralled by this promising western enterprise. They had the financial means but little or no farming know-how.[6] This presented an opportunity for Issei after they completed their railroad contracts, for they hired on easily as farm laborers. Most Japanese immigrants had farming experience and a healthy respect for agricultural work, since farmers were more highly regarded than trade or industry workers in Japan. By 1910, Hood River had the largest population of Oregon Japanese (468) outside Portland.[7] Local resident Athalie Lage remembered Issei apple pickers who worked and lived each fall on the Pooley farm. She saw Issei men outside the bathhouse on Saturday evenings, "in line with their brushes and their soap, ready to go in and take their turn." Eventually, Issei workers lived upstairs in her family's tenant house. "They were friendly, very clean, very nice people and tended to their own business. . . . Many of them came back year after year. They always brought Nabisco wafers, or other candy. . . . Just men and no women. . . . They had an interpreter . . . I remember them singing now and then. . . . They worked long hours, and when they were through working, they were gone."

The demand for Issei labor (and the incentives offered to them for accepting employment) actually became a driving force for Issei settlement in the Hood River valley. That pressure also made them distinctly susceptible to exclusionist threats. Some private landowners, eager to clear the densely forested valley basin and fertile volcanic bluffs, offered Issei five-acre plots of stumpland or brushland for clearing fifteen acres.[8] (This followed a gesture in the late 1800s by Nathaniel and Mary Coe, the first permanent settlers, who offered free land to settlers who would build businesses in town.)[9] The work was physically demanding and so dangerous that others shunned it. Saving their meager earnings, Issei gradually acquired acreage and became landowners without expending capital. Instead of being situated in colonies adjacent to Japanese neighbors as was typical in California and Portland,[10] their farms became interspersed among those owned by white landowners throughout the rugged, forested valley.

Issei women became crucial to the development of permanent communities. Though men had arrived as sojourners intent on earning money and returning to their native Japan, the grim realities of their arduous physical labor and low wages made financial security a distant dream. The aging men also wished to marry, since continuing the family name by producing successors was important in Japanese culture. Then, too, the Gentlemen's

Agreement of 1907–8, forged between the United States and Japan, had severely restricted Japanese immigration. Passports were granted only to laborers returning to the United States and to their wives, children, and parents. Picture bride marriages, based on an exchange of photos and letters and stipulating rigid standards for men's wages and savings, appealed to Issei bachelors and immediately flourished in this country. It is likely that more than half the married women who arrived between 1910 and 1920 were picture brides.[11] While women composed just 14 percent of the Issei population in 1910, ten years later, they constituted 35 percent of the total. During those years in Oregon, the population of Issei women increased fivefold to more than 1,300. By 1920, the Hood River Issei population was more closely balanced, with a ratio of three women to four men.[12]

Women did question their decisions to come to this new land. Mam Noji's mother, Asayo, confessed that when she entered a rustic hovel, the smallest house she had ever seen, "I felt like crying." The woodstove, raised bedsprings, and outside bath and toilet were equally strange. "There was nothing I liked about America," she lamented. As a newcomer, she would need to learn quickly. Her husband taught her to cook and sew, and she performed laundry and housekeeping chores for a neighboring family while also working on the family farm. To save money, the couple shared a home with three other families until the Nojis and their four children moved to the top of their new barn.[13] As is typical of all struggling immigrant families, they cooperated with one another to meet everyday needs.

"For a woman in those days, there was no Sunday!" exclaimed Sho Endow's mother, Tei Endow. "I made breakfast, cleaned the house, washed by hand, and still had to weed strawberries." Wives worked ten to fourteen hours a day with their husbands, then returned home to domestic chores.[14] "They were working harder than the men," insisted George Akiyama. Faced with the economic realities of immigrant life in America, Issei women adopted gender roles different from those that were customary in Japan: wives, mothers, homemakers, and laborers.

## AN IMPROVING ECONOMIC PICTURE

Struggling Issei farmers lived frugally, saved scrupulously, worked long hours, and used enterprising strategies and mutual support systems. They earned incomes while their apple seedlings matured by experimenting with strawberries, cane berries, and asparagus planted between rows as

"There was no Sunday!" exclaimed Sho Endow's mother, Tei Endow. She joined her husband in the strawberry field in addition to handling household and child-rearing chores. (Aya Endow)

quick cash crops. Issei shared farm equipment and formed a farmers' association in 1914, which studied current reports on farming practices and met with representatives of the local growers' cooperative. By 1920, three-fourths of Hood River's 351 Issei, the third-largest population of Japanese in the state, had become farmers. Each earned an average annual income of $1,200. Seventy owned a total of 1,200 acres, part in timber, an average of 17 acres per farm, and they leased an additional 850 acres. In fact, they owned more than half the 2,185 acres owned by Issei in Oregon, and their parcels were larger. By this time, valley Issei cultivated 75 percent of the valley's strawberries and shipped fifty thousand crates of asparagus.[15]

After World War I, three factors favoring the Issei also added to acrimony in the valley. First, strawberry prices had risen, rapidly improving Japanese farmers' economic situations. Second, able to purchase more property, they started building homes and diversified by planting pears. Third, when the big freeze of 1919 severely damaged most apple trees, winter pears proved more resistant to subzero temperatures. As Issei joined the local Apple Growers Association and began to prosper, the number of exclusionist attacks in the valley increased.[16]

Local resident Lucile Wyers recounted: "As long as the Japanese people were poor . . . the Anglos, as they call them, were okay with that. But

Mam Noji's father pruned the limbs of his fruit trees during the winter. (Chiz Tamura, ca. 1935)

when they began to actually buy property and the Japanese began to own orchards and become competitors with the Anglos, they saw it as a threat.... That seems to be a human characteristic: to be afraid of anything that is different." In an assent that would have twisted implications for the valley's ethnic future, a 1923 editorial in a local newspaper maintained that if Issei had remained "common, unskilled laborers, they might have been tolerated, just as Mexicans are today." It went on to surmise, "Eventually it dawned upon some of the white farmers that here was a competitor who, by his methods and standard of living, might eventually gain control of the rich valleys of Oregon."[17]

Lauren Kessler, in *Stubborn Twig*, her book about the prominent Yasui family of Hood River, explained it this way:

While the Japanese were being criticized for wanting to control rather than join American society, for not taking on the trappings of their new home and for being visibly and unalterably different, they were in actuality feared for the opposite reason: they were beating Americans at their own game. In California, in Oregon and in Hood River, *issei* were practicing the Protestant work ethic with an intensity that overwhelmed their white neighbors. The Japanese were devoting themselves to work, teaching their children the meaning of hard labor, delaying their own gratification. They were the new Puritans. And the old Puritans didn't like it.[18]

If Nikkei were becoming competitors, there were abrupt consequences en route to the finish line. Some Americans believed that immigrants and their children should remain in their place, on the bottom rung of the socioeconomic ladder.[19] Along the West Coast, alarms warning of an impending "yellow peril" and "little brown men" resounded in newspaper crusades, roused by nativists and labor unions. President Theodore Roosevelt curbed Japanese immigration through his Gentlemen's Agreement with Japan, prompted by potential consequences for U.S.-Japanese relations after San Francisco segregated Japanese students.[20] In all three Pacific states, Nikkei success in agriculture provoked anti-Japanese coalitions to rail against Japanese landownership. While Japanese operated only 2.5 percent of farms along the Pacific in 1920, and those farms were just one-fourth the size of others, their average value was 23 percent higher, due to the Nikkei's labor-intensive, high-yield farming methods. And though less than 4 percent of the farms were in Oregon,[21] Oregonians were no less outspoken. Those from Hood River, where Issei owned larger plots of land interspersed among their neighbors, became exceedingly vocal.

### ANTI-JAPANESE ACTIVISM

By 1917, Hood River, the county seat of its namesake county, was a town of eight thousand with substantial commercial buildings, streetlights, a railroad depot, a Carnegie library, and new churches. Local women had become active voters, and the Columbia Gorge Highway connected the town to Portland. Agriculture was thriving, as four fruit companies merged to form the Hood River Apple Growers Association, and a new state Mid-Columbia Experiment Station organized to advise farmers.[22]

That year, community leaders also had another mission: to overcome the burgeoning Nikkei threat. Their goal was to prevent Japanese from purchasing property. Four years later, Hood River state senator George Wilbur introduced Oregon's first bill, similar to California's Alien Land Law of 1913. Though it was withdrawn because of the State Department's interest in keeping Japan on the Allies' side during World War I, it was the forerunner of Oregon's Alien Land Law of 1923.[23]

Hood River residents were not dissuaded from their commitment to rid the valley of Japanese competitors. They had already organized social, fraternal, and service organizations, including Odd Fellows, Rebekahs, Masons, the University Club, book exchanges and discussion groups, a pioneer association, a merchant association, and the commercial club.[24] In 1919, locals formed the Anti-Alien Association, vowing to neither sell nor lease land to the valley's Japanese and to oppose the further immigration of "Asiatics." The association had three main issues. It feared that "Jap encroachment" on farmland would transform the valley into a Japanese colony. It was concerned about Japanese farmers' low standard of living and substandard dwellings and rumors that Issei profits were sent to Japan rather than invested at home. It also viewed the high birth rates (reportedly equaling 10 to 20 percent of the local population, although the married Japanese population was just 1.5 percent) as part of a plan to overrun the valley. Local Issei, led by English-speaking proprietor and community leader Masuo Yasui, proposed a conference and offered a threefold compromise: to prevent further immigration of Japanese, limit their future land purchases, and improve their homes and gardens. Ultimately, the association declined the offer, vowing to continue enacting state and federal legislation against Japanese.[25]

In 1920, exclusionist activities in Hood River drew statewide notice. "'The Japanese Question' is more acute in Hood River than in any other place in Oregon," concluded a state report on the Japanese situation. Compiled by state legislator Frank Davey, the study called attention to the economic and expansionist alarms spreading through the valley. Davey's report noted that Japanese in Hood River "went first into the parts where very few farms existed . . . and, after years of incessant hard labor . . . produced many farms on which white farmers later settled and now outnumber the Japanese." He noted, stereotypically, that Japanese were "particularly adapted" to work on vegetables and berries because of "their short stature." Observing that the "present Japanese birth rate was high, owing to the fact that nearly all Japanese families now in Oregon are at the stage of highest productivity," he predicted a declining birthrate in ten years. Davey's report became a critical factor in Governor Ben Olcott's declaration that he intended to "curb the growth of the Japanese colonies in Oregon" and "preserve our lands and our resources for the people of our own race and nationality."[26]

Early anti-Japanese sentiments, though intense, were directed against the "entire race" rather than against individuals. A government document,

"Prejudice in Hood River Valley," contended that Anti-Alien Association meetings and activities were more "moderate" and restrained, at least in the beginning, because of previous amicable relationships between residents and Nikkei and because many recent valley settlers had college educations. The majority of white settlers drawn to the valley by the apple industry were retired businessmen, army and navy officers, and young college graduates, according to the document. They respected Nikkei as "quiet, well-behaved residents" who took "immaculate care of their orchards." It is also likely that, because Japanese farms were scattered throughout the valley and not segregated in ethnic colonies as in other areas, more personal, day-to-day contacts with Nikkei tempered the valley residents' hostility toward individuals. Then, too, newspaper editorials discouraged abusive attacks while supporting the need to check the Japanese population. A *Hood River News* editorial described the Japanese as "law-abiding, thrifty, hardworking, up-to-date in their methods" and "not entirely impossible as neighbors." While it advocated justice for those already in residence, it countered that "they cannot become citizens." Finally, it affirmed Hood River representative L. N. Blowers's backhanded compliment, "These people are nice people so long as they are in a minority." While the *Hood River Glacier* newspaper admitted that Japanese were "here to stay and their qualities outweigh any faults," it maintained that the valley "just could not countenance more Japanese moving in."[27] Likewise, the *Oregon Voter*, a conservative Republican weekly, warned that if Japanese landowners in "one of the paradises of earth" were not checked, the West Coast racial problem could be likened to that in the South. "Just as surely as two times two is four, that whole valley will pass ultimately into the hands of Japanese owners," it warned. Then, predicting consequences if the American Legion investigated these supposedly menacing Japanese land buyers, it quoted correspondent David W. Hazen's prophetic statement in the Portland *Telegram*: "The whole world is going to hear of the Hood River Post of the American Legion before long."[28]

Elsewhere in the state, resistance to Japanese immigrants also surfaced. In 1919, when George Shima brought a handful of Japanese potato experts to central Oregon to raise seed potatoes, the county farm bureau opposed the venture, forcing Shima to limit the number of Issei laborers and, eventually, to withdraw. Similar movements prevented Issei settlement in nearby Prineville and in Medford, located in southern Oregon. A mob of locals in the coastal town of Toledo drove out twenty-two Issei mill workers after disarming and beating sheriff's deputies who had been called to protect them.[29]

By 1923, the Columbia Gorge Highway and the Mount Hood Loop Highway brought a surge in tourism and, with it, renewed building in this "destination and pleasure resort." The Columbia Gorge Hotel, service stations, and car dealerships appeared, as did a creamery and soft-drink bottler as well as businesses related to the fruit industry, such as vinegar brewing, canning, spraying, and shipping.[30]

That year Oregon also gained legal grist for its battle against the perceived Issei threat. After legislators introduced unsuccessful bills in 1917, 1919, 1920, and 1921, the state finally passed its Alien Land Law, forbidding aliens ineligible for citizenship from owning or leasing land. (This followed legal precedents set by California, Washington, Illinois, Minnesota, Kentucky, Oklahoma, and Texas.) The Anti-Asiatic Association, American Legion, Oregon Federation of Labor, Portland Chamber of Commerce, and Ku Klux Klan were strong proponents. Hood River's representative Blowers voiced the majority opinion: "I wish Commodore Perry [who opened Japan to relations with the United States] had stayed home and minded his own business. . . . Boys, Hood River is behind your bill." Issei got around the law, however, by making land purchases in the names of their American-born children, friends, or business acquaintances. The next year, the federal Immigration Act of 1924 prevented aliens ineligible for citizenship from entering the country, although those who were residents could still travel back and forth.[31]

Only temporarily deflated, fears of Nikkei competition rebounded. During the Depression, which began in 1929, many locals who had overplanted apples became resentful of Issei whose pear orchards were beginning to thrive. "How did the Japanese happen to find out that one could make money on pears, while we were going broke raising apples?" they asked. Mayor Joe Meyer complained, "The farmers of this valley object to competing with Japanese farm labor—where all the family gets out and works on the land."[32] In this charged atmosphere, even local youth began to question the actions of Nikkei. One resident recalled making a purchase when he was a youngster at the Yasui Brothers' Store on Oak Street, which sold both Western and Japanese goods. "The proprietor got out this abacus and started pushing all these beads around. I did not trust that because he worked so fast that I thought sure I was going to get gypped a few cents. So after it was over, I figured it out with pencil and paper. He was correct."

Though the community stalled during the Depression, changes occurred. A new hospital opened in 1932; three years later, a new warehouse provided cold storage for valley fruit and a distillery began producing spirits from local fruit. In 1938, Bonneville Dam began generating electric power west of Hood River on the Columbia. Hood River growers were shipping fruit across the country as well as to Europe, South America, and Scandinavian countries.[33]

## COVERT ACTIVITIES AGAINST NEIGHBORS

With hostilities growing in Asia and Europe, the Hood River county sheriff cooperated with the Federal Bureau of Investigation (FBI) to conduct covert activities in the valley. The roots of that action took hold in 1936, when President Franklin D. Roosevelt requested information about suspect U.S. organizations. Working with the U.S. Army and the U.S. Navy, FBI director J. Edgar Hoover set up an intelligence unit tasked with creating lists of "dangerous" nationals, citizens, and political groups.

By 1938, the unit had collected 2,500 names of individuals and maintained intelligence files for those considered "potential enemies to our internal security." Suspects were assigned to three categories: A for those affiliated with Japanese organizations deemed to be controlled by the Japanese military or government, B for those considered "less dangerous," and C for those with limited ties to Japan, such as Nikkei businessmen or those involved with cultural organizations. No distinction was made between Japanese nationals, the Issei, and American citizens, the Nisei.[34]

From 1937 to May 1942, deputized Hood River citizens spied on all valley residents of Japanese descent, not only Issei but Nisei as well. These members of Sheriff John H. Sheldrake's paid surveillance team monitored the activities of 130 Nikkei families. They also guarded installations such as the Union Pacific Railroad station and bridges, the Oregon Lumber Company at Dee, the Bridge of the Gods and Hood River Bridge, the valley's five water supply systems, the telephone company, the county garage, and a busy local intersection. (Not all the guards necessarily understood the impending threat, however. Jan Kurahara, former county commissioner, told of two newly deputized guards who carried .22s and kept watch over the railroad tunnel for several days before finally concluding, "This is ridiculous.") Shopkeepers and businesses (even mail order catalogs from companies such as Sears and Montgomery Ward) reported names of customers who purchased shotguns and shortwave radios. In his biography, *Ganbatte*, Kurahara reported that his family's neighbors received "very good wages" (four times what he received for working on the farms at that time, or one dollar compared to his twenty-five cents an hour) to spy on Nikkei during the five years before they were forced to leave the valley.[35]

Acutely conscious of the community's increasing agitation, Nikkei avoided direct dealings with outspoken individuals and groups, confining their contacts to friendlier folk. They also tried to counteract negative attitudes by discussing issues with other Nikkei and pinpointing typical problems. They fully recognized that the actions of a few could reflect on the entire community. As early as 1921, after Japanese in Portland and The Dalles had been arrested for breaking prohibition laws, members of the local Japanese Farmers' Association vowed to control their consumption of liquor, despite its cultural significance: "Never go out when drinking. Never offer drinks to visitors. No more making wine at home."[36] Nisei George Tamura explained the precautions Nikkei took in later years, "If we did something wrong, the public would say, 'Well, the "Jap" did this.' And that took in everybody. We didn't like that, so we'd discuss it and tried to stay out of trouble."

The Issei had a saying they had learned in Japan: "The nail that sticks up gets hammered down." Despite the Nikkei's efforts to demonstrate citizenship and avoid calling attention to themselves, antagonism against them would rise to new heights. And the hammer would fall.

PART II

# WORLD WAR II

# THREE

# "Why Didn't You Tell Us the War Was Coming?"

## COMMUNITY FALLOUT

## FROM PEARL HARBOR

O N the morning of December 7, 1941, the Akiyamas were busy pruning peach trees in their orchard on Hood River's west side. Glancing across the rolling Cascades, "we saw all these planes go by before lunchtime," George's brother Sab recalled. His mother worried, "Oh, I hope the war hasn't started."

War did seem imminent. Since Japan's decisive victories in the Russo-Japanese War of 1904–5, the tiny nation had emerged as East Asia's military powerhouse. The country that had once been viewed as primitive and isolated was not only rapidly industrializing but reasserting itself militarily through its invasions of Manchuria and China. Japan's expansionist tendencies and its search for raw materials were becoming a threat to U.S. and European colonies in Southeast Asia. During the summer of 1941, when Japan seized southern French Indochina, the United States froze Japan's assets, cut off its oil shipments, and pledged to retaliate over further attacks.[1] Now the island nation, strangled by a resource-poor and floundering economy, was on the offensive.

The attack on Pearl Harbor, however, came as a shock to the Akiyamas, as it did to other Nikkei and Americans across the country. West of Hood River, members of the Imai family were at work in their asparagus field when news broke. "What the heck is going to go on now?" worried son Shig. Sagie Nishioka was fertilizing the family orchard in Dee that Sunday. "Anger kind of crept up on me. I just could hardly believe it, really. . . . I heard someone say they might send us to Japan." The Aki-yamas were among Nikkei families from the lower valley who had been cleaning the downtown Japanese Community Hall in preparation for a talent show the following week. They had hoped to raise money for indoor plumbing. Frightened by the news of Pearl Harbor, they canceled the show and rushed home.[2]

"Where's Pearl Harbor?" wondered Ed Shoemaker, son of a Hood River anti-Japanese activist. Around the country, others echoed his question. The surprise air strike was a blow to the U.S. Pacific Fleet at its main naval base on the Hawaiian Islands (then a U.S. territory). The assault left more than 3,500 Americans killed or wounded, eight battleships sunk or dam-aged, and 160 aircraft grounded. The next day, the United States declared war on Japan, recognizing that the aggressor nation had also attacked Malaya, Hong Kong, Guam, the Philippines, Wake Island, and Midway Island. Germany and Italy, honoring their 1940 pact with Japan, declared war on the United States, which had actually been waging a silent war against Germany, sending military equipment and troops to Europe since mid-1940. Now the United States, allied with Great Britain and the Soviet Union, was immersed in a war that spanned both hemispheres.[3]

SHATTERED PEACE

On the mainland, astonishment, confusion, terror, and mounting anger shattered the peace. President Franklin D. Roosevelt called an emergency evening meeting of his cabinet and congressional leaders. Hawaii's gov-ernor placed the islands under martial law. The West Coast became an "armed camp," with thousands of U.S. troops on twenty-four-hour alert, bivouacked in barns and trenches. The military set up command offices in schools and hotels, installed observation posts at key vantage points, and camouflaged artillery and antiaircraft guns along the beaches. In San Francisco, the mayor declared a state of emergency, and police blocked traffic in the city's Japan Town. Seattle's U.S. Marine Corps recruiting sta-tion enlisted seventy-eight men in three hours. Oregonians mobilized for war with a grim realization that the mouth of the Columbia was the point on the mainland nearest to Japan. Fighter planes dispersed from Port-land to strategic airfields, ready to intercept enemy aircraft. Two sentries guarded each Portland bridge, guards doubled up at other posts, and an appeal went out for more civil protection volunteers in the state. Hunters and military veterans armed with deer rifles patrolled harbors and sand dunes along the coast.[4] Bonneville Dam, on the Columbia River, was sand-blasted black in order to camouflage it after cattle scratching their backs on power lines prompted alarmist fears of saboteurs and overhead aircraft.[5]

"We were propagandized to be afraid," said Hood River political activist Lucille Wyers. She braced for another attack as residents scanned the skies for signs of Japanese bombers. "I hung a coat over the kitchen window," recalled Wyers, complying with the blackout, which extended from 1:30 to 7:30 A.M.[6] "We were told that the Japanese might come and bomb." Even private toilet routines became a public matter. One local woman shone a flashlight during an evening trip to her outdoor toilet and received an admonishing phone call from a watchman atop nearby Van Horn Butte. Citizens signed on for shifts at two aircraft watchtowers, one on the uptown heights and one near the river.[7] Local watchmen guarded strategic bridges, railroads, water supplies, power plants, and other public facilities. Floodlights illuminated headwaters around springs, and the public was warned to stay away. Rumors spread that local Japanese might poison the water in Crystal Springs reservoir, considered particularly vulnerable because it was on Issei property. (This perplexed Nikkei, since the reservoir supplied their drinking water, too.)[8] When the county enrolled guards to monitor a nearby dam, local Pat Cosner volunteered himself and his friend Yukio Kajikawa as lookouts. Officials quickly turned him down.

The Nikkei population, now vulnerable, was just a small segment of the national, state, and county population. In 1940, there were 126,947 people of Japanese descent nationwide, less than 1 percent of the population, whereas the almost 140,000 Nikkei in Hawaii composed 38 percent of the territory's people.[9] While the three Pacific Coast states contained 88.5 percent of the country's Japanese,[10] Oregon's 4,071 Nikkei made up a mere 3 percent of the country's Japanese and only one-third of a percent of the state's population. Portland's Multnomah County had 968, the highest number of Nikkei in Oregon. Though Hood River was home to just 11 percent of the state's Nikkei (and Nikkei in the county composed less than 3 percent of its residents), it still held the second-highest number (462) in Oregon.[11]

Valley Issei, encouraging their sons to serve honorably as American citizens, had already feted six young Nisei draftees at send-off parties (*soko-kai*) held at the downtown Japanese Community Hall.[12] Now the Noji and Akiyama families agonized, concerned about Mam's and George's welfare.

According to Mam's sister, Chiz, "There was nothing we could do . . . but just wait and see what would happen."

For the Akiyama family, repercussions came quickly. While George was in the service, he received a letter describing unexpected "visitors" at his family's home at three in the morning on Monday, December 8:

> My sister [Kiyoko] wrote to me and said they came and got my dad. He was president of the Japanese Issei society here. . . . They took all these Issei, the men who were heads of the organizations. . . . All these Americans thought maybe they were spies, you know. Actually the Hood River Issei society was just to help each other out because most of the men didn't understand English. Well, I thought, that's the way war is and you can't do much about it! But I was really kind of angry. I was here in the army. There wasn't much I could do about it.
>
> The FBI came to the family's house in the middle of the night, ransacked the drawers and everything. My mother had her mother's picture up there on the dresser. They took that picture and just threw it on the floor. My mother really took that hard. She was crying, she said. The FBI threw out all the papers they could find—anything written in Japanese. . . . The rest of the kids were . . . just shocked, just stood there and watched.

Tomeseichi Akiyama, president of the local Japanese Society, was among more than seven hundred Issei community leaders on the West Coast taken into custody by the FBI that evening. Their names were prominent in the A, B, and C categories of the joint FBI and military list of suspects (see ch. 2), and they were arrested without warrants. By mid-February, 2,192 Issei, including 5 from Hood River, had been arrested and taken into custody, along with Germans and Italians. They were now considered enemy aliens.[13] (Jailed first in Portland, the elder Akiyama was imprisoned at Justice Department internment centers at Fort Missoula, Montana; Fort Sill, Oklahoma; and Camp Livingston, Louisiana. He would not see his family for thirteen months.)[14]

Federal and local restrictions on Issei affected the daily lives of Nisei as well. The government immediately froze the assets of the Issei (though they later lifted the ban, allowing families to withdraw enough to cover living expenses) and barred them from taking public buses, trains, and planes. Hood River County judge C. D. Nickelsen and Sheriff John Sheldrake restricted Japanese nationals to their ranches through the end of the month unless accompanied by white Americans, as a "precautionary and protection measure to head off any untoward incident" by a community member. Within the next two months, Issei were forbidden to gather in groups and, along with "unnaturalized aliens" from Germany and Italy, were required to carry identification certificates bearing their photos and fingerprints. Insurance companies notified Issei that their home fire insurance policies were canceled by mailing them checks for the unexpired portions of their policies. Many Nisei complied with regulations, hoping their gestures would bring favor on their parents. Although they were citizens, they also turned in the requested firearms, cameras, and shortwave radios.[15]

The FBI continued to take action against Issei, authorizing warrantless searches of their homes and properties. During February, in cooperation with county and city officials, it conducted a two-day "dragnet for aliens" in Hood River. At the Nishimoto home and farm, four FBI agents spent three hours searching for contraband. When they found a small bullet in the woodshed from Otoichi Nishimoto's pheasant hunting, they jailed him for three months in Portland and then in Montana. At the Endow home, officials hauled away a four-foot-high,

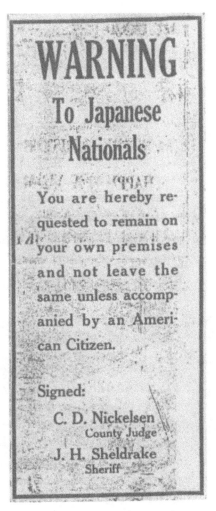

At the end of December 1941, the Hood River county judge and sheriff restricted Issei to their property, as a "protection measure." (*Hood River News*, December 26, 1941)

wooden RCA Victor shortwave radio after searching the family's beds, drawers, and closets.[16] The search of the Noji family's home was merely a walk-through, because the sheriff said he knew Kichizo, the Issei father.

The *Hood River News* reported that the 151 searches resulted in a "negligible catch of 'enemy' aliens" and "not one case of illegal possession of arms." Authorities, it said, jailed four Issei men when they discovered stumping powder and a shortwave radio receiver on the men's property. They also confiscated cameras, radios, guns, and dynamite. Reports did not mention, however, that the guns were legally owned sport weapons and that farmers used dynamite to blow up stumps when clearing land. Along the West Coast, the FBI eventually seized a total of 2,592 guns, 199,000 rounds of ammunition (most from one sporting goods store), 1,652 sticks of dynamite, 1,458 radio receivers, 2,015 cameras, and other contraband items. There was not one proven case of sabotage or espionage among the West Coast Japanese population.[17]

## "EVERYBODY WAS AGAINST THE JAPS"

"An almost reflexive racism of the general public" became palpable, according to historian Roger Daniels.[18] Government officials' denunciations of the loyalty of resident Japanese combined with unfounded accusations from the military to rouse an already nervous public.[19] This triggered sensational reports from the media and rumors that spread like wildfire among the population amid lobbying by special interest groups, politicians, and citizens alike. West Coast newspapers flashed incendiary headlines, including "Flaming Arrows Pointed toward Seattle" (*Seattle Post-Intelligencer*),[20] "Japs May Fly All the Way to Idaho" (*Idaho Daily Statesman*),[21] and "Officials Feel Japanese May Try Anything; Jap Strategy Map Told (*Hillsboro Argus*).[22] An article from the *Oregon Journal's* front page, headlined "FBI Designated As Only Agency to Detain Japs," informed law enforcement agencies that "any complaints with reference to Japanese aliens" should be immediately referred to the FBI.[23] The *Oregonian* showed a large photo of two sheriff's officers arriving at a county jail with an Issei "prisoner." The accompanying caption described "precautions against espionage and sabotage." That same day, the Chinese consul in Portland issued certificates to Chinese citizens, lest they be mistaken for Japanese.[24] (Two weeks later, *Life* magazine published "How to Tell Japs from the Chinese," explaining that Chinese wore the "rational calm of tolerant realists" while "Japs, like

General Tojo, show the humorless intensity of ruthless mystics.")[25] Across the Columbia from Hood River, the Skamania County sheriff arrested and held twenty Issei for the FBI, though she had not discovered a single act of sabotage. Rumors circulated along the West Coast about Japanese gardeners who hid shortwave transmitters in their garden hoses, farmers who grew flowers that took the shape of an arrow pointing toward the airport when viewed from the air, and even University of California class rings found on the fingers of Japanese pilots who had been shot down.[26]

In Hood River, "stories of sabotage were on every hand," according to businesswoman Arline Moore in her postwar letter responding to questions from the editor of the *Dartmouth*. Nikkei were accused of training for fifth-column work at the Japanese Community Hall, teaching Japanese language to Nisei children in preparation for a takeover by Japan after the war, and knowing the full plans for the Pearl Harbor bombing as early as August. Rumors spread that they would kill Caucasian friends during a U.S.-Japanese war and that innocent games of sport were actually military training.[27] Several men, it was said, were signaling Japanese planes, and an Issei man returning to Japan had become an officer in the Japanese army. There was increasing skepticism: Why was there a wireless radio in the back of the Yasui Store? Why did an Issei woman send money to her child in Japan after the harvest? Was it a coincidence that the Japanese Community Hall's fall cleanup and box burning occurred on Pearl Harbor Day? Had all Nikkei known what was going to happen?

"Everybody was against the Japs," observed a local resident and long-time deputy sheriff. In the minds of many, there was no distinction between the Japanese across the Pacific and those living in the valley. Issei were branded as "enemy aliens." Even Nisei became suspect, although they were American citizens whose average age was just nineteen, and two-thirds of them had never been to the land of their ancestors.[28] Businesswoman Moore noted, "The populace [was] literally scared 'pink' and actually seemed to think the few thousands of Japanese people living among our 130 or more millions were some sort of supermen endowed with the ability to travel unseen to any point and there commit unlimited sabotage without being caught in the act."[29]

Rumors began to pass muster as fact, and Nikkei GIs and their families felt the scrutiny and increasing scorn of their neighbors and acquaintances, who often crossed the street to avoid encounters with them. Some conveyed their suspicions in direct ways. "We were accused of having farms near military installations, by the airport and everything," recalled Mam Noji. "As a matter of fact, the farm was there before all these installations! Some of my friends were asked by friendly *hakujin*, 'My gosh, why didn't you tell us the war was coming?' They thought we had a line to Tokyo, you know, that Tojo was talking to us. It was ridiculous." Shig Imai's brother Hit was just as baffled by accusations lobbed at his family. "A lot of people, especially Caucasians, would come and say, 'You dirty Jap. You caused all that.' But we didn't cause all that, you know. . . . We were victims because we were that nationality."

Other community members demonstrated their skepticism indirectly. "They had a joke that they caught a 'Jap' who had arms up [his] sleeve, 'arms' meaning 'weapons,' you know," remembered George's brother Sab. "You notice even your Caucasian buddies kind of stayed away from you in school." Other nonverbal messages signaled that relationships had changed. "The attitude of the public was definitely evident by the stares they gave you," remarked Sagie Nishioka. "One time I went to the office to pay a telephone bill. Everybody was staring at me with a funny look. It looked like everything just came to a halt."

The widening chasm, even between former neighbors and friends, seemed palpable, though not expressed in words. "With the advent of Pearl Harbor, I think there was an invisible barrier separating us from our friends and them from us," explained Toru Noji, Mam's younger brother. "I don't recall that there was an overpowering offering on their part to express their sorrow for the event or us expressing our shame for the atrocious act inflicted upon them by our country of heritage. Perhaps this was because there was so much concern and worry about the things that had to be done."

The slanderous talk caused some Nisei to look askance at their parents, even though they had been raised to respect authority. "Gee whiz," mused Sab, whose father was interned by the FBI. "Possibly some of the Issei are spies? The government wouldn't do that unless they had reason. . . . In times like that, I think you might even get a feeling you don't trust the fellow sitting next to you. We grew up believing Uncle Sam did no wrong, you know? His word was like God's word. It was the law. We didn't question his mores, the way I grew up. . . . It kind of gives a person maybe a guilt feeling to think that way about your parents, but in times like that, you start suspecting Issei."

Nikkei did make special efforts to show support for the country that most had called home for the past thirty to forty years. Early in January 1942, 148 Hood River Issei sent Oregon's governor Charles A. Sprague a collective pledge of loyalty, a logistical challenge because of restrictions on travel and group meetings. They vowed, "We love this country so much that we wish to live here permanently, obeying American laws, policies and administration always." Issei pledged their "loyalty to the Stars and Stripes just as do our children who are patriotic American citizens" and expressed gratitude for their treatment by courteous American friends. The cover letter from Reverend Isaac Inouye, minister of the Hood River Japanese Methodist Church, noted that sixteen of their sons were serving in the U.S. Army.[30] Issei and Nisei formed neighborhood committees to promote sales of war bonds and stamps. (Mam's mother served as local treasurer for families in her area.) The Mid-Columbia Japanese American Citizens League (JACL), a regional chapter of the national organization of American-born sons and daughters of Japanese parents, declared its loyalty exclusively to the United States. Nisei also pledged to serve this country, noting that many were already in the armed services while others awaited the call to enlist. In Portland, Salem, and Ontario, Oregon Nisei similarly proclaimed their loyalty, as did Nisei students at the University of Oregon and Oregon State College.[31]

Not everyone viewed Nikkei with suspicion. Three days after war broke out, local youth took a stand, publishing a plea for tolerance in the Hood River High School newspaper:

> To those of Hood River—if you please
> They are our friends—these Japanese.
> Not "Japs," or even Japanese.
> They are Americans, our schoolmates these.[32]

Some residents, like those students, distinguished between "bad" Japanese across the Pacific and those they knew in Hood River. One reasoned that he did not consider his Nikkei acquaintances to be Asian, explaining, "Only if it was those that I didn't know could they be Japanese." Others recognized the disparity between the treatment of immigrants from Japan and those from Germany. According to Howard Rice,

"The Japanese were so discernible because of their appearance, but the Germans could blend right in."

## GROWING ANTI–JAPANESE AMERICAN SENTIMENT

The distinctiveness of Nikkei, however, became a liability and inflamed public perceptions as the war progressed. Like a whirlwind gaining momentum with each new rumor, sensational media depiction, and lobbying effort, anti-Nikkei sentiment grew from mild skepticism to distrust and eventually to hysteria. The more closely Nikkei were identified with the enemy overseas, the more intense the public scrutiny and the more obscure the line between Issei aliens and Nisei citizens became. Prominent syndicated columnists from California whipped up anti-Nikkei sentiment with their calls for evacuation. Henry McLemore, a columnist for Hearst newspapers (who had long warned of a "yellow peril"), urged the United States to "herd 'em up, pack 'em off and give 'em the inside room in the badlands. . . . Personally, I hate the Japanese. And that goes for all of them." In the wake of a call by Walter Lippman, dubbed the "dean of American political commentators" by some, there was a fivefold increase in letters to the White House calling for the removal of Nikkei.[33] Along the West Coast, editorial support for the rights of Nikkei evaporated as the press relayed accounts based more on rumor than fact and became "government publicists" rather than "watchdog[s]," according to Lloyd Chiasson, mass communications scholar.[34] His study of twenty-seven West Coast newspapers revealed that only four had endorsed constitutional rights for Nikkei; however, within two months, by February, those four would retreat and support displacing the Nikkei. Likewise, Pacific Northwest news editors' initial backing of Nikkei rights diminished after authorities removed Issei from strategic areas and eventually buckled, aligning with the views of exclusionists and the government's eventual order, according to Floyd McKay, journalist and scholar. In Seattle, news headlines increasingly referred to "Japs," an odious term that too often became synonymous with "Japanese Americans." Three months into the war, the pejorative appeared in nearly half the Seattle Times' headlines.[35]

Oregon dailies also reversed their positions, McKay reported. Within ten days of the war's onset, the Oregonian had taken a stand for fair play in the treatment of Nisei, the Oregon Journal pleaded for "toleration," and Salem's Capital Journal decried the "unjust suspicion" of loyal Nisei. As military setbacks in Asia altered public sentiment, support for Nikkei began to dissolve. Midway through February, as the country debated the fate of its West Coast Nikkei residents, 80 percent of citizens polled by the *Oregonian* favored evacuating all Issei, while 36 percent supported evacuating Nisei. (These results were slightly higher than the results of similar polls in California.) By the end of the month, the *Oregonian* supported evacuation as well, rationalizing it as a means of protecting Nikkei from race riots. Salem's *Oregon Statesman* did the same, under the pretext that Nikkei might enjoy greater physical safety away from emotional citizens.[36]

Hood River's two weekly newspapers differed in their approaches. The more colloquial *Hood River County Sun* projected shifting positions more typical of other Oregon newspapers. In "Our Local Neighbors," its first editorial after the war began, the *Sun* cautioned against "idle rumors, malicious gossip and thoughtless acts." Two months later, in a column titled "English Is Our Language," it expressed aggravation with Japanese who professed loyalty and devotion to their adopted country yet did not speak English. "When one is in Rome, one does as the Romans do!" the *Sun* chided.[37] In contrast, the more objective and balanced *Hood River News* regularly reported events in the Nikkei community and, after the war began, printed letters and pledges of loyalty from Nikkei individuals and groups, creating a literary community forum. Buoyed by editor Hugh Ball, who had lived in Japan and written about its citizens, the newspaper referred to Issei and Nisei, rather than the generic and potentially misleading "Japanese." In a January editorial, he reminded the community, "We are all of alien origin." When Nisei voluntarily submitted to fingerprints, he commented on their loyalty, "There should be no fear of the status of the Nisei." In a February editorial, "One Problem Can Create Another," he took a different tack, advising that moving both generations of Japanese inland could create a serious problem: caring for their extensive orchards so that the neglected properties would not adversely affect white residents' farms. They had, he reminded his readers, gained their land legally and retained titles to it.[38]

The anti-Nikkei bandwagon was accelerating, however, overtaking isolated voices of caution. Veterans' groups jumped on, demanding that all Japanese be removed from the West Coast. The American Legion was particularly well organized, having passed an anti-Nikkei resolution at its national convention every year since 1919. In January 1942, the Portland Legion post resolved that "this is no time for namby-pamby pussyfooting," urging "vigorous, wholehearted and concerted action" on mass incarceration and mailing its resolution to more than six hundred western posts and Chambers of Commerce. Oregon Legionnaires in Clatsop, Klamath Falls, Seaside, Drain, Corvallis, Gresham, and Sutherlin followed through with their own statements, and at least thirty-eight posts in Washington endorsed evacuation. Four other Oregon veterans' organizations also added their support.[39]

When the congressional Tolan Committee held hearings in Portland late in February as part of its investigation of evacuation, leaders from Hood River spoke out. "National defense comes first," testified J. E. Klahre, speaking for the delegation representing the local Chamber of Commerce, Civil Defense Council, Apple Growers Association, and American Legion. Estimating that Japanese properties constituted 16 percent of the valley's orchards, they offered to take over those farms. County judge C. D. Nickelsen, who also chaired an ad hoc Japanese Evacuation Committee, urged Attorney General Francis Biddle to remove the Japanese. For safety reasons, the Chamber of Commerce Board of Directors petitioned federal and state authorities to remove all persons of Japanese ancestry, native or foreign-born, and place them under guard. The lumber and sawmill workers' union in upper valley Dee urged Oregon governor Sprague in February to declare a state of martial law in the county until enemy aliens were removed. In March, Hood River Elks followed suit with a unanimous resolution to remove Nikkei, because it was "likely" that they had already arranged to strike the United States as "fifth columnists and saboteurs."[40] Elsewhere in Oregon, isolated civic organizations joined the call to expel Nikkei.[41]

Only a handful of groups and individuals spoke out on behalf of the Nikkei, including the Federal Council of Churches and the Fair Play Committee organized by University of California academics. In Oregon, two private citizens proposed plans to protect Japanese Americans: The Oliver plan would allow prominent citizens to serve as guardians of Japanese Americans and permit others to post good conduct bonds for friends who then would not be sent to camps. The Lewis plan would allow Nikkei to volunteer for federal work programs in eastern Oregon.[42] A Far East authority at the University of Oregon, Harold J. Noble, made a public plea for tolerance, urging, "The Japanese citizens of this country are overwhelmingly loyal. . . . We must fight this war as a nation, not as a mob." A former missionary in Japan, Azalia Emma Peet, was the lone dissenter at the Portland Tolan Committee hearing, challenging the ethics of evacuating "law-abiding, upright people of our community." Twenty-one conscientious objectors in Cascade Locks took a stand against removing the Japanese.[43]

In contrast, the American Civil Liberties Union did not support Nikkei, and the Oregon affiliate remained silent. The Portland Council of Churches maintained that the federal government should pay evacuation costs but did not protest the proposed evacuation itself. Few Portlanders in the religious, academic, and civil rights communities had personal connections with Nikkei, which contributed to the lack of an organized defense against or challenge to mass internment, according to historian Ellen Eisenberg. Churches, the Red Cross, the YMCA and YWCA, and peace associations declined to speak out.[44]

## FUELING EXECUTIVE ORDER 9066

The preponderance of anti-Nikkei voices bolstered bureaucrats, who moved the country toward an unprecedented course of action. Early in February, congressional delegates on the West Coast (led by Senators Hiram Johnson of California and Mon Wallgren of Washington) urged President Roosevelt to evict West Coast Japanese Americans. Two weeks later, Oregon's governor Sprague reversed his earlier position of support and cabled the Justice Department with his own solution: "I do not believe measures now being taken are adequate and urge further and prompt action to remove this menace and recommend internment." He closed by requesting "positive protection for Americans, with decent treatment of Japanese." Governor Sprague's action followed the gubernatorial candidacy of his secretary of state, Earl Snell, a war veteran, who defeated him.[45]

Perhaps the most outrageous claim came from Lieutenant General John L. DeWitt, commander of the Western Defense Command responsible for the security of western states. Equating resident Nikkei to the enemy, he recommended to Secretary of War Henry L. Stimson in February that Japanese be excluded from the West Coast: "The Japanese race is an enemy race and while many second and third generation Japanese born on United States soil, possessed of United States citizenship, have become 'Americanized,' the racial strains are undiluted. . . . The very fact that no sabotage has taken place to date is a disturbing and confirming indication that such action will be taken."[46]

In Washington, D.C., the War Department and the Justice Department engaged in an administrative tug-of-war as DeWitt's views collided with those of Attorney General Francis Biddle, FBI director J. Edgar Hoover, and others who opposed evacuation because there was no evidence of imminent sabotage or attack. Curtis B. Munson, a businessman assigned to conduct an intelligence investigation, had affirmed that there would be no armed uprising of Japanese and that there was no more cause for concern about the disloyalty of Japanese than of any other racial group. Regarding the Nisei, he conceded, "The Nisei are pathetically eager to show this loyalty." Likewise, Lieutenant Commander K. D. Ringle of the Office of Naval Intelligence discounted any plans for mass action against those of Japanese ancestry.[47] Eventually, however, the fate of West Coast Nikkei was decided by a rolling tide of political consensus, public opinion, and, historian Greg Robinson concludes, the president's belief that Japanese Americans were still "adjuncts of Japan" and "presumptively dangerous on racial grounds."[48] In effect, the consequence would be a victory for the War Department, which would assume authority for implementing the exclusion program.[49]

On February 19, 1942, President Roosevelt signed Executive Order 9066, authorizing military authorities to designate "military areas . . . from which any or all persons may be excluded." The order was based on the premise that one's ethnicity determined one's loyalty, that unsubstantiated military accusations were sound, and that concerns for security outweighed the rights of ethnic minorities.[50] The U.S. government, entangled in wartime fears and suspicions, thus succumbed to unfounded conspiracy theories, alarmist campaigns, political pressures, and racist hysteria. Military rule would deny American citizens their constitutional rights, as directed by the president. In other words, Japanese Americans were presumed guilty, without charges or evidence, simply because of who they were.

The government placed more sanctions on Nikkei. In March, DeWitt issued Public Proclamation No. 1, designating western Washington, Oregon, and southern Arizona as evacuation areas and encouraging Japanese to move voluntarily. The army ordered a curfew, confining all Issei and Nisei to their homes between 8 P.M. and 6 A.M., under penalty of arrest. That restriction also applied to Italian and German aliens, but, unlike the strictures placed on Nisei, it did not include their American-born children.[51] Nikkei could travel only within five miles of their homes, preventing trips downtown to purchase farm equipment and clothing. (The local high school band teacher, determined that his star cornet player perform at the spring concert, smuggled Shig Yamaki to school in the trunk of his car.)[52]

Ultimately, plans for evacuating Nikkei evolved from "voluntary" to compulsory.[53] Along the West Coast, 120,313 would be exiled, and there would be no distinction between the Issei and the Nisei, who were Americans by birthright and composed 73 percent of the population.[54] Hood River Nikkei would have just six days to make arrangements for selling or leasing their homes and property, storing their belongings, and packing what they could carry. Forced to leave their homes, they did not know where they were headed or when—or even if—they would be permitted to return.[55]

Mam Noji reflected on those dark days: "War changes things. . . . We looked like foreigners, even amongst our own people. We were different. . . . War brings out the best and the worst in people, you know?"

# FOUR

# *"Fighting for Good Uncle Sam"*

## NISEI ENTER THE MILITARY

**W**HEN war broke, there were already 3,188 Japanese Americans serving in the United States armed forces. Another 19,000 would ultimately serve in Europe, the South Pacific, and else-where.[1] Nisei servicemen had varied responses to their prospects in the military as well as to the suspicions, restrictions, and inequitable treatment they faced.

### PREWAR INDUCTIONS

"When it comes to bingo or keno, my number doesn't come up, but when it came to the draft, I was real lucky," joked Mam Noji. After draft notices arrived for Noji and other young Hood River Nisei during the months before the war, they accepted their lot as citizens. "Young people have to respond to the call," explained Noji. "That's part of growing up."[2] When George Akiyama's draft number came up in November 1941, his parents were adamant that he serve honorably. They advised, "Do your best. Don't be afraid to die for your country."

Others volunteered. Just out of high school, Sho Endow was the eldest of four children in an Odell valley farming family. Resigned to his fate, he enlisted during the spring of 1941, admitting, "It got worse and worse, as far as war talk was concerned. . . . Everybody's gonna eventually end up in the service someplace." Just home from a summer job working in the pea fields after his sophomore year at Whitman College in Walla Walla, Washington, Harry Takagi hitchhiked to Hood River and found his draft notice awaiting him. Hoping to make use of his private pilot's license and studies in pre-medicine, he enlisted for three years so that he could choose his branch of the service rather than serve in the infantry.[3]

The Nikkei community, proud of its young sons, had honored them with send-off parties at the downtown Japanese Community Hall. At the March 1941 tribute for Bill Yamaki, the first local Nisei inductee and volunteer, Nikkei community leader Masuo Yasui urged, "Go now and serve your country with loyalty, honor and pride."[4] In November, locals feted Akiyama, Noji, and Kenjiro Hayakawa with farewell speeches and a community potluck.[5] Issei expressed pride in their sons' newest roles as American citizens by preparing their favorite Japanese delicacies.

From the onset of their military service, however, Nisei saw that their treatment was different from that of other inductees. Neither Noji nor Akiyama was allowed to enter the U.S. Army Air Corps, which each preferred over regiments entrenched in armed combat. Other non-Nikkei valley residents had a choice, but "the only place they wanted us was in infantry," Noji complained. "Discrimination started from induction. Infantry—that's the bottom of the list, you know." Neither the navy, the marine corps, nor the air force accepted Nisei.[6]

Resigned to his lot as an infantryman (though the circumstances of war would change that), Noji began basic training at Camp Roberts, California. On Sunday, December 7, the aftershock of Pearl Harbor jarred his world:

> We were given our first weekend pass down there in Camp Roberts, so some of us went up to Salinas. On the return, the bus driver stopped at a café for coffee. When he came back, he said, "Damn it. Japan bombed Pearl Harbor!" Oh my God, I thought. We didn't even know where Pearl Harbor was at that time. But we knew that that boded no good for the rest of us.
>
> When we got back to camp, things really changed. There were guys patrolling the area with guns on their shoulders, you know, on guard. We were in the middle of training, but they cut us off right away. No more basic. No more training. They took us off KP [kitchen patrol], which suggested maybe they thought we'd be poisoning the food. We were not trusted anymore. Gosh, what a terrible time.

After war was declared, without a clear national policy, army commanders had discretion in how they handled their men. Several hundred Nisei were honorably discharged from active duty. Some were transferred to the Enlisted Reserve Corps (a forerunner of the U.S. Army National Guard and Reserve) and then sent home.[7] In a rare instance, Harry Takagi's commander spoke to all the Nisei in his unit and acknowledged their American citizenship.[8] More typically, officers kept Nisei on active duty but stripped them of their arms, swapping their guns for mops and rakes. Most officers reassigned Nisei to detail work, menial assignments such as cleaning barracks and latrines, scraping paint off windows, picking up cigarette butts, or doing yard work. Akiyama and Noji were among the more fortunate, designated to drive jeeps and trucks in the motor pool. Even Nisei sergeants and corporals were relegated to menial duties. This inequitable treatment was just the first of numerous violations of the Selective Training and Service Act, which had been enacted the year before the war began. The Selective Service System's nondiscrimination clause mandated "equal and fair justice" and specified that there should not be discrimination because of one's "race, creed or color."[9] Actually, Noji countered, "We Nisei were all treated the same—discriminated against." Early the next year, the army moved most of the Nisei soldiers to Arkansas, where they were assigned to perform more non-battle-related tasks.[10] Remembering the long train ride from Camp Roberts in California to Camp Robinson in Arkansas brought bitter recriminations from Noji:

> We were wearing uniforms but they put a guard on us! They put an armed guard on us, watching us, you know! Boy, what a comedown. And they warned us to keep the blinds down. . . . That's the way it was when Pearl Harbor hit. It was a bad day. We were all categorized apart from the rest of the army. What really got me was when they put an armed guard on the train going to Camp Robinson! . . . Everybody picked on us, you know. Psychologically we were abused. . . . It's pretty hard to put into words, but when you're in uniform and you're treated like a prisoner, you wonder what you're doing in the service.

During the first few months after Pearl Harbor, the Selective Service permitted local draft boards to make their own judgments about induct-

Four Hood River Nisei began their basic training at Camp Roberts, California. From left: George Akiyama, Tot (Taro) Asai, Harry Tamura, and Mam (Mamoru) Noji. (Mam Noji/Lloyd and Diana Noji, January 1942)

ing Japanese Americans.[11] In Hood River, Gresham, and Portland, Oregon, the draft continued as usual. Harry Tamura was enrolled at auto mechanic school in Portland during the winter lull in farmwork. He and his three siblings had grown up doing orchard chores, knowing their parents needed their help. When he noticed his draft number approaching, though, there was no question what he would do, as a representative of his family. "I figured it's my duty to volunteer. . . . That was no dilemma for me. I'm an American citizen. I was glad to go!" A few days after the United States entered the war, Shig Imai and Kats Sato submitted their names at the local draft board. By January 6, both were called in. "It turned out that if you passed the physical, you just kept on going," chuckled Imai.

When Sagie Nishioka was inducted, he worried about his widowed mother and two younger siblings (just ten and fifteen years old), who would be left with full responsibility for the family farm. "To run the farm would have been a hardship if I left. That was really a concern. But Caucasian friends told me, 'Well, you don't have to worry about it. We'll take care of it.' But," he added soberly, "I don't think it ended up that way." Unlike white farmers and their sons, Nishioka and other Nikkei were not eligible for deferments as essential agricultural workers.[12]

Frank Hachiya was eager to serve. A Kibei who had been educated in Japan for four years, he was staunch in his faith that American ideals respected the integrity of individuals regardless of race, color, or creed. The principled young man was a political science major at the University of Oregon. "Some despair because they think an individual can do nothing, but history has taught us that an individual can change the map of the world," he'd written Vienna Annala, a former teacher. Hachiya's idealism was intact. "I'm positive that when the dark clouds of war clear away, that we will realize that the grave situation existing now was just caused by misunderstanding and in reality there is friendship." After Pearl Harbor, Hachiya volunteered for service as a language translator. Though his mother and brother still lived in Japan, he posited, "The only way I can help them is to aid in freeing Japan of the military party."[13]

### INDUCTING NISEI DURING THE WAR

While the army vacillated on how to use Nisei, it also grappled with whether to induct more. The Selective Service became more and more averse, however, to accepting Nisei into its ranks. Draft boards began reclassifying them as IV-F, unsuitable for military service. New regulations adopted on September 14, 1942 (but observed earlier) reclassified Nisei as IV-C, "aliens not acceptable to the armed forces, or any group of persons not acceptable." At the same time, any further Nisei induction was banned.[14] The situation made little sense to Shig Imai's brother Hit. "We were I-A when the war started, right? So we were fit for Selective Service. But after the war started, all the Japanese American nationality was denied being soldiers 'til 1943. I figured it was a government deal. There's nothing you're gonna do about it."

The army position on Nisei inductees was not set, however, and wavered during the next few months. Assistant Secretary of War John J. McCloy was intent on reviving Nisei military service, for the purpose of what he referred to as their "rehabilitation." Most Nisei were loyal and all citizens had the right to serve their country, he contended. Prompted by the director of the Office of War Information, Elmer Davis, War Department officials also recognized that enlisting Nisei soldiers would deflect propaganda from Japan that the conflict was "a racial war" and was caused by racial discrimination. The JACL, led by Mike Masaoka and the organization's president Saburo Kido, lobbied hard to show that Nisei were "ready and willing to die for the one country we know and pledge allegiance to." General John DeWitt opposed the proposal because it stood in direct contrast to the government's premise that evacuating Japanese Americans was a "military necessity." Besides, how could they possibly determine the loyalty of Japanese now when it had been deemed impossible one year before? Over General DeWitt's strong objections, however, a plan began to take shape.[15]

On February 1, 1943, President Roosevelt announced the formation of a Nisei combat team. It would be segregated and composed solely of volunteers. "No loyal citizen of the United States should be denied the democratic right to exercise the responsibilities of his citizenship, regardless of his ancestry," Roosevelt proclaimed. "The principle on which this country was founded and by which it has always been governed is that Americanism is a matter of the mind and heart. Americanism is not, and never was, a matter of race or ancestry," he declared,[16] even as more than 100,000 Nikkei were incarcerated behind barbed wire.

For military officials, implementing the Nisei combat plan was analogous to walking a tightrope. Integrating Nisei with regular troops would have been problematic, they believed, because other American soldiers would likely not agree to serve with Nisei. Then, too, an integrated unit would have been inconsistent with the practice of segregating black troops. In order to confirm their readiness for military service, it was necessary to ascertain the loyalty of Nisei, who were, at that time, under military control in so-called relocation centers in the country's interior regions. Ultimately the War Department and the War Relocation Authority combined forces and instituted a registration process for every Nikkei in the camps who was eighteen or older. The program had a dual purpose: to screen Issei and Nisei applications for "leave clearance" (clearance to leave the camps indefinitely for work or school) and to screen Nisei for military service.[17]

Intended to promote goodwill, the process became confusing and contentious. Early in February, poorly trained registration teams dispersed to ten inland camps, where West Coast Nikkei had been sent, and administered what became known as "loyalty questionnaires." Nisei men and women both received the forms, as did Issei, whose median age of fifty-one was well beyond draft age.[18]

Two particular questions among the forty were troublesome. Question 27 asked the internees, "Are you willing to serve in the armed forces of the United States on combat duty, wherever ordered?" What if they would be willing to serve if drafted but were reluctant to volunteer, Nisei wondered. How could they defend a country that incarcerated its own citizens? Might an all-Nisei outfit be sacrificed as cannon fodder? Question 28 asked, "Will you swear unqualified allegiance to the United States of America and faithfully defend the United States from any or all attack by foreign or domestic forces, and forswear any form of allegiance or obedience to the Japanese emperor . . . ?" For Issei, who were ineligible for U.S. citizenship, would renouncing their Japanese citizenship make them stateless? Was this a trick question meant to confirm prior allegiance? If Nisei views differed from those of their parents, would they be separated?[19]

Harry Takagi pondered his future while studying at the Military Intelligence Language School at Camp Savage, Minnesota. Shortly after Pearl Harbor was bombed, he had been so pleased to learn about his neighbors' congenial acts that he had written a letter to *Time* magazine, which was published in the February 2, 1942, issue:

Sirs:

I am a Nisei, an American citizen of Japanese parentage. Like many other Niseis, I am in the service of my country. This war has hit us harder, probably, than any other portion of the American society. It has caused suspicion to be cast on us, not because we have done anything of a suspicious nature, but because of our race. Let me assure you that we know and love only one country. . . . We Niseis are willing to fight and to die if necessary for America and the principle for which it stands.

Harry A. Takagi
Camp Grant, Ill.[20]

Later that month, the government issued evacuation orders for West Coast Nikkei. Hoping to allay his confusion, Takagi sought a more balanced perspective about Japan's wartime situation. Rather than rely on what he viewed as one-sided U.S. mass media portrayals, he turned to Frank Hachiya, a former high school classmate who had lived in Japan for four years. As a result, Takagi recalled, both young men decided that "it would be better for us to remain patriotic Americans despite the indignities we were suffering."

Early in 1943, Takagi and other Nisei stationed at Camp Savage answered loyalty questionnaires. In Takagi's mind, the most pressing questions were worded to the effect of "Do you understand democracy?" and "Do you believe in the American system of government?" To the first, he replied "yes" and to the second question, "undecided until the relocation problem is clarified." By that time, Takagi's family and other West Coast Nikkei had been removed from their homes and confined in government "relocation camps." As for the military, Nisei were not yet accepted for the draft, but the army was so desperate for translators that Takagi and others had been urged to solicit volunteers. Takagi was frustrated to discover that the FBI had grilled his former classmates at Pomona College in California and Grinnell College in Iowa, asking questions akin to "Would you have no qualms about being in the foxhole with Sgt. Takagi?" A month or two later, an officer called Takagi again regarding his earlier response to the question about believing in the American system of government. "After thinking it over, I decided to change my answer to 'yes' and crossed out the previous reply, since Nisei were again allowed to join the army by then."[21]

Others weighed their responses just as carefully. Takagi's friend Frank Hachiya wrote to a former teacher in February 1943, "I am very happy over the recent news, that of recognizing us Nisei as loyal Americans. . . . We are all determined to do our utmost to prove this new rule is right."[22] Hit Imai reflected, "Here I was an American citizen and I don't know anything about Japan. So the only thing I knew was 'Serve our own country.'" Imai was the third of five Imai sons to serve his country while, across the Pacific, an uncle was in the Japanese navy.

By March 1943, only 1,208 Nisei had volunteered for the army as a result of the tumultuous registration process, less than half the quota of 3,000. They composed 5 percent of those eligible for the draft (between eighteen and thirty-seven years of age) who had answered "yes" to questions 27 and 28 in the loyalty questionnaire. Among them, 800 passed their physical exams.[23] By the end of the war, a total of 2,355 Nisei from the camps had entered the U.S. armed forces.[24]

Out of the mainland volunteers and three thousand volunteers from the Hawaiian Islands, the army formed the 442nd Regimental Combat Team. On April 13, 1943, the 442nd began assembling at Camp Shelby, Mississippi, memorable for the torrential rain that overflowed roadside gullies, turned roads into swamps, and produced red clay mud that coated shoes and socks.[25]

While Nisei were maneuvering in the mud and preparing for service to their country, General DeWitt was testifying to the House Naval Affairs Subcommittee in San Francisco: "A Jap's a Jap. They are a dangerous element. There is no way to determine their loyalty. It makes no difference whether he is an American citizen; theoretically he is still a Japanese, and you can't change him. You can't change him by giving him a piece of paper."[26]

## BASIC TRAINING

Young recruits at Camp Shelby were, however, immersing themselves in basic training. Their days were consumed with physical conditioning, beginning with fundamental drills on military discipline, the care and cleaning of equipment and weapons, day and night patrolling, and map reading. They lived six in a tent, recalled Harry Tamura. Their day began with reveille at 6 A.M., followed by roll call, breakfast, and morning drills that included formations, marching, and M-1 rifle range practice. "It wasn't bad at all," he maintained. "We were young and healthy, and I think I enjoyed all that marching." At the same time, the longer hikes became a challenge. At first, Sagie Nishioka wondered whether he'd be able to survive the twenty-mile march and the obstacle course, climbing up and down a ten-foot wall within a specified time. "Everything had to be done in a hurried manner," he claimed. Sho Endow recalled the four-hour hikes with disdain. After performing office work at Fort Richardson, Alaska, he found the change to sixteen weeks of training was abrupt. "When we went to Camp Shelby, they took a company out for eight- or ten-mile hikes. We could hardly make it! The first hike I can remember, we started out about eight o'clock and came back about two in the afternoon. That was supposed to have been about ten miles. After fourteen, fifteen weeks, why, you can make that in about four hours."

Chester Tanaka characterized the Nisei GIs as spunky and scrappy in his book *Go for Broke*:

They ate K-rations and cursed the man who invented them. They blasted the guys in the rear echelons who grabbed all the Lucky Strikes and Camels and left them with Chelseas and Sensations to smoke. They drank warm beer and were happy to get it. They took off as fast as any GI when the MPs started sweeping the Off-Limits areas. . . . They were typical, run-of-the-mill American GIs. However, there were some differences. They liked rice. Three times a day. They had strange sounding names . . . ; almond eyes . . . ; black hair . . . ; and brown skin.[27]

They were also in a quandary over GI uniforms, for the average Nisei was five feet four and weighed just 125 pounds. "These fatigue pants," complained George Akiyama, "the smallest one was 34–36. Great big baggy pants, inseams about fifteen inches long." Akiyama was five feet four and had a thirty-one-inch waist. Nisei were so small that the army shipped WAC (Women's Army Corps) clothing to Camp Shelby.[28]

Mainland Nisei faced another challenge of sorts when they met the Nisei from Hawaii. Originally the Hawaiian Provisional Infantry Battalion, they dubbed themselves "One Puka Puka," the 100th Infantry Battalion. When three thousand of them completed training in Wisconsin and joined the mainlanders at Camp Shelby, a kind of "sibling rivalry" erupted.[29] Nisei from Hawaii, who tended to be fun-loving, generous, and group-spirited, and who spoke their minds freely, became a bit resentful when they arrived to find that the mainland draftees, who composed only 30 percent of the Nisei combat team, had filled all the noncommissioned officer positions. In their pidgin English, they dubbed mainlanders "kotonks," for the sound empty coconuts make when they hit the ground. Mainlanders, who had grown up as members of a smaller minority group and where prejudices were evident, were more timid, individualistic, and wary of others' views. They referred to their island partners as "Buddha-heads," derived from the pidgin term "buta head," or "pig head."[30] The rift between them would dissipate on the war front, where, as George Akiyama would explain, "They start respecting you."

Rural Hood River Nisei were shocked by another form of cultural diversity: the color distinctions and racial prejudices of the American South. When they arrived in Hattiesburg, Mississippi, state representative John Rankin delivered a speech titled "Jap Invasion of the Southland." White civilians "socially snubbed or ignored" the young men, and the local USO (United Service Organizations) excluded them from dances, so Nisei traveled thirty-two miles to Columbia during their off-duty hours, according to 1943 army intelligence reports.[31] Two and a half months later, their relations with the "white people of Hattiesburg" were characterized as "friendly," though "not on a particularly cordial plane."[32] The Jim Crow laws, however, were particularly noxious. While bars and nightclubs in

Hattiesburg catered to GIs, it was clear that services and facilities were different based on one's color. Though their officers directed Nisei to use facilities for whites, some Nisei were aghast at segregation policies. "When I took a streetcar, I always liked to go in the back," explained Fred Sumoge. "They stopped me and said, 'Sit in the front.'" He was surprised to learn that blacks were not permitted to board buses unless there was space. Even the army theater posted a separatist sign: "Colored Seats from the Left Rear Corner." Sumoge observed: "Maybe I'm a little better off—or they're worse off. . . . Even in the uniform, fighting for their country, they're soldiers in uniform—and still discrimination. We were getting the same thing: discrimination."

## DIFFERENT WAYS OF SERVING

During the early years of the war, two Hood River Nisei served as cooks. Harry Tamura was among several who answered his unit's call for volunteers. After attending cooking school at Fort Leonard Wood, Missouri, he became one of two cooks (along with two second cooks, mess sergeants, and noncommissioned officers) to return to Camp Shelby, where Nisei recruits trained for six weeks before going overseas. "I was in charge of the meal. If something went wrong with that meal, I was to blame," he explained matter-of-factly. Working twenty-four-hour shifts from noon until noon, Tamura and his second cook prepared meals for two hundred on a coal stove, ensuring that food was ready and palatable when "the boys" returned from drills. For breakfast, they typically prepared scrambled eggs (using real eggs), bacon, toast, and coffee. Steak was not served often enough to satisfy the troops, but far and away the least favorite dish was okra, a slimy southern vegetable prominent in army rations. Sagie Nishioka also volunteered to be a cook, considering that "at least I'd learn something instead of wiping windows." After working as a cook's assistant, he would become a cook for the 442nd in Europe.

Several Hood River Nisei worked in special services. During his medic training at Camp Grant outside Chicago, Shig Imai, a slight 150 pounds, found favor in his squad. While practicing as litter bearers, his buddies chose to carry *him* in the litter, as he was the lightest member of their squad. A self-taught, hunt-and-peck typist, Imai became mess officer clerk at Camp Grant Station Hospital. Eventually he transferred to the Prisoner of War Processing Company, where he compiled records of prisoners of war (POWs) for the Red Cross, including photos, fingerprints, and personnel files. Imai's final assignment would be with the POW cadre in Hawaii, guarding captive Koreans from Saigon.

Harry Takagi also spent his first year in the military at Camp Grant, where his two years of pre-med studies served him well in the medic corps. After practicing with bandages and splints for eight weeks, he trained as a surgical technician, assisting with appendectomies and surgery on hemorrhoids, hernias, and tonsils. By October 1942, when the army desperately sought Japanese-language translators, recruiters asked Takagi to volunteer. Though he declined, he was directed to study languages anyway and, as previously noted, studied Chinese and Japanese languages at Pomona College, the University of Denver, and Grinnell College. After also training to intercept radio messages at McDill Field Air Force Base in Florida, Takagi would return to the Military Intelligence Language School at Fort Snelling, Minnesota.[33] Expounding on the vagaries of war, he wrote a former teacher, "The doctrine of love instead of hate seems to have disappeared behind the smoke-screen of dictatorships and intense nationalism. I only hope that this will soon be won, for every day of warfare means a day of suffering by the multitude of innocent humanity who suffer the consequences."[34]

Shig Imai was not promoted because of a photo the FBI found during its wartime search of his parents' home. (Sheri Imai-Swiggart, 1942)

## A QUESTION OF EQUITY

As they prepared for war, Nisei GIs recognized other disparities in their military treatment. Shig Imai had tolerated the army initially limiting Nisei to the infantry as well as his post–Pearl Harbor transfer to detail work. But he was exasperated that he was not gaining a single stripe. (This situation would not change over the next two years. While searching the

Imais' Hood River home during the spring of 1942, the FBI discovered a photo of Camp Grant that Imai had mailed to his sister, marking his living quarters. This immediately became part of his military record. "I just wanted to send a picture the PX was selling," Imai explained. "They were on a fishing expedition. . . . After that, I got to be a corporal. Then I got three stripes and that was it." Upon his honorable discharge in January 1945, Shig Imai would reach the rank of technical sergeant.)

Most officers in the Nisei battalion were white. The War Department's organizational plan of January 22, 1943, stipulated that all officers down to company commander must be "white American citizens."[35] Just a few Nisei, those trained in college reserve officer programs, advanced to lieutenant and captain. Yet the intelligence and schooling of Nisei qualified them as officers, according to Bill Hosokawa, news editor and author. The average IQ among members of the 442nd was 119, 9 points higher than the requirement for officer candidate school and the highest of all infantry units in the army; the battalion also included more college graduates than any unit of its size.[36]

Nisei GIs did not feel that the military or their government trusted them, causing them to wonder whether they and their families were, in fact, mainland POWs. "Nobody else was treated the way we were," maintained Mam Noji. "After all, Germany declared war on us. Italy declared war on us. But none of them were segregated like we were. Germans and Italians all retained whatever privileges they had. They took away all our civil rights." At the same time, Nisei felt they had little recourse but to withstand the military's drudgery and inequities. "We are not a rebellious people. We tend to do what we are ordered to do, you know—especially in those days. . . . Oh, we didn't like what we were told to do. But then who does in the service? We wanted to be forthright American citizens, and we tried to do the best we could even though I think we were betrayed by the government. No question about that. We did the best we could under the circumstances. We were in no position to argue with anybody. We were at the bottom. . . . *Shikataganai*—'can't help it.'"

The War Department would not implement an equitable policy for Nisei until January 1944, when they would be reclassified "on the same basis as other citizens." Now, rather than simply volunteering, Nisei would again be eligible for the draft.[37] Altogether, 22,500 Nisei would serve in the U.S. military during World War II. Eighteen thousand of them would join segregated units in Europe and Hawaii, including the combined 100th

Battalion/442nd Regimental Combat Team, while the remainder would fulfill the demand for Japanese-language translators in the South Pacific. Nisei would, in fact, be overrepresented. Not only would the proportion of Japanese Americans in the army be 20 percent higher than their representation in the population,[38] but they would also have the highest percentage of service members of any other ethnic group serving.[39]

In a letter to a neighbor, Noji laid bare his loyalties: "There are many Japanese American men in uniform like me . . . intent on keeping this country of ours as our forefathers intended it to be."[40] Despite the adverse conditions they faced, Akiyama, too, was firm in his conviction. "We still wanted to be good citizens. Here we were fighting for good Uncle Sam, we used to say."

# FIVE

# "The Two-Sided Sword"

## WARTIME CHANGES FOR

## JAPANESE AMERICAN FAMILIES

I N the weeks and months following the bombing of Pearl Harbor, Nisei GIs' distress about their families' welfare overshadowed their own wartime dilemmas. George Akiyama's father was interned in a Justice Department detention center, and his mother and four younger siblings tended the family's thirty-five-acre farm. Likewise, Sagie Nishioka's widowed mother and his school-age brother and sister were pruning, fertilizing, irrigating, and handling other off-season chores on their seventeen acres of strawberries, pears, and cherries. With the absence of their family patriarchs and eldest sons, the Akiyamas and Nishiokas strained to manage farm responsibilities in addition to making day-to-day household decisions. Even intact families of local Nisei soldiers struggled with the consequences of Executive Order 9066. Overcome with fractured hopes and gnawing questions about their grim future, they wondered: How would they cope? What would become of their farms and homes? Then all too soon: How would they face life in exile?

During those tenuous times, there was limited communication between GIs and their families. "I did make a few phone calls to Mother, but she asked me not to call because she was sure the phones were tapped," explained Mam Noji. "In those days, we had party lines. Neighbors could hear the ring and all pick up. I'm sure they were monitoring all Japanese families. When all this was happening and we're in uniform a thousand miles away, it weighed on you."

George Akiyama served in the U.S. Army while his father was imprisoned in a Justice Department internment center in Missoula, Montana. George's mother (left) sent this photo to her husband. (Itsu Akiyama, 1942)

## PREPARING TO LEAVE

After the FBI rounded up George Akiyama's father with other Issei leaders, the worried GI kept in touch through his sister Kiyo's letters. He learned that his father had been confined in the Multnomah County Jail in Portland before being transferred to camps in Montana, Oklahoma, and eventually Louisiana. Brother Nob had driven their mother the four-hour round-trip to Portland so that Mr. Akiyama could give his wife instructions for fertilizing and pruning the orchard. "She knew quite a bit, but she was just adjusted to following orders, not giving orders," explained younger brother Sab. After Executive Order 9066 was issued, George, the eldest son, was given a two-day leave so he could arrange for a neighbor to lease the family orchard. The *Hood River News*, withholding George's name, editorialized about his return, noting, "In more normal times there would be no evacuation of parents of sons serving in the United States Army."[1]

Provoked by the rumor mill and confused about whether they would be able to return, panic-stricken Nikkei became victims of opportunists who purchased or leased their possessions and property at a fraction of their value. "Caucasians came to buy our cow and calf," recalled Mrs. Akiyama. "They told me, 'This is forty dollars. This is fifty dollars.' I would just reply, 'All right.' We had a Fergie [Ferguson] tractor. We sold it, because we did not know whether we would return."[2] Mam Noji's sister, Chiz, remembered selling items for "practically nothing." Even their parents' new bedroom set had to be sold because "we didn't know whether we were going to come back."[3]

Former Hood River resident Min (Minoru) Asai described the chaotic situation: "Since the proclamation by General DeWitt, Japanese people were trying to get our business in order, trying to store our household items, sell what we could and lease our properties to anyone that would buy. We were in a very weak position. Many of the people sold all their worldly possessions at nowhere near their value. Many Japanese lost almost everything."[4] They had much at stake, for three-quarters of local Nikkei farmers owned their property. And the value of Nikkei farms was more than seven times greater per acre than others on the West Coast.[5]

Ads appearing in the classified section of the local newspaper depicted the haste and fear that accompanied the government's harsh actions with the onset of war:

For sale: Cow, fresh soon; also two-year-old Heifer; also Laying Hens. N. Hamada.
For sale: Team of young horses, 1300 lbs. Cheap for cash. K. Uyeno, Parkdale.
For lease or sale: Fifty acre tract: Consisting of 19 acres of apple trees; 10 acres of pears: Bartlett, Bosc, D'Anjous; 4 acres of cherries; 5 ½ acres of fine asparagus ranch; remaining acreage, wooded land. Free irrigation water. Orchard has received excellent care. Nobuo Kobayashi.[6]

Like other Nikkei families, the Nojis had cleared the land, planted trees, nurtured their farm, and, after seven long years, finally brought their forty acres to the point of bearing fruit. Not surprisingly, the fate of their young trees was their biggest concern. Leaving their farm equipment and fertilizer, the family asked for little compensation from their property caretakers, requesting only, "Just take good care of our orchard."[7]

When local businesses sold out their stocks of suitcases, Nikkei resorted to ordering footlockers from the Montgomery Ward catalog. Storing and selling larger items and loaning others to friends and neighbors, they packed only the necessities (bedding, toilet articles, clothing, eating utensils, and personal effects), mindful to take only what each person could carry.[8]

## "A MOTLEY CROWD"

They looked like "kind of a motley crowd," milling around and carrying their prized possessions, observed Dr. Stanley Wells, whose medical practice was located several blocks from the Union Pacific train depot. Toting duffel bags and suitcases with assigned family numbers dangling from their clothing, 431 residents boarded the rickety train. Sixty soldiers stood watch, joined by local and state law enforcement officials and several hundred locals. It was just six days after Civil Exclusion Order No. 49 had posted official news of their evacuation and six weeks since the first West Coast evacuation from Bainbridge Island, Washington, on March 31.[9]

Hood River Nikkei, toting as much as they could carry, board trains to a destination unknown to them at that time. (Billie Stevens, Hood River County Extension Service, 1942)

Local newspapers reported a buoyant atmosphere, free of hostility and characterized by "a holiday spirit" among the evacuees.[10] In contrast, District Attorney Teunis Wyers observed that "many of the older folks wept and I think most of the younger ones were quite satisfied that they would never be permitted to return." He discerned "the practically unanimous reaction" among townsfolk and farmers of the valley that "they must never return—that their coming here was wrong and that the valley is far better off without them. One hears this even from those who had close personal friends among the evacuees."[11]

Nikkei viewed their departure with despair. The mother of veteran Sho Endow recalled that their leaving was "somewhat quiet and reserved. We tried to suppress our feelings and leave quietly and with goodwill. . . . But my husband and I commiserated with Mr. and Mrs. [Katsusaburo] Tamura, crying together about our fate."[12] Mam's sister Chiz was worried, recalling, "It was a sad feeling. We didn't know if we would ever come back again. We thought maybe they might even send us to Japan." George Akiyama's older sister, Kiyo, expressed her anguish, writing, "I just couldn't keep from crying. . . . I never felt so down-hearted in all my life."[13] Younger brother Henry tried vainly to remain upbeat. "Although most people feel very low, I . . . will keep my chin up."[14]

Shortly after their May 13th departure, a statement from the Mid-Columbia Japanese American Citizens League appeared in the *Hood River County Sun*: "To the People of the Mid-Columbia and to the People of the Northwest: As we go forth from this majestic area in the midst of the Cascade Range, we leave with long years of love for this friendly community. . . . While we are temporarily exiled, these memories of friendship and the love for our homes will be the invaluable source of comfort and consolation to us. . . ."[15]

On the train, armed soldiers stood guard and blinds were lowered, adding to the tension and eeriness of this unwelcome journey to a destination unknown. When a young Nisei returned from the lavatory in pitch-black darkness, he wandered up and down the aisle, gingerly feeling his way among passengers, trying to find his father.[16] Jostled passengers tried to sleep as the train pitched back and forth, careening up mountains, through tunnels and over construction bridges, and then braking every few hours to cool the engine. Past Portland and Eugene to Klamath Falls, Oregon, then on through Redding, Sacramento, and Fresno, California—the panorama through the grimy windows shifted from evergreen-draped mountains and snowcapped Mount Hood to grazing sheep and unfamiliar date palms and orange trees.[17]

The trip was eye-opening in another way for many rural residents, whose ties to their farms as well as the forested mountain terrain that discouraged travel, had virtually confined them to their own communities. A surprised Sab Akiyama reflected, "I didn't know there were that many Japanese in Hood River. In the olden days I knew the people in Oak Grove, and that was about it. We didn't associate much with Parkdale or Odell . . . I'd never been beyond Portland."

## LIFE IN CAMP

Hood River Nikkei finally arrived at Pinedale, a thousand miles from home, one of sixteen temporary quarters set up by the War Department. A former mill site in the desert near Fresno, it was enclosed by an eight- to ten-foot mesh fence topped by several rows of electrified barbed wire. Searchlights scoured the darkness from towers manned by armed guards. Weary and anxious Nikkei, herded through registration lines and issued blankets, were assigned to hastily constructed, unfinished tarpaper barracks. A single lightbulb with a drop cord hung inside each spare room; army cots with bare springs and thin mattresses were the only furnishings. Ceilings were open so that even the most private conversations next door were easily heard.[18]

George Akiyama's youngest brother, fifteen-year-old Henry, conveyed his day-to-day musings in letters to Vienna Annala, his teacher and principal at Oak Grove School:

How is everybody back in the best community of the best place in the whole world? I am quite fine and so is everybody else except the heat is getting me so don't be surprised if I fade out of this world. I saw about 6 persons faint out with sunstroke yesterday. It must have been about 130 degrees in the sun. . . . Yesterday we got word not to drink any more water because it is impure. I took my smallpox and third (last) typhoid shots yesterday. My arm sure is sore today. . . . I feel low, ready to cry. . . . Although this may be a great personal sacrafice [sic] to all of us, it is so little we can do to help our country win this horrid war and we are all proud to have done one small cooperation.

I'm so lonesome and broken-hearted down here. . . . We Hood River small boys 15 and under played 3 softball games, all being with White River, Washington boys. We won the first two and lost the third. . . . I don't know what to write. There is nothing hardly happening around here so how's everything back home? . . .[19]

George's twenty-four-year-old sister also wrote about life in camp:

We are warned to keep a distance of 10 ft. from the electric fences. I understand a little boy was shot in the leg when he chased after a baseball near the fence. I feel so sorry for those soldiers guarding us. It is so hot and they are on their feet walking back and forth all day long. I imagine that it certainly is a tiresome task. Many people collapsed from the terrific heat and all ready [sic] one Hood Riverite passed away. No privacy in any way whatsoever here. We can hear the nextdoor neighbor clear as ever. . . . People stand in line and wait for hours for meals. On hot days it's really terrible. We've had many cases where people collapse right in line. . . . I miss Oak Grove and Hood River's water. Oh! If I could only have a glass of that water! Our days for washing are Mon, Wed & Sat.

Eating canned meat has made everyone sick. I heard 75% of the people are suffering from stomach trouble. . . . If it isn't too much trouble, could you open up my little trunk. I have my electric plate pushed way in the bottom. I'll have to drink hot water or cocoa from now on . . . they have no preparations for the ill here. . . .[20]

The dry desert heat became so unbearable that Mam Noji's father improvised a cooling system by pouring water on the cement floor and then lying *under* his cot. Later, he confessed that he thought he'd been sent to Pinedale to die.

As soon as the more permanent facilities were completed, residents moved again, the second time in two months. Hood River Nikkei were transferred from Pinedale Assembly Center to quarters in northern California. Tule Lake was one of ten "relocation centers," as the government designated them although President Roosevelt himself called them "concentration camps."[21] The ten camps were located on isolated federal property in Arizona, Arkansas, California, Colorado, Idaho, Utah, and Wyoming. "Godforsaken spots in alien climes where no one had lived before and no one has lived since," mused historian Roger Daniels.[22]

Their new home was a dry, isolated lakebed. Shaggy willow trees, sagebrush, and desert grass stubble were the only vegetation that survived Tule Lake's arid climate and ten inches of rain each year. In his novel *Tule Lake*, Nisei Oregonian Edward Miyakawa aptly described the setting: "The dry heat burns the dirt loose from the earth. In gusts and whirlwinds it blows hundreds of feet above Tule, abrades our faces and filters into our eyes and throats, burning and strangling."[23] Security continued to be heavily enforced, with barbed wire fences encircling the camp and armed guards posted vigilantly in watchtowers nearby. Barracks were arranged in sixty-four community blocks, each sharing centralized mess halls, toilet facilities, showers, and laundry rooms.

Nisei made efforts to adjust to the extreme climate changes and seemed to alter their ideas of what was normal, as Henry Akiyama explained:

If I don't watch out, I might be a roast hen pretty soon . . . there's only one good sized tree inside this project. . . . The mosquitoes and ants make short work of me and how! Everything down here is dead as usual. Four of us Freshmans [sic] have made a club called the "Blackhawks." We Blackhawks go snake hunting up "Castle Rock" here. Succeeded in getting three rattlers so far. We sell the meat so we may raise some money for our treasury. . . . Boy what a dead fourth of July it was this year. There were ballgames and . . . a nice program at the outdoor stage which drew approximately 8,000 Tuleans there that night. But still this fourth lacked something. Maybe it was the folks back in Oak Grove, maybe the peacetime emotions. . . . They opened a Pee-Wee softball league here. . . . Block residents have done a lot trying to put up recreation facilities such as volleyball or see-saw.

Today I witnessed the worst dust storm ever to visit this colony. . . . Clouds gathered above, the wind started to howl, and when I looked southward, I started home as fast as my legs could carry me . . . I got home just in front of the storm which lasted about 20 minutes without a let-up. I couldn't even see the next barrack all that time. Lots of dust got in our apartments through the cracks too. . . . When my dad came inside after about 10 minutes of it, he looked like he had a mud coating all over his head. I couldn't stop laughing.[24]

Winter was just as harsh when temperatures dipped to twenty degrees below zero,[25] as Chiz Tamura noted: "In the wintertime, it was really

When Harry Tamura (right) and army buddy Chik Aoyama visited his family at the Tule Lake concentration camp, family members recall that the GIs preferred talk of food rather than army life. (Harry Tamura, 1943)

cold. We burned a potbelly stove. They would bring coal to the middle of the barracks, and people would rush over and get what they could. The latrines, you know, we had to go outside. We would take walks around the blocks. But there were always those guard houses. . . . After awhile, you just accepted it and felt that was your life. We had no control."

Some Nisei sons serving in the army were able to visit their families while on leave and witnessed camp life firsthand. When Harry Tamura stepped off the Greyhound bus, the gravity of his family's situation overwhelmed him. "When I got to the gate there and the camp barbed wire fence, I really felt sad for my parents and for the Japanese people. . . . It really bothered me."

Obstacles for their families were all too evident. "You had to get permission to go in and permission to get out. So it was sort of like, really, a prison," Sagie Nishioka observed after visiting his family in camp. "Of course, living conditions were not too good . . . There was very little privacy. . . . Army food was a lot better. . . . The Army had more meats, you know." Nishioka contrived a three-tier rating system: Hospital food was tastier than army food but camp food was the worst of all. (Feeding evacuees cost just forty-five cents per day, sometimes falling as low as thirty-one cents. This conformed to the government's requirement that evacuee meals should not cost more than army rations, which were set at forty cents per person per day.)[26] Kenjiro Hayakawa was more blunt after visiting his family at Tule Lake. "Living there was a waste of time. Their lives they could enrich better instead of staying confined. . . . People could be in business, people could be in school, people could be like everybody else. Everything is held back."

Before he shipped out to Europe, George Akiyama paid a brief visit to his parents and four siblings, who had been transferred to Camp Minidoka in Idaho. (Mr. Akiyama had rejoined his family early in the year after his thirteen-month imprisonment in Justice Department internment centers.) "They just coped like the rest of them—hoped the war would be over soon and we'd be coming back safe. My mother said, 'Be a good soldier. Don't embarrass the family. Go to church whenever it's possible.' I remember that."

Mam Noji was denied the chance to visit his family a month before he shipped out to the South Pacific. "My parents were in Tule Lake. At that time, that was a restricted area [within the military zone]. That really made us unhappy. Probably our last chance to see our parents, you know."

EFFECTS OF CAMP

The Nikkei had already been segregated by the government because of their ethnicity, and, for some, the war severed the once-sturdy bonds between them. The federal government had administered controversial and poorly explained "loyalty questions" in an effort to screen Nikkei for military induction, work permits, and clearance to resettle outside the camps, as discussed in chapter 4. Those who answered that they would serve in the armed forces and those who swore unqualified allegiance to the United States (also forswearing allegiance to the Japanese emperor) were deemed "loyal" and transferred to other camps. Those who refused, misinterpreted the questions, or failed to register were branded "disloyal" and isolated at the Tule Lake camp, which became the designated segregation center. As a result, more than eighteen thousand Nikkei were segregated at Tule Lake while the rest were dispersed to other camps. Hood River "loyals" transferred to Minidoka, in south-central Idaho near Twin Falls; Heart Mountain, in northwestern Wyoming; and Jerome, in southeastern Arkansas.[27]

Their incarceration[28] lacerated the souls of Nikkei, especially the American-born Nisei, eroding their hard-fought dreams of succeeding in mainstream America. "Most of the Nisei lived with the thought that as long as they were citizens, they were immune to this treatment, but they have found out the hard way," GI Frank Hachiya explained to a friend in camp. Viewing the situation as a resident of both the United States and Japan, he philosophized, "The source of all this ill treatment being forced upon us is the inconsistency between the theory and the practice of democracy."[29] Nevertheless, Nisei permitted themselves a more charitable view of their incarceration, recognizing both sides of the dismal situation.

"It was kind of a two-sided sword," reflected Sab Akiyama. "As a teenager, you had no restrictions. My dad was gone [interned in a justice detention center because he was an Issei community leader], and we were provided with shelter and food. You could just do whatever you wanted to do during the day. There were no chores, except I used to wash dishes at the mess hall." Recalling a similar carefree attitude, Hit Imai added, "You didn't have any responsibility. Just let the government do this and that. If you're in the camp, well, though you have responsibility, there isn't much you can do about it." Tellingly, he added, "At that time, I thought I was having fun."

Adults young and old recognized that daily routines in camp were a complete contrast from their unrelenting labors on the farm. "On the other side, we got to see people at home we would never see that often," admitted Noji's sister Chiz Tamura. "Mom and Dad found some friends they had known in Japan. They got together and visited. This was the first time they ever got to rest. That was the good part, I guess, if there was a good part."

Similarly, Mrs. Akiyama told her family that camp was "like a vacation," disclosed son Sab. "She wasn't out there early in the morning splitting wood and starting the fire and cooking breakfast and coming home to cook lunch, then go out and work and come home and cook supper. It was entirely different. . . . She enjoyed the time she was allowed to do craft things. At home, she never had time for anything like that. If she had any time, she was sitting and patching, darning socks or shirts." Women unwittingly became the "happiest people in the relocation center," maintained Christian minister Daisuke Kitagawa. He observed that, liberated from lives of continuous drudgery, women found camp life to be like a well-deserved holiday.[30]

As despicable as it seemed, life in camp did offer welcome relief for

Sagie Nishioka's widowed mother and two young siblings. "Being the old-est, I kind of felt responsible for the family," he explained. "In some ways, that relocation camp kind of helped me out because I knew that they would at least provide them food and stuff."

There were shortcomings to this freedom from responsibility, however. For one, the cohesive family unit splintered. In camp, the once self-reli-ant Nikkei were now dependent on the government for their basic needs. Communal living, which meant Nikkei ate in mess halls and used cen-tralized bathroom facilities, limited precious family bonding time and separated residents by age group and gender. With Nisei less reliant on their parents, the influence of Issei, especially men, weakened as did their traditional roles as family providers and decision makers.[31] "Even after my father returned, the folks still didn't have much authority because there was no way to hold you down," explained Sab Akiyama. "You really didn't have to obey anybody. You got your meal. You had your bed. There's noth-ing to do but just kinda wander around. It was a funny life . . . I mean, you kind of lost all purpose in life for awhile. The family unit disintegrated."

"Just one year in this camp and we will all be 'bums,'" lamented one Nikkei at Tule Lake, deploring the breakdown of morale among young people.[32] Life inside barbed wire was definitely taking a toll. Local news editor Hugh Ball, dispatched to two camps by the governor to assess work release possibilities, observed that the young Japanese Americans he knew as "fine, loyal American citizens" were "rapidly degenerating into cynics, whose ideas are based upon what they believe is the utter hopelessness of their future." He characterized them as "formerly active young men, largely raised in conformance with American ideals, now inmates of an enemy aliens' camp, largely without healthy occupation of an objective type, with plenty of time on their hands to mourn their fate."[33]

For Nisei, who reminded themselves that they were still American citi-zens, the denial of their civil rights was the most pronounced and egre-gious of offenses. "We were treated as prisoners and criminals when we had not committed any crime," Min Asai insisted. "The only reason we were there was because we had Japanese faces and the military thought we might harm the war effort."[34]

Indeed, the U.S. Constitution should have protected the almost 88,000 Japanese Americans under its jurisdiction.[35] Yet Nisei were denied their rights as natural-born citizens. In fact, as the JACL, the largest Nikkei civil rights organization, has noted, their forced removal and incarceration violated six articles of the Bill of Rights. Among the guaranteed rights they were denied are freedom of speech and the press, in being forbidden to use the Japanese language; freedom to practice religions other than Christianity; the right to be secure from searches without warrants; the right to a speedy and public trial, to be informed of the charges against them, and to have access to legal counsel; the right to not be subjected to cruel and unusual punishment, as represented by inadequate conditions in the assembly and detention centers; and the right to vote.[36] Those rights were revoked even in the nation's highest courts, as when, in 1943, the U.S. Supreme Court ruled against Hood River Nisei Minoru Yasui, who challenged the curfew order in Portland. The justification was, simply, "military necessity."[37]

It was difficult to be detained behind barbed wire while one's siblings were serving in the U.S. armed forces. Members of Mam Noji's family expressed their frustrations. "Mam was representing the family. Then, to have his family incarcerated in camps, it just did not seem right," remarked his sister Chiz. "We were still citizens. . . . It wasn't constitutional, was it?" Mam's brother Toru concurred. "The greatest shame . . . was the denial of our citizenship and the constitutional protection that we thought that we had. I recognized that there was the possibility that our Issei parents could or might be interned but never thought that we Nisei as U.S. citizens would or could be incarcerated. This was a shocker and hard to believe that it could happen in this country."

Mam described learning of his family's incarceration as "a kind of low blow to me."[38] "Here I was in uniform a thousand miles away. Wrong place at the wrong time. But when they strip you of your citizenship—all the rights that we had taken for granted, you know—that wasn't worth the paper it was written on. When it comes right down to it, it didn't mean a darn thing. We put a lot of weight on that. That was really a big disappointment. The sacrifices we had to give!" Unfortunately, as the perils of World War II continued, even more sacrifices and setbacks lay ahead.

# SIX

# *"Getting Shot from Ahead of Us and Behind Us"*

## WAR IN THE SOUTH PACIFIC

**H**EADED for the South Pacific battlefront, Mam Noji gazed across San Francisco Bay from the top deck of a cargo Liberty ship. In only a few minutes, the enormity of his future would become apparent. "When Tot [fellow Hood Riverite Taro Asai] and I were going underneath the Golden Gate Bridge, he says, 'I figure that we've only got a fifty-fifty chance of seeing that bridge again.' Until then I never thought of not coming back. Fifty-fifty's not good odds, is it?"

Marksmanship practice on the ship did not bolster Noji's confidence. "For the first three days we were accompanied by a big Chicago cruiser, a big battleship. We felt pretty good about it. One day, my gosh, we were all alone. We felt like a big target out there. And every day a few sailors on our ship would let loose a balloon and practice. They never even came close to it, you know. That didn't do our morale too much good."

### MILITARY INTELLIGENCE SERVICE

Noji, Asai, and Frank Hachiya were specially trained Nisei linguists in the Military Intelligence Service (MIS), considered to be the U.S. Army's "secret weapon." They worked as Japanese-language translators and interrogators for the Intelligence Division of the U.S. Army (G-2).[1] Dubbed the "Yankee Samurai,"[2] they would become the eyes and ears of the Allied forces and would be instrumental in breaking the Pacific stalemate. Dispersed to duty with front line units from Great Britain, Canada, Australia, New Zealand, India, and China, the MIS would serve in every major campaign and every major battle in the Pacific.[3]

In order to defeat Japan's army, the U.S. military determined it would need hundreds, if not thousands, of linguists. Beginning in the spring of 1941, it laid the foundation for a language school, assuming that Nisei soldiers would be ready candidates. Unraveling the Japanese language, considered more complicated than most European languages, was a daunting mission, however, "almost beyond comprehension," according to Brigadier General John Weckerling, the intelligence officer in the South Pacific who organized the school. Two separate alphabets and thousands of Chinese characters composed the written symbols, and the spoken language used different forms depending on rank or class. Military commanders in the Japanese army, confident that foreigners could not possibly intercept their messages and translate their complicated language, neglected to code their wartime communications. Japanese soldiers spoke freely, labeled their minefields, carried personal diaries, and even disregarded security while handling military documents. As a result, Nisei, who had been criticized for an upbringing that included Japanese language and culture, became indispensable for their wartime service: translating captured Japanese documents and interrogating prisoners of war.[4]

"The military were desperately scraping the bottom of the barrel to find some of us," admitted Noji. "There was almost zero amongst American people who could speak Japanese language. . . . They were so desperate to find people who understood some Japanese—and I put myself at the lower level. They had to have us!" Indeed, the army had overestimated Nisei linguistic skills, hoping that a few weeks' study of Japanese vocabulary, military terminology, and combat intelligence would suffice. Most Americanized Nisei had managed to converse in Japanese with their parents but had little experience reading and writing the complicated foreign characters (and certainly no exposure to Japanese military language). In 1941, a survey of the first 3,700 enlisted Nisei showed that only 3 percent could speak fluently. Another 4 percent were considered proficient, and 3 percent would be eligible only after "a prolonged period of training,"[5] according to historian Masaharu Ano. Even then, one-fourth of GIs in the first class failed to graduate.[6]

Kibei, defined by U.S. intelligence as those Nisei having three or more years of schooling in Japan, particularly after age thirteen,[7] were more fluent in both written and spoken Japanese. In a college autobiography, Frank Hachiya shared his perspective on balancing his marginal positions between two cultures: "When you know the language of one people, you know the people and understand their problems. So the first step to promote better understanding between the nations is to have as many people as possible who have the knowledge of both."[8]

As the war progressed, the format and standards for recruiting linguists loosened while the military tried to meet the huge demand from all branches of the U.S. military as well as Allied forces throughout the Pacific and Southeast Asia. In July 1942, the army began to recruit Nisei from the camps. But by late 1944, few Nisei selected for language training were proficient in Japanese or any language other than English.[9]

Even as pressure increased to recruit more Japanese linguists, the process became mired in bureaucratic orders. First, the War Department mandated that Nisei could not serve overseas. It was only after lobbying by intelligence officers that the order was rescinded, and Nisei linguists were permitted to serve in all branches of the U.S. military. Second, President Roosevelt's Executive Order 9066 excluded Nikkei from the West Coast, which necessitated moving the army intelligence school inland from San Francisco's Presidio.[10] After a nationwide search for a locale that would "accept oriental-faced Americans . . . fighting with their brains for their native America," the school's commandant, Colonel Kai E. Rasmussen, met with Governor Harold E. Stassen and determined that Minnesota "not only had room physically but also had room in the people's hearts."[11]

TRAINING AT CAMP SAVAGE

Formerly a shelter for elderly, indigent men in the southern outskirts of Minneapolis, Camp Savage became the new site of the Military Intelligence Service Language School in June 1942. Early on, its deficient physical conditions and the demands of its curriculum seemed apt preparation for the sometimes haphazard and extreme nature of combat and intelligence duty. When Noji joined the first class of two hundred students and their fifteen instructors, the poorly equipped cabin classrooms lacked furniture and textbooks. Classes commenced nevertheless, even as Noji and his classmates studied on the cold concrete floor.[12] Their rigorous coursework extended from 8 A.M. to 4:30 P.M. and was followed by study in the evening. The classroom pace was so rapid that after lights-out at 11 P.M., overwhelmed students often crammed for tests by taking flashlights under their blankets or sitting in the latrines. (This led late-night officer patrols to turn out lights and send the harried men to bed.) Time for weekend study and relaxation was limited, since the men practiced mandatory field maneuvers in preparation for their dual roles as soldiers and linguists. On Saturday mornings, they were expected to pass weekly tests.[13]

In December 1942, after six months of intensive study, Noji graduated in Camp Savage's first class of linguists. He had one major misgiving: "We were given a few stripes and ordered for duties. There were three *hakujin* in my own class. They all got commissions. That was a big difference that kind of bothers you, you know?" White classmates gained automatic commissions as second lieutenants, while Nisei earned promotions of just one or two levels and remained in the enlisted ranks. Even Nisei who served as instructors for their promoted white classmates emerged with ranks no higher than sergeant.[14] That situation would not change until 1944, when the visiting chief of army intelligence questioned why a Nisei civilian was giving military commands; afterward, a Nisei finally received a commission.[15]

By June 1946, 6,000 men would train at the language school, which was moved to larger facilities at nearby Fort Snelling, Minnesota. Of those, 3,700 would serve in combat areas, attached to some 128 units, including those of other international forces.[16]

## "COOL RECEPTION IN THE TROPICS"

Among the first one hundred Nisei linguists headed for the Pacific theater in December 1942,[17] Noji landed in the French territory of New Caledonia, east of Australia. There, encamped in coconut groves frequently drenched by steamy rain showers, his ten-man MIS team joined the Forty-third Division, a National Guard unit of New Englanders. "We had a cool reception in the tropics. I'm sure there were guys peering through the corners and looking at us through the tents, you know, wondering who these strange-looking guys were. Only one fellow came out to greet us. . . . Probably few of these New England boys had seen an Asian, and they suspiciously viewed us from a distance. . . . This awkward situation resolved itself once our unit engaged with the enemy, and they realized our mission and what our capabilities were."[18]

Japanese forces were boldly driving southward to seize territory in the

Philippines, Southeast Asia, and Indonesia. In the first seven months after crippling the U.S. Pacific Fleet at Pearl Harbor, Japan had gained control of territories extending east and west from Burma to the Gilbert Islands (in the Central Pacific) and north and south from the Aleutians to the Philippine Islands. Bolstering its offensive against the weakened Allied Forces and continuing its South Pacific expansion,[19] Japan began building an airstrip on Guadalcanal, in the midst of the Solomon Islands in the Central Pacific. This tactical move not only threatened U.S. supply lines to Australia but provided a strategic base from which to dominate nearby islands. By also securing New Guinea, the world's second-largest island, Japan would be in a position to invade Australia from both the north and the northeast.[20]

Following a decisive victory in June 1942 at Midway Island in the North Pacific, Allied forces prepared to take the Solomon Islands, New Guinea's northeastern coast, and eventually Rabaul, the island base for 100,000 Japanese soldiers. They struck with two lines of offense: Operation Cartwheel called for General Douglas MacArthur to advance U.S. and Australian units from the southwest to the northern coast of New Guinea, while Admiral Robert Ghormley (succeeded by Admiral William "Bull" Halsey) would begin the offensive by heading up the Solomon Islands from Guadalcanal.[21]

Beginning in August 1942, a series of fierce naval and air battles on Guadalcanal left the outcome in doubt until the Allies secured the island in February 1943.[22] One evening, Noji and his unit experienced the terror and thrill of witnessing their own fighter air show:

On April first 1943 Japanese bombers were en route to bomb Guadalcanal. Their escorting Zeroes were met by our fighter planes, mostly sleek P-38's. We occupants of Russell Island were audience to the frightening "show" overhead as they chased each other for the kill. . . . The Zeroes would burst into flames as soon as they got hit in a vulnerable place. We witnessed many Zeroes plunging earthward with smoke trailing their spiraling descent. Whenever this scenario took place, the whole island reverberated with loud yelling and hand clapping approval much like when your team scores against the opposing team in sports. When the remaining Zeroes scooted for home base, we, the audience, were simply exhausted from the excitement and intensity.[23]

After Noji took part in clean-up operations on Guadalcanal, his unit advanced thirty-five miles northwest to the Russell Islands. There, the Allies defeated the enemy, firmly establishing themselves in the Solomon Islands, which was viewed as a natural highway to the South Pacific. When enemy troops retreated toward Japan's main Southeast Asian base of Rabaul, they abandoned their supplies, including steel drums full of rice. The opportunistic GIs pounced. "We Nisei had gone without rice for so long, we hungered for it. So, even though the rice was in a rusted drum, we cooked some over open fire. It tasted terrible!"[24]

For "green and untested, scared soldiers," this introduction to armed combat presented myriad tests: "The jungle is an eerie place with insects and strange noises. In the pitch dark a scared and nervous man can see and imagine all kinds of frightening things and when someone shoots 'something,' all hell breaks loose. It was rumored later that we were shooting at each other more than against the enemy. You shoot first and then ask questions, you know. . . . The learning process can be deadly.'"[25]

The next Allied target in the Solomons was New Georgia Island, two hundred miles up "the Slot" (the waters between the islands) from Guadalcanal. In June 1943, the amphibious assault began when marine corps and army forces landed on nearby Rendova Island and did not end until New Georgia was finally secured in October.[26] In preparation for the invasion, Noji's unit had boarded an LCI (landing craft, infantry), a shallow craft for fifty to sixty that could maneuver close to the beach. His first campaign was terrifying:

When we were going into battle, we hit a storm. It seemed the upper structure of the craft was meeting water on both sides as it listed from one side to the other. And it seemed the thick single steel plates on the side of the boat would surely crack in the heavy sea. Many got seasick in short order. We could see two destroyers laying down smoke screens to camouflage our landing. When we were to get off the ship and go into another craft to make a landing, I think this was the first time we ever went down a rope ladder off the side of a ship.

. . . When we got off the landing craft and were wading through the water—it probably came up to above my knee—I could see bullets landing on both sides of me. Both sides now! I never expected to be shot at, you know. So when we got to this coconut tree, we all started hugging the base of it. . . .

That was a scary moment for us "green people." When we landed, this one kid just cried because he's so scared. Yeah, that was a tough introduction to war.[27]

The daybreak landing on Rendova Island on June 10, 1943, was captured in a photo published in the November 12, 1990, issue of *U.S. News & World Report* (with Noji's silhouette visible), headlined in its "Medal of Honor" special report.

## INTERROGATING JAPANESE POWS

During the New Guinea campaign, Noji had his baptism of fire, when he interrogated his first POW, a Japanese pilot who had been shot down.[28] "I approached this meeting with much apprehension because my *nihongo* [Japanese language], by any measure, was inadequate. And he was a pilot, the cream of the crop in most any country. Here I was trying to talk to him in conversation that was maybe third- or fourth-grade school level."

There were important considerations, however, when approaching Japanese POWs. "We were taught at school that a warrior considered it a disgrace to be captured. My foremost thought was to talk him out of committing suicide. I told him, 'It would be more helpful to your own country if you would help rebuild it instead of committing suicide.' I don't know whether I succeeded or not." Japanese soldiers were in a precarious situation. They not only followed the samurai warrior code of Bushido, which values honor above life, but had been indoctrinated to believe

When Mam Noji showed his parents this photo of himself interviewing a Japanese prisoner of war, he cut out the POW on the left because he was worried about their feelings.
(Mam Noji)

that their capture would lead to torture. So the MIS followed a simple procedure set up by the Allied Translator and Interpreter Section (ATIS), the American military intelligence center in Brisbane, Australia: First, ensure that the prisoner's wounds are treated; second, offer a cigarette; and third, make no threats during the interview.[29]

On another occasion, Noji became unnerved when POWs prostrated themselves in front of him: "I entered the compound and, my gosh, every one of them got up and did *gassho* [a prostrated bow in which the forehead touches the ground]. I think they felt a sense of relief that a *nihonjin* [a Japanese person] would come into their compound with a sort of friendly face. They couldn't understand English . . . I think they expected to be abused by American soldiers. . . . When it was time for me to leave, they also returned the *gassho*. That was embarrassing, and I didn't know how to respond, you know?"

Noji and his cohorts spent the bulk of their time translating documents captured from the enemy, a tedious, full-time job. "Guys would bring in armloads, buckets. When the enemy's running away, they can't destroy everything. So we got a lot of stuff . . . G-3 [military operations division] wanted to know what outfit we were facing, what their capabilities were, and where they were going." As it attempted to piece together a portrait of the enemy, its location, strength, and plans, the MIS sifted through mountains of captured documents and data collected from POWs.[30]

### ON-THE-JOB TRAINING

Despite six months of intensive schooling day and night, there was much on-the-job training. More than once, resourceful Nisei sought help from POWs: "GIs turned everything in that had Japanese characters, and we had no cross-references to match. Dictionaries and reference books were woefully inadequate and way behind the times—thirty to fifty years, it seemed. There was a nameplate that had characters for air, pressure, and machine. This had us stumped. So the next time I interrogated a POW, I asked him what it was. He pondered over this for some time and finally said, 'Wakari ma shitta. [It is understood.] SUPA CHAJA desu.' Ah, so it was a supercharger!"[31]

In teams of ten, with one officer, the MIS cooperated to eavesdrop on the enemy's tactical orders and radio messages and translate battle plans, defense maps, newspapers and magazines, nameplates from military equipment, diaries, and even letters home. For those unfamiliar with Japanese politics and government, the task was especially taxing. But Kibei, who had been schooled in Japan, were much more proficient with the fast-paced conversations and technical terms. So the combined team of Kibei and Nisei managed the Japanese-to-English interpretations. Sometimes their results were so accurate and timely that artillery teams ambushed enemy posts just minutes after receiving their messages.[32]

Indeed, MIS translations enabled Allied commanders to avoid surprise attacks, anticipate enemy actions, and plan successful counterattacks. Noji recalled, "There was a time in New Georgia that our unit had a difficult time getting past a certain hill. It was not for lack of trying. The hill was shot up and blasted so badly there was not a blade of green grass or a standing tree. By some fortune, a map of their defensive position was turned in to our tent office. We translated it and passed this information to G-2 and we were able to bypass their defense. I'm sure this kind of information was turned in everywhere MIS was present."[33] Other MIS successes were instrumental in defeating the Japanese military: MIS translators produced a five-volume, alphabetized list of forty thousand Japanese army officers by rank and assignment, which was distributed to all Allied forces in October 1942. In April 1943, they decoded an enemy radio message, enabling U.S. fighters to shoot down the plane of Admiral Isoroku Yamamoto, commander in chief of Japan's Combined Fleet and architect of the Pearl Harbor attack. After Admiral Mineichi Koga's "Z Plan" fell into the hands of Philippine guerrillas in May 1944, the MIS's translation helped derail Japan's counterattack in the Central Pacific and led to the decisive defeat of its fleet in the Philippine Sea.[34]

By the summer of 1944, General MacArthur's joint forces in the southwest had seized the Japanese base at Rabaul and were leapfrogging across New Guinea's northwestern shores. The aim was to force Japanese troops to retreat to their islands. As planned, U.S. troops were converging in a step-by-step amphibious assault across the Central Pacific, led by Admiral Chester W. Nimitz. The drive to free the Philippines from Japan's three-year domination began on A-Day (Assault Day), October 20, 1944, when Allied forces bombarded the island of Leyte from sea and land. Their goal was to drive across the island and capture Japan's port at Ormoc Bay. As the troops met in brutal warfare amid monsoon rains (thirty-five inches in six weeks), MIS teams parachuted into the island's remote mountains, gorges, and jungles where they could eavesdrop on enemy conversations and negotiate enemy surrenders.[35]

Frank Hachiya gave up his furlough in Hawaii and volunteered for a dangerous mission to interview a Japanese prisoner of war in the Philippines. (Homer Hachiya, 1942)

## A GUTSY MISSION

Technician Third Grade Frank Hachiya joined the MIS on that pivotal mission. Having interrupted his furlough in Hawaii in order to temporarily replace an ill Nisei, he chose to complete the campaign. "I'll not be back in time for Christmas," he wrote a friend. "Instead, celebrate it in some muddy foxhole with can of GI rations." The Thirty-second Infantry Regiment was heading through two parallel ridges that had been infiltrated by the enemy. Attached to the Seventh Division, twenty-five-year-old Hachiya volunteered for forward duty so that he could interrogate a prisoner, a precarious move for one who resembled the enemy.[36] Accounts of what happened next vary.

The *Honolulu Star-Bulletin* quoted Lieutenant Howard M. Moss, Hachiya's commanding officer:

> The units in an adjacent ridge got another prisoner, and Frank volunteered to go over and interrogate him. He had to cross a valley in which Japs were known to be. It was essential to get the information from the prisoner of war immediately, as some of our units were in a bad spot. Frank was given permission to go by the lieutenant colonel, who sent him

with infantrymen as a bodyguard. They started out, and when they got to the bottom of the valley, Frank outran his bodyguards. He also started hollering to the Japs in the valley when a sniper let him have it at close range. Frank said he emptied his gun into the sniper. He then walked back up the hill, where he was given plasma, and started for the hospital. He was bleeding badly and had to have transfusions as well as plasma.[37]

The *Hood River News* printed a statement from Headquarters, Seventh Infantry Division, on March 4, 1945:

Hachiya, a regimental interpreter, requested special permission to accompany the patrol. En route, three enemy soldiers were seen to run into a bamboo thicket on the edge of a deep and heavily-wooded gorge. Hachiya went to the spot and tried to "talk the enemy out." He entered the thicket alone, saw a faint trail into the gorge and requested permission to pursue the enemy and try to capture them. He was required to take a two-man patrol, but moved out rapidly ahead of the patrol in going down the gorge. After proceeding about 100 yards, a 12-man enemy patrol in the bottom of the gorge opened fire. . . . After being hit, and while lying helpless on the ground, he fired a complete magazine at the enemy, driving them up the ravine.[38]

Another version ascribes the bullets that struck Hachiya to a totally different source. According to journalist Bill Hosokawa, in *Nisei: The Quiet Americans*, Hachiya volunteered to be dropped behind Japanese lines. "Invading GIs mistook him for an enemy infiltrator—an ever-present danger facing the Nisei—and shot him as he was making his way back to American lines."[39] Still, Hachiya delivered maps of the Japanese defenses to an American officer, an act credited with saving the lives of hundreds of fellow soldiers. Budd Fukei, journalist and author of *The Japanese American Story*, also described Hachiya being "mistaken for an enemy" by invading American soldiers, but writes that he "managed to crawl far enough forward to lay at an American officer's feet a complete map of the Japanese defenses for Leyte."[40] A 1991 commemorative editorial in the *New York Times* and memoirs by Nisei in the MIS similarly reported that invading Americans mistook Hachiya for an infiltrator.[41] Even an accolade delivered by Oregon congressman Al Ullman in the 88th Congress in 1963 attributed Hachiya's death to being "mistakenly shot and killed by his own comrades."[42]

What is not in dispute is that Frank Hachiya died several days later, on January 3, 1945. He received blood transfusions and plasma, but a bullet had punctured his liver.[43] This bold and principled young American, how-ever, would become a cause célèbre throughout the United States and play a part in countering racist acts in his hometown.

Without a doubt, wartime service posed dangers far beyond the armed combat that Technician Third Grade Hachiya and Noji experienced. As Noji explained, the Nisei's resemblance to the enemy meant threats could come from both the front and the rear:

> We were all warned about infiltrators coming to our area, Japanese in American uniforms. Gosh, we fit that bill, you know? At first, whenever we went out of our area, we had a fellow soldier accompany us. Well, I gotta tell you, one time a fellow came up to me and said, "I had you in my sights." (He didn't tell me why he didn't pull the trigger.) One MIS guy hadn't taken a bath in so long he took his clothes off and jumped into a pool of water. Immediately he got surrounded by Marines who were either gonna capture him or kill him. He had to talk real fast to get out of that pickle. The enemy's our cousin. We all look alike, you know? We were getting shot from ahead of us and behind us.

Nisei knew that if they were captured, they, like other Allied troops, would have been subject to torture or execution.[44] Almost as unsettling was the uncertainty each time Nisei interrogated POWs. "We all had cous-ins over there that were in the Japanese army. . . . That would have been a bad day if I'd had to interview somebody named Noji."

## BATTLESHIPS, HIDDEN HOWITZERS, AND FOXHOLES

After two months of air and marine strikes bolstered by heavy ground fighting, the Allies surrounded Japanese forces and captured Ormoc Val-ley. Having secured Leyte island, the troops moved north to the main Philippine island of Luzon. There, in January 1945, they launched a mas-sive invasion at Lingayen Gulf, driving one hundred miles south to the capital city of Manila. Allied forces conducted raids to free more than five hundred prisoners of war.[45] After duty in New Guinea, Mam Noji and the Forty-third Division joined MacArthur's assault on Luzon, where Noji remained until the island was secure in the summer of 1945. The sights and sounds of war left him awestruck. "I tell you, the invasion of Luzon in the Philippines is something I'll never forget. Our convoy anchored in Lingayen Bay. Boy, as far as you could see from horizon to horizon, big battleships. Big ones! And they were all shooting. Big huge guns! When they're firing those big guns, the recoil of the guns actually pushed the ship back a little ways, you know that?"

MIS Nisei were not infantrymen, yet they were exposed to the same bombing raids and artillery fire as their units, Noji recalled. Calculated planning, split-second actions, and extreme discomfort could mean the difference between life and death. "In the Philippines, the Japanese had big howitzers, short-barreled cannons that shot shells in a high arc.[46] What they would do is lob the shells over. Howitzer shells don't go straight. They move back and forth, sideways and back and forth. I thought I was really going to get hit, so I dove in the nearest foxhole. There were guys already in there, and I was protecting those guys with my body!"

Digging foxholes on the coral banks of the South Pacific was such grueling work that GIs typically blew out the holes with dynamite that they got from engineers. Sometimes their defensive positions required sleeping in foxholes, particularly awkward during the recurrent tropical rainstorms. A foxhole did not assure one's safety, Noji explained. "One of my friends was sleeping in this foxhole, but the plane flew over and dropped a bomb. It didn't hit him. But it hit close enough that he got buried. So no guarantee goes with foxholes."

The subsequent Allied captures of Iwo Jima and Okinawa (the southernmost island in the chain leading to Japan) exacted huge human tolls on both sides. It was only after the United States dropped atomic bombs on Hiroshima and Nagasaki, on August 6 and August 9, 1945, respectively, that the Japanese government surrendered, ending more than three and a half years of war.[47]

## CLASSIFIED DOCUMENTS AND AMERICA'S "SECRET WEAPON"

The MIS's wartime contributions were well documented. When the war ended, Nisei linguists in the South Pacific had translated two million documents with more than twenty million pages, interrogated fourteen thousand Japanese prisoners, and worked with front-line troops in every Pacific campaign.[48] "One of the generals says we shortened the war by two years," reflected Noji. "Nobody will be able to prove it, but it's a nice thing to say." He was referring to General Charles Willoughby, General MacArthur's chief of staff for intelligence, who also maintained that Nisei in the MIS saved more than one million American lives. "Never before in history," General MacArthur declared, "did one army know so much concerning its enemy prior to actual engagement as did the American army during most of the Pacific campaign."[49]

The Nisei's military ranks, however, did not reflect the soldiers' value. Not only were they passed over as team leaders in favor of their white peers (who often were much less fluent in Japanese), but few received promotions, though more than three-quarters had attended college. White Americans working alongside Nisei received promotions at a rate of three pay grades, according to Joseph D. Harrington, author of *Yankee Samurai*.[50] That system would not change significantly until a month before the end of the war, when the War Department issued its Table of Distribution on July 29, 1945. The number of lieutenants then increased from 38 to 300 and captains from 26 to 116. Still, few MIS Nisei would advance higher than staff sergeant, and most commissions were much lower in rank.[51]

But Nisei in the MIS were also not headliners. In his study of these linguists, Masaharu Ano observed, "There existed few war heroes among them, although several won citations. In general, what they accomplished was neither exciting nor sensational. Their weapons were language, skill, and intelligence, not bayonets and machine guns. Their tactic was persuasion rather than destruction."[52] Documents related to the accomplishments of these Japanese American intelligence specialists were classified during the war in order to ensure that this military asset remained a "secret weapon against Japan." Despite the enormity of their wartime contributions, these "Yankee Samurai" would remain unknown to much of the general public.[53]

# SEVEN

# "From Somewhere in Europe"

## WAR IN EUROPE

F ROM somewhere in Europe. So far I'm in good health. Hope you people are okay," George Akiyama wrote to his mother at Tule Lake. "I always told her, 'I'm okay.' I couldn't tell the location. I couldn't tell her what the next battle was or anything. And just signed, 'From somewhere in Europe.'"

By 1943, Europe was in its fourth year of war with Nazi Germany, and, as Chester Tanaka explained in *Go for Broke*, Hitler was well within reach of dominating Europe:

Austria, Belgium, Czechoslovakia, France, Hungary, North Africa and Poland were ground under the iron heel of the Nazis, and smaller or more distant countries were intimidated or eliminated. England and Russia were under siege. Italy, Germany's Axis partner, bristled and chafed under Hitler's iron collar. The juggernaut of the greatest war machine the world had ever known was crunching inexorably toward global domination.

The Allied Forces of the free world (U.S., Great Britain, France, and Russia) united to oppose this Nazi advance. Led by Gen. Dwight D. Eisenhower, the Allies formed three tiers of defense through their northern, central, and southern armies. The southern unit, commanded by Gen. Jacob L. Devers, eventually included the Nisei.[1]

By August, George Akiyama had left the United States for Europe by way of North Africa, a queasy trip aboard a slow, swaying vessel that traveled only nine miles an hour.[2] "Of course, I got seasick. I really suffered. It took us three weeks to get over there on a small Liberty ship. I said, 'How come it takes so long?' Somebody said they don't go straight. They kind of zigzag to miss the submarines." After the ship stopped briefly in Oran, Africa, the wobbly-footed GIs finally debarked in Naples, Italy.

The southwestern coastal city of Naples, above the ankle of Italy's boot, had become the crossroad for the Allies' initial assault on Italy and the Germans' forceful counterattack. The combined British and U.S. forces in the Allied Fifth Army had gradually forced the enemy northward toward the sea. The Germans retaliated by destroying the harbor at Naples. After three weeks, the Allies finally captured the city, but at a cost of fifteen thousand casualties.[3] For Akiyama, the first glimpse of Naples's war-torn rubble was haunting: "The town was really damaged—all bombed, big buildings in ruins. A lot of people lost their homes . . . they picked up a lot of these galvanized, metal roofing sheets, you know. They had that leaning up against the outside wall that was left. They were huddled under there, living. They were cooking food with a little wood fire on the street. So I thought, 'Boy, this war is really bad. . . . It's a good thing we're gonna stop them before they get over to the United States.'"

### THE 100TH BATTALION IN ITALY

Akiyama became a replacement in the 100th Battalion, born from the all-Nisei Hawaiian Provisional Infantry Battalion, a unit that had also trained at Camp Shelby and had suffered many casualties.[4] "Since my name started with 'A,' maybe I was one of the first ones they picked up," he reasoned. He trained at "Repo Depot" (Reposition Depot), a few miles north of Naples, where long evening marches were the norm. "Being a truck driver, I was really out of shape! . . . I got blisters on my feet. Boy, I didn't know if I could take it or not." The toughening-up process included target shooting and backpacking over hills and sand dunes at night. Weary men eventually returned at midnight or one o'clock in the morning.

The GIs' encounters with innocent children, clad in tattered clothing and shoes without soles, brought daily reminders of the ravages of war: "We were cooking out in the field, eating out of our mess kits," continued Akiyama. "These Italian kids didn't have food. . . . Every time we ate, they're all lined up out there. . . . Any leftover food, they had a can. We poured our food in there and they were glad to get it. . . . A lot of the soldiers threw cigarettes out. You didn't have to worry about cleaning up. The kids would pick up all those butts for their parents. So I thought, boy, it's really rough on the kids."

As Allied troops mobilized to push the enemy northward, the Germans were entrenching their troops along the Volturno River, which flows north of Naples. In September 1943, the 100th Battalion attached to the Thirty-fourth Red Bull Division, the first U.S. division to enter combat. After forcing Nazi troops to retreat from town after town amid showers of rain, snow, sleet, and "screaming meemies" (six-barrel rocket launchers, or *Nebelwerfers*), the 100th, still barraged by artillery and mortar fire, forded the swift, icy current of the Volturno. It went on to overtake six key hills in its march toward Cassino, on the Gustav Line, the Germans' mountain defense protecting the main route to Rome.[5]

At the time of the first attack on Cassino, Allied advance troops had established a beachhead on enemy shores at Anzio, west of Cassino. The ten-mile-square plot of flat seacoast became the site of a two-month stalemate: Allied forces were hemmed in by German sharpshooters encamped in surrounding hills, but Germans were unable to overcome the Allies' beachhead. Early in June 1944, the 100th spearheaded a drive up Italy's western coast and wiped out the last enemy defenses on the road to Rome. Rome was wrested from the clutches of the Nazis on June 5, 1944, the day before Allied forces landed at Normandy.[6]

## THE 100TH BATTALION AND 442ND REGIMENTAL COMBAT TEAM COMBINE

Depleted by nine hundred casualties, the 1,400 men of the 100th Battalion became attached to the recently arrived 442nd Regimental Combat Team.[7] The combined 100th, 2nd, and 3rd Battalions replaced the 1st Battalion, which had sent replacements to the 100th in Italy. Because of its distinction on the battlefield over nine months, the 100th retained its designation. Thus, the new unit officially became the 100th Infantry Battalion and the 442nd Regimental Combat Team.[8]

The day after Rome fell, Allied armies continued their advance up the front of Italy's boot. The battlefield baptism of the Second and Third Battalions was gruesome. "First time I come in contact with the enemy, I got shot

Three months after Sho Endow's L Company received Bronze Stars for valor, he was struck by shrapnel during a battle in Bruyeres, France. (Shirley Cree)

at, pinned down with machine gun. It was north of Anzio on the way up to the Arno River," recalled Sho Endow. "The Germans always had a setup on the road or someplace where they'd pin you down. All they have to have is a couple guys with a rifle and a machine gun and know that you're gonna come up this road. . . . That'll keep you down." The 100th managed to stage a surprise counterattack, and brought the town of Belvedere under Allied control. As Endow's L Company advanced toward Leghorn (Livorno), the western seaport that supplied German troops,[9] it lost most of its men in a battle: "Fourth of July of that year we got one of the worst casualties of the company. Went out with 130-some people and come back with 26 or 27. That was really a rough one. Then they pulled us back down to Naples to reorganize and get some more people in the outfit. That's why you don't . . . get to be buddy-buddy unless you're pretty close. Acquaintances were short."

Through three weeks of combat in July, the 100th/442nd merged as a fighting unit, liberating a dozen towns as it forced the Germans north.[10] Endow and members of his L Company earned Bronze Stars for valor. "We just kept on going 'til we stopped at the Arno River," he explained. "The Germans were pretty well protected by the river on the other side. They were still pretty well organized. If we didn't push them, why they probably would have pushed us back in the ocean."

George Akiyama takes a break from guard duty on the French side of the Maritime Alps, along the border with Italy. The goal of the 100th Battalion was to prevent Italians from moving toward the French border. (George Akiyama, 1945)

On September 1, 1944, the 100th/442nd achieved its goal and crossed the Arno River under heavy enemy fire. The price of the battle for the forty miles of countryside from Rome to the Arno was heavy: There were nearly 1,300 casualties—more than a quarter of the unit's total strength, including 239 killed, seventeen missing, 972 wounded, and forty-four noncombat injuries.[11]

## OFF TO FRANCE

The Allies appeared to be on the verge of winning the war in Italy and driving Hitler's weakened armies north toward the Alps when officers made a controversial decision. Generals Eisenhower and George Marshall (U.S. Army chief of staff) called on seven units, including the 100th/442nd, to help invade northern France. So later that month, Nisei GIs retreated from the Arno River in Italy to the valley of the Rhone in France. They landed in the southern port city of Marseille and then traveled by freight car to the country's northeastern battleground.[12]

"We were up there one month before we took our shoes off," recalled Akiyama of the bitter cold and rain that was "like what we had in Hood River. . . . A lot of them got trench foot.[13] . . . Some of them couldn't get their shoes off, their feet were so swollen." The heavy rain soaked their olive drab wool uniforms, filled their foxholes, and turned to ice overnight.[14]

Conditions were extreme, but the stakes were high. With the battlefield edging toward Germany at the north and east, Hitler ordered Nazi troops to stand firm along the Rhine River, running between France and Germany, at all costs. The determined enemy zeroed in on bridges and junctions, devising every scheme imaginable in an effort to hold its ground, including minefields, booby traps, specialized rockets, and mortar fire. If they were to overtake them, the Allies would need to break through the Vosges Mountains in eastern France, cross the Rhine, and advance into Germany. Critical to that plan was the quaint northeastern town of Bruyeres, a rail center and fork in the road that had been under Nazi control for four years. The mission of the 100th/442nd would be to take the town.[15]

## BRUYERES

Bruyeres lay in a valley dominated on three sides by four conical hills, dubbed Hills A, B, C, and D. The steep slopes of each were covered with thick pine forests and underbrush that seemed to conspire with dense fog to camouflage the heavily mined ground and multiple machine-gun nests.[16] A Seventh Army report would cite Bruyeres as "the most viciously fought-for town" in the long march against the Germans.[17]

Hill A, the key to taking Bruyeres, was assigned to the 100th, and the unit advanced on October 15.[18] Akiyama recalled the terrifying torrent of fire from the invisible but well-fortified and determined enemy. "Every time you hear a shot going up, you're scared. You don't know which is the enemy and which is friendly." After a few days, vigilant GIs could discern the different shells. "That whistling sound—the one that overshoots—you could hear it go *shhhh*. But the one that's gonna land near you, that sound gets real sharp, like a big mosquito." The fearsome German 88, effective against tanks and aircraft, gave the enemy an edge. "That was the most feared shell they had. . . . Most artillery—when they shoot it—it takes so many seconds to go up and land. But this 88 is just like a rifle. It's straight. When they shoot that, boom! It just hits you . . . within a second or two. You don't have time to duck or anything. . . . Boom, bang! That's how fast it goes."

Tromping across hillsides, unnerved soldiers could smell human flesh as they dodged body parts. "I even saw a dog chewing on a dead German's brain," recalled Akiyama. Along the way, he and other GIs inspected homes for concealed enemy soldiers. "We go up to the house and ask them, 'Are there any Germans hiding in there?' The woman who comes out says, 'Oh, no, no, no. No Germans.' We say, 'Are you sure?' So we go in there and search the house. Find two, three Germans hidden in the basement. Have to shoot them out. Of course, the family are hostages, so they're not gonna admit it."

Making their way through villages infiltrated by the enemy, infantrymen were just as vulnerable, recalled Endow:

There were brick buildings with slate for their roofing, so every time a point detonating shell would come over, they'd burst right over the top of this slate. Then you'd see a clutter of slate coming down on the street. They had fir trees in there, probably eighteen to twenty inches in diameter.... You take a point detonating shell, when they hit the top of the trees [the dreaded "tree bursts" of cascading steel and wood fragments], that explodes it, see, and people walking underneath might get shrapnel and knock their heads off.... Once you get your head knocked off, the first aid people don't even come.

Soldiers frequently witnessed death, even when walking down an alley, as Akiyama explained:

We were all spread out fifteen to twenty feet apart. Then they shelled us again.... A lot of them were 88s.... You take cover in whatever place you can find. If you're out on the road, you usually find a ditch to protect yourself. In that little alley going through town, there's no ditch. But some of those storefronts, they had little open doorways—I ducked in one.... We were ducking for a minute, a minute and a half, two minutes. Then they signaled to go forward. Each one motions the next one to come forward. I signaled my assistant squad leader, "Okay, we're going." He doesn't answer. So I run back to him and I said, "Hey, Fred, we're gonna go." He doesn't answer.... He's on one knee with a rifle in his hand and he's dead. His eyes were wide open, his mouth was open, and he's bleeding out of his mouth.

From the first days of battle, GIs like Akiyama had already forged a strong team spirit that prevented them from abandoning their wounded comrades, regardless of the risks to their own lives:[19]

> A Hawaiian boy got hit from the shrapnel. He was moaning. He had a large wound right through his belly, and his intestine was hanging out. He was in pain bad, and he could hardly move. So a bunch of us jumped out of the foxhole and tried to help him. The Germans . . . see us out there and they just throw more shells. We had to take cover in the foxhole, and here he's laying out there. Then there's a lull. You know, artillery doesn't come solid. They shoot like heck for three, four minutes. Then there's a little lull. Then they start in again. We had to move him to a safer place . . . I see a tank out there. . . . I jumped up there on that tank, and I found a raincoat. We buttoned it together. We found a couple of poles. We ran it through a sleeve, kind of tied things up, made it like a homemade stretcher. . . . Finally we were able to move him.

Being at war required vigilance in mind and body, even after a full day at the battlefront. "You fight all day, you're tired, and you have to dig a foxhole at night with a little shovel," explained Akiyama. "You dig about a foot sometimes, then you run into a big old boulder. . . . Sometimes you have to dig two, three places before you can dig a hole deep enough to hold you. Without the rocks and stuff, you could dig it in about half an hour. But it could take about forty-five minutes to an hour." Cramped foxholes, the soldiers' dirt motels, were generally three feet in diameter and three and a half feet deep.[20] One night, Akiyama's squad members heard him vomiting in his foxhole. "They thought I was getting strangled by a German. I said no, I just didn't feel good. Something gave a funny odor. That night, we dug our foxholes when it was dark. That morning, I looked around, and, heck, there was a dead German soldier just laying about seven, eight feet away."

In the dead of night, there was guard duty, and then the dreaded night patrol. Each man in the eight- to twelve-member squad took his turn, explained Akiyama. "We have three squads in the platoon. You always have two, three men guarding all night. . . . You don't know when the enemy could creep up and toss a grenade. Twenty-four hours a day, you gotta be alert!" Fatigue was deadly for one nearby squad after Germans took advantage when they all fell asleep. Night patrol was particularly odious. "Four, five men go out at night with a compass and kind of feel their way to find out where the Germans might be. That's scarier than when you're with a bunch of men."

Against stiff artillery, machine-gun, and mortar fire, the 100th Battalion took Hill A to the west of Bruyeres on October 18. Within two days, Bruyeres was free, and Hills B, C, and D were in Allied hands. After the Germans retook Hill D, Companies F, H, and L penetrated enemy lines and launched a successful attack from the rear.[21] Sho Endow, in Company L, became a casualty: "I think it was October the 20th, 1944, when I got hit. I was out in the front lines moving up at nighttime.... You could hear the Germans on the other side, shouting orders to put their mortar up.... Finally you get one. It was shrapnel from mortar. I was hit in the back, right around the belt line. If I'd got one inch over, I'd probably have been killed right there because it probably would have hit my spine." Medics carried Endow to the field house. The next day, he was flown to Naples, where he would remain hospitalized for ninety days.

## THE LOST BATTALION

Despite counterattacks that left their units surrounded and cut off from supplies, Nisei soldiers staved off the Germans and liberated Biffontaine and other towns around Bruyeres.[22] But after ten days of vicious fighting broken by less than two days of rest, the exhausted men of the 442nd, their ranks depleted, were sent into battle again. Their orders: rescue the Lost Battalion. More than two hundred Texans in the First Battalion, 141st Regiment, were trapped on a ridge four miles into enemy territory in the Vosges Mountains and cut off on all sides by six thousand fresh German troops. Two battalions in their own regiment had failed to reach them, and the Texans were low on food, water, and ammunition.[23] German prisoners revealed that Hitler himself had commanded that the trapped battalion be held at any cost: no hostages, no survivors.[24]

In freezing rain and dense fog, the 442nd dodged artillery fire and "screaming meemies" while maneuvering along nine miles of winding paths and steep, forty-five-degree ridges thick with sixty-foot pines and strewn with mines. Supporting them were the 522nd Field Artillery Battalion and Cannon Company, the 232nd Engineer Company, and other tank, chemical, and mortar battalions. They were little match for German tanks, however.[25] George Akiyama, who was carrying ammunition for his troop's bazooka shooter, had an encounter with a tank that was too close for comfort:

> We sneaked our way up there close as we could get. We found a pretty big tree where we kind of protected ourselves. The bazooka shooter said, "Wait 'til that tank comes by." You shoot at the side and try to knock the track off or shoot at the back—the motor is at the back, you know. So you try to get the tank disabled.
>
> You could hear the Germans talking. I betcha they were fifty, sixty feet away. There was a thicket of vine maple, so you couldn't see the tank. But you could hear the Germans talking. You could hear those tanks. Boom! Boom! Revving up like they're getting ready to take off. Turned the throttle on, like these kids with their hot rods, you know. Boom, boom! Boy, I was scared! I was scared of the tank. Boy, if they ever see us, we're gone! And it just so happened that they turned around and took off. . . . So that saved our lives.

U.S. troops loaded five light tanks with ammunition and headed up the steep and muddy mountain. When the Germans opened fire, Akiyama and nineteen others "fearlessly resisted with their individual weapons and the machine guns emplaced on the tanks, neutralized a considerable portion of the concentrated fire and enabled the tanks to reach friendly forces." Members of his platoon received the Bronze Star for "heroic achievement."[26] In Akiyama's words, "We were just sitting ducks on the tank. . . . We had to fight our way up there by foot just to force the Germans back. We couldn't go much faster!"

After five continuous day and night battles, the 100th/442nd broke through and rescued the Lost Battalion. The units had suffered more than eight hundred casualties to save 211 Texans, all that remained of the original 275. Now the Nisei looked forward to having some time to recuperate—but there would still be no time. As soon as Major General John E. Dahlquist learned of the rescue, he ordered Nisei troops to drive Germans off the next ridge, where the enemy seemed to be "dug in like moles." They fought for nine more days before the German troops finally withdrew.[27]

Only a small number of Nisei appeared at a dress review General Dahlquist ordered to honor them on November 12. When he rebuked officers for the scant showing, a colonel reportedly answered, "General, this is the regiment. The rest are either dead or in the hospital." The combat team, which had numbered 2,943 men the month before, now amounted to less than half its regimental strength. Undaunted, the next day, the general sent the Second and Third Battalions back into the fray to forestall an enemy counterattack.[28]

The Nisei's military successes made them the center of another battlefield of sorts: army generals engaged in a tug-of-war over who would get to command them. "Every division in the 5th Army insisted that the 442nd be assigned to it," revealed Major General Alfred M. Gruenther. After the invasion in France, General Jacob L. Devers appealed all the way to the Joint Chiefs of Staff to hold on to the 442nd. "One would think that the 442nd RCT was the only unit in Italy the way you fellows are squawking about giving it up!" remarked a War Department officer. This time, General Mark W. Clark's arguments won out. In March 1945, after six months in France, the Nisei regiment secretly returned to Italy.[29]

## RETURN TO ITALY AND THE GOTHIC LINE

This time, their mission was to crack the western sector of the formidable Gothic Line in Italy's rugged Apennine Mountains. The saw-toothed Apennines form a spine up the Italian peninsula, dividing the east and west coasts. To the northwest, the wide, flat Po River valley leading to the Austrian Alps represented the last barrier against Germany. For nine months, the Germans had constructed what, up to this point, had been an impregnable stronghold, the Gothic Line, forcing fifteen thousand Italian slave laborers to drill trenches into the rocky terrain and fortify them with concrete. This fortress of more than 2,300 machine-gun nests gave the enemy an unobstructed view of approaching armies. Even bombing and strafing by Allied planes had failed to drive out the Germans.[30]

It seemed implausible that the Nisei regiment could succeed where others had failed. After much deliberation, a perilous strategy was devised: they would scale the Gothic Line's sheer cliffs (some towering three thousand feet) at night and prepare for a dawn assault. On April 3, the men of the 442nd advanced. George Akiyama took part in the frontal attack against Georgia Hill, the first of the peaks rising from the west coast at the thigh of Italy's boot:[31]

As we hit there at daybreak, the Germans just opened fire on us. They shot machine guns, throwing their hand grenades. They had a whole bunch of land mines planted here and there. . . . We're firing at the machine guns . . . but pretty hard to get them. Just their heads were sticking out.

Our squad leader stepped on a mine. . . . It reminded me like when you're a kid playing with a firecracker—where you place a can on a firecracker. Watch that can go up in the air thirty, forty feet! Boom! You could see his shoe and foot flying up in the air, thirty, forty feet. We're pinned down for a whole day there! Oh, we might have made forty, fifty feet up the hill but we couldn't get much further. They were shooting so much. We couldn't get them out with rifle fire.

The sight of Germans high above them, peering from dugouts fortified with sandbags, protected by minefields, and tossing grenades while firing machine guns made a takeover seem doubtful. Still, Akiyama's A Company concocted a risky plan:

We had to get those Germans up there. They were just up on top, shooting at us all day. . . . You couldn't get them by shooting, since we knew they had a safe dugout up there. So the next day the only way we thought we could get them was to go up with a hand grenade and throw it in their bunker. Well, two of us volunteered to go up there. We each carried two grenades apiece. . . . Each of us got four more from our squad members, stuffed in our pockets. And we crawled up there. The others were shooting, trying to divert their attention on top with their machine guns. We just sneaked up there, crawling with a rifle in our hands.

I was leading, and he was following me. I got up to about twenty, twenty-five feet. It's real steep, so the Germans couldn't see us. And on the top there's a little flat place. I got within twenty-five feet probably. And I see this German with a rifle. He's looking toward where our men were down the other way. All of a sudden, he turned, and he saw my helmet, I guess. He had his rifle pointed at me—and I still see his face. He shot at me, and I shot back at him. There happened to be a little rock in front of my helmet. . . . His bullet struck the rock, and it glanced off and hit my helmet. My helmet rolled off. The lieutenant—he was watching from down below—saw that, and he says, "Oh, there goes Akiyama." He thought I was a downer. But I fooled him. I wasn't even hurt. I couldn't believe it myself. So then we got up closer, and we threw our grenades in there.

Those Germans were "really tough," conceded Akiyama. "You know, they picked up our grenades, and they threw some back at us. I couldn't believe it!" He seemed unaware that his own indomitable grit, as well as that of the men in A Company, far surpassed that of the protected enemy. In just thirty-two minutes, the men of the 100th drove the Germans from the fortress that had resisted Allied attacks for more than five months.[32] The next day, their replacement platoon found several dead Germans in a high bunker, one, with a large hole in his head, likely Akiyama's victim. The Silver Star Akiyama earned for his "extraordinary aggressiveness" and gallantry in action also cited his humanity in crawling through a mined area to administer first aid to a wounded soldier lying ten yards from the enemy.[33]

Within three days, from April 5 to April 7, 1945, Nisei soldiers achieved what had once seemed inconceivable: forcing the Germans to their knees on all nine hills of the Gothic Line. Next, they pushed northward toward Carrara, Italy's marble-quarrying center. On April 13, 1945, luck was not on the side of the 100th/442nd, which thrust forward so quickly that its artillery could not keep pace. The Germans, moving in from their vantage point in the mountains, hammered two advance battalions as well as the Third Battalion, encamped in Carrara.[34] Sagie Nishioka would become one of their casualties.

Nishioka's role as cook was to prepare and transport meals for the men of G Company, which would overtake a German hill and fort by the next day.[35] When troops were at rest, he cooked meals. When they were on the front lines, he carried boxes of K rations[36] to the fighting front: "I think we had to get up at five, and we had those gas stoves. In the course of the day we would have to take freshly made coffee to the front lines besides supplying the K rations. They were canned meat and crackers and stuff like that. Spam was the most popular. . . . We used to take three to four hours to go up the hill to deliver the boxes. I remember one time we got there at midnight. Boy, was I tired." After hoisting twenty-five-pound boxes of supplies up steep hillsides, Nishioka and other cooks carried wounded GIs on stretchers when they descended.

On the evening of April 13, twilight was fading into darkness when Nishioka rose from a log after reading his Bible. Fifteen feet away, the town residents' dirt-covered, dome-shaped shelter was suddenly barraged by German artillery in the nearby mountains. Nishioka's reaction was immediate:

I could tell from that sound from the gun as to where the artillery shell was going to land. . . . That's one of the reasons why I jumped in this slit trench that I had dug. I went into the slit trench—a hole in the ground big enough so your body will fit—when I thought the third round of artillery was coming close to me. . . . For a strange reason, I placed my legs where my head usually would be. This shell explosion broke both of my legs and caused other damage to my body. Now if I had my head where my legs were, I wouldn't be sitting here. There's no question about that.

Nishioka was blown out of his slit trench and found himself atop a pile of dirt with an urge to remove his shoes. He prayed that he would see his family again—and wondered what would become of them if he didn't. Hood Riverite George Kinoshita drove Nishioka by jeep to the field station thirty minutes away. When he arrived, the severely injured Nishioka, whose only pain medication was aspirin, almost gave up. "I wanted to get it over with. I was in such pain, I almost asked the armed sentry to shoot me." Shrapnel from an exploding 88 shell had punctured Nishioka's stomach and the right ventricle of his heart, and both his legs were broken.

Back on the battlefield, Nishioka's companions joined Allied armies to clean up along Italy's western coast, by the Ligurian Sea. In fierce artillery fights from Carrara northward, the combined forces doggedly pursued the Germans, sweeping forts, securing hilltops, and liberating towns, including the strategic Aulla, Germany's pathway to the coast. The demoralized German troops retreated north to the Po River, battered and without supplies. Overwhelmed by this full-scale diversionary tactic combined with the Allies' successful assaults on Bologna and the Po Valley, they surrendered unconditionally. The war in Italy ended on May 2. Five days later, Germany surrendered. By May 7, 1945, the war in Europe was officially over.[37]

For the 100th/442nd, the imminent peace had come at a price. In its seven major campaigns, the regiment suffered the highest combat casualty rate of any in the U.S. Army. The 9,486 casualties, all Purple Heart recipients (awarded to members of the armed forces who are wounded or killed in action), equaled three times the number of soldiers.[38] Lieutenant General Mark W. Clark, commander of the Fifth Army, explained that while injured soldiers typically maneuvered to stay in the hospital or ship back, "Here the 100th/442nd men were actually going AWOL to get back to their unit."[39] The so-called Purple Heart Battalion went all out to depict the motto it had adopted from Hawaiian crap shooters: "Go for Broke," or, in George Akiyama's words, "Give it everything you got." The liberty torches on their red, white, and blue shoulder patches were apt symbols for the eighteen thousand men, more than six hundred of whom paid with their lives.[40] Though their battle was coming to a close, the war-weary survivors were unaware of another conflict taking place on U.S. soil, fought by Nisei from their own hometown.

# EIGHT

# *"I've Got a Lot of Fighting to Do Right Here"*

## CHARGED WITH

## WILLFUL DISOBEDIENCE

**F**RED Sumoge anxiously shined his shoes and donned his khaki, Class A dress uniform. Word had drifted out that President Roosevelt was going to visit the army camp where Sumoge was stationed on that Easter Sunday in 1943. "Hey, gonna see the president!" he chortled as he adjusted the folds of his hat. Sumoge's optimism, however, was short-lived. By sundown, his ardor would dissipate, replaced by feelings of humiliation, betrayal, and anger. The astonishing events of the day would also launch him on a trajectory in his military service that would extend from Fort Riley, Kansas, to Fort McClellan, Arkansas, and lead to his court-martial and imprisonment with twenty others. Ultimately, it would perpetuate court-martial appeals that would go all the way to the Pentagon.

Verbal sparring was atypical behavior for Sumoge. He grew up in the orchards of western Hood River's Oak Grove and described himself as "kind of quiet" as a child. Following his older brother, Yoshio, around, he "didn't have to say much" and relied on his sibling to do the talking. When he made a purchase, he simply handed his money over and waited for the clerk to complete the transaction. Even as he grew older, he was described by a classmate as "a quiet personality of few words."[1]

Signs of impending war with his parents' homeland (which he had never visited) became apparent after Sumoge graduated from high school. While working for an Issei grocer in Portland, he recognized trouble brewing between Japan and the United States. Crew members from Japanese ships, who regularly purchased goods from the grocery, began to leave port on ships with empty holds. "Any nation that boycotts another nation means they're starting a war," Sumoge surmised as the government froze Japanese assets in the United States, ending trade with Japan. The day after Japan bombed Pearl Harbor, the FBI arrested his employer (the president of Portland's Japanese Grocer Association) along with other prominent Issei and placed them in a Justice Department internment center. "The FBI knew just where to go," Sumoge declared. "It seemed like it was all arranged."[2]

Though Sumoge had registered for the draft early in 1941, he did not receive his notice until after the war began. With the signing of Executive Order 9066 in February 1942, he supposed he might land "in prison in the concentration camp" instead. Whatever the orders, though, he was sure of his response. "I got the notice. I went. . . . We were discriminated [against], . . . but really, what can you do?"

Sumoge's basic training began in March 1942 at Camp Robinson, Arkansas. Each company was composed of two hundred men, including fifteen Nisei assigned to their own five-man tents.[3] Sumoge's sergeant introduced Nisei to the other men by assuring them, "They are not Japanese from Japan. They're United States citizens, just like you and me." Well, that's true, thought Sumoge. "You know, it's good; we're citizens. So we trained. Nothing other than basic training."

The preparation seemed pointless, however, when other units shipped out eight weeks later, leaving the Nisei behind. Some remained at Camp Robinson, while the army dispatched the rest to Fort Leonard Wood, Missouri, a small number to other camps, and around six hundred to Fort Riley, Kansas. Sumoge remembered that Nisei at Fort Riley were segregated into a "Japan Town" and the army declined to issue them firearms or helmets. Instead, their military service was reduced to menial tasks: mowing lawns, chopping weeds, shoveling manure, cleaning, and working in the motor pool and at the target range. "I took basic training to fight. What am I doing here?" Sumoge wondered.[4] Within a year, the army sent two-thirds of the Fort Riley Nisei to Camp Shelby, Mississippi, where they joined Nisei volunteers from Hawaii in combat training. Of some 160 remaining Nisei (about half of whom were Kibei), about 30 served at the post's headquarters while the remainder formed two detachments at Fort Riley's Cavalry Replacement Training Center (CRTC). There, some fifteen miles from the main camp, they unloaded freight trains and continued performing other tedious chores.[5]

## NISEI ON GUARD DURING PRESIDENT ROOSEVELT'S VISIT TO FORT RILEY

Then came Easter Sunday, April 25, 1943. Fort Riley would be the fifteenth of nineteen stops for the president's sixteen-day train tour of military posts, naval stations, and war factories in the country's southeastern quadrant. Roosevelt's second wartime tour was "conducted in strict wartime secrecy" and was "carefully guarded." At Fort Riley, all military personnel were expected to line the roadside to welcome the commander in chief when he attended Easter services with some fifteen thousand military personnel. At the same time, security precautions included evacuating buildings along the travel route[6] and getting "potential subversives" out of the way. Early that morning, suspecting a "disloyal conspiracy" among some Japanese American soldiers at the camp, officers sent forty-two of them to mend fences and dig posts ten miles away.[7]

Awaiting further commands, some 120 Nisei soldiers fell out in columns of 4 along the west side of their barracks. Instead of heading toward the parade grounds, however, they were ordered to march in the opposite direction. Tramping uphill and down along a winding embankment lined with small trees and bushes, they arrived twenty minutes later at Republican Flats, a clearing in the dry bed of the Republic River.

The bewildered men halted fifty yards in front of a huge aircraft hangar, the Motor Mechanics School Building where the CRTC's motor pool was stored, banked on one side by a steep hill. Atop the hill, half a dozen soldiers standing at twenty-foot intervals aimed .30 caliber machine guns their way. Straight ahead, only one side door of the building was unlocked. The wary Nisei marched single file through the open door, with two soldiers pointing rifles at them. Once inside, six second lieutenants, four armed with .45 automatic pistols, ushered them to four tiers of temporary bleachers in a corner of the cavernous building. The door was then locked. A colonel ordered, "All eyes front. No talking."[8]

The atmosphere was at once cold, confrontational, and beyond belief. Tears welled up in the eyes of some of the younger GIs. "We figured out we were prisoners," Sumoge remembered thinking, "you know, guarded by machine guns. MPs [military police] were kind of nervous. . . . They were outnumbered." After a while, Tow Hori raised his hand. He had to go to the latrine. Officers talked it over and consented to latrine calls, ten at a time. With pistols again drawn and pointed, they marched ten Nisei to the latrines, warned them to come out as soon as possible, and then escorted them back to the bleachers before designating ten more. "Hours and hours just sitting there, and we can't even talk," Sumoge recalled, decrying their treatment. "I wasn't sure that I would live through it." But if he did, he vowed, "there was going to be trouble."

Finally, after almost four hours, officers ordered the Nisei out, marched them back to their barracks, and dismissed them. It was around two thirty. By then the president and his party had toured the center, eaten lunch, and returned to the train.[9] An uncharacteristic silence, a despondent hush, fell over the GIs. Lunchtime had long since passed, but cold cuts and cereal were available at the mess hall, they were told. Few responded. When white soldiers asked where they had been, there was little they could say to explain the unimaginable turn of events. Most Nisei simply "moped around" the barracks, forgoing their typical Sunday exoduses to "Junk Town" (nearby Junction City). Lost in their musings, many sat on their bunks, hanging their heads. Even that Sunday night at mess, their usual spirited exchanges were replaced with glassy stares, futile mumblings, and an aura of dejection and betrayal. It would be weeks before some could speak of the day's unmistakable slight.

"They treated [us] like prisoners. We were in the U.S. army uniform. We were one of them . . . I don't see why anybody wouldn't be angry about that," maintained Sumoge. He began to raise questions and challenge his treatment: "You don't trust me. You have to guard me. What am I doing here? I want to get out. Put me in the concentration camp with my family." Hori concurred. "Your own army pointing guns at you. . . . They treated us like POWs. And then they tell you to go out and fight for your country. How could we do that?"

Their families' experiences had a strong impact on how Nisei viewed their positions in the military. Over the past year, the other ten members of Sumoge's family had been uprooted from their Hood River home and twenty-two-acre orchard. Leaving strawberries soon to be harvested, they also lost a seven-acre plot when they were unable to pay taxes. Now they lived in the arid lakebed of Tule Lake concentration camp in northern California. "They're in prison there," worried Sumoge, as doubt about his country's leaders grew. "So at times I thought, 'All the Japanese are in the camp. They could bomb it.'" Four months later, Sumoge faced another reversal. His request to visit his parents during his first furlough in September 1942 was denied because Tule Lake was within the West Coast zone prohibited to Nikkei. "I'm a U.S. soldier and I can't see my parents? Get me out of the army," he exclaimed.

The increasing weight of discrimination became more and more distressing to Sumoge. His family was incarcerated, treated like the enemy, and the warehouse detention at gunpoint tainted his view of the military. That feeling intensified after Hakubun Nozawa wrote to the War Department about the incident at Fort Riley. Army officials intercepted his letter, confined him to barracks for thirty days, and demoted him from private first class to private.[10]

What neither Sumoge nor the other Nisei knew was that an investigation by the War Department's own officials was revealing problems with Fort Riley's security measures. George Inagaki, executive secretary of the Japanese American Citizens League's Southern District Council, had mailed a disgruntled Fort Riley GI's letter to Colonel William P. Scobey, general staff executive to the assistant secretary of war. The letter likened treatment of Nisei GIs during Roosevelt's visit to that of "prisoners of war."[11] Colonel Scobey responded quickly: "The action of the Commander of this camp in subjecting the Nisei soldiers to this humiliating position certainly was totally unjustified and will not be tolerated by the War Department." Requesting facts before conducting an investigation, he did express hope that "Nisei would not expect realization of the complete position of a citizen."[12]

Scobey's superior, Assistant Secretary of War John J. McCloy, had a stake in the success of Japanese American GIs after shepherding the Nisei combat team through the War Department. "The whole idea of making these men good combat troops is completely negatived by destroying their self-respect or the assumption of their loyalty," he claimed. "They are all carefully screened men."[13]

The six-page investigative report concluded that Nisei soldiers were not discriminated against and security measures were reasonable and necessary; it also recommended no future action be taken.[14] Labeling this "unsatisfactory," Colonel Scobey queried: "Was the inspecting officer attempting to give protective cover-up to someone? . . . When did the classification of Kibei or Buddhist become conclusive proof of disloyalty? . . . Why were the 72, presumably loyal Japanese Americans, confined?" Forecasting "I don't think they will be loyal very long," he maintained that the situation could have been handled "without confining them, causing them to lose self-respect and breaking down their loyalty to their government, the army and their officers."[15]

A month later, Captain Smith W. Brookhart, Jr., compiled a sixteen-page report based on testimony from twenty-two officers, although he cited no Japanese American soldiers. Security measures varied widely, he concluded, for each of the three commanders had developed his own security plan. At the Cavalry Replacement Training Center, officers—one of whom conveyed his belief that Japanese American soldiers were "No. 1 potential subversives"—confined all of their men. As a result, the CRTC's measures were the most stringent: vacating and guarding buildings that bordered the president's route; confining civilian employees, officers' wives, and guests at the service club with armed guards; holding cooks and other personnel at recreation halls; freezing traffic and foot movement; and detaining Nisei soldiers at the Motor Mechanics School building. Captain Harold J. Crase, who was in charge of the school, requested arms for guards posted inside the building in order to protect the million dollars' worth of stored equipment. (He recalled that soldiers played cards, gambled, and read, although Nisei remembered that they sat on bleachers, forced to face forward without talking.) Outside, armed sentries, who typically patrolled when the school was not in session, continued their guard. In contrast, officers in the quartermaster detachment allowed Nisei to remain in their barracks during the president's visit, while in the headquarters detachment, a substantial number of Nisei joined their units at the Easter service attended by the president.[16]

Since most communication for the president's visit was oral, due to the need for secrecy, resulting security measures were inconsistent, Captain Brookhart's report concluded, and subordinate officers' actions at the CRTC were "no more than ill-advised and excessive zeal" in trying to ensure the president's safety." One commander was singled out for his "prejudice against all Japanese American soldiers"; the Nisei soldier whose letter sparked the investigation likely belonged to his detachment. Brigadier General Robert W. Strong was so dissatisfied with that captain's handling of troops that he intended to recommend that the officer be relieved until he learned the captain would be transferred out of the country.[17] (Tow Hori recalled the dreaded captain storming into the shower while he and another Nisei were bathing and then confining them to barracks for thirty days because they had been speaking Japanese.)

In his report, Captain Brookhart recommended no further action but did direct Fort Riley's commanding generals to take corrective action in order to prevent a recurrence. This meant little more than creating a central chain of command that would assure uniformity and eliminate "excessive zeal and poor judgment" among subordinate officers.[18]

Colonel Scobey expressed his frustrations: "It becomes difficult to develop loyalty on the part of these soldiers when they are all looked upon, classified, and treated as subversive." Officers at the CRTC who had closer relationships with Nikkei soldiers viewed them as "loyal and trustworthy," he admonished.[19]

There were "unnecessary and harsh restrictive measures," concluded Assistant Secretary McCloy. He also took issue with the view of some officers that Japanese American soldiers were "No. 1 potential subversives." Maintaining, "I have yet to learn of a single case where a Japanese American in the Army has been guilty of a subversive act," he continued that "for the most part, they make excellent soldiers with a high regard for their responsibilities."[20] Three and a half months after the incident, the army's "corrective action"[21] was of little consequence to the Nisei, who remained unaware of the military's investigation into their complaints.

It was at this point that Sumoge began to speak out. When a Nisei sergeant admonished a Kibei for talking in Japanese, he stuck up for the GI. "Let him speak. It's a Japanese unit. We're all discriminated against. You're discriminated against, too." As punishment, Sumoge drew dishwashing duty, eight hours a day for several months. Ironically, washing dishes at the officers' service club worked to his advantage, for he earned thirty dollars more than his typical sixty-dollar monthly wage and did not have to work outdoors during the twenty-degrees-below-zero winter weather. He believed that his isolated kitchen duty precluded his receiving the loyalty questionnaire (first distributed to Nikkei in the camps) when others at Fort Riley did, as discussed in chapters 4 and 5.

Though the questionnaire was not an issue for him, Sumoge did begin to consider his future. "Why stay in a place where they don't trust you and treat you like a prisoner?" he asked himself. In particular, he opposed the notion of a Nisei combat team. "I don't trust this army. And I don't like segregated units. We're all on the same boat. . . . You might sink the boat." When he finally visited his family after they were transferred to Heart Mountain, a camp in Wyoming outside the West Coast prohibited zone, he confided in his father. Sumoge had decided to express his feelings to the military. "Now we're going to the combat unit. That's when I'm going to really argue my side of it. . . . So I could be dead when I'm arguing. . . .

If you resist in the army, they could shoot you," he assumed, recalling the weapons that had been pointed at him at Fort Riley.

A month after the Fort Riley incident, Nisei volunteers from Hawaii and the mainland assembled at Camp Shelby, Mississippi, to form the Nisei combat team. By January 1944, the War Department had reinstituted the draft for Japanese Americans. Now Nisei would be ordered for combat training.

At that time, Fort Riley and Fort Leonard Wood, Missouri, held the two largest contingents of Nisei already serving in the U.S. military. Joining some 150 soldiers drawn from other camps, they would form the Thirty-third Infantry Battalion and train as replacements for the 442nd Regimental Combat Team, which was suffering mounting casualties, in Europe. The Thirty-third, composed entirely of Nisei (with Kibei representing about one-sixth of the battalion) would be the first such group to train at Fort McClellan's Infantry Replacement Training Center in Arkansas. Most had been drafted before the outbreak of war. All had been relegated to work as menials for the previous two to three years. Some one hundred, like Sumoge, came from Fort Riley, where they had felt the sting of military distrust, and all but a few had arrived by troop train just three to four days earlier.[22] Corporals, sergeants, and privates first class were, by and large, stripped of their ranks. The shadow cast at Fort Riley eleven months earlier began to lengthen as the men sought answers to their mounting questions when they arrived at their new base.

## THE QUESTION OF COMBAT DUTY AT FORT MCCLELLAN

The Thirty-third's six hundred men at Fort McClellan were divided equally into three companies. Companies A, B, and C camped along the vast hillsides: five men to a tent, two rows of tents per company, each company's tents advancing separately up the hills out of sight of the others. At the juncture where the hill leveled off along a gully, a large wooden structure at Company Street served as battalion headquarters.

Monday, March 20, 1944, was a peculiar day from the outset. After breakfast, the Thirty-third was to begin eight weeks of combat training, and men from Company B began to gather near headquarters. Fred Sumoge was among them. Already distressed by the discrimination his family was enduring and his own struggle with military inequities, he became even more incensed by local news reports that Nisei had all volunteered for combat.[23] "It's a lie. Everybody was talking about that." Now he was determined to express his views. "I wanted to see the company commander, so I had an appointment Monday morning. . . . There were a lot of people by the headquarters there, so I thought everybody's got an appointment. . . . People were hollering they wanted to see the company commander. I just stood there. I'm not the only one, but I had an appointment." (The Friday before, an angry officer inadvertently helped Sumoge to schedule his appointment. When Sumoge failed to salute him., the second lieutenant escorted the errant private to headquarters and ordered the meeting. Sumoge, grateful for the help, thanked the perplexed junior officer.)

Kenjiro Hayakawa, a Kibei from Hood River who had been inducted a month before the outbreak of war, had his own reasons for being at headquarters that morning. "I was drafted, so I wanted to serve, but I wanted to tell the company commander that I'm not fluent in English and I can't understand. . . . I had no intentions to ask the commander a favor. I just wanted him to understand our situation," he explained through his wife's translation.

Hayakawa understood little English and spoke even less. Born in Seattle in 1919, he had lived in Japan for seventeen of the first eighteen years of his life before returning to the United States to assist family members at their Hood River farm. His English schooling was limited to just two months each winter over three years. At the age of twenty-two, Hayakawa entered the army in November 1941 and completed thirteen weeks of basic training. (Like many Kibei, he had returned to the United States to avoid Japan's military service. Yet he accepted the draft in this country matter-of-factly, because it "wasn't the Japanese military.")[24] After transferring from Camp Roberts, California, to Camp Robinson, Arkansas, Hayakawa worked as a nurse in the hospital ward, where he spoke in Japanese to Kibei and in spotty English to others. "They showed us what to do and how to do it. Then I learned what the instructions were," he explained. Once he arrived at Fort McClellan, Hayakawa was demoted from technician fifth grade to private first class, though his job remained the same. Disappointed that his commander had not taken steps to simplify the language portion of his training, Hayakawa waited his turn that Monday morning.[25]

Eventually more than one hundred Nisei congregated outside the orderly room across from battalion headquarters.[26] Each had his own reasons for seeking an appointment with the commanding officer. Still, over

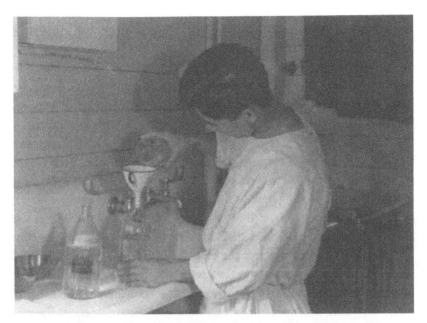

Nurse Kenjiro Hayakawa prepares for surgery in the hospital ward at Camp Robinson, Arkansas. (Kenjiro Hayakawa/Wendy Hakayawa, 1942)

the past week, with little to do by day and no officers at their barracks in the evening, it was evident that the men, especially the Kibei, had discussed their frustrations day and night. As Sumoge expressed it, "Everybody was unhappy." But, he added, "I didn't know everybody had the same idea." Hori recalled, "Each had an idea of what to do. Some didn't have nerve. Kibei hardheads had their minds made up."

Sergeant Edward McDonald, the scheduling officer, appeared at the entrance, and when soldiers refused to divulge their reasons for requesting meetings, he ordered that they fall into two ranks. "There was all kinds of talking back and forth," remembered Sumoge. "I know one or two in the big crowd were hollering and mad." Then Sergeant McDonald used a derisive term that Sumoge would not soon forget. After some described their families' plights in the camps, the officer called them "yellow-bellied Japs," according to their testimonies (an action the sergeant denied). Several broke ranks to protest this insult, which caught the attention of Major William Aycock.[27]

Major Aycock commanded Corporal Jesse Ballinger to march the men between the tent rows, and they proceeded for forty to seventy-five yards before their four-column formation stopped. In their testimonies, the men and officers disputed what had occurred. Major Aycock insisted that he addressed the soldiers in a loud voice, commanding, "You men will march to the field house." The men claimed the major did not speak to them as a group nor did they know where they were going. Corporal Ballinger heard two or three say, "This is as far as we go," before they all stopped. The men stated that they bunched up and stopped after several ahead of them had stopped. "The front stopped so I stopped too. I don't know why we stopped," explained Hayakawa, who stood in the middle of the fourth column. Sumoge, in the second column, was surprised, too. "The people in front stopped, so I stopped. And who was in the front? Nobody knows." Major Aycock testified later that he ordered the men to the field house a second time and explained that refusing to obey orders was serious. The men said they did not hear the major's second order though they did hear him ask anyone who was in the group by mistake to step out. No one moved. Then Corporal Ballinger asserted that he requested the name of each individual, and all the men refused. The men remembered the first three Nisei shaking their heads, after which the corporal walked past the columns without stopping or speaking, a gesture they did not understand. All agreed that the major placed the men under arrest and instructed Lieutenant Frank Lawson to summon the military police. Shortly after seven in the morning, MPs loaded forty-three men (all from Company B, all from Fort Riley, and most of whom were Kibei) on four to five trucks and drove them to the camp stockade.[28]

Around the hill beyond the battalion headquarters and men's tents and farther down the main road to the left of the stockade, the rest of the company gathered at the field house, unaware of those outside the headquarters. After morning roll call and formation, Brigadier General Wallace C. Philoon gave a brief welcome speech. Then members of each company were ordered to collect helmets and M1 rifles in the supply tents. Some fifty refused, congregating instead along the embankment above, on Company Street. MPs marched the resisters to the stockade, too. By afternoon, others, mostly Kibei and the majority from Fort Riley, broke ranks and joined them. Some, remembering the brigadier general inviting them to see their company commander if they had any problems, joined the sequestered men the next morning when their entreaties were ignored. Within thirty-six hours, there were 106 men from Companies A, B, and C confined behind the big double gates of the stockade.[29]

The stockade, located in a large yard lined with guard towers and barracks, was completely surrounded by a ten-foot-tall barbed wire fence. That night, as the imprisoned men slept on a barrack floor, searchlights swept across them and a loudspeaker warned them not to stick their heads out of the windows. At ten the next morning, the men crowded into the stockade mess hall, which was sealed off from the kitchen with sheets of plywood. Early arrivals sat on benches arranged like pews along a middle aisle, while Sumoge and others stood three deep in the back. Lieutenant Colonel Johnston spoke from a small podium, and his booming voice was intimidating, even when the 442nd Battalion's soft-spoken Captain Tanimura translated his words into Japanese. Hori recalled the lieutenant colonel saying: "You men are charged with insubordination. Insubordination in time of war is akin to mutiny punishable by death, according to the Articles of War." Sumoge remembered him threatening, "If this happened in Germany or Japan, you know what would happen." After the officer asked whether the men were loyal to the emperor, he insisted that the army's business was to train men for combat and that it could do nothing about their problems. He then gave them a choice: Those willing to train for combat were to exit by the right door. Those not willing should leave by the left door. They had approximately ten minutes to ponder their decision.[30]

Silently, the men walked single file down the center aisle. Seventy-eight exited to the right,[31] rejoining their companies and abandoning their attempts to talk to an officer about any problems.[32] Twenty-eight went to the left and were charged with violating the sixty-fourth Article of War: willful disobedience of a lawful order of a superior officer.[33] Hayakawa and Sumoge were among the twenty-eight.

"I did so," explained Hayakawa, "in the hope of bringing my problems to the attention of higher officials."[34] Sumoge recalled, "My mind was made up. I didn't have to think." The stakes were high. Remembering Lieutenant Colonel Johnston's threats as well as the weapons that Fort Riley soldiers had aimed at them, he and others presumed their ultimate sentence might be death. "We were expecting anytime they'd come with a machine gun," recalled Sumoge. "Anything could happen."

Meanwhile, the *Pacific Citizen*, the national JACL's newspaper, kept the Nikkei community informed through articles based on Associated Press reports. On March 25, 1944, it wrote that twenty-eight pre–Pearl Harbor inductees had refused to submit to military training and that they had received most of their formal education in Japan and returned to the United States shortly before the war. Sumoge's experience contradicted all those statements, for he had been inducted three months after the war began and had never been to Japan; he also recalled being one of several Nisei among the twenty-eight, all schooled in the United States. According to a quotation from Brigadier General Wallace C. Philoon, commanding officer of the Infantry Replacement Training Center, the men had become "indoctrinated with the philosophy of the Japanese people" and refused to salute the flag.[35]

An investigation followed. Over twelve days, Captain Merrill R. Wiseman oversaw an inquiry into each of the twenty-eight cases.[36] "Now this is the chance to talk to somebody," exulted Sumoge. Finally finding a receptive ear, he divulged his feelings to each of the three officers who interviewed him. "The main thing," Sumoge maintained, was to "fight discrimination." He described his predicament, saying, "Look, I have no home to go to. They took my home. My parents and family are all in a concentration camp. Now they don't trust me in the army. Now you say, 'Go fight for this country.' What am I going to fight for? . . . I think I've got a lot of fighting to do right here." Of attacks against Kibei, he insisted, "The Kibeis are more loyal than I am. They had two countries, and they chose America."

At Sumoge's investigation hearing on March 27, Major Aycock, First Lieutenant Lawson, and Colonel Ballinger spoke as army witnesses, and in his testimony, Sumoge continued to unload his frustrations:

> They always kick us Japanese Americans around like cattle. . . . We have been discriminated against in the army for the last two years. . . . We are fighting for protection of this country and the protection of our home and our form of government. That is the way I felt and I don't have any of those things . . . I think I don't in the first place belong in the Army. . . . They told us we were volunteers and we were going to get 17 weeks training and go overseas and "you might as well make the best of it." . . . I want to have my reasons clear before I go . . . I don't have any home to go back to. . . . If I am going to do the duties of a citizen, I want to get the rights of one . . . not more but as much.[37]

Kenjiro Hayakawa's language limitations became clear early in his hearing. After affirming his first and last name, he answered, "I cannot understand English" when Captain Wiseman requested his rank, organization, and serial number. As a result, Captain Tanimura translated statements by Major Aycock, Lieutenant Lawson, and Corporal Ballinger for Hayakawa, who declared through the interpreter that "a lot of misunderstanding" occurred because of his lack of language proficiency. Rather than make a statement, Hayakawa asked questions about the nature and process of a general court-martial. Yes, capital punishment was a possibility, and yes, there would be an interpreter at his trial. In response to the last query, Captain Wiseman affirmed, "That is not a promise, but a regulation."[38]

## COURT-MARTIAL

The trials would go forward. Captain Wiseman recommended that both Sumoge and Hayakawa face general courts-martial. Sumoge would be tried on April 12 and 13, 1944, and Hayakawa on April 20 and 21, 1944. They would be among twenty-one of twenty-eight Nisei to face military criminal trials during the next month. Sumoge was one of three who was not Kibei.[39]

A fair trial seemed improbable to the Nisei private, who felt victimized by discrimination and accepted defense counsel only after coaxing. "We're all *nihonjin* [Japanese] and they're all *hakujin*. . . . We know we're not going to get a fair trial," Sumoge reasoned. His general court-martial took place in a Fort McClellan courtroom before a panel of ten officers. Two military lawyers, or judge advocates, prosecuted the case, and two military lawyers served as defense counsel. Sumoge was arraigned at 2:13 P.M. on April 12, 1944:

> Charge: Violation of the 64th Article of War.
>
> Specification: In that, Private Fred F. Sumoge, Company B, 33rd Training Battalion, Infantry Replacement Training Center, Fort McClellan, Alabama, having received a lawful command from Maj. William B. Aycock, his superior officer, to march to the Field House, Fort McClellan, Alabama, did at Fort McClellan, Alabama, at 0700, on or about 20 March 1944, willfully disobey the same.[40]

Sumoge pleaded "not guilty" to both the charge and the specification.

Major Aycock, Corporal Ballinger, and First Sergeant McDonald testified about the incident outside battalion headquarters, and Captain Wiseman, the investigating officer, gave details of the official inquiry, testifying that he followed procedures from the *Manual for Courts-Martial*. The defense regularly objected when testimony went beyond the charge against Sumoge and challenged the use of self-incriminating quotations from Sumoge. Before the first day of court concluded at 2:40 P.M., the defense moved unsuccessfully for a verdict in favor of Sumoge, based on a lack of proof that "the accused" had received the command, that the alleged command was willfully disobeyed, and that the command, if given, was not personal (as defined in *Winthrop's Military Law and Precedents*) and had not been proved as coming from Major Aycock.[41]

At 7:45 A.M. the next day, the court informed Sumoge that he had a choice. He had the right to become a witness on his own behalf and be questioned by defense, prosecution, and the court; he could make an unsworn statement without being questioned; or he could remain silent. Sumoge chose to take the stand, and the defense continued to object to including his testimony from the investigation, in particular, his statement that ". . . unless this is straightened out here or in Washington I can't train. . . ." Four Nisei witnesses from Company B also testified, three often answering that they did not recall or had not heard what had happened and two of the three objecting to some questions that could incriminate them. The defense closed by arguing that Sumoge did not "willfully disobey," since he did not receive the order and it was neither personal nor understood. His attorney also maintained that any violation of orders that took place after the time specified in the charge and admissions made during what he contended was an "improper investigation" should not be considered. The prosecuting lawyers countered that, while the matter of whether the major gave the order should be decided by the court, there was no testimony that anyone gave an order to stop. Sumoge had voiced "a lot of reasons" not to train. Furthermore, they contended that others could be present in a group at the time of a so-called personal command and that the series of incidents combined to form one transaction.[42]

While Sumoge felt that his defense had served him well, he had one reservation: he did not get to read a statement he had labored over for two days. The four Nisei who had been tried during the past four days had received sentences of twenty (for two men), twenty-five, and thirty years, which they communicated by signaling with their fingers through their barrack window. Heeding his counsel's advice, Sumoge omitted the statement. His one-and-a-half-page handwritten missive had disclosed potentially self-incriminating views: "Something was wrong. There was a problem. We had to fight for democracy, not overseas, but here in the United States of America for equality of rights and treatment. No segregated unit. No inhuman treatment. No racial discrimination. No families in concentration camps. . . . Things may have been different if after basic training we stayed together with this non-segregated unit and as a regular American military unit, work and fight together anywhere in the world."[43]

Recalling the weapons he had faced at Fort Riley, Sumoge imagined the worst. "You could be shot. You have to prepare for death because you're fighting the army." Besides, he opined, "I figured . . . I died once, anyway, or twice. . . . I wasn't afraid of death." He considered his first brush with death to have occurred on Easter Sunday at Fort Riley, and the second with the colonel's threat at the Fort McCallum stockade. So he was prepared when the verdict came just before noon on April 13. Sumoge was pronounced guilty. He was sentenced "to be dishonorably discharged [from] the service, to forfeit all pay and allowances due or to become due, and to be confined at hard labor at such place as the reviewing authority may direct for twenty years."[44]

A week later, at 9:32 A.M. on a hot and sultry day, Kenjiro Hayakawa faced his own court-martial. "That was a total mess!" he recalled, sensing that the nine youthful judges "didn't want to be there." He was facing the first trial of his twenty-four years, and a more serious atmosphere would have reassured him. "The judges were talking among themselves, eating candy."

Proceedings in Hayakawa's trial followed the format of Sumoge's. The charge and specification were the same, as were Hayakawa's pleas of "not guilty" to both. Sumoge's attorneys also defended Hayakawa. Major Aycock, Corporal Ballinger, and First Sergeant McDonald again testified about the events of the morning. This time, McDonald presented the noon roll call naming the forty-three men who were absent, and First Lieutenant James P. Mallon of the military police spoke about marching the men to the post stockade. Similar to Sumoge's trial, the defense frequently objected to references to orders not included in the charge and concluded the officers' testimonies with a motion to find Hayakawa "not guilty on specification." As before, the court denied the motion.[45]

After he was apprised of his rights as a witness, Hayakawa took the stand. His statement, given through Technical Sergeant Tom Oye's translations, reiterated that "most of the time" he did not understand English-language statements and completed tasks by doing "the same things the others did." Would he have fought against Japan? "I would be willing to fight against Japan," Hayakawa explained, "but first I would like to have my feelings expressed to the government and an answer or solution given . . . because since I was inducted into the Army I have suffered discrimination and also my relatives have been evacuated from the West Coast and have suffered not only property damage but also personal humiliation because of such evacuation. If the government would grant full rights to those citizens of Japanese ancestry and would grant returns for such losses suffered . . . I would be very willing and glad to fight against Japan." But was he willing to train anyway? "I was willing to take training even if satisfaction was not granted," Hayakawa answered.[46]

Three Nisei witnesses from Company B each testified that they did not hear the officers' orders, and two objected to some of the questions from the prosecutors and the court. When the court reconvened at 8:00 A.M. on April 21, 1944, Major Aycock and First Sergeant McDonald answered more questions before closing arguments. As in Sumoge's case, the defense emphasized that Hayakawa had no intent to disobey ("he did what the other fellows did") and that the group's intent could not be assigned to him by implication. Despite having family members in Japan and the "confusion that was in his mind," he was willing to fight Japan. If there was reasonable doubt that he understood and willfully and intentionally violated an order not given to him personally, he could not be convicted under the sixty-fourth Article of War. Meanwhile, the prosecution contended that after three years in the army, Hayakawa could understand the simple command "You will march" and that he was unwilling to train until he had a solution to his problems. No, he was guilty as charged and should be punished.[47]

"At the court-martial, they asked me questions, and I answered them," Hayakawa remarked. Satisfied that he had verbalized his main concern ("Take us out of the camps"), he was disappointed that he had "no chance to say anything they didn't ask me." Shortly before 10:15 A.M. on April 21, 1944, the court announced its verdict. Kenjiro Hayakawa was pronounced guilty. He was sentenced "to be dishonorably discharged," forfeit all pay, and be confined at hard labor for ten years. Speaking matter-of-factly, Hayakawa reflected, "I had no idea what would happen to me. . . . Whatever the sentence, *shikataganai* [it couldn't be helped], because I disobeyed the order. I just had to take the consequences."

The consequences would be confinement in the United States Disciplinary Barracks at Fort Leavenworth, Kansas. Now Hayakawa and Sumoge would be among twenty-one convicted "Fort McClellan discipline barrack boys," known as "DB boys." Though both were quiet by nature and avoided calling attention to themselves, their individual concerns had overcome their preference for the periphery. They were Americans in U.S. military uniforms. Yet they faced the scourge of discrimination in the army as surely as their families did in the camps. So they spoke out against their families' discriminatory treatment at the hands of the government. And they resisted what they viewed as the inequitable and punitive actions the military took against Nisei servicemen. Still, these men were not just citizens but soldiers who had defied military orders.

"I wouldn't cause any trouble, but if trouble comes to me, then I'll have to fight it, see?" Sumoge explained. "So," he added slowly, "a lot of trouble came to me." The men's personal convictions about what was right and just aroused emotions deep inside each of them and gave rise to uncharacteristically bold and outspoken deeds. As Sumoge wrote in his court statement, rather than fighting in Europe and Japan, they were waging a battle on American turf.[48]

# NINE

# "Discard My Uniform for Good"

## THE END OF THE WAR

**W**ELL, that was good news! We know we're gonna be able to come home now." George Akiyama was at the Allied supply base in Leghorn, Italy, when he read about Germany's surrender. The bold headline plastered across three-fourths of the newspaper's front page flashed the welcome words: "PEACE AT LAST."

The war had been long and gruesome, exacting a worldwide death toll of 55 million. For forty-five months, Americans had waged war on two overseas fronts against the Axis aggressors. Allied with Great Britain and the Soviet Union, U.S. troops invaded North Africa and Italy and then joined the D-Day landing that led to the liberation of France and Belgium and forced the Nazis to retreat from France to Germany. Blocked by Soviet troops from the east, ravaged by bombing in Berlin, and leaderless after Adolph Hitler's suicide, Germany finally surrendered in May 1945. On the Pacific front, U.S. troops island-hopped, seizing weaker islands, stranding Japanese armies on island outposts, and cutting off Japan's supplies of raw materials. After halting the Japanese advance to Australia in the Battle of the Coral Sea, the United States eventually overwhelmed Japan at Midway and Guadalcanal before retaking the Philippines at Leyte Gulf. Bitter fighting and heavy losses at Iwo Jima and Okinawa still did not force surrender, but the United States' newly tested nuclear weapons did. Atomic bombs leveled first Hiroshima and then Nagasaki under purple-hazed mushroom clouds and fireballs that instantly killed 170,000. Japan surrendered on

August 9, 1945, five days after the second bomb. World War II was over. At last, the men—though laden with burdens from the war—could head home.[1]

## THE WOUNDED

Some were already Stateside. Sho Endow was on duty at Camp Robinson, Arkansas, ten months after being hit by shrapnel in Bruyeres. Ninety days of hospitalization in Naples had not healed him, so Endow, one of the "walking wounded," recovered at Harmon Army Hospital in Longview, Texas, before taking sick leave to visit his family in Payette, Idaho. Despite his slow recovery, Endow was committed to serving until the end of the war—just not any longer. "I got to thinking," he

George Akiyama reads news of the war's end while at the 100th Battalion's command post in Leghorn, Italy. (George Akiyama, August 1945)

remarked wryly, "if I'd stayed in, I might have been a drunk when I got out. A thirty-year drunk."

Sagie Nishioka was hospitalized at Fitzsimmons Medical Center in Denver, Colorado, when word reached him of the war's end. "Sheer relief" came over him, he recalled, though he told himself that had the war ended twenty-four days earlier, he could have been spared his dismal condition. Immobilized in a body cast up to his chest, Nishioka had been told by a doctor that he'd never walk again. Though that prognosis proved to be wrong, medical procedures were extensive and painful. Once, though, there was a welcome surprise. Following surgery to graft flesh from his stomach onto his left leg, Nishioka developed an infection and a 103-degree fever. The young patient was understandably "just feeling lousy" the next day when General Dwight D. Eisenhower, former commander of Allied forces in the Mediterranean theater, appeared at his bedside while visiting the hospital. "I remember you boys when you were in southern Italy," he

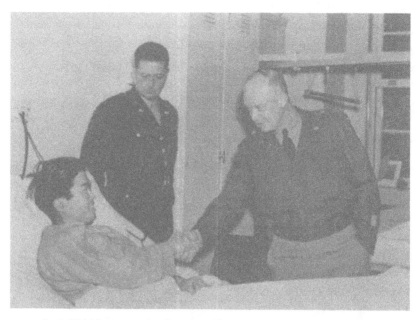

Sagie Nishioka, recovering from one of his sixteen surgeries, was surprised by a bedside visit from General Dwight Eisenhower. "I didn't even shave," he remarked. (Sagie Nishioka, 1945)

told Nishioka before the fifteen-second buzzer signaled that it was time to move on to the next patient. The ailing Nishioka, one patient among many in the four-thousand-bed facility, had not expected Eisenhower to visit him personally. "I didn't even shave that morning, for goodness sakes!" Yet the visit was as uplifting as the general's demeanor. "Generally when you see a general, they don't smile like that," he noted. There was little else to smile about, however, for Nishioka's hospitalization would extend another four months, for a total of eighteen months. He would endure sixteen operations and twenty blood transfusions, lose forty pints of blood, and emerge with a full disability and his right leg shortened by two and a half inches.

## THE RELEASED

Mam Noji was also in the States when the war ended, after thirty straight months of overseas duty. The functions performed by the Military Intelligence Service were so critical that translators were denied leaves until 1945.

Frank Hachiya's family held his memorial service in the mess hall of Block 37 in the Minidoka concentration camp in Hunt, Idaho. Junkichi Hachiya, Frank's father, is seated to the right of the altar. Friend Harry Takagi, on leave from the army, is standing at far right. (Carolyn Brady, 1945)

"We were considered at one time invaluable," he explained, "so no matter how many points we accumulated, we weren't eligible to go home." His break came toward the end of the Philippine campaign, and he was lucky enough to be selected for temporary duty in the States. Boarding a transport ship in Manila, he and five thousand anxious GIs from all categories followed an unexpectedly circuitous route home. Zigzagging across the Pacific and passing through the Panama Canal, their ship cruised through the Caribbean and up the East Coast to land at Newport News, Virginia. From there, Noji boarded a train and completed the final leg of a homeward trek that lasted five weeks. When the war ended, he became eligible for discharge. "After more than 46 months," he sighed, "I was able to discard my uniform for good."[2]

Frank Hachiya remained in the Philippines, his body interred in Grave 4479 of the U.S. Armed Forces Cemetery outside the town of Palo on Leyte Island.[3] Mortally wounded in January 1945 after volunteering to reconnoiter the enemy's position on the front lines, he was memorialized at services in both Hawaii and Idaho. In February, Gold Star Mothers included Hachiya when they honored their deceased sons at a flower-filled auditorium in downtown Honolulu's Harris Memorial Church; men who had served with him at Kwajalein and Eniwetok islands joined friends to pay their respects.[4] Across the Pacific, a more austere service took place at the Minidoka concentration camp in Hunt, Idaho. Family and friends crowded into Block 37's mess hall for the Konkokyo service, chanting sutras and containing their grief. No War Department representative was present, but close friend Harry Takagi stood in uniform.[5] Few personal effects remained: Japanese-English and English-Japanese dictionaries, a pair of shoes, and a face towel. But more than anything, Mr. Hachiya cherished his final memories of his son. At their parting near the gate at Tule Lake a year and a half earlier, the father remembered encouraging his son and warning against cowardice in battle. "Do not worry, Dad. I know what my duty is," Frank had smiled back. Mr. Hachiya stoically and justifiably declared, "I am proud of my son's supreme sacrifice for his country."[6]

### THE DECORATED AND THE UNRECOGNIZED

Citizens across the country demonstrated pride in their war heroes. When the men of the 100th/442nd sailed into New York Harbor, cheering crowds waved American flags while city firefighters thrust their hoses skyward to form welcoming trajectories of spraying water. In Washington, D.C., the combat team marched down Constitution Avenue to the cadence of rousing Sousa marches amid applause from six thousand spectators, including government workers granted longer lunch hours to join the celebration. When a drenching June rain caused an aide to consider canceling the White House ceremony, President Harry S. Truman retorted, "After what those boys have been through, I can stand a little rain."[7] Before he pinned an unprecedented seventh Presidential Unit Citation on their colors, the president congratulated the men: "I can't tell you how very much I appreciate the privilege of being able to show you just how much the United States of America thinks of what you have done."[8]

Indeed, this all-Nisei combat team had become the most highly decorated unit of its size and length of service in U.S. military history. Its seven Presidential Unit Citations were unparalleled for such a unit, and it earned five of those during its brutal month of fighting for Bruyeres and the Lost Battalion. Men of the 442nd gained such high acclaim that one colonel at an awards ceremony privately commented, "The only thing wrong with this outfit is it has too damned many heroes."[9]

## THE UNRECOGNIZED

Neither parades nor fanfare greeted the invaluable men of the Military Intelligence Service when they returned from the war. In the eyes of Colonel Sidney Forrester Mashbir (commandant of the Allied Translator and Interpreter Section intelligence center in Brisbane, Australia), "No group had so much to lose. Capture would have meant indescribable horrors to them and their relatives in Japan." It would be impossible to determine, he added, "how many hundreds of American lives and how many billions of dollars were saved" because of the Nisei's contributions to military intelligence.[10]

Nonetheless, the accomplishments of the MIS remained a well-kept secret from the general public and the press. As long as no one, including the Japanese military, knew that the United States had the ability to translate Japanese documents, the U.S. military retained an edge in the Pacific. As a result, the MIS's operations, techniques, and capabilities became "America's superb secret weapon."[11] The minimal honors the MIS received reflect that secrecy, for during the war, it was awarded only a single Distinguished Service Cross among honors for individuals, and there was no Presidential Unit Citation. Since the teams, composed of up to ten men, were attached only temporarily to their combat units, their names were not listed in morning reports and they were not easily recognized for their accomplishments as a group;[12] there was also little documentation of their contributions and no centralized database.[13] Neither did their military ranks signify their contributions, for they earned promotions at one-third the rate of whites who worked alongside them. One month before the war's end, however, some one hundred Nisei gained commissions as officers.[14]

Men of the 100th/442nd also had questions about the equity of military honors. "There should have been more Congressional Medals," maintained Sho Endow, who noticed that, despite so many Nisei acts of bravery, few seemed to be recognized for rewards. No member of the combat team had received a Medal of Honor (approved by the secretary of war); instead, each request was downgraded to a Distinguished Service Cross (approved by an army commander), although individual feats rivaled those awarded the Medal of Honor in other units.[15] Not until JACL leader Mike Masaoka raised the issue with Senator Elbert Thomas, chair of the Military Affairs Committee, did the military posthumously honor Private First Class Sadao S. Munemori, a Nisei from George Akiyama's Company A who smothered a grenade with his chest to save his buddies.[16] Ironically, an officer who had previously declined to accept the 100th in his command eventually signed one of its seven Presidential Unit Citations. It was General Dwight D. Eisenhower who acknowledged the 100th/442nd and the 232nd Combat Engineer Company, through his signature, for their breakthroughs along the Gothic Line.[17]

On the battlefield, there had been suspicions of racial prejudice. After the 100th decimated enemy defenses outside Rome, the men relished the thought of being the first unit to march through the city. Instead, on June 4, just six miles away from the city, they were ordered to halt on the roadside while the First Armored Division passed by. Not until 10:30 the next evening did the Nisei finally arrive, but they rode in trucks and stepped out at an assembly area a few miles northwest of the city. The official U.S. Army campaign history did not mention their critical victories, nor did a *New York Times* report, which credited another regiment without detailing the 100th's spearheading efforts.[18] Four months later, after the bloody battle to free Bruyeres, public credit eluded the entire 442nd. The secrecy of the Vosges mission prevented it, according to General John E. Dahlquist. Since Germany knew the 442nd was fighting in Italy, divulging its takeover of Bruyeres would convey critical intelligence that the military front was shifting from Italy to France, he explained in a telephone call to the 442nd's headquarters. (Colonel S. L. A. Marshall, former journalist and later military historian, complained that the War Department's "air of mystery" about Nisei troops fed suspicions that they were untrustworthy.)[19]

GIs consistently complained about General Dahlquist's callous treatment of their battalion, though they were unclear whether his lack of combat experience, his poor leadership skills, or his views of Nisei were to blame. After the Third Battalion liberated Bruyeres, the general restaged the takeover with the Second so that the press could capture the event on camera. Next, General Dahlquist ordered the 100th to take Biffontaine; this action, which battalion leaders viewed as the senseless pursuit of a farm town, required an uphill death charge that left the men trapped two miles deeper in enemy territory. When Biffontaine was in hand after brutal house-to-house fighting, the general again sent the exhausted men out, this time to rescue the Lost Battalion, which had become trapped as a result of his command. "Get the men out there crawling and get the Krauts out of the holes," he had demanded. At one point, a furious Colonel Alfred Pursall defied the general: "I won't let you kill my boys."[20] By the time the men rescued the 211 trapped Texans, their units were decimated, with just twenty-five riflemen remaining in Companies K and I combined. General Dahlquist immediately pushed them onward to the next hill. The men, forced into innumerable death traps with virtually no recovery time, sensed that they were considered disposable.[21] Colonel Gordon Singles, commander of the 100th Battalion, refused to shake General Dahlquist's hand at a full dress review. Colonel Young Kim, the 100th's operations officer, charged that the commander had "violated every principle of leadership and tactics."[22] Still, there was no thought of mutiny, Akiyama related. "Just do what you're told in the army."

Nisei soldiers sensed inequities and mistrust in other areas of the service, too. Sagie Nishioka felt that officers imposed tougher training standards on the Nisei. During practice maneuvers, officers told the Nisei that "we had to do a little better than the Caucasians." The extra effort did pay off when members of the 442nd achieved higher maneuver scores, he concluded. George Akiyama also noticed a difference in how commanders treated them. "They always had us go into the toughest fighting. Where other units couldn't do it, we did. . . . Nobody complained or anything." Mam Noji's indignation reached beyond military service to the crux of Nikkei wartime treatment: "Here our families were all removed from the coast and put in internment camps. Yet they needed their sons to serve in the army. Gosh, whoever heard of such a thing? . . . Nikkei are denied all privileges of citizenship, yet they want volunteers to serve in the army. How misguided can a government be? . . . Those were terrible times."

## THE DISTRUSTED

Kenjiro Hayakawa and Fred Sumoge also held strong feelings about wartime discrimination. In their case, circumstances at Fort Riley, Kansas, and Fort McClellan, Arkansas, compelled them to confront the issue head-on. After facing court-martial for willfully disobeying a superior officer, each had been sentenced to confinement and hard labor at Fort Leavenworth, Kansas.

Like other Hood River Nisei in uniform, the two had vowed allegiance to their country. And, not unlike the others, they were concerned about their wartime treatment—the government's toward their families and the military's toward them. Beyond that, however, they differed from their valley peers. Instead of complying with orders, Hayakawa and Sumoge had registered their dissent against the regimented and disciplined military system. By doing so, the men's behavior was also out of character with the sense of moral obligation, loyalty, obedience, and self-restraint emphasized by their Issei parents.

Despite the discrimination their families faced, the two had willingly trained from the beginning, because, as Sumoge claimed, "We're citizens." Experiencing what they believed was inequitable military treatment, however, they changed their views. After both were denied the chance to voice their concerns to their superiors, they expressed their frustrations outwardly, as when the normally quiet Sumoge refused to salute a junior officer.

A military unit's morale depended on how soldiers viewed their organization and its demands, according to sociologist Tamotsu Shibutani, and this had a major effect on their performance. Shibutani's study of the atypical Company K at Fort Snelling's Military Intelligence Service Language School drew revealing parallels with other Nisei at Fort McClellan. When the men believed they were treated unjustly—and their leaders insisted on enforcing regulations without regard to their frustrations—they tended to become resentful, especially when forced to perform tasks they viewed as useless. As they began to question the legitimacy of the military structure, the men became increasingly averse to following orders. Shibutani characterized this as demoralization, a gradual breakdown and reluctance to comply with norms, a process that became pronounced when the unit encountered an obstacle.[23]

Central to Sumoge's and Hayakawa's thinking was their belief in the principles of the Constitution: their responsibilities to protect it and the rights it guaranteed them. The men's decision came at a critical point and was influenced by their growing distrust of the army. It involved examining their concerns and principles in light of their military duty. It meant making a choice. Ultimately, they opted to voice their concerns rather than lose any hope of expressing themselves. So they were among the indicted twenty-one who chose to exit through the left door of the stockade rather than begin combat training.

For the first six months after their sentencing in April 1944, the men remained at Fort McClellan's stockade. Sumoge remembered collecting rocks as part of a work crew while offering reassurance to the scared young MP who kept one hand on his gun. "Don't worry. Put your gun away. We're not going to go anyplace," he told the MP. "Why don't you go lie down and sleep? I'll wake you up when we're ready." Not surprisingly, the two became friends. Sumoge and other imprisoned men also built a cement canal.

Those twenty-one Nisei were eventually transferred to the federal government's first penal institution, Fort Leavenworth, which had been established in northeastern Kansas in 1875. The imposing twelve-and-a-half-acre prison complex was enclosed by stone walls fourteen to forty-one feet high, strung with razor wire, and interspersed with twelve guard towers. The U.S. Disciplinary Barracks was a federal maximum-security prison for men from all branches of the armed forces who had been court-martialed as well as conscientious objectors and hardened criminals serving long-term sentences. Dubbed "The Castle," its eight wings of cells branched out from a shallow gray dome in the center of an octagonal hub. Each five-by-eight-foot cell contained a mattress on a metal-frame bed, a stainless steel toilet, and a small, wall-mounted shelf that flipped up to form a table.[24] The men followed a monotonous routine, lining up outside their cells before marching downstairs to the main floor mess hall, lining up to march back to their cells, and then lining up again to go downstairs for work, showers, or haircuts. The twenty-one Nisei discipline barrack boys kept fit, walking down and up innumerable times from their cells at the top of the eight floors. Sumoge recalled missing dinner after inmates threw a lightbulb that shattered on a sergeant's desk. When he was forced to miss a meal on his birthday, thoughts of his mother's cooking, especially her savory *maze-gohan* (rice mixed with vegetables), were all that sustained him.

"I idled away," muttered Hayakawa, whose "hard labor" at Leavenworth dwindled to collecting trash on prison grounds and picking up eggs and cleaning a large chicken coop outside the prison. "I sawed bits of wood, made *geta* [Japanese wooden clogs] and a lot of airplanes, anything I could make by carving with a pocketknife." Sumoge worked in the prison radio lab, while others handled secretarial duties, electrical work, or outdoor chores. During the last few months, he weeded beets at the farm colony outside the barrack walls. Though the men were unguarded and isolated, they worked steadily without thoughts of running away. "They might shoot us or put us back in and give us another ten years," he reasoned.

The men, who believed they were holding to their principles and "fighting for democracy," noticed one redeeming aspect of the penal system. "Really, no discrimination. Everybody in the same boat," claimed Sumoge. Nonetheless, he and others voiced their displeasure by crooning Cole Porter's "Don't Fence Me In."

Ever so slowly over the next fourteen months, changes in their sentences began to tilt in their favor. In April 1945, four months before the war's end and after a year of imprisonment, the office of Secretary of War Henry Stimson reduced Sumoge's sentence to ten years and did the same for others whose confinement exceeded ten years. At the same time, that office denied clemency to Hayakawa because of the "serious nature of the offense" and the "relatively short period" he had been confined. In August 1945, when news of the war's end drifted upward to the eighth floor of Fort Leavenworth's disciplinary barracks, men began cheering, "*Yare yare*" (How glad I am), according to Hayakawa. For Sumoge, that milestone meant little. "We were still prisoners," he realized. Three and a half months after the war ended, in November 1945, the secretary of war reduced the men's sentences to three years through a special clemency action by President Harry S. Truman.[25] Finally, in May 1946, after twenty-five total months of imprisonment, all twenty-one of the men experienced the elation of liberty when they were released, one or two at a time over several weeks. "I was free so I was happy," exulted Hayakawa. Likewise, Sumoge proclaimed, "I was just like a bird let out of a cage. Hey, you're free, so fly all over." The men exited the big gate at Fort Leavenworth wearing new black suits and felt hats with ten-dollar bills and bus tickets home tucked in their pockets. Still, the joy of freedom was diminished by the stigma they carried on their release papers: "Dishonorable Discharge."

## THE RETURNEES

The war years had been oppressive in ways that were unique to each of the Hood River men who served in the army. The GIs earned seven Purple Hearts (six for being wounded and one for killed in action), two Silver Stars (for gallantry in action), and nine Bronze Stars (for heroic achievement).[26] Those men bore injuries—whether physical, emotional, or personal—that would impede their adjustments at home. A few were celebrated; many were not. Most, whether they received accolades or faced accusations, were reluctant to discuss what they had experienced. And although they simply wanted to return home, their hearts were heavy. "We kept thinking about all the friends we lost," grieved George Akiyama. Then, too, they worried about the reception they could expect at home. "If we return to Hood River, will the white people there make trouble for us?" Sagie Nishioka wondered. "And if we do go back to the farm, will I be able to work it again with my legs so busted up?"[27] Regrettably, the men would face a hometown chill and little gratitude for their wartime sacrifices, whatever they may have been.

PART III

# AFTER THE WAR

# TEN

# "No Japes Wanted in Hood River"

## THE HOOD RIVER SITUATION

**W**HAT a lowdown thing to have done," exclaimed Mam Noji. The action by citizens in his hometown struck a visceral blow at Noji's service to his country and discredited his parents' forty years of sacrifice in their adopted homeland. What's more, news headlines across the country were describing his community in venomous terms. Even in the South Pacific, he overheard MIS buddies whisper sympathetically, "One of them guys is from Hood River."

Nine months before the war's end, Hood River residents were making headway in growing fruit and continuing with community life as usual. They voted the Republican ticket in the November 1944 election (except for the state attorney general, a Democrat but a Hood River native), giving Thomas Dewey a forty-eight-vote lead over Franklin Roosevelt in the presidential race. Mayor-elect Joe Meyer rolled the first ball at the Hood River Bowling Alleys' grand reopening. Hi-Ho crackers sold for $.21, a two-pound jar of orange marmalade for $.33, and a head of lettuce for $.10 at Eby's Food Market. J. C. Penney advertised rayon crepe holiday dresses for $7.90 and men's suits for $29.75; Goodyear tires cost $16.05 each; and Hackett Furniture Store offered a four-piece mahogany bedroom suite at $79.50. For entertainment, the Rialto featured Wallace Beery in *Barbary Coast Gent* as well as *Rosie the Riveter*, and the Cascadian showed *The Deerslayer*. Apple and pear production was at near-record levels, with both exceeding one million boxes and Extra Fancy or Fancy Anjous bringing $4.10 a box. In order to meet growth needs, the Apple Growers Association cooperative opened a new warehouse in Parkdale.[1]

That same month, an act by a local veterans' organization became a hotly contested public issue that would incite debate across the country. On November 29, 1944, American Legion Post No. 22 defaced a war memorial it had erected fourteen months before. The honor roll, which ran along the upper section of the entire east wall of the county courthouse, was composed of wooden plaques that displayed the names of more than 1,600 young men and women from the county who were serving in the armed forces. Sometime that evening, Legion members dashed black paint over sixteen of those names. All sixteen were of Japanese Americans. The reason, the organization declared, was its belief that these young men were citizens of Japan and subjects of the emperor of Japan.[2]

Overseas, Hood River Nisei were shocked and agitated when they read the news. "It was kind of a dirty deal," commented Shig Imai. "Nothing less than an insult," added Noji. "Here we were risking our lives, you might say. And it wasn't good enough to be on the board."[3] Several aroused Nisei took pen in hand. "I was kind of angry," recalled George Akiyama. "That's the reason I wrote a letter to *Life* magazine . . . I wanted the rest of the country to know what the situation was. I got a reply from the Legion post in New York. . . . They welcomed me and said as soon as you get discharged, you're welcome to join our American Legion."[4] From an island near New Guinea, Sergeant Taro Asai expressed surprise at this "most cruel gesture." His name meant more than just an inscription on the board, Asai maintained, for it stood for one of democracy's ideals.[5] From France, two months after his brother was wounded in action, Sergeant Johnny Y. Wakamatsu of Hood River penned more acrid words:

> . . . Remember, we did not volunteer unless we thought that as Americans it was our duty. Many have died believing in Liberty, equality, and the pursuit of Happiness. Many more are crippled in various hospitals here in France, England and back there in the states.
>
> Your actions and policies are not American; they do not give us the treatment of loyal American soldiers. Really it is too bad that the Hood River Legion Post must follow such UnAmerican ideals. I regret that I was reared and educated in such an unjust community with such narrow-minded so-called Americans.

Disgustedly yours,

1st Sgt. Johnny Y. Wakamatsu, France[6]

The soldiers' hometown community had grappled with the question of its absentee population even as Nikkei headed from the train depot to camp. A week after Nikkei left the valley in May 1942, the *Hood River County Sun* commended the nearby Bonneville American Legion post's stand that aliens be deported within two years if they did not become citizens. It declared, "If living in America is not worth becoming an American citizen, we feel that one should not be allowed to live in America." The paper did not, however, acknowledge that only "free white persons" were eligible for naturalization at that time.[7]

Hood River's struggle with its economic and demographic situation was coming to a head. White valley residents had long been frustrated by Issei farms interspersed amid their land, by competition from the Issei's success with strawberries and pears, and by the Issei purchasing and leasing property in their citizen children's names in order to get around the alien land law. In a January 1943 newspaper poll, 352 residents (reportedly representing a cross section of the county) made their views public. A whopping 84 percent did not want Japanese to return after the war; 9 percent would admit only citizens; 5 percent favored their return; and 2 percent were undecided. (Those results showed that local disapproval of Japanese returning was almost three times stronger than shown in results for four other Western states, where a a reported 31 percent would not permit Japanese to return.)[8] The *Sun* followed up by taking umbrage at the more moderate reporting about Nikkei by the valley's other news weekly. "They must never return," it urged, predicting "bitterness and violence the like of which we have never had before."[9]

Meanwhile, American Legion Post No. 22 was leading its own determined anti-Japanese campaign, reverberations of which would stretch across the nation. The veterans' organization protested against Nisei serving in the armed forces for it had long been suspicious of what it saw as Japanese residents' evasion of land laws, high birth rates, loyalty to Japan, withdrawal from community social life, and acquisition of property and wealth to the detriment of other locals. Legionnaire Kent Shoemaker spurred on the campaign, motivated by unfinished business from his term

Hood River's American Legion post urged Nikkei and their families not to return home once the federal government rescinded orders that had excluded them from the West Coast. (*Hood River News*, December 22, 1944)

as the first post commander in 1919. At that time, his efforts to "keep more Japs from buying more land in Hood River" were squashed by "sneaky cunningness and the violation of our state law by the Japs." Post No. 22's new campaign was another effort to "preserve Hood River County for the standard way of living and the way of life . . . a majority of the people in Hood River want."[10]

In the first week in January 1943, the local American Legion post resolved to prevent those of Japanese ancestry from returning to the valley and to deport all Nikkei to Japan. It proposed an amendment to the U.S. Constitution that would "deprive all American-Japanese of their claimed citizenship." (In its newsletter, *The Bull*, the local post's commander, Jess Edington, claimed, "No one can be top half foreign and bottom half American and do us any good.") This dramatic action aligned with the position of the Oregon State American Legion commander, who two months later urged posts to support interning the Japanese, and with the national American Legion, which had passed anti-Japanese resolutions annually from 1919 through 1943.[11]

World War I veterans and key proponents of the Anti-Alien Association two decades before, the Legionnaires were now prominent townspeople. Leaders included a lumber company executive, a banker, a fruit grower, the manager of an oil company branch, two realtors, and five merchants. Four were past presidents of the Rotary and Lions Clubs and the Chamber of Commerce. With the influence of its members in county agencies, Post No. 22's resolution provoked similar actions elsewhere in this community of less than twelve thousand. The local Chamber of Commerce quickly followed suit at a meeting where at least two of the five voting board members were also Legionnaires. At the end of the month, the Hood River Lions adopted like resolutions, and by June, the Hood River City Council fell in line.[12]

During the spring of 1943, in an effort to mediate the heightened tension in the community, the *Hood River News* reminded its patrons that in less than forty years, these "aliens of an Asiatic race" had gone from being welcomed with open arms as a solution to the labor shortage to being branded as undesirables who should be deported.[13] In May, the paper quoted a student from the Tule Lake concentration camp, where several hundred local Nikkei were detained: "If we are regarded as prisoners of war, we're getting excellent treatment, and no fooling. If we are regarded as United States citizens, as most of us are, all I can say is that this is one hell of a note."[14]

Meanwhile, the valley community championed an aggressive, extraordinarily successful war bond campaign in support of the war effort. With Legionnaires among those at the helm, Hood River distinguished itself as the only county in the nation to double its Series E bond quota on its Fifth War Loan drive, and it topped all counties in the state with sales in excess of $750,00 on its sixth. War bond fever was infectious. Hundreds of exuberant locals attended rallies at the Victory Center, exhorted by speakers standing on a dais in front of the county memorial wall. Precinct captains and workers solicited residences in the thirteen county regions, while merchants placed displays in store windows and ads in newspapers.[15]

Within those drives, however, racial overtones were evident. In a November issue of the *Hood River News*, nineteen ads appeared on twelve pages, several as large as a quarter page. Two ads resourcefully tied their messages to the enemy, with the foe limited to the Pacific. A Paris Fair department store advertisement read: "Thousands of Americans are still in Jap prisons. What will YOU do about it? Remember Corregidor? Remember the pictures of grinning Japanese soldiers guarding American prisoners? We're out to wipe the grins off their faces. . . . Buy at least one extra $100 war bond." A J.C. Penney Company ad ran with the image of a U.S. soldier superimposed on the islands of Japan: "Next! 6th War Loan." Eby's grocery store announced, "Once there was a man named Bill . . . For three years he fought Japs. . . . WAR BONDS—to have and to hold!"[16]

## LEGION POST NO. 22'S RESOLUTIONS

Just as assiduously, the Hood River Legion post continued another crusade. On November 4, 1944, it passed a resolution to prevent the sale or lease of property to those of Japanese origin and to appraise and purchase all land they currently owned. It also voted to investigate property titles transferred to Japanese after 1923, the year of Oregon's Alien Land Law. (The next month, the post followed through by boldly suggesting to the government's Office of Alien Property that the holdings of Masuo Yasui, who had been interned by the FBI, should be vested if he were guilty.)[17] In "A Statement on the Japanese," a ten-page pamphlet rationalizing its action, Post No. 22 cautioned that the "clever, well-organized and well-disciplined minority among us" was scheming to dominate the Pacific slope. They were implementing their plan through the "old sure game of infiltration by reproduction," by deliberately lowering the value (and forcing the sale) of adjoining land, and by crowding out others in the valley. Besides, it accused, the heads of Japanese families had met almost nightly before the bombing of Pearl Harbor, and "every adult Japanese in this valley knew what was brewing. NOT ONE TOLD!" Now the Legion post planned to prevent the "rapid and sure Japanization of our little valley."[18]

It was the post's second November mandate, however, that stirred the nation and plagued the community. It resolved to remove the names of Nikkei soldiers from the community's memorial plaque on the corner of Second and Oak. Legionnaires challenged these GIs' status as Americans because, they contended, the men were dual citizens of Japan and the United States. Their names would not be replaced, the post vowed, until either the men completed their tours of service or a decision was rendered on their dual citizenship.[19]

Up to that point, the legality of dual citizenship had been so obscure that, by and large, local Nikkei families had overlooked it. Under Japanese law prior to 1924, children of Japanese citizens automatically became subjects of Japan. (The United States also followed this universal practice of jus sanguinis, or right of blood, conferring citizenship on children of Americans even when they were born in foreign countries.) The United States, however, also practiced jus soli, or right of the soil, issuing citizenship to those born in this country. Technically then, Nisei who were born before 1924 held both American and Japanese citizenship. After December 1, 1924, Japan enacted a law that required parents to register their children at a Japanese consulate if they wished their offspring to be Japanese citizens and allowed Nisei to renounce that citizenship.[20] Unaware of these details, veterans George Akiyama, Sagie Nishioka, Mam Noji, and Harry Tamura (all born before 1924) denied having dual citizenship and devoutly affirmed their American citizenship.

By the morning of November 30, then, sixteen Nisei names had been eradicated from the memorial board: George Akiyama, Masaaki Asai, Taro Asai, Noboru Hamada, Kenjiro Hayakawa, Shige Shigenobu Imai, Fred Mitsuo Kinoshita, George Kinoshita, Sagie Nishioka, Mamoru Noji, Henry K. Norimatsu, Katsumi Sato, Harry Osamu Takagi, Eichi Wakamatsu, Johnny Y. Wakamatsu, and Bill Shyuichi Yamaki.[21] Isao Namba's name, mistaken for Finnish, was not removed. The names of other Nisei were not listed on the board because they had registered for the draft outside the valley. These included Sho Endow, Sumio Fukui, Frank Hachiya, Setsu Shitara, Fred Sumoge, Nob Takasumi, and Harry Tamura.

## HOOD RIVER HOTBED

The tiny, rural community was deluged with publicity, as the press circulated the story and rapidly editorialized. Headlines overwhelmingly reprimanded the Legion post and its commander: "A Nosegay for Mr. Edington" (*New York Herald Tribune*), "Americans vs. Americans" (*St. Louis Post-Dispatch*), "Hood River's Blunder" (*New York Times*), "A Nomination for the Award for Most Contemptible Deed" (*PM*), "An Un-American Act" (*Detroit Free Press*), "Hood River Legionnaires Blotting a Glorious Escutcheon" (*Salt Lake Tribune*), "Not So American" (*Chicago Sun*), "Example That Ought to Shame Us" (*Des Moines Register*), "Dirty Work at Hood River" (*Colliers*).[22]

Two newspapers contrasted the pastoral agricultural community with the Legion post's harsh action. After lauding the valley's orchards and apples, the *New York Herald Tribune* raised issues of religion. The paper asked to which "strange and cockeyed gods" the Legionnaires made obeisance, then questioned whether they had perused the sayings of a man in another valley—the one near the Sea of Galilee. Similarly, Royce Brier, in his "This World Today" column for the *San Francisco Chronicle*, chastised the men in the "smiling and beautiful orchard country" for their prejudices against sixteen men with "brownish pigment" in their skins. New York's *PM* suggested that the local Legion's temperament qualified its members to belong to the Ku Klux Klan and proposed that Oregon's governor send the military to restore the American soldiers' names. Likewise, Ed Sullivan, in his "Little Old New York" column in the *New York Daily News*, proposed that the American Legion "hammer some American history into the Oregon post." Commentator Burno Shaw of the Blue Network radio station in New York sent a telegram to Post No. 22: "Are you doing same with Americans of German and Italian and other European enemy ancestry?" Several dailies equated the post's deed with Nazi Germany's tactics. "Discrimination on account of racial origin is the enemy's weapon, not ours," chastised the *New York Times*; the *Salt Lake Tribune* berated the post for "imitat[ing] the methods of our enemies and betray[ing] the ideals of America and the Legion"; and the Catholic Church's *America* likened the post's actions to "taking a leaf direct from Hitler's book." Editors at the *Des Moines Register* analyzed the Legion post's "A Statement on the Japanese" and pronounced it "full of half-truths, misleading facts and inferences, and demagoguery of the worst sort." Taking a jab at the closing line, "Call us fascists if you will," it responded simply: "Well, that tempts us."[23]

Conversely, other papers rationalized the Post No. 22's maneuver. The *Democrat-Herald* in Albany, Oregon, ruled out the valor of Nisei GIs because they did not fight Japanese forces. Pendleton's *East Oregonian* joined the *Democrat-Herald* in accusing Japanese of a plot to "out-breed" whites. The *Eastern Oregon Review* refused to take potshots at Hood River. Familiar with news items that the American Legion post in Hollywood, California, had just accepted a Japanese member and that a New York post had invited the sixteen Hood River Nisei to join, it conceded that the Hood River Legionnaires were the best judges of their situation. The *Bellevue Herald* in Iowa commended the Legion post's foresight for considering the "big problem" with "millions of Japs" now that the war was over. "Are they going to be allowed to buy up the west coast?" it asked.[24]

Stirred by the broad and biting press coverage, citizens across the country reacted to the brouhaha. With sentiments ranging from outrage and disgust to shame or even amusement, Americans put pen to paper and mailed emotional missives to Hood River newspapers and to the Post No. 22 itself. Their stamped, three-cent letters and one-cent postcards arrived from Massachusetts, Florida, Oklahoma, Indiana, Kansas, Wyoming, California, and Washington, among other states, and from across two oceans.

A torrent of protesters assailed the act. One New York City writer mailed the *New York Times'* editorial to the Hood River Legion post with a single word scrawled above it: "Shame!" Even East Coast high school students chastised the valley, exclaiming, "Hood River is an American community. LET'S SEE IT ACT THAT WAY!" Some writers expounded on American ideals, urging the post to study the Constitution's preamble. Many pointedly questioned whether the names of GIs of German and Italian descent had been removed, and a Floridian expressed bemusement, noting that few Americans could claim the status of indigenous Indians. The most vehement protests came from those who likened the post's actions to "nazi tactics," mocking "Heil Hitler! Greetings Hirohito." Letter writers gave the community new labels, including "Berlin" and "Berchtesgaden" (Hitler's retreat in Germany). A number attacked the valley where it was most vulnerable—its economic pride—vowing never again to eat Hood River apples. Seeking to remedy the situation in her own way, a New Englander requested the names and addresses of the sixteen fighting Americans so that she could send her apologies. Relationships were no closer between these men and the Pacific "beasts," she declared, than between the country's founding fathers, who loved democracy, and members of American Legion Post No. 22.[25]

Young men serving in the military were so indignant about this assault on their "brothers in arms" that they inspired a war correspondent with the Seventh Army in Europe to write, "If the Hood River, Oregon, American Legion Post hasn't been getting much mail lately, it can stop worrying." The GIs "bitching loud and long" wrote letters to President Roosevelt and to congressmen as well.[26] Their impassioned letters, especially from those who had witnessed the sacrifices of Nisei firsthand, were compelling.

In Europe, it had been little more than a month since the valiant Nisei in the 100th Infantry Battalion and the 442nd Regimental Combat Team had saved the Lost Battalion, suffering heavy casualties. An officer wrote from France, "No man would scratch one Japanese American's name from an Honor Roll and live if any officer or ex-officer of the 442nd was present." A private reported, "People back home ought to know that if it wasn't for the Nisei, a lot of their sons would be dead. . . . Our boys don't say they are as good as we are. They say they are a helluva lot better and have more guts." I Company, one of the first units to break through to the Lost Battalion, had been left with only 8 of its 185 men. Five members of that company vowed, "If the Japs have to fight their way back into Hood River, you can rest assured that the second platoon of 'I' company will be with them."[27] From the South Pacific, where Nisei had performed critical intelligence work, a staff sergeant invited complainers to travel across the Pacific to where "thousands of American, British, and Indian soldiers will testify as to the gallantry of these boys." Another infantryman challenged, "If I ever take a stand such as your post did, I hope someone shoots me quick. . . . Don't get any false ideas about my being a Jap lover—but right is right." More than three hundred servicemen in the Pacific wrote letters to the *Hood River News*, all but one critical of the post's action.[28]

Among locals serving overseas, some admitted to being tongue-tied when they first read about their hometown's actions. They quickly found words. Sergeant Jim Lill waxed nostalgic about the "good old days" when "people were more angry at poor fruit prices and harvesting weather than they were with each other." It was exasperating, he wrote, to see the precepts he was fighting for coldly violated at home. "Hatred is a natural brother of war," he affirmed, "but it should end with the armistice." Three Hood Riverites, Kenneth and Don Butzin and Hal Lyon, requested that their names be struck from the memorial unless Nisei names were replaced. One local explained that he no longer claimed he was from Hood River because "I haven't felt like an argument." Lieutenant Chuck Swanson visited the *Hood River News* office to laud the roles of local Nisei who taught intensive Japanese-language classes and played "important and hazardous parts in operations." Had his brother not died for his country, he added, he was certain Captain Tommy Swanson would have disdained an honor roll on which names were removed simply because they belonged to men with brown rather than white skin.[29]

For another family, the issue provoked an intergenerational clash. The Coast Guard's Helen J. Merrill wrote that she had "lost all pride" in her birthplace and was sure her grandfather would never agree with the local Legion's action. Though she was "not a Japanese lover," she continued, she thought the town should "put those names back." Her grandfather, a local resident, confronted his granddaughter in a letter the following week, asserting that the issue was citizenship and loyalty, not color. Besides, he questioned, "Why did they not forewarn us before Pearl Harbor if they were true American citizens?"[30]

The escalating controversy enveloped other Legion posts, Legionnaires, and even government officials. Eight American Legion posts followed Hood River's lead by removing the names of Nisei servicemen from their honor rolls. Wolverine Post 360 in Reading, Michigan, the post in Cheney, Washington, and the chaplain for Post No. 1 in Portland, Oregon, protested. Legionnaire and War Relocation Authority (WRA) assistant director Robert D. Cozzens expressed outrage, accusing, "You desecrate the grave of the unknown soldier." Even Secretary of War Henry Stimson weighed in against such "unworthy discrimination" against Japanese servicemen.[31]

Of the almost four hundred letters that Post No. 22 received from GIs, Legionnaires, ministers, and other citizens, two-thirds opposed its move.[32] Yet supporters of the post's actions did not mince words. "Stick to your guns," exhorted Legionnaires from Portland, nearby Gresham, and Lomita, California. "Get your heart in America and the Japs out!" exhorted Oregon state senator Earl Fisher on his official stationery. "'Praise the Lord and pass the ammunition!' is our prayer, Amen." One writer likened Nikkei to a national "cancer" that should be immediately removed. "What this country is in need of besides a good five cent cigar is a few more Americans with guts enough to clamp down on the Jap loving element in our borders," a Texan asserted, while an Oregonian advised, "Treat them as we do the American Indian." Some feared racial characteristics that could never be typically American. "If one drop of (friendly) negro blood flattens the nose and kinks the hair," another Texan queried, "what will gallons of enemy Jap blood do for us?" A number shared the view of an Oregonian that "a Jap is a Jap no matter where he was born." Writers' economic interests also emerged. A Washingtonian applauded the Legion post's call to dispose of Japanese property and quickly positioned himself as a buyer, while another Oregon resident offered suggestions for boycotting Japanese businesses. Some perceived the Nikkei's lot during World War II as pampered and dismissed their role on the battlefield. A local GI in the South Pacific equated nationalist Japanese to Nikkei at home: "I don't know whether I can go back and live alongside those little —— or not. Right now I think one of us will have to move out, and I'm not about to move." A Washingtonian proposed anti-Japanese parades in coastal cities, with displays of "Remember Pearl Harbor" and "My son died in Japanese prison" banners.[33]

Organizations entered the fray. The American Civil Liberties Union, Portland's Council of Churches and its branch of the National Association for the Advancement of Colored People, and San Francisco's Committee on American Principles and Fair Play condemned the action, as did Friends of the American Way in Pasadena, California. In January, the Hood River Ministerial Association and rural Odell Methodist Church resolved that their county erect a new honor roll listing all citizens' names. Standing firm in its support for the post, the Pasadena Ban the Japs Committee telegraphed, "Our white boys can win war without Japs." Statewide, the ultimate purpose of Oregon Anti-Japanese, Inc., in Gresham and Portland was clear.[34]

Even locals not inclined to speak out took sides in the mounting debate. One wrote of his consternation at how many Japanese children attended public school in "one of the best parts of this valley." Displaying a confused view of the Nisei military role and lifestyle, the disgruntled resident complained that, after the war, Japanese would "return to some of the very best farm land in the United States" while "the boys" were "fighting to keep these same Japanese from encompassing the whole world." Those native sons would come back to "marginal lands in hand to mouth existence," while the "unappreciative, unassimilative, incompatible Japs live here in luxury and under the very protection of the same government that they are now seeking to destroy." These people "multiply like flies" and "can live on a few handfuls of rice a day." Their endurance would force competitors to work eighteen hours a day throughout the year, he objected in letters to both local newspapers. In opposition, Hazel V. Smith did begin with an admission that allowing "Oriental immigration" might have been a mistake. Yet, "two wrongs never make a right," she continued. Rather than blame "these boys" for atrocities in another land, Smith urged, "Let us first win this horrible war, then fairly and calmly settle our internal difficulties." Esther Kesti equated local actions to atrocities committed across the ocean, while Jack Hanser tagged "selfish greed" as the root of the problem: "The ones doing the most yelping are getting rich—and I do mean rich—off these same Japanese places."[35]

It was W. Sherman Burgoyne's letter in the *Hood River News*, however, that would make him the target of a public crusade three weeks later. "Every person in Hood River County . . . is disgraced," wrote the minister of the downtown Asbury Methodist Church. Maintaining that "the Courthouse belongs to Hood River county and all its people," he proposed that residents redeem themselves in the eyes of the world "by placing all the names of our service men and women on the walls of our Courthouse." In a letter to Post No. 22 the following week, he distanced himself from his statement, explaining, "Personally I don't think any group of foreign language or habits should be allowed to congregate in a single place, no matter what race they may be. It keeps them from thinking and living 'American.'" Striking a balance in his letter, he suggested that the local Legion separate the matter of the postwar return of Japanese to their homes from the removal of names from the honor roll, which he and other Ministerial Association members were against. (The *Hood River News* published Reverend Burgoyne's public letter alongside correspondence from Superintendent Frank H. Smith of the Methodist Church's Board of Missions and Church Extension. Smith claimed that the American Legion post was a disgrace to the state of Oregon and that Hood River was in "first place as the chief opponent of the Army policy.")[36]

Despite the outcry across the nation and overseas, Hood River Legionnaires staunchly held their ground. In their official reply, published in several local and state newspapers, members conceded that they were willing to replace the names of young "citizens of Japan" once they received official documents confirming that the men had renounced their foreign citizenship. But there were other issues: What was the hurry in allowing Japanese to return? Was the war really under control on the strategic Pacific Coast? "Let us not pass on another racial problem to our children's children such as the one we have inherited," they declared. Finally, pledging to uphold law and order, they denied claims that their motives were economic, closing with "This is our America and we Love it!"[37]

Members of the media, including New York and Colorado news writers, poked holes in the post's claim, as did a seventeen-page government analysis of race relations in Hood River titled "Prejudice in Hood River Valley: A Case Study in Race Relations." The WRA report concluded that while, on one hand, Legionnaires sought to clear themselves of being driven by economic motivations, on the other hand, they were attracting support to "keep evacuees out on the basis of the very motivations they were denying." In sum, the study determined that the Legion post had three motives for its charges: First, those of Japanese descent were disloyal, dual citizens who were decisively aiding Japan's bid for domination of the Pacific and should be considered aliens until they renounced their allegiance to Japan. Second, Japanese were resisting assimilation by segregating themselves, sending their children to Japanese language schools, and living frugally. Third, Japanese planned to "control the wealth of the Valley" through their high birth rates and their "squeeze play," which forced neighboring white landowners to sell their property. Actually, Nikkei operated a mere 8 percent of farm acreage in the valley and made up just 7 percent of the valley farmers. WRA records did show that more than 80 percent of the 154 Nikkei older than fourteen years of age were involved in agriculture.[38]

By the middle of December, a change in government policy muddled the fractious situation even more. Two and a half weeks after Nisei names had been removed from the memorial plaque, the federal government rescinded Public Proclamation No. 21, meaning that, as of December 17, loyal U.S. citizens could no longer be detained in the camps. To counteract the government's measure, local Legionnaires moved quickly to discourage their former neighbors from returning. The next issue of the weekly *Hood River News* posted an ad addressed to them: "Statement to Returning Japanese." The hometown veterans warned their Nisei counterparts, "FOR YOUR OWN BEST INTERESTS, WE URGE YOU NOT TO RETURN" and offered a salve by pledging to help Japanese get "a square deal" when they disposed of their holdings. Early the next year, the Legion post even investigated the idea of holding a special election for gauging public opinion about the return of Japanese. It became clear, however, that these views would be immaterial, for the decision was in the hands of the government.[39]

With the advent of a new year, the public campaign took a strategic, more provocative turn. From the early 1900s, anti-Japanese agitation had aimed attacks at the "entire race" but had avoided persecuting individuals. The 1945 campaign continued to berate Nikkei as a group but now singled out individual Nikkei. The first move on January 12, 1945, came in the form of a quarter-page ad summarizing the Selective Service status of Japanese in the county. Among 106 registered American-born Japanese in Hood River, the Legion post maintained that 19 were Class IV-C, considered "unacceptable" by the War Department. "It seems that this classification was set up to accommodate DISLOYAL Registrants born in the United States," it stated and listed the names of the nineteen Nisei. That information had in fact been accurate only during the chaotic year after Pearl Harbor. Draft boards had reclassified Nisei first as IV-F (unsuitable for military service) and then officially, after September 1942, as IV-C (aliens not acceptable to the armed forces). That classification was revoked after President Roosevelt announced the formation of the Nisei combat team in

February 1943. Within two weeks of the ad's publication, Nobuo Takasumi wrote that the falsehood got his "dander up," protesting that he was I-A (the highest eligibility rating) and would be inducted that very week. Two weeks later, the commander publicly retracted the post's faulty implication about Private Takasumi.[40]

## ADVERTISING CAMPAIGN

The next series of public notices was designed to discourage Nikkei from returning to the valley. Each ad, up to a full page, was designed and written under the byline of Kent Shoemaker, longtime county clerk and former Chamber of Commerce manager. Now he initiated a full-throttle effort to recover lost ground from his previous anti-Japanese campaign as post commander, printing six intermittent ads in two local papers from January through March 1945.

Shoemaker's first notice, "So Sorry Please, Japs Are Not Wanted in Hood River," served as "an open letter to W. Sherman Burgoyne." In the first of two ads meant to refute the minister's criticism of Legion Post No. 22, he reprinted the post's inflammatory brochure "A Statement on the Japanese" and ended with a pointed "Yours for a Hood River without a Jap." (The closing was undoubtedly a play on Reverend Burgoyne's letter to the editor on January 5, 1945, signed "Yours for the American Way.")[41]

The second full-page ad, published a week later, featured a map, two lists, and the following poem:

> Hood River, Golden Valley in the hills,
> Who is to possess its acres and its rills?
> A horde of aliens from across the sea?
> Or—shall it be a Paradise for you and me?

Shoemaker made his point by inserting a map of an upper valley farmer's property surrounded on all sides by Japanese farmers (including Mam Noji), illustrating the "squeeze method" that was allegedly being used to expel white landowners. Next to the map was a list of Nikkei and their eighty-eight pieces of property. His goal over the coming weeks was to place a check mark in front of each property, indicating that it was sold. Especially daunting, however, was Shoemaker's admonition: "You Japs, listed on this page, have been told by some that you would be welcome

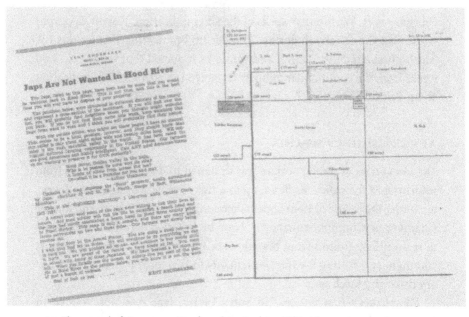

The second of six newspaper ads seeking to deter Nikkei from returning home featured a map of Japanese properties "squeezing" out white landowners and a list of 480 residents who purportedly did not want their neighbors to return. (*Hood River News*, February 2, 1945)

back in Hood River. This is not true, and this is the best time you will ever have to dispose of your property." Listed below were the names of 480 locals who had signed petitions and represented "neighbors whom you thought might welcome you back." Shoemaker continued his warning: "If you do not find [your neighbor's] name this week, keep watching this page from week to week and I think you will eventually find their names."[42]

The third ad, published the following week, listed transfers of land owned by Japanese and the names of thirty-five who had purchased Nikkei property since the bombing of Pearl Harbor. Before listing 421 more petition signers, Shoemaker highlighted their chilling vow: "We, the undersigned residents and taxpayers of Hood River County are one hundred percent behind Hood River Post No. 22, American Legion in ALL their efforts to keep the Japs from returning to this county."[43]

In his fourth and fifth notices, both published in February, Shoemaker rallied support by describing a well-attended anti-Japanese mass meeting outside Portland and quoted public figures and reading materials as a way of boosting his cause. Advocates of running out the Japanese included Walter M. Pierce, former Oregon governor; Monrad Wallgren, Washington governor; and George Wilbur, former Hood River state senator. Wilbur had, in fact, chanted, "They are yellow, we are white. We are Christians, they are pagan. We cannot live together, nor can we assimilate them." Retired educator T. S. Van Vleet's *Once a Jap, Always a Jap* concluded that "the Jap is just an 'educated,' unbridled, sadistic, modernized barbarian." Shoemaker also cited several *Reader's Digest* articles as supporting evidence. "Let us keep Japan for the Japs and Hood River for our own prosperity," he urged and listed a total of 384 more names.[44]

## THE NATIONAL AMERICAN LEGION OFFICE RESPONDS

Coincident with this vigorous campaign, the national office of the American Legion was scrutinizing the most highly publicized of its more than twelve thousand posts. Not only had Hood River's controversy cast a pall on the reputation of the entire Legion, but the War Department had begun raising questions as well. Eight days after the Hood River names were stricken from the memorial, national commander Edward N. Scheiberling requested details from the post; within a week, Commander Edington and six members of the Hood River post responded with explanatory letters, emphasizing that their issue was not race discrimination but one of "unassimilable aliens." Just two weeks after the national commander denounced the return of West Coast Japanese as a national safety hazard, Scheiberling took a different stand on the Hood River GIs:

> After a thorough investigation and after a review of all of the data submitted by you, I believe it will be to the best interest of the war effort and of The American Legion to restore at once to the honor roll the names of those removed, with the exception of one individual, who, I am advised, was discharged dishonorably from the Army. . . . The American Legion has taken a very definite position regarding Japanese nationals but that has no bearing on the status of these men whose names were removed from your honor roll. . . . The American Legion has always maintained that bigotry and race hatred have no place in American life, and the action of this one individual post of more than 12,245 posts of The Ameri-

can Legion, was ill-considered and ill-advised and contrary to the ideals and purposes for which The American Legion is organized.[45]

The national commander's telegram hit "un-like a buzz bomb," but "it did drop right in the middle of Hood River Post," provoking discussion at a "high pitch," according to Shoemaker. Proposed solutions ranged from replacing the names to taking the board down, with repercussions threatened for both actions. It would be one and a half months before Post No. 22 voted to accede to the national Legion's request. Members had originally tabled the matter; then, in February, they defied Scheiberling's recommendation by announcing that they deemed it "inadvisable" to take action. Their change of heart came on the heels of another proposed investigation that could have jeopardized the post's charter. (Many viewed this as an empty threat. Oregon's state Legion commander, Penn C. Crum, a former Hood River commander, claimed that the post had broken no clauses in its charter.)[46]

Five weeks later, seven weeks after the national Legion commander's statement, and thirteen weeks after the names had been removed, the fifteen names were finally repainted on April 9, 1945. Ironically, with the new boards, nails, and hooks, Nisei names appeared more prominent with their freshly lacquered strokes. The country took notice, too, and offered mild accolades. National commander Scheiberling sent a telegram lauding Legion Post 22's "mature and deliberate consideration" and recognizing that "the nation and the American Legion are the better for your latest action." *Survey Midmonthly* reported, "Democracy won another round against racial hatred"; the *Pacific Citizen* (the JACL's newspaper) joined the periodical in crediting "the people of America" for fomenting fair play. The *Hood River News* editorial "To Err Is Human" urged that the community suppress its hard feelings and thrust the incident into oblivion. Likewise, the *Oregon Journal* cautioned, "To allay racial and nationalist distinctions is difficult in peace, more difficult in the heat, passion and prejudice of war."[47]

Still, local Legionnaires were unwilling to fully concede. Commander Edington made it clear that replacing the names did not change the post's view on Japanese returning to Hood River. As if to prove his point, a sixth ad appeared two weeks later, capped with the demeaning title "NO JAPES WANTED IN HOOD RIVER." ("Japes" was a combination of the words "Japs" and "apes.") The gist of the message was a take-off on Secretary of the Interior Harold Ickes's contention that Japanese Americans should be able to relocate outside the evacuated areas, including in the East. Shoemaker circumspectly urged *all* Japanese to "Go East, follow Mr. Ickes' advice, and go east of the Mississippi river." He also berated WRA director Dillon Myer for seeming to be more interested in helping "Japes" to secure jobs after the war than in coming to the aid of their own sons. Topping off the final ad with the names of four hundred more supporters and a mail-in form for sending more signatures, Shoemaker underscored his intent by again signing the ad "Yours for a Hood River without a Jap."[48]

## LOCAL NISEI CASUALTIES

While Americans at home were debating the loyalty and rights of Nisei servicemen, those at the center of the controversy were tending to the business of defending the country. A month before his name was removed from the honor roll, Private Eichi Wakamatsu had been wounded in France; four months later, he was awarded a Good Conduct Medal for exemplary conduct. Within two months of writing to protest the Hood River Legion's removal of his name, George Akiyama earned the first of two citations for heroism. The Bronze Star recognized his "heroic disregard for personal safety" while resisting enemy fire to help rescue the Lost Battalion in France. Three and a half months after George Kinoshita's name was obscured, a local news column cited the "Dee Boy" and nine other Oregonians in the Second Battalion for their front-line combat high in the French Alps.[49] In the Philippines, Frank Hachiya sacrificed even more. He died the month before the national American Legion commander requested that Nisei names be returned to the memorial. Hachiya was posthumously awarded the Silver Star, and his death provoked a flurry of heartfelt responses contrasting the bravery of his deed with the shame of his community. Headlines expressed the country's disdain: "Sgt. Hachiya, Spurned by Legion Post, Dies Hero's Death in P.I." (*Honolulu Star Bulletin*), "Private Hachiya, American" (*New York Times*), and "His Comrades Understood" (*Hood River News*).[50]

Citizens unleashed even more diatribes at the Hood River Legion post, labeling its act "despicable, un-American, and shameful." A New Yorker lashed out, "You cannot hurt Hachiya now—but see what you have done to yourselves!" Three disgusted infantrymen from Florida reproached the post for "knif[ing] fighting men in the back," while Friends of the American Way in Pasadena queried, "Can you keep his name from your honor [roll], and call yourselves good Americans?"[51]

## NEWS MEDIA AND THE OREGON LEGISLATURE

During the heated controversy, local weeklies had taken opposing positions but avoided outright clashes through their more measured approaches. The *Hood River News* did not print editorials that directly addressed the issue (though it did deride the western state Granges' moves toward a "white" America and refuted a San Francisco writer's reference to Hood River's "apples of intolerance"), but editor Hugh Ball obliquely communicated the paper's position through the outside editorials and letters he chose to publish. In the seven weeks following the Post No. 22 incident, Ball reprinted six editorials from other presses—two from *The Dalles Optimist*, a neighboring weekly, and four from national dailies. With titles such as "An Un-American Act," "Is This Americanism?" "A Question of Racial Prejudice," and "Not So American,"[52] they conveyed the paper's critical view. Through those seven weeks, the *Hood River News* printed twenty-five letters in its Public Opinion section. While locals composed a little more than half the letter writers, the balance of sentiment was definitely one-sided. Of the published letters, 88 percent opposed the post's actions, with only two letters supportive and one neutral. By mid-January, the paper had reconsidered the merits of serving as a public forum versus the potential of stoking an already heated debate and concluded it would cease printing opinions.

In its January 19, 1945, issue, the *Hood River News* introduced its Public Opinion section with a proviso. Since both sides of the honor roll controversy had been heard, it asserted, the overall interests of the community would be best served by a period of calm reflection. "No useful purpose can possibly be served by lending this column to the fanning of the flames of dissension, at a time when the utmost unity is of the highest importance." Holding to its well-considered intentions, however, was impracticable. The following week, it reprinted "Legion and the Japs," a statement by the national American Legion vice commander pledging constitutional protection to returning Japanese and lamenting that undue emphasis on minority issues could deter the achievement of peace. In March, after accepting and publishing the fifth of Shoemaker's exclusionary, paid public notices, the newspaper followed up by printing two letters critical of him.[53] All in all, Ball's more circumspect oversight of his weekly's pages heightened community discourse while laying bare the controversial issues and, ultimately, proffering indirect support for Nikkei.

Through the same seven weeks, the *Hood River County Sun* made its position clear through intensity, though not frequency. Its single editorial harked back to the brazen caveat it had issued almost two years before: "THEY MUST NEVER COME BACK." The consequence if they did return, the paper had earlier maintained, would be "bitterness and violence the like of which we have never had before." In its first issue in January 1945, the *Sun* had renewed its warning while recalling a local correspondent's observation about "how much the white people had done and how little Japanese had reciprocated." Few in the county wanted them back, and, in surprisingly more genteel terms, the paper expressed hope that "those that wish to return will think twice." In an interview for New York's *PM*, *Sun* editor John Travis claimed that previously skeptical locals now agreed that "maybe the means is worth the end." Considering the Japanese community a "little spot of empire," he added a new accusation: that the Japanese emperor paid Issei a bounty of twenty-five dollars for each child registered with his government. In addition to publishing all six of Shoemaker's notices, the *Sun* printed six letters, four supportive of the local Legion post. One letter writer made a fresh comparison with American Indians: "We are keeping the true American, the Indian, on reservations. What a shame that he has not the privilege the Jap, who is our enemy and is at war with us, has. Can't you see the chance we are taking?"[54]

Those who sought to abrogate Nikkei rights placed their hopes in the U.S. Congress. By February 1944, county judge C. D. Nickelsen had appealed to Oregon's congressional delegates to bar Japanese from the county, state, West Coast, and country. The previous year, two anti-Japanese legislative memorials, or petitions, had called on Congress to prevent Nisei from serving in the military and to deport all Japanese. Adopted by the U.S Senate, those memorials died in a House committee. Two similarly unsuccessful memorials in the 1945 Oregon legislature called for the deportation of alien Japanese and Nisei with dual citizenship (or those whose disloyalty had been proved) and the exclusion of Japanese from the Pacific coast for the duration of the war. Judge Nickelsen had denounced any concessions on behalf of the Japanese, citing the treatment of American prisoners in Japanese war camps by "murderous race-devotees of the SUN-GOD of oriental ideology." Leveraging support from legislators, Nickelsen also advocated that a petition "signed by each and every citizen of the city and valley" be forwarded to U.S. Representative Lowell Stockman. "We must not let up on our insistence that the Japs be deported," he warned.[55]

A year later, Oregon did pass a bill intended to strangle the livelihood of Nikkei.

Similar to the state's 1923 legislation, aliens could neither own nor lease land, but Issei had used a loophole in that law and purchased and farmed land in their children's names. The 1945 Alien Land Law made that impossible. Now, if they lived and worked on the land, they were subject to criminal prosecution: a maximum of two years' imprisonment and a five thousand dollar fine. Even more injurious, Nisei could be prosecuted if their parents occupied or labored on their property.[56]

Thus it was that, although Nikkei had official sanction to return to their homes in 1945, more practical matters concerned them. How would their neighbors and former friends treat them? What would be the condition of their farms and homes? And would they be safe?

# ELEVEN

# "Ninety Percent Are Against the Japs!"

## VETERANS AND THEIR

## FAMILIES RETURN

I T took *some* bravado to return," observed Mam Noji in early 1945. Members of his family were among the first to return to their beleaguered valley after the government finally permitted Nikkei back on the West Coast in December. By January, however, only one out of six Nikkei had left the ten government camps,[1] and rumors of intimidating receptions discouraged others.

Bold, early adventurers experienced bursts of hostility along the West Coast: "Terrorists" dynamited and burned the fruit packing shed of a Placer County truck farmer, the first of thirty attempts in that California county to frighten returning Nikkei. Three grocery clerks in South Pasadena, California, quit in defiance of their proprietor's orders to serve Japanese customers, whereupon rising sun graffiti appeared on the market and a telephone caller threatened, "I'm going to shoot you on sight." Also in California, someone fired shots at the Cressey home of a Nisei veteran who was entertaining another Nisei veteran in uniform. A barber in Parker, Arizona, ejected a wounded Nisei veteran from his shop. Las Vegas, Nevada, pronounced itself 100 percent anti-Japanese, views supported by the highest state officials. Anti-Japanese rallies took place in Brawley, California; Bellevue, Washington; and Gresham, Oregon.[2] By late February, New York *PM* reporter Charles A. Michie would report that just five hundred had returned home to the West Coast and explained the low numbers as due to "details of removal from camps" and because "some are plain damn scared." Michie added that thirty-three thousand chose to head east and seventy-eight thousand still remained in the camps.[3]

## A "PLAGUE SPOT"

Hood River and its 11,500 valley residents were especially in the public eye. New York's *PM* cited the farming community, along with California's Placer County and Washington's White River Valley, as one of "three isolated plague spots in the Northwest" for "ruthlessly resisting efforts of American citizens to take possession of their own homes." The *Pacific Citizen*, published by the Japanese American Citizens League, named Hood River one of two national sites of "undemocratic" anti-evacuee movements. A writer for the *Saturday Review of Literature* labeled Hood River a "test area" where prejudice against Nisei ran the highest and, according to the War Relocation Authority, attracted the most national interest. A local merchant and community activist writing for *Asia and the Americas*, Arline Winchell Moore, classified the situation as "one of the most shamefully un-American programs of persecution of a minority group ever witnessed in this Land of the Free."[4] William Worden, writing in the *Saturday Evening Post*, described the effects of infectious wartime paranoia: "War hysteria, old economic resentments and fear for lucrative jobs or contracts combined with simple race fanaticism to make easy the job of the professional anti-Japanese drum beaters. The disease was infectious." He highlighted Hood River as his first example.[5]

Despite such censure, anti-Japanese attitudes persisted. "Ninety percent are against the Japs!" Hood River mayor Joe Meyer blasted in a stunning pronouncement. "We trusted them so completely while they were here among us, while all the time they were plotting our defeat and downfall. They were just waiting to stab us in the back. . . . We must let the Japanese know they're not welcome here." American Legion Post No. 22 continued its anti-Japanese campaign, predicting bloodshed if Japanese returned. Rumors spread that one Nikkei had already been beaten and that "reception committees" at the train depot would discourage returning evacuees. Stationery notes displayed a photo of an orchard valley with "There Is No Room in This Picture for Japs" imprinted beneath. One Legionnaire, a local wholesaler opposed to affixing "Jap names beside American names on any list," added his own searing questions: "Would you move into a Jap community? . . . Would you marry a Jap (Ameri-

Hood River's Victory Center was a rallying site for its six successful war loan campaigns. Names of county residents serving in the armed forces covered the courthouse wall. (Ralph Vincent, The History Museum, Hood River, 1945)

can born or not)? . . . Are you willing to see Jap communities grow and enlarge in our cities to the point where their clannish, slavish economic cancer fouls the life blood of American commerce and economic balance so that their descendants finally own the country? Are you willing to see Japs elected to public office? Would you have your son serve under Jap-American officers? Would you let your daughter marry a Jap? Do you think a Jap-American is just as good a citizen and asset to the U.S.A. as you are?" Anyone who answered yes, he declared, "should seek admission to Japan." In fact, that same Legionnaire skeptically noted that this country did not need the help of "a handful of American-born Japs to fight in its army and to observe our military methods in order to betray the United States at some later date."[6]

"Jingoism pays no heed to sacrifice," declared Richard Neuberger, writer for the *Saturday Review* and future U.S. senator from Oregon, citing extremists who roused anti-Japanese groups along the West Coast. Oregon State College dean of men U. G. Dubach had stated in the local high school auditorium, "Japanese will never become thorough Americans." All were Shintoists who had been trained that they were chosen to rule the earth and that the emperor was descended from gods, he maintained. The Americanism Educational League in Los Angeles offered to arrange a mass meeting in Hood River, similar to its well-attended Jap Return Protest in Brawley, California.[7]

"The fears and antagonisms of the general public were fanned to a white hot heat," observed Arline Moore, owner of Moore Electric Shop in downtown Hood River. "Race baiting became the topic of every social and civic gathering. The aim . . . was definitely to arouse feeling to the point whereby the laws of this country could be changed and the Japanese people, citizens and aliens alike, could be arbitrarily removed to Japan." The atmosphere was so heated that federal officials arrived to assess the local situation. The Oregon State Police survey of prominent valley citizens indicated that only one among the nine interviewed believed there would be mob violence. Two interviewees, however, anticipated fires or assaults, and a newspaper editor reported rumors that several residents carried firearms and had threatened to "shoot the first Jap on sight."[8]

"Plain, damn scared." Such was one government official's characterization of returning Nisei. Even the return of a uniformed GI (home on business a year and a half earlier) had been the topic of a local editorial titled "Not Well Received," urging that it was "very unwise" for Japanese to return.[9] The trepidation of Hood River's Nikkei multiplied with the publication of each of Kent Shoemaker's cautionary notices. One Heart Mountain resident described his thoughts: "It gives you a funny feeling to see your name in your local paper listed with the other Japanese they are trying to keep out and to see the names of people you thought were your friends on a petition saying they want you to stay away. I have seen the names of my neighbors on two sides. Maybe I'll see the names of the rest of my neighbors sometime."[10]

EARLY RETURNEES

With more eyes across the nation cast on them, early Hood River returnees became self-conscious newsmakers in January 1945. For three weeks in a row, local front-page news accounts covered speculation about their return until the eventual arrival of the first three Nikkei. The week-by-week sequence unfolded through headlines in the *Hood River News*: "Ray

Sato to Be First Japanese to Return Here," "No Nisei Have Yet Returned," Three Nisei Return To Valley Homes."

The first week's news item reported that the T. Satos and K. Nojis were the only families planning to return at that time. The following week, the newspaper disclosed that baggage for two Nisei had arrived and that a "reception" committee was organizing to persuade Japanese "not to plan to return to their homes." Finally, the third week, three Nisei fruit growers who had "good reputations in their respective communities" arrived. The two Portland papers reported their return, one on the front page, the other noting there was "not a single demonstration." The *Pacific Citizen* similarly announced their return in an issue that also listed, in eight columns, the names of 363 Nisei war casualties in Europe, including five fatalities.[11]

While Mam Noji was continuing U.S. military intelligence work in the Philippines, his younger brother became one of the first three to return to his hometown. Sat (Satoru) Noji joined Ray Sato and Min Asai, all young Nisei fruit growers whose homes were ensconced in wooded slopes along the shadows of Mount Hood's towering snowscapes. On January 12, 1945, the three young men (who had been working in the Midwest outside the military zone) cautiously arrived by train at the local depot, braced for a hostile reception. To their relief, the "welcoming party" did not materialize. Instead, WRA representative Clyde Linville met the three and drove them to Sato's home seventeen miles south of town, where they lived together for a few days as a safety measure. Suspicious when they heard gunshots and wary because of rumored lynchings, burnings, and beatings, they were spooked by nothing more than the sound of popping ashes in the fireplace. Confronted with children's jeers of "Japs! Japs! Japs!", glassy-eyed stares from merchants who denied them service, and widespread accusations of Japanese infiltration, the trio withstood an agonizing reentry. When even former classmates and friends turned their backs, the large, soft-spoken Linville became a welcome ally, commuting sixty miles each day from Portland to check on their well-being. His advocacy, including pressure on Standard Oil's head office to force local fuel delivery to their farms, made it possible for the men to "stick it out."[12]

Apprehensive about Noji's return, his parents and sister decided to join him, despite negative newspaper reports and friends who warned that they were "crazy to go home" so soon. In doing so, they became the first family with Nisei in the military to return to the valley. Others cautioned the Nojis that the situation was far too dangerous, mindful of the newspaper notices. "Scared to death once they were home," they jumped at every sound and stayed close to their premises, counting on Sat to take care of household errands. They scoured filth from the run-down house that had been quarters for orchard workers and tended to the rodent- and worm-infested apple and pear trees. Still, the Nojis considered themselves fortunate. WRA representative Linville buoyed them with his daily visits, and several neighbors surprised the distraught family by offering beds, canned raspberries, and other goods. Most reassuring, however, was the propriety of their caretaker, R. J. McIsaac, who had kept their orchard in better condition than many others (considering the wartime difficulty of hiring workers), maintained meticulous records, and had given the Nojis honest financial returns. "Don't be afraid," he comforted them as they redoubled their efforts to make a living.[13]

### VETERANS RETURN

Nisei veterans returning from their overseas duties had more difficulty. Newly arrived in Oregon from Germany, Harry Tamura decided to hitchhike from Portland to Hood River. "A few cars slowed down, and they knew I was a Japanese, I imagine, so they went on. And so I said, 'Well, this won't do me any good.' I went back to Portland and caught a bus." Purple Heart recipient Sagie Nishioka fared no better. "I went into the Shell service station downtown in Hood River. The attendant said, 'We don't sell gas to you people.' I was . . . riding the car in uniform and still it happened."[14]

As citizens who had served their country, Nisei veterans expected a warmer, more respectful welcome. Postwar Hood River resident and veteran Jan Kurahara, in his autobiography *Ganbatte*, lamented, "It is amazing what a uniform doesn't do for you. . . . I should have been wearing a Japanese Imperial Army soldier's uniform for the disrespect the U.S. Army uniform was getting. I was told that they wouldn't serve me nor would anybody else in town." Sab Akiyama received similar treatment when he disregarded the "No Japs Allowed" sign at the Rockford Store he had once frequented in his Oak Grove community. Still wearing his uniform, he asked for a pack of cigarettes. "We don't have any cigarettes," the proprietor replied. "Oh, I'll have a glass of beer," Akiyama countered, noting men swigging ale at the bar. "Can't you read that sign?" the irate owner asked before ejecting him from the store. It was likewise an affront when a downtown barbershop denied service to brother George Akiyama, despite the

Silver and Bronze Stars and seven other decorations on his uniform. After the barber waved his razor and threatened, "I ought to slit your throat," Akiyama simply walked out, mumbling, "Boy, you're worse than some of those Germans we fought." By chance, air force captain Sheldon Lawrence, a resident of upper valley Parkdale, had witnessed the entire incident. Though he and Akiyama were not acquainted, the officer drove west to Oak Grove and trudged the final half mile up the Akiyamas' snow-covered hill so that he could apologize. In a letter to the *Oregonian*, Captain Laurence denounced "such unjustified prejudice and insults" to "some of the nation's best fighting men." Criticizing those who "have not yet grown up," he added prophetically, "perhaps millions of returning veterans will help them."[15]

After serving in the U.S. military for three years and nine months, Mam Noji expressed his regret. "You hate to think we were fighting for these people who would deny you these kinds of services." In mid-January 1945, the *Hood River County Sun* reported that all stores on the town heights displayed "No Jap Trade" signs. The *Pacific Citizen* recounted a Nisei veteran's first sight upon returning home: a sign reading "No Cigarettes, No Negroes, No Japs." Eventually, there were signs on almost every store; some were paper, some painted, and some covering entire windows. It was so difficult for Nikkei to purchase goods in downtown Hood River that many drove to The Dalles, twenty miles away. That led one clerk in that Mid-Columbia town to guffaw about his competitors, "I hope those guys stay crazy up there. We get a lot of business." Hood River, in fact, lost thousands of dollars in revenue because of its merchants' stands. The situation came to the attention of the WRA when a Nisei telephoned Victor McLaughlin, a Minidoka official in charge of relocation and work release. "Mac, these guys won't sell me groceries over here," he explained. After McLaughlin and Linville tried unsuccessfully to solve the problem with the town's mayor, an impatient Major General J. A. Ulio, adjutant general of the army, flew in to confront the town. "Here we are fighting a war for our lives and you're telling a citizen that they can't buy groceries in your town!" the two-star general chastised the mayor and city council. He threatened to put the entire town under martial law "at the point of a bayonet" if the situation did not change by 5:00 P.M. the day of his visit. It was not long before the visiting McLaughlin's phone at a local hotel began "ringing off the hook," and the downtown Safeway store reportedly offered a pickup-load of free groceries to the Nisei.[16]

Nisei veterans and their families struggled to reestablish themselves despite being "treated like so much trash," as one Nisei veteran explained. By May 1945, twenty-one families had returned to the valley. Arline Moore described their trials: "Under the stress of the evacuation, many had sacrificed their equipment at terrific losses. Trucks, sprayers, tractors with less than one year of service had been sold for two to three hundred dollars, but could not be replaced for as many thousand. Goods left stored with persons counted [as] friends were missing. Homes had been broken into and things [were] either wantonly destroyed or carried away."[17]

Cars revved their motors down Nikkei driveways late at night, neighbors stole gas from pumps and tools from sheds, and anonymous callers phoned hate messages. Scoundrels regularly broke the Asai family's window, where they displayed their "Sons in Service" flag, its four stars representing four of their five sons who were serving in the army. One returning family discovered that their home had served as a chicken coop while they were gone. Many found that the caretakers of their farms had harvested the fruit for their own profit but sacrificed future harvests by failing to properly care for trees and by abusing the land. Some gave unfair returns for renting the farms. Though Nikkei were still members of the Apple Growers Association cooperative, which packed and distributed valley fruit, many had to rely on friends to deliver their crops, as packers refused to handle their produce, threatening to strike unless they could process boxes from other growers first.[18]

Nikkei returnees faced other tests. When Min Asai and a Seattle Nisei met the WRA's Linville for lunch at the Hood River Café, the waitress served only one glass of water—to Linville. Management did not allow her to serve Japanese Americans, she told the men. The optimism of Nisei became measured. "Nobody told me to get the hell out except for one guy and that's it," explained Sho Endow after he was "kicked out" of a downtown auto parts store. "The guy says, 'Well, I can't sell you anything.' I says, 'Okay.' Walked out. What's the use?" Nikkei were bothered when they recognized their own guns and rifles—confiscated by the sheriff's office before the war—in the gun cabinets of private auction customers or friends of the sheriff.[19] A neighbor of the Nojis approached Mam and offered to purchase the family's farm. "We wouldn't have a place to go," Mam responded, for the family could not even fathom selling and leaving their thirty-year investment in the land. Still, the determined neighbor persisted, "Well, you could move." Their postwar challenges sometimes seemed as insurmountable as those the Nisei GIs had faced overseas.

Although the return of Nisei servicemen had little effect on adamant valley exclusionists, the testimonies of other newly arrived veterans did, as Captain Laurence had maintained. "The returning Caucasian GIs were, almost to a man, loyal to their Japanese brothers in arms, and those who had served in any area where Japanese-American soldiers had fought were all loud in their praise," explained Arline Moore. As George Akiyama saw it, "That's when things started changing. That's when the veterans gave the older people heck." Early returnee Sato noticed that servicemen "defended the Nisei and the Valiant Nisei war hero." A decorated army captain returning from the South Pacific challenged his father's anti-Japanese business practices, demanding, "What in the hell is this I hear?" and the discriminatory sign came tumbling down. After Lieutenant Colonel Wallace Moore spoke to high school students about his shared exploits with Nisei GIs, treatment of Nisei youth at the school improved.[20] Not all were persuasive, however. Ed Shoemaker, son of the architect of Hood River's anti-Japanese campaign, returned to the valley in 1945 after four years as an air corps engineer in England. Having befriended Nisei at school (where they composed one-third of his high school class), he was "embarrassed" and "ashamed" by his father's actions. It made little sense, however, for him to cross his father, who was "too hot" and set in his ways, he explained.

Nikkei were buoyed by the smallest gestures of goodwill from principled and courageous neighbors and friends, even from those whom they did not know. One month after the government announced that those of Japanese descent could return to the restricted West Coast and a month and a half after Nisei names had been expunged from the honor roll, a tiny nine-line classified notice appeared in the *Hood River News*: "Any Japanese-American soldier home on furlough will find friendship, good food, warm bed and peaceful atmosphere in comfortable home of Joe Haviland and June Eaton Haviland, one and a half miles west Columbia River highway. No phoning necessary. Welcome at any hour."

The Havilands' offer was intended to show "the boys" that they had friends who appreciated their service. Two weeks earlier, June Haviland had written to the local American Legion post, advising them, "When one makes an error, it is always best to quickly admit it—right the wrong by saying it was a mistake—then there's quiet on the Homefront!"[21]

Some stalwart citizens did emerge to defend the rights of Japanese Americans. Arline Moore's downtown shop became a haven where Nikkei could congregate without fear. When storeowners denied service to Japanese Americans, the jovial great-granddaughter of hardy 1844 pioneers collected their shopping lists and made purchases for them—despite her limp and need to use a cane. Former teacher Frances Moller, known for her bluntness, marched into stores with "No Jap trade" signs and loudly expressed her displeasure: "My maiden name is Oberteuffer. That's German, you know. . . . Will you sell to me?" She also publicly chastised a Legionnaire who hired high school students to frighten an Issei widow and her daughters late at night while her Nisei son was still serving in the army. (After the Mollers invited veteran Tot Asai to dinner, the Elks Club blackballed husband Elmer. "I've had Elks to dinner too," he retorted.) R. J. McIsaac, reputable caretaker for the Noji orchard, owned McIsaac's Store in upper valley Parkdale, twenty-five miles south of town, toward Mount Hood. Despite "Jap Lovers" graffiti that appeared on his store windows, he refused to concede to customers' threats of a boycott, going so far as to stock Japanese goods. A respected community leader, he successfully continued his business and also wielded influence on the board of the AGA cooperative, where he served nearly fifteen years, six as president.[22]

The most public Nikkei defender was Reverend Sherman W. Burgoyne of the downtown Asbury Methodist Church, whose pointed letters and statements made him a target for the first of Kent Shoemaker's infamous newspaper ads. The tall, burly minister had never known or spoken to a Nikkei, having arrived from southern Oregon two months after their evacuation. "It was an un-American thing to do," he explained. "I would have protested as loudly if the names of Jews, Negroes, Catholics, or any other group had been removed." Even after wife Doris's brother became the victim to a Japanese sniper on Guadalcanal, the Burgoynes were outspoken. "My brother died to secure 'liberty and justice for all,'" declared Doris, disavowing the connection others saw between Nikkei families and Japanese imperial troops.[23]

A group of principled locals took to heart the closing words of the Pledge of Allegiance when they formed the League for Liberty and Justice, aiming to counter valley intolerance. With Reverend Burgoyne as their spiritual founder, members took steps to defend valley Nikkei and thwart

Businesswoman Arline Moore and Reverend Sherman Burgoyne, leading advocates for restoring Nisei names on the county honor roll, examine the names on the courthouse wall. (Homer Yasui, June 16, 1946)

the propaganda that unfairly branded them. League members mailed letters to newly returned Nikkei, expressing sympathy for their "shameful, unjust and unnecessary ordeal" and offering help "to offset some of the wrongs." Fifty-plus league members convened twice a month and volunteered to meet returnees at the train depot, shop for them, and drive produce trucks to warehouses when workers declined the Nikkei's fruit. League president Avon W. Sutton wrote to chain stores, including J. C. Penney and Safeway, urging them to accept Japanese business and published, at his own expense, a newspaper notice titled "Witch Burning." In his May 1945 statement, Sutton denounced intolerance and harassment that he likened to the "Salem witch burning spirit," querying, "Shall we write into the Bill of Rights, 'For Caucasians Only'?. . . Let us not burn any witches in Hood River." Two weeks later, the league bought space in the newspaper to reprint an army officer's flaming response to his hometown paper. From Europe, Lieutenant Colonel James M. Hanley took editor Charles F. Pierce of North Dakota's *Mandan Daily Pioneer* to task for his jocular remark, "A squib in a paper makes the statement that there are some good Jap-Americans in this country but it didn't say where they are buried." As the commander of five thousand Nisei in the 442nd's Second Battalion, Hanley could easily recount acts of Nisei courage and berated signs of racial prejudice. In closing, he challenged the editor: "Come on over here, Charlie. I'll show you where some good Jap-Americans are buried." In a quest to promote cultural relations, the League for Liberty and Justice presented educational programs, including a WRA film, "Challenge to Democracy," about life at the Heart Mountain concentration camp. It also introduced speakers such as Sergeant Henry Gosho, a Bronze Star veteran of the famed Merrill's Marauders. Gosho was among the hardy Nisei who reopened the road to Burma by fighting and marching through seven hundred miles of dense Burmese jungle, all behind enemy lines. The league urged local pastors to support these efforts to defy prejudice by addressing intercultural themes in their sermons.[24]

In other actions, the state extension service and the federal government sponsored three talks by economist Dr. Joaquin Ortega about race prejudice as a deterrent to peace. The Hood River Ministerial Association took a stand, posting a newspaper ad in May that condemned race hatred as a means for achieving an economic purpose.[25]

The anti-Japanese campaign took on herculean proportions, more antagonistic than the valley's earlier segregationist stance. Rather than focus on Japanese as a group, the new crusade targeted individuals, for, as *Hood River County Sun* editor John Travis claimed, "the means is worth the end" if it achieved a "Hood River Valley for whites only." Race, the economy, and community pressure became defining factors. As early returnee Min Asai explained, "Money, racial prejudice, economic self-interest, political profit, and patriotism were in combination a potent source for social actions."[26]

## RACE

Acts such as the ones described above, undertaken in the name of patriotism and allegiance to country, appeared to mask antipathy for nonwhite races, or, simply, racism. That became evident when people with names that could be mistaken for Japanese began to suffer similar consequences. Seven months into the war, when vaccine serum for influenza was limited, valley resident Mildred Alijoki telephoned the county health department, only to be told that no serum was available. After a neighbor received the vaccine, Alijoki called back, repeating her request in a heavy Finnish accent. Again she was refused. Disturbed by an outbreak of influenza in Oak Grove, the determined mother finally ushered her children into the health office. "Oh, you're not Japanese," the staff told her apologetically. "Yes, we do have vaccine." Constance Nastasi's new neighbors were aloof and belittling, mistaking her Italian last name for a Japanese name until they met her husband after the war.

Others went further to show disdain for nonwhite neighbors. Outside of town, a Legionnaire who owned a sand and gravel screening plant refused to make deliveries to Japanese, forcing them to haul the heavy aggregate on their own and collecting their payments in a "Jap Gravel" fund for hard liquor. One local farmer robustly contended, "Uncle Sam made a mighty big mistake in letting Japs come into the country." How about Catholics? "Well, Catholics always caused a heap of trouble where they was." Jews? "Jews got all the money without working for it." Negroes? "We don't want niggers in Hood River any more 'n Japs." What about Indians? "Indians is no damn good. Get a little liquor under their belts and they're as dangerous as a blizzard in January." There was no easy resolution. The Hood River Legion post's own literature had used racial terms in berating the unassimilable "top half foreign and bottom half American," underscoring its vow not to "pass on another racial problem to our children's children."[27]

In uncensored, personal letters, Post No. 22's officers explained their position to the American Legion national commander and let loose their views on race: "After forty years of experience we are convinced that we cannot Americanize the Japanese," wrote local commander Jess Edington. Any race not assimilable by marriage had no place in the valley, maintained Decatur Baldwin, worried that there would be "little place for the white race on the Pacific coast." Kent Shoemaker, keen on following through with his failed attempt in 1919 to prevent Issei from settling, vowed to "carry on the fight to rid Hood River of every drop of Jap blood."[28] As veteran Jan Kurahara lamented, "All you had to do was have a Japanese face, and you'd had it."

## ECONOMICS

Leaders of the anti-Japanese movement denied that economics was a factor in their movement. "As we have said time and again," Kent Shoemaker retorted, "there is no economic issue involved in our action. This is our America and we love it. Can *any* good American blame us for wanting to preserve this beautiful valley for *our* posterity?" Still, each of his six ads had attacked Nikkei land acquisition and sought to "keep MORE Japs from buying MORE land in Hood River." Mayor Joe Meyer disclosed his own bias: "The Japanese came into this valley, picked up good land here, crowding out the whites. . . . The Japs had money here during the depression, when nobody in the valley had any. . . . The farmers of this valley object to competing with Japanese farm labor—where all the family gets out and works on the land. . . . The Japs have all the good land."[29]

Hood River native Jane Franz Rice, a local newspaper correspondent and longtime school cook, was forthright about the problem. "I think there was a cloud of jealousy. I am sure of it. The Japanese were very successful in what they did. They were good stewards of the land. After the war, . . . the white people that took over really reaped a lot of the benefits from the money received from the crops." Then, too, there was the matter of compensating Japanese property owners and returning the prosperous farms. "The Japanese had cleared the ground, had planted the stuff, and it had just gotten to the point where they were finally making a little money off of it, when wham!" gestured Constance Nastasi, upper valley resident and wife of a GI. Paul Sanstrum, working as a manager at Safeway after returning from military service in the Pacific, similarly spoke of consequences. "A lot of people took over the Japanese farms and tried to do a good job taking care of things. Others used up all of their fertilizer, used up their paint, wore out their equipment and everything. That's where the greed was." Athalie Lage, homemaker and widow of former state legislator Riddell Lage, agreed. "Certain ones just took everything, ripped everything off a place, took all the machinery and everything they had and kept it or sold it. The Japanese would come home to a place that had really been ravaged." Even the WRA admitted that the public's insensitivity to pilfering and vandalism "encouraged the lawless to commit increasingly bold acts at the expense of the absent owners."[30]

The local Issei's prowess on the land—dating back to their clearing the forested valley when they arrived—was a distinct factor in the valley's economic strife. As discussed in chapter 2, the Issei entered into a unique arrangement with novice landowners and took on this hazardous labor in exchange for marginal acreage scattered around the valley. By 1920, with their intensive and cooperative farming practices and family-oriented work ethic, Hood River Nikkei were becoming successful farmers and owned more than half the total acreage owned by Japanese in the state. Locals, including Shoemaker, the county clerk, accused them of violating state laws prohibiting Issei land purchases, controlling the best crops and orchard land, and conspiring with other Japanese to dominate the three western states.[31]

Thirty years later, a new motive arose—profiteering from successful Nikkei farms. Before the war, crops from local Nikkei farms were valued at $5 million and contributed 25 percent of the valley's total fruit production, though Nikkei made up less than 0.5 percent of the population. (Japanese Americans produced 90 percent of the county's asparagus, 80 percent of the strawberries, 35 percent of the pears, and 30 percent of the apples.) By then, Hood River County led the state in the value of its fruit harvest, valued at $2.2 million in 1940. Other farmers recognized the chance to acquire Nikkei's well-tended and productive farms for a pittance, just as many acquired belongings when Nikkei left the valley.[32] Sho Endow admitted, "Neighbors signed the paper and guys I went to school with . . . made lots of money. They hid behind the apple tree to stay away from the war." One local Nisei orchard that rented for $1,000 a year grossed $50,000 per year for its caretaker during the owner's three-year absence. Another forty-acre orchard rented for $250 annually, while the tenant grossed $25,000. The *Oregonian* condemned those profiteers for playing on "war-inspired hatred of the enemy to eliminate an economic minority." With economics still the underlying theme, the WRA differentiated between the valley's earlier rancor in the 1920s to prevent Japanese farmers from acquiring *more* land and the wartime drive in the 1940s to prevent Nikkei from returning to land they *already* owned. It also claimed that anti-Japanese proponents used property interests as a means to gain public support while otherwise denying that economics was an incentive.[33] "Our parents were all hardworking people, and they made a success of areas where others had failed," observed Mam Noji. "Because Japanese as a whole did so well, other people envied us. . . . They didn't want us to come back and resume our place. . . . Call it greed, if you wish. I'm sure fair-minded people are not too proud of what happened."

## PRESSURE

More than anything, social, political, and economic pressure from those who held the reins of local power became overwhelming. Nikkei, as well as those who supported them, often suffered from paralyzing efforts that interfered with their personal choices and how they conducted their day-to-day business.

At the time of the war, the American Legion in Hood River was a "well-oiled political machine," according to Reverend Burgoyne. Though not large in number, its members held sway in every major office and organization in town. "If you didn't play ball with the Legion, you'd get frozen out," he added. The Legion's "dictatorship" over the small town had gone unchallenged ever since the earliest settlers could remember.[34]

Taking care of twenty-five-year old unfinished business with the Issei, Shoemaker was the architect of the full-scale advertising and petition campaign. He disputed the contention that agitation in the valley was the work of just thirty radicals by circulating petitions around the valley and including locals in the full-page newspaper ads he penned. "Some farming districts have signed ninety nine percent," he wrote the Legion's national commander. Shoemaker also affirmed that, in the heated debate after Scheiberling's telegram, he "led the opposition," defying those who would restore the names or take the board down. Stirring the pot further, he likewise applied pressure on the national commander, asserting that the Nisei names "can never be replaced without splitting Hood River Post, Hood River County, possibly the state of Oregon and even the three western states," resulting in "sure blood shed" when some agitators had "three or four beers under their belt."[35]

Scheming to force Nikkei out by cutting off their supplies, six stores led the White Supremacy program, even refusing sales to GIs. When members boycotted businesses that sold to Japanese, others joined for fear of being boycotted themselves. The owner of one Odell community store report-edly received threats of arson if he allowed Japanese to shop. A West Side store owner who shed tears when parting with the Asai family posted a "No Jap Trade" sign on his window when they returned. Insurance com-panies would not cover Japanese, mindful that a lawsuit judged by a jury of peers was a sure loss. Some succumbed to pressure even though they were "friendly inside their hearts," as Noji put it. Another Odell grocer illus-trated this with his own cautious measures. "Come after dark," he whis-pered to Nikkei. "We'll sell you anything you want." A few, like veteran Paul Sanstrum of Safeway, withstood the power group that included two people embittered by their sons' deaths in the Pacific. "If you turn out the Japanese, you have to turn out the Germans and the Italians," he told them. In fact, welcoming the Japanese was good business, Sanstrum added with a laugh. "I got them all!" Nikkei were indeed limited in where they could buy groceries: downtown at Safeway or Hess, twenty miles south to McIsaac's in Parkdale, twenty miles up the gorge to The Dalles, or sixty miles west to Portland. Barckley's was their only drugstore, Field Furniture downtown was willing to sell them home furnishings, they could eventually buy autos and gasoline at Garrabrant, and Moore's sold electrical supplies. All the barbers were Legionnaires with influence over beauty parlors, so Nikkei were forced to travel for haircuts.[36] "It was very uncomfortable to live here," conceded local resident Athalie Lage. "Most of us just went along with the tide and didn't question, which was a mistake, I am sure. But we were not leaders; we were just country people."[37]

Residents were also pressured to sign petitions. Members of the Grange circulated forms urging pledges of support for "every legal means to pre-vent the return of the Japanese people to the West Coast." Some entreaties came at meetings. Others occurred at people's homes. Constance Nastasi remembered two men threatening, "Well, your house could burn," if she did not acquiesce. Living with her daughter and mother in a two-story, shingled home while her husband served as a paratrooper in Europe, she was vulnerable enough that she decided to sign, despite her dissenting views. A local farmer observed, "There was pressure all right. . . . Sign it or else. . . . Everybody was real stirred up, naturally." Others saw through the circumstances that caused some people to sign in spite of their true sentiments. "If you are surprised to see certain names on the intolerant list," Wally Miller, active in the League for Liberty and Justice, wrote to a valley Nisei, "I can personally assure you that many of them were browbeaten into signing and they merely lacked *guts*." Some questioned whether names were added "willy nilly." (One resident was surprised to find her father's name—misspelled—on a petition, though he had taken the side of Japanese Americans during a heated family squabble.) Nisei, too, acknowledged the influence that community leaders could have. "I was surprised to see some of those names," exclaimed Sab Akiyama, "but I think when you're just a follower in a community, there's a lot of pressure from the people in power. If you have a few leaders who have a hold of the community, they can just about make everybody think the way they want. We had quite a group of old Hood Riverites who were really prejudiced." Arline Moore also maintained that "two out of every three persons didn't care to refuse a neighbor," and none expected to see his or her name published in the newspaper. Many were newcomers, and few had dealt directly with Japanese. Moore noticed that either many had signed several times or their names had been reprinted.[38] An analysis of the names did show that of the 1,857 names printed in five issues of the *Hood River County Sun*, 37 appeared twice and 3 appeared three times, for a corrected total of 1,814 names.[39]

Those who "stuck their necks out to help" Nikkei were criticized. Reverend Sherman Burgoyne and his wife, Doris, were foremost among them. "It was a terribly lonely fight in the beginning," the pastor confessed of his war on words with Post No. 22. Legionnaires excoriated him, according to written accounts, expressing sentiments such as "We've been running this town for 25 years, and you just can't get away with it!" He was dubbed a "Jap Lover," and someone threw a rock through the parsonage window. He was frozen out of the Rotary Club and other civic groups and could find no buyers for his ten-acre ranch. The Burgoynes were turned away from the same stores that denied Japanese. Doris, shunned by coworkers after dashing from her bank teller's booth to greet early returnee Ray Sato, eventually quit her job.[40]

Support from Reverend Burgoyne's congregation also dissipated. Although leaders at Asbury Methodist Church had unanimously supported his return for a fourth year in 1945 and the Methodist Church's Board of Missions initially sided with him, members did not openly stand behind him, and families stopped attending the church. "No one knows how hot it was for us," explained Doris Burgoyne. "We expected to be beaten up or run out of town any moment."[41]

Sacrifices by those who withstood the label of "Jap Lover" did not go unnoticed by returning Nikkei. "Can you imagine the kind of pressure they must have had?" queried Mam Noji. "Those people who befriended us were also ostracized almost as bad as we were. I think we have to take our hats off to people like that." Min Asai also extolled those who "gave us faith again in America and democracy."[42]

Nikkei and their advocates nevertheless recognized the consequences of wartime pressure. "We had to remember that in the war, there's war hysteria. . . . A lot of people did things that I'm sure they regretted," conceded Noji. In a letter to him, Moore pointed out the intensity of peer pressure, noting that many were "just falling in line with the popular trend." Then, "to save face, they could not back down."[43] "I think it was the powerful people talking," Kurahara admitted. "If the person is powerful enough, you don't want to refuse them anything. I think that's how most of the names got on the petition." Trying to empathize with those in that situation, Noji wondered, "How would we have reacted under that kind of pressure? Some of these people have regretted having signed those petitions. Yeah, we recognized the names. In a crisis like this, it brings out the worst and brings out the best in people."

Still, understanding the roots did not resolve the conflict. When WRA director Dillon Myer stopped at Hood River in April 1945 during his tour of West Coast "hot spots," Legionnaires invited themselves to his meeting. After Myer presented plans for resettling evacuees, the twenty-some "guests" insisted on jobs and homes for *their* returning GIs and called for a vote on whether "Japs" should return to Hood River. In the end, Myer managed to deflect the ill-intended vote. A valley native writing to the *Hood River County Sun* reacted to another WRA speaker's discussion of the rights of Japanese Americans by asking, "Am I entitled to constitutional rights? . . . Have the American Japanese become more worthy of constitutional rights because of this war?" Spring newspaper ads for war bonds continued to use defamatory images and text linking Nikkei to the Japanese enemy. In a May issue, a picture of three haggard, wounded veterans at a cemetery was offset with the caption "American prisoners say: 'We want to get back at the Japs!' Match their spirit in the mighty 7th war loan drive." On the page facing it, another ad read: "Remember the first Tokyo bombing?" After characterizing how pilots captured by the Japanese had been barbarously treated, it implored, "Buy—and hold—More War bonds!"[44]

Their hometown's sullied image easily deterred two other GIs. Newly released from Fort Leavenworth's disciplinary barracks in May 1946, neither Fred Sumoge nor Kenjiro Hayakawa considered returning permanently. "I heard bad things," explained Sumoge. "That little town, I think I read someplace, was the worst city in the U.S. as far as *nihonjin* [Japanese] discrimination. . . . It started with this *nihonjin* honor roll. . . . I just can't think of living there." For six months, Sumoge did rejoin his family at their fifteen-acre strawberry, cherry, and apple farm, which had been without care during the war. Finding work driving a one-and-a-half-ton truck at another farm, he hauled and unloaded almost three hundred forty- to fifty-pound lug boxes of apples per day at the AGA warehouse, which, by the fall of 1946, was accepting produce from Nikkei farmers. Hayakawa's relatives no longer resided in the valley after losing their farm lease at the end of the war. While visiting friends, however, he and Sumoge met again. "What are you doing here?" the surprised Sumoge asked his compatriot. Despite more than two years of imprisonment together, they did not know they shared ties to the discredited valley.

## THE HOMEWARD PULL

The ruthlessness of war, combined with economic lust and racial prejudice, continued its debilitating hold. In May 1945, twenty-one Nikkei families again resided in the valley. By the following year, only 40.3 percent (186 of 462) of the prewar Nikkei had returned, low compared to the 68.9 percent who returned to the entire state.[45]

Tiny Hood River, now famous for more than its fruit, had garnered a virulent reputation across the country. In its study "Prejudice in Hood River Valley," the WRA ended on a cautionary note: "The old organization and the old attitudes still exist in Hood River—in some ways worse than before—and will undoubtedly be called into play at the next opportunity. If the friends of the evacuees and 'fair play' are content with the small victory given them by the temporary support of public opinion and official action (both the result of widespread publicity) and drop the local fight, the 'Hood River Incident' will continue far into the future."[46]

## TWELVE

# *"You Could Feel It"*

## RESETTLING IN THE COMMUNITY
## AND ELSEWHERE

O'ER the land of the free and the home of the brave!" Two hundred voices swelled to sing the "Star Spangled Banner" when Mid-Columbia Japanese Americans welcomed their sons home from war late in December 1946. Though their families' freedoms had not remained intact, as the national anthem pronounced, through their wartime service, Nikkei had demonstrated that Americanism was their lifeblood. This assemblage was a visible sign that valley Nikkei were back—a heartfelt homage to the young men who had brought them honor as well as a bold message to the community that had dismissed them. They had struggled to recoup their wartime losses, withstand a backlash of community sentiment, and bring normalcy to their lives. Now heartaches of the past and ordeals of the present gave way to this single evening's tribute.

The banquet was a colorful testimonial to Nisei veterans in both words and music. Dedicated to the memory of Frank Hachiya, it included a tribute to the fallen soldier by Reverend Sherman Burgoyne, a local proponent of the Nikkei. The evening's guest speaker, an assistant division commander from Fort Lewis, in Washington, recognized Nisei servicemen's outstanding war record in Italy and France. Posing the oft-asked question, "Can they be trusted?" Brigadier General Joseph A. Cranston responded that "the highest percentage of Nisei volunteers came from the Pacific Northwest." The officer's ringing words left no doubt about his view of Nisei GIs' allegiance: "They were just as eager to fight the Japanese as they were to fight the Germans. . . . There should be no distinction between the Nisei and any other Americans who serve in the army of the United States. They have every right to say: 'I have fought a good fight; I have finished my course; I have kept the Faith!'"[1]

Nikkei and white friends joined in the celebratory program. Ray Yasui served as toastmaster, veteran Mam Noji extended greetings, veteran George Akiyama gave a response, and Bessie Watanabe and Ochiyo Nishioka performed "Il Bacio," a violin duet. Among the friends of the Nikkei who were there, Reverend James Brown offered the invocation, while Doris Burgoyne and Boyd Miller sang solos, Forrest Durland played "Bumble Boogie" on the piano, and W. B. Durland rendered a version of "Star of the East" on his musical saw. Even the venue was telling, for the Hood River Café had denied service to Nikkei just the year before.[2]

### REMNANTS OF HOME

Although they put up a brave front, there was no denying the challenges that dogged Nikkei daily since their return. Indeed, the valley whose residents once enticed Japanese immigrants with labor incentives had publicly renounced them during the war. Petitions bearing the names of more than 1,800 signers printed in local newspapers, the erasure of Nisei names from the downtown memorial plaque, and support for exclusionary legislation had proclaimed a harsh message: "Japs" were not welcome.

Resettling alongside neighbors who had condemned their return took "a lot of courage," admitted Ed Shoemaker, a wartime air force engineer, whose father led the valley's anti-Japanese campaign. Referring to the removal of Nisei names from the veterans' wall, he added, "That was a crime. I think it was jealousy, small-mindedness. I think it was just fear of the Japanese taking over the valley. I was ashamed to be a Hood Riverite," he confided.

Speaking of the maelstrom of anti-Japanese voices and actions, Mam Noji observed, "The unscrupulous had usurped properties, stolen equipment, ruined valuable orchards, and made a mockery of 'duration contracts' on businesses and farms. To be sure, there were courageous and fair-minded small groups that urged 'fair play.' . . . Sorrowfully, the mood was such that they themselves were ostracized and fingered for their noble stand. Compassion, sympathy and understanding were in very short supply."[3]

Those shortcomings were immediately evident when Nikkei reclaimed their property and belongings. Rogues had broken into the Nishiokas' home, smashed their furniture, and stolen other pieces. An arsonist set fire to the Tamuras' shed. Someone killed the Akiyamas' chickens and shot holes through their spraying machine, and the local garage refused to repair their machinery. After downtown businesses would not sell farm tools to the Akiyamas' youngest son, the downcast teenager found the tires in his truck deflated and fluid drained from the radiator's crankcase. Caretakers who had leased the Akiyamas' farm and home during the war helped themselves to the family's belongings, taking everything but six Japanese plates; they also cured bacon inside the house, leaving an acrid odor in floors saturated with rancid fat.[4]

Most Nikkei farms suffered three or more years of gross neglect. The Akiyamas' four acres of asparagus had become a field of weeds one and a half feet tall that they removed and hauled away by the truckload. Then, too, "the orchard was run down," asserted son George, who was discharged ten months after his family returned. "It wasn't sprayed properly, wasn't pruned properly. The first couple years they could hardly get a very good crop. They had to get the trees back in shape. That took a couple of years." And they worked "thirty hours a day," according to his younger brother Sab. Nor did the Akiyamas receive compensation for the produce sold during the three wartime years when the caretakers leased the farm. (Their contract permitted caretakers to keep profits if they cared for the farm and paid property taxes; the couple, however, neither worked the farm nor paid the Akiyamas.)[5] Sagie Nishioka worried just as much about his widowed mother and young siblings. Four months before his military discharge, his family returned to a home with shattered windows and indifferent farm upkeep, which he charitably attributed to the labor shortage. "Most of the farm had to have a man to do the work. . . . Why, it did produce hardship." After the war, in fact, only one-fourth of West Coast Nikkei farmers returned, and these typically were landowners.[6]

To be sure, the adjustment for returning Nikkei was stressful, whether they were home from the warfront, from camp, or from work release programs. Scholar Tetsuden Kashima characterized this postwar period as the "crisis of readjustment."[7] He was referring to the unsteady transition of Nikkei from the confines of camp, but the term is just as appropriate for returning veterans, who struggled mightily to normalize their lives. For them, the physical and emotional impact of war was just as disabling.

After the war, the Akiyama family hauled away one-and-a-half-foot-high
weeds from their four acres of asparagus fields. This photo of the family at work
appeared in a War Relocation Authority magazine. (George Akiyama, June 1945)

### THE PERSONAL, SOCIAL, AND ECONOMIC PRICE

Physical effects of war immediately took their toll. After forty-six months
in the military, Mam Noji returned home in August 1945 with a Bronze
Star for his service in the Philippine liberation. He promptly showed
symptoms of malaria, which could occur up to a year after exposure to the
parasite. "One moment you're sweating and the next moment you had to
have a blanket because you were freezing . . . I spent a miserable month," he
explained. More than 500,000 GIs contracted the disease during the war.[8]
"Walking wounded, most of the time," was how Sho Endow described his
condition after shrapnel pierced his back. Despite ninety days in a Naples
hospital and five months of Stateside rehabilitation, Endow's wounds
affected nerves along his spine. As a result, "it takes a long time to get
things done," he conceded. For Sagie Nishioka, even after eighteen months

in the hospital, a single step felt as if he were "walking on needles." Though he disproved a doctor's prognosis that he would never take a step again, Nishioka found that the act of walking—so simple before—required calculated planning. "Even today, I always have to figure out a way to get to my destination with the fewest steps possible," he disclosed. Each of Nishioka's footsteps brought a reminder of his sacrifice—and the price of war.

Emotional sores from battle afflicted veterans long after they returned. Even familiar noises could provoke unexpected reactions. "I remember overseas when we went for a rest in France on the coast, there were palm trees swaying and making a hissing sound. . . . It would remind you of the artillery shell coming over your head," recalled George Akiyama. "Men all ran for cover!" If the swish of palm fronds could instill fear, a rifle shot was likely to produce the jitters they called "shell shock." "You hear that shot and you feel like somebody's shooting at you," Akiyama admitted. "You remember being shot at. You rehash the whole thing. . . . You dream about it, have nightmares." The mental wear and tear of war had long-term, haunting effects. "Things like that bother you. It stays a long time with you. You relive those scenes where you see people getting killed or injured." Those flashbacks and other reactions characterize post-traumatic stress disorder, commonly associated with combat and other psychologically distressing events beyond the normal range of human experience.

Whether Nikkei were returning from the battlefield, camp, or work, they shared psychological scars from their wartime experiences.[9] This became apparent when they encountered former friends and neighbors, whom most had not seen for three or more years. Those first meetings were often awkward and hurtful. "People that once were your friends, and whom you trusted in and worked with, would turn the other way when approached and have nothing to do with you. Some were loyal to us to the very end and some were in the 'middle' wondering which way to go or what to say. Unbelievable!" remarked Ray Sato, one of the first three civilian returnees to the valley.[10] Similarly, acquaintances averted their eyes when Jan Kurahara saw them downtown. "They would try to look away from you, hoping that maybe you wouldn't recognize them, trying to be as nonchalant as possible . . . you get the feeling nobody wants you here. All of a sudden it makes your ancestry more potent." Mam Noji's emotions ran just as deep. "It hurts. Your feelings for friends turn upside down. You could see it in their faces. We had the wrong kind of face. We had the wrong names."

How were they to react when former friends snubbed them? Nisei veterans' words evoked raw emotions. "We didn't cause the war, but then they still blame us because of our nationality," Hit Imai remarked. "I resented being called a 'Jap,' especially after the war," exclaimed Johnny Wakamatsu, who had reenlisted for four more years despite combat injuries he sustained in France. "As I went into Barclay's [pharmacy] on the heights, one kid said to another, 'That's a Jap.' I told them the next time I heard that word that I would slap the —— out of them." Sho Endow was skeptical. "What's the use? We always knew that some of them were a-holes so we never did talk to them." Nisei did became sensitized to mixed messages. "They might speak nice to you in front of you, but behind your back, you don't know what they're saying," observed Hit Imai. "You could feel it," added Harry Tamura. "They'd say 'hi' to you. But you could feel it. . . . You can't do anything about it . . . so you just let it go."

Keeping a low profile seemed the simplest solution. "Why provoke a confrontation, you know?" asked Mam Noji. "In those days we had a lot of doubts about our acceptance." Shig Imai explained his actions. "Try not to raise a lot of fuss and try to get along as much as we can. We didn't socialize too much then. . . . You're in situation where . . . *shikataganai*. You're just stuck with it . . . so you just go along." Such Japanese cultural norms, including *enryo* (deference, restraint) and *gaman* (internalizing emotion, persevering) strongly affected Nikkei reasoning, tying their fate to forces beyond their control and promoting conformity, reserve, and compromise in their approaches—even a sense of powerlessness.[11] "I tried not to carry these grudges too much in my mind," accorded Sagie Nishioka about the "constant pressure of being put down. . . . So I sort of lived with it, you might say."

"Being who we were was detrimental to our health," concluded veteran Jan Kurahara, in explaining the Nikkei's decision to limit their socializing at first and thus avoid certain rejection. With few exceptions, they kept their pain hidden, their feelings to themselves. Sab Akiyama was honest about his view of the war as a seventeen-year-old. "It's like a victim of rape. You think, 'There must be something wrong with me that the government could treat me this way.' . . . You felt like, 'It was partly my fault that we were interned.'" But the shame of being considered a second-class citizen and being classified an enemy alien by the army was "the deepest wound," Akiyama grieved. "If you sit and just think about it, it kind of hurts." For Noji, there was the resultant feeling of powerlessness. "We had to follow along. We were in no position to argue with anybody. We were at the bottom. We were all immature; most of us were very young yet, a lot in our teens. . . . We were like sheep; we followed orders." Reflecting on the scars of racism that formed the "prevailing ingredient of their lives," Togo W. Tanaka (a publisher and former editor of *Rafu Shimpo*, the Los Angeles daily Japanese-language newspaper) queried, "Is it any wonder, then, that my generation—in common with blacks and chicanos—should find subconscious inhibitions in their responses to their environment?"[12]

In *Years of Infamy*, Michi Weglyn described these emotions as a "castration: a deep consciousness of personal inferiority" that inclined Nikkei to avoid encounters that could increase their pain. Keeping low profiles, following along, rationalizing their actions, and repressing their feelings typified defense mechanisms that Amy Iwasaki Mass attributed to a Nikkei means of self-protection against psychological pain, an attempt to maintain their sense of integrity and self-worth.[13]

Their suppression of feelings and memories also led to an unwritten code of behavior: Nikkei avoided talk of their wartime ordeals, forging a "social amnesia," as termed by Tetsuden Kashima. Sidestepping unpleasant topics even among themselves eased their discomfort, and avoiding confrontation helped them achieve *wa*, or harmony, explained Kashima. Hit Imai said of their incarceration, "We never did talk about it, and I don't want to bring it up because why should I bring up all that hardship we went through?" When the veterans returned, they, too, avoided talk of the discipline barrack boys, conversing instead about the "trivial, the humorous or the non-threatening moments," according to Kashima. "Court-martial is not a good thing," allowed Fred Sumoge, one of the DB boys. "Maybe that's why others didn't want to talk about it or ask about it." Instead, he recalled, he spent time "minding my own business."[14]

The Nisei's extreme sensitivity about how others viewed them and how their actions reflected on themselves restrained their behavior, concluded S. Frank Miyamoto, a notable Nisei sociologist. "If they didn't ask, I wouldn't tell because I had really nothing to tell . . . I don't know, it's one of those things," explained Sumoge. Even during a conversation with former schoolmate George Akiyama about close calls in Europe, his longtime friend asked no questions. "We talked about old times," Akiyama remembered, "about our schoolmates and how I was treated when I came back to Hood River, mostly about our families. We didn't talk about his Fort Leavenworth thing. I knew he was in that bunch. He didn't bring it up. No,

I didn't bring it up. . . . We were both glad we were out of the army." The Nisei style of "quietness" had evolved from living on the lower rungs of a vertical society of unequal power (similar to the social order their parents had known in Japan). With little control over their own lives, they were put in the position of having to earn their rights or prove that these were due them, theorized Nisei scholar James Hirabayashi.[15]

While veterans and their families paid a personal price that was evident in their physical and emotional scars, they also suffered enormous financial loss. Mam Noji's sister noted that her family's seedlings had finally produced young trees mature enough to bear fruit, and at a time when prices were making the business lucrative. Then they were forced to evacuate. "We were just getting even, and so we were looking forward to the years ahead," Chiz Tamura explained. Losing the expected income was "devastating" to the family, who worked years after the war to return their orchard to productivity. The postwar price for fruit was significantly higher. Though prices varied by size, variety, and grade, Extra Fancy Red Delicious apples sold for just $1.50 a box in 1941, while Newtown apples brought $1.60 and Anjou pears sold for $1.75 to $2.15. By 1945, however, apples sold for $3.19 a box after wartime prices that had risen to as much as $5 a box, with some pears selling for up to $7 a box.[16] "You can't sue anybody for anticipated profits," complained Sho Endow. "Whatever the caretaker picked up, we should have been entitled to but we never did go to court."

In 1948, Congress passed the Japanese American Evacuation Claims Act, which allowed Nikkei to claim "damage to or loss of real or personal property." But compensation was minimal. During their hasty evacuations, many families lost the documents and paperwork necessary for their applications. Those who did file claims recovered paltry sums, some as low as 9 percent of the value of their losses. In Hood River and throughout the country, Nikkei received restitution that amounted to just a few cents on the 1942 dollar.[17]

## DETERMINED TO SURVIVE

Losing financial compensation was setback enough; being denied the right to their farms was extreme. In 1945, the Oregon legislature passed an amendment to the 1923 Alien Land Law that tied a knot in the loophole Issei had used to continue working on their farms. The new law not only prevented the first generation from owning or leasing land; it added a new twist: denying them the right to live on those farms and making it a criminal offense to work on them. Four years later, the Oregon State Supreme Court ruled that the law violated the Fourteenth Amendment's equal protection clause and reversed a decision against father and son Etsuo and Kenji Namba for leasing land.[18]

The financial, legislative, and personal challenges were overwhelming, yet Nikkei still allowed for small measures of optimism. Dealing with the wartime trauma prompted a kind of super-patriotism among some Nikkei. After being incarcerated at Camp Minidoka while his older brother George was serving in the 442nd, Sab Akiyama enlisted in 1944 when he turned twenty. "I wanted to volunteer for the service to prove to the other Americans that we're just as good citizens as anybody else. I think most Nisei felt they had to prove themselves." This earnestness to become "better Americans" was a Nikkei attempt to restore honor, observed Weglyn. Others, too, recognized this increased drive to assimilate, to become successful, and to be viewed as "super-Americans."[19] Surviving combat cast their futures in a different light. Mam Noji gained a new appreciation for what life offered. "Over there, you could be standing and the next minute you could be lying down," he recalled. Despite the drudgery he faced in his orchard and the rebuffs he and his family received, George Akiyama conceded, "Farming was easy for me after being in battle. Before my army days, when it got hot doing dusty work at home, we wouldn't work in the afternoon. We'd go swimming. But after I came back . . . , I'd do a lot of disking [using a harrow to break up plowed ground] in the hot dust. My mother used to say, 'Why don't you rest?' I'd say, 'Ehhh, this is easy compared to fighting the war. You don't have to worry about getting shot.'"

Being so close to death brought some nearer to God. "Just think. I could have been killed," Nishioka exclaimed. "I had a particle go through my right ventricle. Whew, that was close. That makes me think I have more faith in God, that there is really a God." George Akiyama had mixed feelings. "I kinda feel guilty. How can you explain somebody five feet from me getting hit and I didn't? . . . So I figured if I come back alive without getting hit, I've got to pay my respect to God."

Once one peeled back layers of time, the same silence, repression, and accommodation that typified the trauma Japanese Americans suffered during the war repeated itself during their resettlement after the war, observed historian Art Hansen. Writing about Tetsuden Kashima's view of the postwar crisis, he summarized the Nikkei plight: ". . . they had to heal divisions within their communities, families, and even themselves. And they had to organize so as to roll back extant discriminatory legislation, repel new anti-Japanese initiatives, and gain long denied citizenship perquisites. At the same time, they had to overcome their *hazukashi* or prevailing sense of shame, however unwarranted. Usually this was accomplished through repression, silence, or forgetting." And while Japanese Americans were striving to achieve outward success, "they still needed to gain inner peace."[20]

The war's impact on Nikkei resettlement was palpable in their physical and emotional responses as well as in their decreased numbers. Before the war, almost 90 percent of mainland Nikkei had lived on the West Coast. Five years after the war, by 1950, fewer than 60 percent would reside in Washington, Oregon, and California. Hood River's postwar Nikkei population would decline by almost half, from 462 to 233.[21]

Eighteen months after the first Nikkei returned, the consequences of war still burned in the words of outspoken community members. Ralph B. Sherrieb, owner of the Rockford grocery store, rationalized his refusal to direct visiting news writers to Japanese farms: "We just don't recognize 'em around here. We don't want 'em and we tell 'em to stay away from us. So far as we are concerned, it's once a Jap, always a Jap." And that, he added, applied to Nisei who had served in the army as well. C. A. Perkins, local wholesaler and Legionnaire, was just as strident: "I don't think it is possible for members of a race so foreign to ours to understand us, to live with us as we live, or to be the same kind of citizens as we are. We have everything to lose and the Japs have everything to gain. I don't believe the United States needed the help of a handful of American-born Japs to fight in its army and to observe our military methods in order to betray the United States at some later date." Even the conciliatory words of Chamber of Commerce manager R. E. Steele rang hollow: "I don't necessarily like the Japanese. I think some may still be unfriendly to the country which defeated their homeland. Others are unquestionably loyal Americans. However, they are now back among us under the laws of the United States. The government has seen fit to allow their return to Hood River. I imagine that settles the issue, regardless of what particular personal feelings we may have."[22]

It seemed that Nikkei had only just begun their journey toward resettling among those who had protested their return. In 1946, local businesswoman Arline Moore wrote in "Hood River Redeems Itself" that there was "still a long road to travel before this 'anti' racial canker is eliminated from the American way of life." A year later, in a letter to the editor of the *Dartmouth*, she was more sanguine: "Some Legionnaires still insist they were right. Most would like to forget it ever occurred. The many GIs entering the Legion will in time swing sentiment in the right direction. Certainly a man cannot serve side by side with another man day after day, sharing the same risks and the same rations, often owing his life to that individual and continue to think of him as unfit for peace time association."[23] Time would surely tell.

# THIRTEEN

# *"Time Is a Good Healer"*

## REBUILDING

S EVERAL months after the war's end, a young upper-valley Nisei's good intentions came to a sputtering halt. Eager to see former white classmates, the younger brother of Mam Noji hosted a reunion at his parents' home. To his chagrin, only one couple arrived, and there was no word—not even a phone call—from the others. "The experience turned me sour to our happy return," Toru Noji lamented, adding that there were plenty of homemade refreshments left.[1] For him and others, the personal pain from war seemed as wrenching as the physical scars and wounds their GI siblings endured. It did underscore, however, the heights they would need to scale if they were to leave behind the depths of their wartime disruption.

### PROVING THEMSELVES

"Being veterans gave us good backbone," offered Mam Noji. "The healing process began as soon as we returned from war." Earnest about rebuilding their lives in an unwelcoming, often hostile, hometown milieu, local Nikkei strived to reestablish themselves economically, socially, and politically. Developing their own sensitized antennae and defensive armor, they steeled themselves against rejection and kept low profiles. Their own self-reliance and citizenship, the personal relationships they nurtured, and their gradual community involvement proved to be important assets. Ever so slowly, if unconsciously, they took minute steps toward reclaiming their stake in the valley—one pace forward, a stride back, another half-step ahead—fending off challenges that trumped them at home and from their state government.

First, however, hard work was the critical antidote. "We stayed home most of the time and worked," admitted Harry Tamura. "When we had to buy things, we bought where they would accept us." His wife, Chiz, described their goal: "You want to raise good fruit and have a good reputation, right?" Shig Imai rationalized this necessary Nikkei lifestyle: "Out here in the country, why, you can work hard all day and go to bed and go to sleep and get up and do it again the next day." A strong work ethic was a must, for their livelihood was tied to their farms' productivity.

After the war, their trustworthiness was just as critical. "We had to do something to turn this notion that we were second-grade citizens," asserted Sagie Nishioka. "They didn't trust us," added George Akiyama. "We had to prove that we were good citizens and loyal Americans." Mam Noji insisted, "We were law-abiding people. We were a quiet people." He recalled a compliment from the local sheriff: "The only problem I had with you people was one or two of you would be driving down the road too fast." The sheriff made this public statement to the Mid-Columbia Japanese American Citizens League, which Noji served as the first postwar president in 1946.[2]

These "good citizens and loyal Americans" remained devoted to those who supported and defended them. In February 1946, they hosted a farewell party for Clyde Linville and other WRA personnel who had aided them. They also avidly supported Reverend Sherman Burgoyne, who led the campaign to reinstate the names of Nisei GIs on the county honor roll. In 1947, Reverend Burgoyne was named a recipient of the Thomas Jefferson Award for advancing democracy, along with Eleanor Roosevelt, Frank Sinatra, and others. Selected from a pool of 1,500 civic, religious, and educational organizations and 500 newspaper editors across the country, honorees were to be feted in New York by the Council against Intolerance in America. "We all felt we had a responsibility to make sure they got there," commented Noji. With proceeds from fund-raisers, the local JACL bought a set of luggage, train tickets, and hotel reservations and presented these purchases along with expense money to the couple.[3]

Once the pastor returned home, there was disappointing news. He would be reassigned from Hood River's congregation of 450 to a tiny church of 89 in Shedd, Oregon (although two Washington State church adminis-trators interceded and transferred him to Spokane). In "No Reward for Valor," Richard L. Neuberger (then a *New York Times* correspondent and later a U.S. senator) praised the "defender of the Nisei" and criticized his "demotion to one of the smallest settlements in Oregon."[4] Clearly, champi-ons of the Nikkei cause faced dismal challenges, too.

It was no wonder, then, that Nikkei developed a form of ESP, or extra-sensory perception. For veteran Sab Akiyama, it was instinctive: "Some-how you could go in a store and tell by their reaction whether you're welcome or not. Then you kind of just walk out—I mean, even without a 'No Japs' sign. . . . You kind of learn to roll with the punches. We grew up with some kind of feeling that you 'don't stick up like a nail' because you're gonna get pounded down."

Also under a veil of self-doubt, valley newcomer and veteran Jan Kura-hara described how he detected cues: "After awhile, you can feel people out pretty easily. If they smile and they talk to you, generally that indicates they kind of want to be friends. . . . If they're not very friendly, I stayed away from them." This radar for spotting those who were "anti" (a com-mon term among Nikkei) became a key ingredient of postwar coexistence. It illustrates what sociologist Frank Miyamoto observed as a key difference between non-Nikkei and Nikkei interpersonal styles: Japanese Americans were sensitized first to the feelings and motives of others and second to themselves. They viewed themselves as they thought others saw them, which meant "they entered interactional situations with their brakes on."[5]

That tentativeness in Nikkei encounters was not lost on the mainstream community. "Many of the Japanese held back just a little bit," observed Lee Foster, retired agricultural extension agent, "to see how we were going to accept them." There was a reason. A national publication illustrated the valley's repressed race hatred with a quote from a local farmer: "I don't like those lousy Japs, but I'm not doing anything about it because I'm mixed up in a lot of farm deals with them." Even the Sansei, third-generation Nikkei, became savvy about blank looks and grimaces, like the five-year-old who whimpered, "Daddy, they don't like us in there, do they?"[6] The message was clear. "We knew who the unfriendly people were," Mam Noji main-tained. "We tried to avoid them, and they probably tried to avoid us, so we got along all right."

Nikkei inched ahead, developing trust through their few personal ties and gradually broadening their connections. "I overcame the belligerence by approaching people one at a time, instead of tackling them as a group," explained Kurahara. "I got to know more and more people that way." Then, too, while locals at first discriminated against Nikkei on strictly racial terms, an interesting phenomenon became apparent. "They seemed to be more selective, separating those whom they had personal acquaintance with from the others," Kurahara observed. A white resident shared that perception, claiming, "If I knew somebody, I never thought of them as Japanese. Only if it was someone that I didn't know could they be Japanese."[7] Gradually, the circle was beginning to widen, for, as Kurahara explained, locals began to understand "that we were just people too."

Mindful that the WRA had cautioned against gathering in large groups, Nisei observed how their parents' ethnic enclaves had contributed to the racial divide. Issei, confined by language and work, stuck closer to home and associated mainly with one another. Now it was essential that Nisei not isolate themselves and instead reach out to locals. As she got to know their neighbors, the spouse of one veteran expressed her hope, "Maybe they're just thinking, 'Well, I guess these Nisei aren't so bad after all.'"[8]

Eventually, other veterans and citizens began to show appreciation for the Nisei's war record: "Those boys were damn good soldiers, never backed away from anything." While there was continual pressure on businesses to exclude Nikkei, some began to soften. A few hardy residents told merchants they would not patronize stores where "a soldier with the Silver Star or a wounded man receiving his fortieth blood transfusion was not welcome." To rile those labeled as "race haters," some brave souls put on showy demonstrations of friendship "every time a Caucasian saw one of his Nisei friends downtown."[9]

In 1946, within a year of their return, more businesses began to serve Nikkei. Their reasons varied, including a desire to regain lost business, pressure from organized and independent community members, and a sense of justice. Those exchanges were not always heartfelt, however. One merchant who advocated "fair play" in business still demonstrated his prejudice: "Who wants a Japanese as their social equal? Who wants a Japanese as a close neighbor? Who wants intermarriage? I don't want these things, but that is beside the point. We can and have lived together in this Valley before, we can do so again."[10] Not surprisingly, Nikkei had long memories when it came to storekeepers who had once turned them away. A grocer in outlying Odell got this response when he solicited a Nisei: "I heard my money wasn't any good at your store." When Standard Oil Company also sought to regain Nikkei business, a veteran responded, "As long as Shell's bringing gas, why should I quit?"

Though Nisei took steps to avoid isolating themselves, they remained cautious. When other Oregon Nikkei encouraged them to become politically active and demand a public apology from the Hood River Legion post, locals declined. No, their approach would be low-key. Little by little, they fended off challenges—personally, locally, then with the government—without stirring up bitterness, "without being too visible or too vocal." Keeping a low profile, they quietly donated money to appeal the 1945 Alien Land Law that barred Issei from living and working on their own farmland. A chronology of the Mid-Columbia Japanese-American Citizens League simply stated: "In the late 1940's JACL helped defeat the Oregon Alien Land Law which was in effect since 1924. (Namba vs. Oregon)." But their well-intended efforts to sponsor cross-community events were only moderately successful. One venture was a joint fund-raiser with a local Latter Day Saints church at the old Japanese Hall in 1947 and 1948. While they shared profits equitably, a gap was apparent. "Each group enjoyed the program and danced with their immediate associates," observed local Arline Moore. "There wasn't even a noticeable exchange of greeting among acquaintances of the two races."[11]

## A FALLEN NISEI SON

The eyes of the state and the nation turned to a fallen Nisei son and ultimately helped to reawaken community consciousness. At the same time, the doubts of a grieving father were finally put to rest. Though Frank Hachiya had died in the Philippines in 1945, a year later, his body was still interred at the U.S. Armed Forces Cemetery outside Leyte Island's town of Palo. Considering the valley's intemperate climate, Junkichi Hachiya worried that he would never bury his son at home. After he confided in Monroe Sweetland (a former Red Cross field director who had befriended Frank in Eniwetok, Marshall Islands) that he "didn't want any more trouble," his son's friend sought resolution. Sweetland, then a newspaper publisher and later a state senator, contacted his counterpart at the *Hood River News*. Hugh Ball, who had indirectly supported Nikkei through the letters and national editorials he published, expressed his hopes. "That was a terrible thing. . . . We ought to make amends. We ought to have a demonstration that we do appreciate Frank. . . ."[12]

On September 11, 1948, three years after his death, Frank Hachiya finally came home, this time with a posthumous Silver Star for gallantry in action. An overflow crowd memorialized him at downtown Hood River's Asbury Methodist Church. "The great and the small" attended, according to the *Oregonian*. State and national dignitaries served as his honorary pallbearers: former governor Charles Sprague, attorney and future chief judge of the U.S. District Court of Oregon Gus Solomon, banker E. B. MacNaughton of First National Bank, national JACL president Hito Okada, attorney Verne Dusenberry (who had successfully challenged the Alien Land Law the previous year), Reverend Burgoyne, and Sweetland himself.[13] Mike Masaoka, national JACL representative, was there. General Mark W. Clark, commander of the Sixth Army, sent a representative. During the simple service, Hachiya's former college teacher Martha Ferguson McKeown let the young soldier's own words reveal his strength of spirit. "The love of one's country, America! It's queer and mystifying, is all I can say . . . life is a gift . . . I shall be grateful of one thing to the war. That is in

Frank Hachiya's body returned to his hometown for a public memorial at Asbury Methodist Church on September 11, 1948, three years after his death. From left: Reverend A. E. Place, Min Asai, Setsu Shitara, Mrs. M. F. McKeown, Monroe Sweetland, Reverend Francis Hayashi, and Mrs. A. E. Place. (*Oregonian*, September 11, 1948)

making me realize life." Friend Min Asai, president of the local JACL, also spoke of how "love of country was foremost in Hachiya's mind. . . . Little we realized as we wrestled and played together that he would prove it with his life." Following the service, Frank was buried under the oaks at the community's Idlewilde Cemetery without incident. The senior Hachiya received the flag from his son's casket, having traveled from Chicago to bury him in the only place Frank had called home. Frank's mother and brother were absent, still in Tokyo, where Homer served as an interpreter for the U.S. Army's Railway Transportation Office. Later, Hachiya's father expressed his hopes to Mrs. McKeown, "If only people of this country will recognize the Nisei as 100 per cent Americans . . . then my son has not died in vain."[14]

## GROWING COMMUNITY INVOLVEMENT

Testing their antennae and strengthening their emotional armor, Nikkei took gradual steps toward integrating within the community. In one case, a fortuitous military connection paved the way. After young Nisei finished work during the winter months, "there was no place to go play," as Hit Imai put it. During the 1940s, bowling was in its heyday as an inexpensive but challenging team sport, and bowling alleys were becoming fixtures in communities. But there was a "whites only" policy in league bowling, according to the American Bowling Congress. At downtown Hood River's bowling alley, proprietor Rene Hazeltine, an ex-sergeant and New Yorker, had no problems with Nisei bowlers. When the lanes closed at ten, he entrusted veteran Harry Inukai with the key, locked the front door, and invited Inukai and four friends (all Nisei veterans) to bowl as late as they wanted.[15] The novice bowlers practiced a couple nights a week until midnight, teaching themselves and setting their own pins. Eventually, the men formed four teams representing the rural communities of Odell, Parkdale, Oak Grove, and Dee. Imai recalled that their bowling night became known as "Nisei Night. And then, what do you know, some of the *hakujin* started to join in, you know, since we were having fun." By 1955, thirty Nisei had formed six teams.

The American Bowling Congress finally changed its requirements in 1951, and Nisei formed league teams in the Fraternal, then Commercial, and finally the City League (considered the most elite). The next year, a few Nisei even accepted invitations to join established white teams. Little by little, they stared down prejudice. "Some people are friendly face to face," recalled Imai, "but you know, behind your back, they've got a different personality. But then pretty soon, you bowl on their team, and they're not that way." Hazeltine himself bucked the community's discrimination by reminding complainers, "I own the lanes, and I can do what I want." One decidedly "anti" team eased off as the teams became more integrated. Finding team sponsors was challenging, however. A local business declined to be a sponsor, even though Imai was a regular customer. "Just because we're Japanese?" he asked, to no response. Eventually, Ted Hackett appliances, Central Sales farm implements, and Garrabrant auto dealers sponsored Nisei teams, a big step since one of the merchants had not readily welcomed Nikkei customers after the war. Soon forty Nisei stepped out on the lanes. Then, in the mid-1950s, a surprising sponsorship evolved. Three Nisei veterans had frequently joined white friends at pinball downstairs from the bowling alley. After they became acquainted, the manager signed on as a sponsor, and "American Legion" was emblazoned on the shirts of a Nisei team.[16]

Returning from the war—even after distinguished service overseas—did not assure the Nisei automatic membership in veterans' organizations. Joining the Veterans of Foreign Wars (VFW) seemed a reasonable option, especially after several Legionnaires protested the anti-Japanese campaign by resigning and joining the VFW.[17] Still, there was no guarantee of admission. In 1947 Tot Asai became the first Nisei to join the local VFW post, though not without creating a stir, as told by his nephew, David Loftus: "An old mail carrier named Leonard put up Tot's name for VFW membership. Two or three months later, he informed Tot that several World War II vets had blackballed him. (It took only three to do it.) In June, a veteran named Price was elected commander of the local post (VFW Post No. 1479), and after several more months of heated debate, Tot was given the nod. . . . [According to the minutes,] Price had broken the gavel trying to keep order, and dissidents quit." Later, an officer confessed his role in the valley's anti-Japanese campaign. "Like a sheep," he told Asai. "I'm sorry, I don't know why."[18] He had clearly been a leader, since he admitted writing the resolution to keep Japanese from the valley, but he showed his contrition by purchasing apples from Asai.

Two years later, Sho Endow joined the VFW, and in 1950, Shig Imai, Harry Tamura, and Mam Noji signed on as well. Attempting to offset negative publicity and promote amity, Mam Noji wrote the following letter to

*Scene,* an international east-west magazine, published under the caption "Harmony in Hood River, Oregon."[19]

> Dear Sirs:
>
> I enclose a picture of Sho Endow, Jr., 31, fruit grower from the Odell District of Hood River, Ore., just after he had been sworn in as commander of the Hood River post of the Veterans of Foreign Wars by Herb Mattieu, past commander, The Dalles (Ore.) post. Koe Nishimoto, also an Odell fruit grower and a Pacific veteran, is the new Hood River junior vice-commander; Harry Tamura, European theatre veteran, is a delegate to the district convention.
>
> Endow's election completes a cycle. He was Sgt. Endow of the U.S. Air Force in Alaska when his name, along with a dozen other Niseis, was removed from the Hood River Honor Roll during the war.[20] But things have changed since then. Thanks to Hood River VFW men like Bob Moore, Evan Jones, Lloyd Nance, and Frank Tate, the Niseis feel at home here. In the first year after the Niseis' return, Taro Asai, a veteran of 30 months in the Pacific, was elected VFW post chaplain. These days, when you talk of Hood River, Ore., there's no ground to associate the name with the wartime incident. Those days are gone. We of Hood River are infinitely more proud of our crisp red apples and luscious pears—and we want people to know that the Niseis have joined hands with their fellow citizens of Hood River.

By 1956, thirteen Nisei had joined the local VFW; eventually, there were ten more.[21]

Joining the American Legion was another matter. "We tried to get the Japanese boys into the Legion," explained Ed Shoemaker, son of the first commander of Post No. 22. "They were afraid to come in, you know. We finally got Bob Kageyama and Setsu Shitara. . . . They took quite a beating for awhile. People just shunned them. That took a lot of guts. . . . Everybody liked them after they were introduced. They were awful good Legionnaires." A new generation of ex-servicemen dramatically defused the tone of Post No. 22 meetings. "They needed some new blood, some new thinking," offered Bud Collins, Post No. 22's historian until his death in 2010, of the more than three hundred World War II veterans (including himself) who joined the twenty-five to thirty World War I veterans. "We disagreed with what they did, but we understood how they did it." A number of early members were World War I veterans whose sons were killed in the second war, and "they thought they were doing something for the war effort . . . but clearer heads prevailed."[22]

Other Nisei joined—or declined—for their own reasons. "I wanted to be accepted," admitted Shig Imai, who became a member in 1950, eventually signing on for life. "I thought it was the thing to do." In 1957, Sagie Nishioka contemplated the local snubbing of Nisei before joining the post in Salem, where he had moved. "It doesn't mean that all the people have adverse feelings about Japanese." For Mam Noji, the pain lingered, even after a 2002 invitation from the Legion's national headquarters. "I told them I really can't join because you were responsible for erasing my name as one of sixteen names on the local honor roll. . . . It poses bad memories for me." Twelve Nisei eventually joined the local Legion. Even nationally, only a small number of Nisei veterans participated in veterans' organizations.[23]

For women in the American Legion Auxiliary, animosities were just as heated. In 1951, Koke (Kyoko) Iwatsuki, whose husband joined the Legion after serving with the MIS, became the first Nisei member. Although the president, Alberta Parker, sponsored her, Iwatsuki faced intense opposition. "We don't want a Jap in this organization! We fought the war in Japan and we don't want Japs here!" some women clamored. The Hood River post commander's wife was adamant. "As long as I'm standing on two feet, you're not going to be in here!" Banging the gavel, Parker ordered the women to their seats. "Koke has just as much right as you people. . . . You don't have sons or husbands who served during World War II." After Parker's stern rebuke, the fifty women voted Iwatsuki in. (Two veterans later apologized to her husband for their wives' actions.) Still, Iwatsuki avoided meetings. "I know where I'm wanted and not wanted. I'm not creating any ill will," she explained. She did try to use her key privileges and met friends at the Legion Hall, but just once. Calling her a "dirty Jap," the cook berated Iwatsuki, exclaiming, "This is for Americans," and then accused her of stealing the key to gain access. "From that day, I turned in my key," said Iwatsuki. "I'm not the punching type. Where you don't want me, I'm not going." Yuki Sato, the other Nisei member, quit soon afterward.

## A STATE CIVIL RIGHTS CHALLENGE

A challenge of a different sort confronted Sagie Nishioka when he sought his first job after the war. The mild-mannered Purple Heart recipient would never have anticipated—or sought—statewide publicity. Nishioka had originally planned to farm and become a rural mail carrier, but his wartime injuries made that unlikely. The GI Bill allowed him to attend Lewis and Clark College, where he earned a degree in business in 1950 before completing postgraduate work at the University of Oregon. Nishioka's top-ranking score on the civil service test for prospective tax examiners seemed promising.

The following headlines of front-page articles in three of the state's prominent newspapers told of Nishioka's change of heart over two days: "'They Didn't Want Me': Japanese War Hero Won't Fight for Job" (*Oregon Journal*), "State Office Repulses Nisei, Violates FEP Law" (*Oregonian*), "Sagie Nishioka to Fight for Tax Commission Job" (*Oregon Statesman*).[24] "My not being hired was based solely on race," explained Nishioka. "The supervisor said, 'Supposing I have an Oregon wheat rancher who has a son who was killed in, say, Wake Island? If he sees you, he might not like it.'"

State labor commissioner W. E. Kimsey charged the Oregon Tax Commission with violating the state's Fair Employment Practices Act, the first state department so accused. Enacted in 1949, the law prohibited racial or religious discrimination in hiring employees. According to Kimsey, Nishioka's name was at the top of a list of three sent to the tax commission. While a state department may select any of the three, the commission's reasoning was the issue. It passed over Nishioka because "the public wouldn't approve dealing with a Japanese." That act occurred during Brotherhood Week, designated to promote racial and religious tolerance and observed from the 1930s through the 1980s.[25]

Newspapers detected a controversy between Oregon tax commissioner Ray Smith and his personnel director, Jason Lee. According to the *Oregon Journal*, Lee, who originally accepted part of the blame, later insisted that superiors blocked him from recommending Nishioka. Smith maintained that he was not involved and first learned of the incident in the newspapers. The *Oregonian* cited Smith's position that Nishioka "was not the type of man he would like to employ in the field." Lee also disassociated himself from the violation, which carried a fine and jail sentence as penalties.[26]

Loath to be in the limelight, Nishioka first vowed to drop the matter. "I won't fight it, because I might win . . . they might consider me unfavorably after I did get the job." Pressed further, he reflected, "I had so many adversities pushed on me, I kind of didn't do anything about it in my mind." But the comment of a Hawaiian infantryman in the 442nd goaded him. "You mainland boys don't speak up," he'd been told. Clearly, there was pressure to "show that I have guts." The next day, Nishioka changed his mind, telling the *Oregonian*, " I'd rather carry it through. I was rather timid or conservative before."[27]

Oregonians spoke out, sending telegrams and letters to the governor's office and to Nishioka. The first telegram protesting the action came from twelve ministers, organized by Reverend Sherman Burgoyne. Another tongue-in-cheek wire congratulated the tax commission: "No one is going to outstrip the great state of Oregon in ratio [*sic*] bigotry and narrow minded provincialism." Two of the sixteen messages to the governor arrived from Hood River. "Will we, by our selfish indifference condemn him to bear the burden of race prejudice also?" queried Mr. and Mrs. Carl Smith. "Of just such things are war and riot bred." Another Hood River resident, Marcia Yuck, wrote, "How the Kremlin must laugh at such 'incidents' in our U.S. Yours for a 100 percent fair Oregon." The American Veterans Committee in Oregon called for the dismissal of the tax commission employees responsible for this "insult to the people of Oregon." Two letters supported the tax commission's action, one applauding Smith for putting "Americanism before party or race" and the other asking that Nishioka's pension be withheld if he took a job.[28] Nishioka received ten personal letters, including one from the Burgoynes, claiming, "Your friends are all jumping in for you." They wrote to Jason Lee and Ray Smith, in addition to the governor, encouraged others to do the same, and told the story to newspapers. Attorney Robert Y. Thornton, a Tillamook state representative who would later become Oregon's attorney general, offered his legal services to Nishioka as repayment for "your great loyalty, devotion and sacrifice."[29]

The governor's position changed in just a few days. On March 28, Governor Douglas McKay's response to letter writers expressed his "utmost confidence" that Kimsey and the advisory committee would work out a satisfactory response. Three days later, after meeting with the Oregon Tax Commission and the Board of Control (which appointed commission members), his tone was different. "Just plain stupid!" he exclaimed. "There will be no discrimination—period."[30]

On March 31, Smith mailed Nishioka a terse letter informing him that he was certified for a position as junior accountant. On the same day, Governor McKay released a statement that cleared the tax commission of any violations. "It has been found that it has not been the policy of the State

Five years after being denied state employment in 1952, Sagie Nishioka was elected state commander of the Oregon Military Order of the Purple Heart. (Sagie Nishioka, June 1957)

Tax Commission to discriminate against anyone because of race, religion, color or national origin." As examples of the state's compliance, the governor cited the Portland Tax Commission's hiring of several Chinese employees. Still, he closed by adding, "I expect all state departments to set an example of conforming to the law. No discrimination will be tolerated." Quoted in the *Oregonian*, McKay stated, "If a man is good enough to fight for his country, he is good enough to hold a job in it in a civilian capacity, no matter what his race or color." From Seattle, where he worked as a post exchange clerk at the army's Fort Lawton, Nishioka accepted the position.[31] Despite the situation, he resolved, "Even though they did that to you, you just had to kind of try to forget about it, try to live the best you can." He would spend his career employed by the Oregon Department of Revenue in Salem.

## NIKKEI ACCULTURATION

Nikkei in Hood River were mindful of their roles in the larger community, not hampered by the language barrier that had limited Issei interactions: "We associated more with Caucasians than our parents did," commented one Nisei. It was important, she maintained, to "get to know each other better." Members of the second generation led the way by opening up their events to other valley residents. In 1948, the Mid-Columbia JACL hosted its first fishing derby, a day of friendly competition for anglers of all ages. The winner, who landed a nineteen-inch, three-and-a-half-pound brown trout, won a Philco portable radio and the trophy's bragging rights for a year. Local businesses and Portland merchants donated prizes, including a Remington electric shaver, a desk lamp, a garbage can, and a sack of rice. Non-JACL members paid a two-dollar entry fee, and members paid a dollar. Three years later, the Issei followed through with their first "interracial activity." The Japanese Methodist Church's chow mein dinner and bazaar was a huge success, with five hundred attending. There were "three Caucasian Americans to one Japanese American," according to one news article, which noted "a pleasant air of friendliness." The following year, the JACL began its tradition of presenting a memorial wreath at the community's Memorial Day services.[32]

By 1951, Nikkei were becoming more visible as employees and as volunteers. The Oregon Lumber Company reportedly became the first major local firm to hire Nisei. Arline Moore, in her article "The Happy Ending: Return to Hood River," touted Nisei variously employed in such jobs as assistant to the Odell packing plant superintendent, nurse at the Hood River Hospital, cook at Pine Grove School, clerk at Pine Grove Grocery Store, dental office assistant, and Bartol Motors car salesman. Nisei began volunteering in the four area fire districts, on the Apple Growers Association board, as Sunday school teachers, and as officers for their local school boards and parent-teacher associations. Besides bowling, they played baseball, softball, and basketball, and three years after their return, those teams were decidedly of mixed heritage.[33]

Changes were imminent for the Issei generation as well. They could finally become naturalized citizens, after the McCarran-Walter Act of 1952 removed race as a barrier to immigration and naturalization. Conscientiously preparing for their new roles, Issei attended citizenship classes taught by Reverend Arthur Collins, minister of the local Baptist church. Armed with English texts and Japanese dictionaries, they practiced writing answers to questions about U.S. history and politics, quizzed one another on the terms of elective offices, and recited the Pledge of Allegiance. Three-fourths of the Issei became new citizens, and they embraced the privilege of voting, the right to own land, and the responsibility of paying taxes.[34]

The older generation noticed a trend among their children. Nisei were becoming increasingly acculturated, adapting to American middle-class life. The process was hastened during and after the war by the Nisei's exposure to new communities, their expanded contacts with non-Nikkei, and the greater confidence that other World War II veterans expressed in them.[35] As the WRA observed, Nisei, "because of the rude shock of evacuation—grew up within a few short months." Becoming accustomed to American-style cuisine, colloquialisms, and customs, it seemed natural that they also began worshipping at local churches with their neighbors and friends. This led Issei to make a decision that enhanced their relations within the valley. During the 1950s, members of the Japanese Methodist Church had begun fund-raising to build their own sanctuary, so that they would no longer have to meet at the Japanese Community Hall. They donated $3,500 out of this fund toward Asbury Methodist Church's remodeling project. The downtown church, in return, allowed the Issei congregation to use its facilities and named a prayer chapel room "Izumi," or "Living Water." Guest ministers from Portland traveled to Hood River to conduct intermittent Japanese-language services for Issei Methodists and Buddhists.[36]

Nonetheless, while Japanese Americans began to be more visible within the broader community, those initiatives did not necessarily diminish their Nikkei-ness. Little could sever the cultural ties and kinship that had been strengthened by wartime challenges. The Mid-Columbia JACL became a community nucleus. In 1962, it held its first annual graduation banquet to recognize the outstanding achievements of the Sansei; two years later, the Junior JACL formed. The valley hosted its first annual Nisei Bowling Tournament in 1965, which attracted Nisei from Portland. Members concocted an ingenious and practical project to fund scholarships for high school graduates. Their valley Christmas card, imprinted with the names of donors (who could forgo sending their own cards), grossed $680 when it began in 1971 and eventually increased to $1,000. The JACL's four most popular events attracted all three generations.[37] At the Issei Appreciation Dinner, the older generation enjoyed teriyaki chicken, chow mein, and other ethnic favorites with entertainment ranging from kimono-clad Sansei performing Japanese dances to traditional Japanese movies. The August picnic brought families together for a potluck, bingo, raffle drawings, and games for all ages, including blindfolded Issei breaking whole watermelons with wooden mallets (a traditional game for seniors in Japan). At Christmas, the holiday potluck featured local talent and a visit from a Japanese American Santa. Nikkei also honored high school and college graduates at an annual banquet.

Ironically, being restricted from some mainstream organizations actually strengthened such Nikkei activities. Even the WRA recognized this dilemma: the unique problems Japanese Americans experienced after the war instilled a sense of group solidarity as their participation in segregated organizations cut off, or at least limited, their involvement in wider community groups. Nisei, half of whom were younger than twenty-one when the war began, were still relatively young and inexperienced. They straddled both Japanese and American cultures. In 1947, the WRA discerned, "Few have attained complete mastery in the customs of either." This contributed, it added, to the Nikkei's "lack of social ease" within the broader community and their desire to consider both Japanese and American culture when making decisions, resulting in "a constrained and self-conscious individual." Jan Kurahara admitted, "Being who we were was detrimental to our health. That's probably why we did what people in our position did best: Not to mingle with the natives unless we were sure of their politics and not to frequent places that we knew were not hospitable to us. Most places would fit this category." Nonetheless, as the war accelerated their acculturation, it hastened the Nisei's maturation.[38]

## A NATIONAL STANCE

It was during the 1970s that the broad Nikkei community, bolstered by the civil rights movement and increased activism of the Sansei, began to speak out against the government's wrongful wartime acts. In 1970, the national JACL passed the first of three resolutions seeking compensation, or redress, for victims of injustice. By the next year, members of the Mid-Columbia JACL had raised $1,250, their goal over three years to support the redress fund. George Akiyama gave his view of the campaign: "I thought it was fair, I thought it was right." Nationally, however, Nikkei voices were not unified, either on their views of redress or on how to accomplish it,[39] although consensus did begin to form.

Several major events gave much-needed momentum to the redress movement. On February 19, 1976, thirty-four years after Executive Order 9066 set mass evacuation and detention in motion, President Gerald R. Ford revoked the order and called for "an honest reckoning . . . of our

national mistakes." In 1980, Congress created the Commission on Wartime Relocation and Internment of Civilians (CWRIC), which, the following year, heard emotional public testimony calling for reparations. That
same year, legal scholar Peter Irons uncovered evidence that the government knowingly suppressed evidence that disproved allegations of espionage made against Japanese Americans. This added to a tide of favorable
sentiment for Nikkei.[40]

*Personal Justice Denied*, the title of the CWRIC's 1983 report, aptly con-
veys its findings. The United States had acted on the basis of "race prejudice,
war hysteria and a failure of political leadership," it concluded. The result:
"a grave injustice was done to Americans and resident aliens of Japanese
ancestry." As a remedy, the commission recommended a congressional
apology signed by the president, establishment of a research and education
trust fund, and compensation of $20,000 to each survivor of the incarcera-
tion. Lobbied by grassroots campaigners in Washington, D.C., and twenty
thousand letters and mailgrams, Congress passed the Civil Liberties Act,
and President Ronald Reagan signed the bill authorizing redress payments
in 1988. The oldest living Issei received the first redress payments in 1990.[41]
Local veterans supported the act. "It was the right thing for the president
to do," Akiyama commented approvingly. Agreed Nishioka, "We were justified in asking the government for an apology and compensation."

### NIKKEI ACTIVISM AND THE HEALING PROCESS

Ever so gradually, Nikkei began to gain a foothold in Hood River. Their
farms and homes were responding to their care, and they were gaining the
trust of non-Nikkei neighbors and friends. And now, at long last, there was
vindication that they had indeed been wronged during the war. The local
community, too, began to recognize the dedication and composure with
which Japanese Americans redoubled their efforts to succeed. In an essay
published in a national journal, one resident lauded their "efforts toward
rebuilding their losses . . . with a courtesy and poise few of us would even
attempt under like circumstances."[42]

Locals in the valley began to meet each other halfway. "Most people in
Hood River are really good people," opined business owner Arline Moore.
"As for the noisy few who started all the trouble, their convictions weren't
as deep." So more and more Nikkei accepted invitations to join in the
broader public life. "We've just got to keep going on and doing something

for the community," remarked Nishioka. Noji agreed. "We had to uphold our end of the community welfare. It's only right that we return some favors. . . . When people were trying to ameliorate differences we might have had, I thought that was a real nice gesture to participate in their organization." Though he avoided the Rotary Club, where one negative vote could have blackballed him, Noji served on the county's irrigation board, hospital board, school committees, Federal Housing Administration Loan Committee, and the Hood River Electric Cooperative Board, of which he was president. Other Nisei veterans served just as vigorously, as chair of the county school board, county commissioner, Chamber of Commerce board member, president of the local Rotary Club, and, regionally, as the governor's appointee to the Columbia Gorge Commission.[43] The benefits were reciprocal. "I get more out of it than I put in," Noji admitted. "The healing process is working pretty good." Their visibility helped. "More and more people got to be better known, and they kind of understood that we were just people, too," added Jan Kurahara.

Nikkei did become better known. Joan Yasui, an early Sansei leader, was the topic of a 1959 news editorial in a state newspaper. Born behind barbed wire at the Tule Lake wartime camp, in 1959, she was elected not only president of Hood River's rural Wy'east High School student body but governor of Girls' State (a youth leadership and citizenship program), selected by high school representatives from each county. (In a twist of fate, the American Legion and Legion Auxiliary sponsored that national and state leadership program.) "May it ever be," the *Sunday Oregonian* concluded, "that a Joan Yasui will have full freedom to enjoy the honors earned by her own ability and personality, regardless of ancestry."[44]

In other ways, Nisei and their parents' homeland became part of the fabric of the community. In 1959, Jan Kurahara was named Hood River's Man of the Year. "It does show how far this community has come in taking the hate out of racial discrimination," reflected Kurahara. From 1965 to 1974, four other Nisei received Orchardist of the Year tributes, among them Mam Noji. Issei Shizue Iwatsuki was named Woman of the Year in 1973 for her work as a public servant, a leader in women's and Christian societies as well as the Methodist Church, founder of the Saga School for Japanese flower arrangement and tea ceremony, and a poet, honored that year by the Japanese emperor. A marble tribute inscribed with Iwatsuki's award-winning poem stands near the entrance to the local museum. In 1977, Hood River joined hands with Tsuruta, Japan, whose rolling hills, snowcapped mountain, meandering river, and fruit orchards made it an appealing "twin sister." Promoted by prominent Nisei fruit grower Ray Yasui, the sister-city program has thrived, with an active exchange program involving schools and citizens. During the spring of 2007, to commemorate the thirtieth anniversary of the program, the Hood River City Council renamed a park at one of its busiest intersections. Officials from both Hood River and Tsuruta marked the event by unveiling a black granite monument engraved with the message "Strong Ties and Friendship Will Last Forever" and planting twenty-three ornamental cherry trees, fourteen at the newly named Tsuruta Park.[45]

For the Hood River Nikkei, rebuilding their postwar lives was arduous, a gradual, often turbulent, process marked by emotional wounds, physical calluses, and lengthy government appeals. It meant awkwardly wading through "the pain, the resentment, the disillusionment and the community dissensions," as described by Tetsuden Kashima. It meant acquiring an antenna-like ability to detect "anti" feelings as well as maintaining low profiles in order to avoid antagonism. At the same time, Nikkei needed to develop their own armor, the better to survive prejudicial acts and comments. Indeed, they had withstood a "bona fide social disaster, replete with long-lasting dislocations and repercussions," certainly defying the popular view that historian Art Hansen criticized as one in which a "model minority" metamorphosed in "a puzzling miracle of race, ethnicity, and culture."[46]

"Imagine the deep psychological wounds the evacuation must have inflicted" on Nisei, empathized a local Sansei. Now, as the elder generation of Japanese Americans, Nisei were conflicted. On the inside, they concealed pain that they struggled mightily to endure, while on the outside, despite their words, they maintained an "impenetrable happy mask" that overcame their "wounded humanity." It was no wonder that, even today, "their hearts are full of unshed tears." Still, their angst has seeped out in subtle ways: through their hesitations or silences, through an overeagerness to see the positive, through occasional, unguarded comments. A study published in 1983 concluded that Nikkei, and Nisei in particular, saw a clear social boundary between themselves and the American majority population.[47]

After the war, their goal was simply to coexist and get on with their lives, as Mam Noji frankly explained. "There were a lot of doubts about acceptance. . . . We either avoided each other or avoided the subject . . . I'm surprised how well we got along, actually." There was one factor on their side though. "Time is a good healer. Eventually even the worst would probably talk to us, you know?"

# FOURTEEN

# *"Guilty of Courage"*

## DISCIPLINE BARRACK BOYS' APPEALS

**B**RANDED with dishonorable discharges, Kenjiro Hayakawa and Fred Sumoge also faced a lifetime of obstacles. Both had been cell-bound in Fort Leavenworth's disciplinary barracks for nineteen months, from October 1944 until May 1946. The stigma of military incarceration haunted them over the next thirty-seven years as they fervently challenged their records, all the way to the office of the president.

### LIFE CHALLENGES

Both Hayakawa and Sumoge visited Hood River after the war, but each ultimately chose to settle in Los Angeles. Their military records hampered them. "I could not get a good job or go to school because of my court-martial and dishonorable discharge," sighed Hayakawa. He moved to Salt Lake City in 1946 and spent three years pressing hotel sheets at his cousin's laundry before returning to Los Angeles, where he worked for ten years as a busboy and then as a night watchman and janitor at Lawry's Restaurant in Beverly Hills.

Sumoge's newfound outspokenness became both an asset and a draw-back as he navigated workplace challenges. In the Chicago factories where he spliced camera film and assembled lampshades, he spoke up against inequity and objectionable behavior. On one occasion, when he realized that others at the camera factory were paid fifty cents more than he was, he requested—and received—a ten-cent raise, earning ninety-five cents an hour in his second month on the job. And after hearing the burly lampshade factory manager swear, Sumoge pulled him aside, requesting that he watch his language and advising him that, rather than yelling when the machine broke, he could improve productivity by quickly repairing the equipment. After accompanying a friend to Los Angeles, Sumoge linked up with Fort Leavenworth buddies and decided he was in California to stay. Though it was "hard to get a job," he said, he finally found work at the Ontra Cafeteria, cleaning vegetables and washing pots. This time, though, Sumoge's sense of fairness had negative consequences. After he witnessed the cook persistently hollering at female employees, Sumoge "told him off." He remembered explaining, "These people are working hard so that you've got a job . . . so don't think you're a big shot. You have no reason to yell at them." A week later, he was fired. He later worked as a busboy at Lawry's Restaurant and as a produce clerk at a Grand Central Market produce stand.[1]

The impact of their courts-martial continued to burden the men. "I didn't think that we deserved all this," maintained Sumoge. "That's not right." Some DB boys immediately challenged their records. "Really going to town" in New York, as described by Sumoge, Hakuban Nozawa sent appeals to General Dwight Eisenhower and the director of Veterans Affairs in New York in 1946 while engaging an attorney to introduce legislation that would allow him to gain an honorable discharge.[2] For the next two years, he sought the "slightest of sympathy" for an early hearing in letters to President Harry S. Truman's secretary, the secretary of defense, the president's military aide, and even the former prosecutor at his court-martial.[3] Nozawa eventually sought help—though unsuccessfully—from George A. Spiegelberg, chair of the American Bar Association's Committee on Military Justice, and from influential liberal, syndicated columnist and radio personality Drew Pearson, based in Washington, D.C., and New York newspaper and radio commentator Walter Winchell.[4] In 1947, Sumoge also attempted, through Portland attorney Gus Solomon, to have a private bill introduced in Congress.[5] Advised that it was too soon after the war to take such action, the men were discouraged but not dissuaded.

## A SELF-APPOINTED CRUSADER

Jump-starting their crusade, a friend of one of the twenty-one released Nisei became the first of two allies to offer a defense. Charles Edmund Zane was indignant at the "obvious and absolute innocence of these Japanese-American citizens, and the obvious prejudice, spite, and cold indifference of the officers involved. . . ." A high school friend of one of the DB boys, he and Mas Kataoka had "a bond like real brothers." At school, they had traded skills: Kataoka tutored Zane in algebra, and Zane coached Kataoka in English. During the war, Zane stored the Kataoka family's Plymouth, furniture, and books and kept in touch by letter. After the war, his charitable nature became evident when he invited the homeless to join him for meals at the Kataoka home, an act regarded dubiously, but graciously, by his hosts.[6]

Zane was deeply affected by his friend's trial record. "These fellows . . . really had faith in what America was supposed to be. . . . They were not unpatriotic. They were not un-American. They were enduring situations that no citizen of the United States and no soldier of the United States should have been expected to take with silence." In Zane's mind, there was one underlying cause. "I think that the most ordinary kind of prejudice was at the bottom of it. . . . If they were guilty of anything, they were guilty of courage." Critical of the "travesties of justice" apparent in Kataoka's trial record, Zane pondered the situation, thinking, "Maybe I can do something about this." After examining the transcript, he resolved, "I'd better read the other ones."[7]

Zane became convinced he could help. From 1946, the year the men were released, he volunteered to take on the task of overturning Kataoka's court-martial and then committed himself to all twenty-one men. A self-described "clumsy college student" at the University of Redlands who did not "write naturally," Zane had plenty of will, but no legal background. Still, he dug in and organized "a lot of meetings" with the men, as Hayakawa recalled.[8]

Zane compiled transcripts of the twenty-one trials and queried the men: What did you and other Nisei talk about on the train to Fort McClellan? (The "secret and immediate transfer" of Nisei to Fort McClellan, answered Sumoge.) What did the men say while marching? ("We must speak to the commanding officer," wrote Sumoge.) Why didn't you step out when Major Aycock requested that of men who did not understand his order? (We were "waiting for explanation.") Zane persisted, compiling the men's applications and identifying discrepancies in trial testimonies, instances of the court's prejudice, and unreasonable claims and conclusions from the prosecuting attorney.[9] Fitting the pieces together like a "giant jig-saw puzzle," he drafted a brief, contacted military and public officials, and bolstered the men's spirits.

In September 1948, twenty-seven months after the men's release, Zane sent twenty-one applications for correction of their military records and five copies of his supportive brief to the Army Board for Correction of Military Records in Washington, D.C. He requested an open hearing and aimed to defend the men "independently as a friend of one of them, as an ex-G.I., and as a citizen whose duty it is to plead against any severe injustice." In the sixty-three-page, legal-size brief, Zane contended that the men were not tried and sentenced on the charge and specification upon which they were arraigned but for incidents that antagonized their officers and for their efforts to "talk things over and get things straightened out in their minds." (The four who spoke out most determinedly against discrimination received the harshest sentences, he pointed out. Fred Sumoge headed his list of names.) This self-appointed defender claimed that the twenty-one GIs were involved "in identically the same way in identically the same incidents" as seventy-eight who were never charged. Therefore, each was "entirely and absolutely innocent." Zane argued that certain officers were wholly at fault for provoking resentment and mental confusion that they ultimately tried to suppress through intimidation and by imposing court-martial sentences. Criticizing Major Aycock as "proud and pompous . . . impatient and harsh," he asserted that "it would have been an easy thing to ease the consciences of these men and to gain their willing cooperation." Zane also maintained that both the pretrial investigation and trial involved improper procedures, demonstrated prejudice, and drew early conclusions about the men. By their questions and unguarded comments, the investigator and various members of the court let slip their assumptions of the men's guilt.[10] In the body of his brief, Zane discussed each trial record one by one, pointing out testimony supporting his case.[11]

## SETBACK AFTER SETBACK

A month later, the Army Board gave Zane his first setback, explaining it did not review cases unless directed by the secretary of the army. The staff would, however, introduce applications to the secretary for his personal decision. After six months, on May 13, 1949, the board's staff notified Zane by letter, stating that there was "no justification for a formal hearing and review of cases." The screening had "failed to disclose any basis for a reasonable doubt of guilt or to reveal any indication of probable error or injustice in their trials or sentences." Bolstered by a six-page recommendation from the Clemency and Parole Board (which did acknowledge that, after December 7, 1941, "discriminations and prejudices became almost intolerable"), it contemplated no further action. At the same time, the Army Board cited another regulation that prevented it from reviewing general court-martial cases "unless directed by the Secretary of War."[12] Somehow, the process already seemed mired in bureaucratic shuffling.

Perplexed, Zane contacted Congressman Gordon L. McDonough of California's Fifteenth District. He believed so earnestly that the men were "palpably innocent," Zane wrote on May 24, 1949, that "even such a novice" as he would be able to obtain justice for them. "Tell us how to get this case heard just once by a completely impartial court," he requested. The next month, he learned that no further action would be taken unless "pertinent and material evidence" appeared that was not in the records. A new amendment to the Articles of War, effective February 1949, did authorize the judge advocate general (JAG), the senior legal officer and chief adviser in each branch of the military, to grant new trials upon good cause. Individuals should apply and would be reviewed separately.[13]

Zane acted quickly. The next week, undaunted, he requested that the Army Board retain the twenty-one applications. Implying that forty-three marching men could stop at the same time because they individually wished to disobey a marching order was "ridiculous," he alleged. "What is happening . . . to the tradition of justice in the United States?" In none of the twenty-one cases was a conviction unanimous, Zane continued. Two-thirds of the court voted for conviction in thirteen of the cases, and three-fourths did so in the other eight. "Two or three honest men in every convicting court voted against conviction," he concluded. Clearly, these Nisei were "victims of vengeance and prejudice," for the trial records were "full of obvious prejudice and improper and illegal procedure." Finally, convinced that the brief he had submitted made those arguments irrefutably clear, he queried, "Was the brief of arguments . . . read?" That same day, June 17, 1949, he wrote a letter to President Truman and was no less ardent. These twenty-one men were "guilty of nothing," he insisted. They were charged and tried "because they stood verbally by their principles." Give the brief to "someone you can personally trust," he entreated the president.[14]

On June 30, 1949, Colonel G. K. Heiss, special assistant in the Office of the Secretary of the Army, responded to both Zane's applications and his letter to the president, stating that there was "no basis for a change in the Secretary's decision." Evidence clearly showed that the men halted without authorized command and did not proceed to the field house. Again, there was no further action contemplated.[15]

Still, Zane was undaunted, now that he had studied all twenty-one trial records. He recommitted himself to the men's defense and wrote a letter to them. "Do not let this discourage you. I am as sure as ever that I can have your conviction reversed to 'not guilty' and more sure than ever of your innocence." He briskly dismissed the army's denial. "I have more proof and evidence than before. I have been re-studying these records during the past three weeks, and am positive that it will be easy to show your innocence to any Court."[16]

In September, Zane appealed to President Truman a second time, refuting Colonel Heiss's one-sentence explanation for denying open hearings. Each of the forty-three men stopped, Zane claimed, because men in front of them suddenly stopped, and "surely every man did not intend to disobey." He also denied Colonel Heiss's statement that the men were given "several opportunities," even one opportunity, to withdraw. There was no "sound reason" those men should not be heard, Zane implored, again asking President Truman to "vouchsafe such a hearing." These twenty-one men were tried while others who had engaged in identical behavior were released without penalty. Zane enclosed a revised, more comprehensive, 122-page brief, developed after indexing details from twenty-one trial records into thirty grids, from which he quoted testimony, deduced discrepancies, and refuted claims against the men. Once more, he begged the president to have the brief read by "someone whom you can personally trust" because "I cannot feel confident of the judgment of Colonel Heiss."[17]

Political pressure was ineffective even when a prominent New York bar member interceded. George A. Spiegelberg of the American Bar Association (who had been previously solicited by Nozawa) sought help from the president's military aide, Major General Harry H. Vaughan, to secure a presidential pardon for the men. In his letter of September 26, 1949, Spiegelberg stated that the Nisei were "victims of perhaps understandable but nonetheless inexcusable prejudice" and that their penalty seemed "nothing short of ferocious." Zane, too, went on the offensive with Major General Vaughan. At the beginning of November, he wrote to the president's military aide, detailing innumerable errors in the JAG's statements. Those inaccuracies ranged from the erroneous information that all the men enlisted or were inducted before December 7, 1941 (eight were inducted after that date), to the trial record's prejudicial statement that men were "demanding" to see their commanding officer (since no witness made that claim), to wide discrepancies in Major Aycock's testimony. This time Zane requested that the twenty-one men be found innocent and be compensated for the suffering that resulted from their unjust convictions. In his third and final letter to the president on November 2, 1949, Zane took issue with "the false, the exaggerated, and the slanted statements" in the JAG memo forwarded by Major General Vaughan. In his view, the president was the sole person who could give these men a fair court. "I beseech from you the chance to defend these men before a court," he pleaded.[18]

Attempting to influence public opinion, Zane sent fifty-five letters to prominent people, organizations, and publications. "I am more than ever convinced of the complete innocence of these men," he averred. Recipients of his lobbying blitz included the American Civil Liberties Union, the American Legion, the Red Cross, the JACL, members of the Supreme Court, the mass media, publications such as the *New York Times* and *Newsweek*, and government and military officials.[19] He galvanized the DB boys, urging them to contact their congressmen and penning a blanket letter. It began:

> Your attention is called to the troubles of a group of 21 men, of whom I
> am one. We know that we have been treated unjustly. We do not know
> what to do about it. We have just been denied a hearing before the last
> regular court empowered to reverse convictions in trials by Army Courts
> Martial. But we are totally innocent of any crime whatsoever, and we
> cannot help believing that we are still victims of the same prejudice
> and indifference by which we have already been sorely punished and
> deprived. We hope that you may be able to help us secure a hearing by
> some impartial court or individual.[20]

The army stuck to its position. Through G. K. Heiss, now a brigadier general, it notified Zane on November 4, 1949, that his latest brief failed to "reveal any basis for a change" in decision. A month later, John Cronkrite, executive secretary of the Army Board, referring to Zane's letter to the president, wrote that he could add nothing further to General Heiss's November letter.[21]

Was vindication implausible? In a July 1950 letter to D.C. journalist Drew Pearson, Hakuban Nozawa admitted, "I am afraid that Army is using tactics to pro-long our case until you forget about the whole things [sic]. Usually their red-tape extends to a year long vacation." That day, Nozawa also confided to Sumoge that it "looks to me that even Zane gave up the case." Not whipped yet, Nozawa rallied their cause: "Sumoge, don't give up the hope—eventually we'll win."[22]

## APPEAL AFTER APPEAL

Zane was not yet defeated. Two years later, in February 1952, he mounted one more appeal to the judge advocate general, submitting thirteen applications for new trials with a revised brief. This time, the six-year veteran of military rebuffs was unapologetically blunt. "Since you are going to reject them, please reject them quickly and lets [sic] get this gesture over with." Zane was so agitated by the army's multiple denials that he spoke his mind freely. "All you ever do is to make bold and absurd statements," he accused, while "unlike you, we offer testimony to prove everything we say." He corrected inaccuracies in military records, supported by examples from his scrupulous analyses of transcripts, and indicated biases signaled by officials' slanted word choices. Zane again condemned the "order-happy" Major Aycock, declaring that Aycock "lied deliberately and maliciously" when alleging that he ordered the men to the field house and offering the major's own trial statements as evidence. Still, he maintained, the trial judge advocate, the chief prosecutor, continually offered "unrestrained exaggerations of what Major Aycock said" as evidence. "Why be honest and straightforward when you don't have to . . . ," demanded Zane, pointing out the introduction of "attached papers" that were not part of trial records.[23]

"Justice? Hell." Zane went on, charging that the Army Board continued to deny allegations that the men had received unfair trials and that their sentences were unduly severe, underlining the prejudices of Major Aycock, Lieutenant Mallon, and members of the courts (the latter tagged as "prigs and bigots"); the prosecutor's "unethical and dishonest tactics"; the "trivial, indifferent, and timid defense"; highly improper investigations of the charges; and the decision to allow many men to answer questions and make statements that were not understandable. Fair trials? "Not by a long shot. Read these and weep (or laugh out of the side of your mouth)," he concluded. "Justice is not the business of the military." Zane's closing remarks forecast the army's response, releasing all the frustration that had coalesced during his six years of futile exchanges:

> I send you these applications for new trials. I send you a brief one hundred and thirty pages long. I send you back your summary of the case and, point by point, my corrections of its dozens of misrepresentations, corrections each of which is substantiated by references to specific testimony in the trial records. You will not have the brief read. It will be determined in your office that it would be inconvenient to reverse these twenty one convictions. You will deny the applications. You will not grant new trials. As an American citizen, I address you with the greatest possible resentment and contempt.[24]

By June 9, 1954, the situation appeared hopeless, even after appeals to General Eisenhower and the JACL. The time limit for submitting petitions had expired on May 31 1952. "It is not considered appropriate that further action be recommended by this office," wrote Lieutenant Colonel A. G. Eger, chief of new trials for the judge advocate general.[25]

"So carry on, carry on," Sumoge declared. "You just keep going. . . . It wasn't easy." Saddled with their dishonorable discharges, Hayakawa and Sumoge settled for jobs that did not require security clearances. Hayakawa's health suffered when he worked as a night watchman and janitor, so in 1960, he and his wife of ten years began a gardening business, which gave them the flexibility to look after their four children.

For Sumoge, the daily routine at Fort Leavenworth's disciplinary barracks had rekindled his career interest. Listening to radio programs in his cell and working in the prison radio lab revived a curiosity in electronics that had begun with a prewar correspondence course. How was it possible for sound to travel through thin air and emerge from a small box? Admittedly "kind of curious" and encouraged by his wife, Sumoge attended technical school at night while working at a produce stand during the day. The inner workings of the radio and television—and later the transistor radio and color TV—fascinated him. Though he was turned down for federal defense work because of his military record, Sumoge became an electronic technician in 1952, servicing radios and TVs for small and large companies, including J. C. Penney.

By the late 1970s, with their freedoms restored after more than two years of imprisonment, Kenjiro Hayakawa and Fred Sumoge viewed their futures with newfound optimism. "You can start to breathe fresh air," rejoiced Sumoge. "You don't see any more guns around. . . . You're not fenced in. You're sort of free."

## A RENEWED CAMPAIGN

Thirty-three years after their release from Fort Leavenworth's disciplinary barracks, a propitious family bond, coupled with a more open-minded climate, became pivotal in the search for justice by Hayakawa, Sumoge, and nine other DB boys. Their interest was reawakened after Tim Nomiyama, one of the men, revealed his secret to a family member. Reluctant at first about the romance between his daughter and Paul Minerich, the grandson of Slavic immigrants, Nomiyama reversed his opinion when he recognized that, despite the discriminatory behavior of some Americans, "white people were good and bad, just like us." After his daughter married the law student, Nomiyama showed his new son-in-law the court-martial papers, which revealed the struggles that had shaped his wariness and search for equity. Young Minerich vowed to fight back for his father-in-law, who invited other DB boys to join and help defray expenses. Of the twenty-one, Nomiyama was able to contact eleven (two from Chicago, one from Japan, one from Utah, and seven from Los Angeles) who agreed to pursue the quest to change their records. (Some were reluctant to open their past to scrutiny, especially if they had not revealed these incidents to family members.)

While Charles Edmund Zane strongly supported Minerich's efforts, ceding responsibility for his eight-year-long case was wrenching. Once stalwart in his belief that justice would prevail, he had found himself powerless to outmaneuver the military bureaucracy and had been stymied by an era in which citizens tolerated incarcerating fellow Americans. In a personal letter to Minerich, Zane revealed his shame, guilt, and sense of failure: "It is hard to see innocent and gentle men, and their families, treated with such cruel irresponsibility by a government supposed to be fair and impartial. . . . If I were going to have a heart-attack or a stroke (or more probably an apoplectic fit), the great rage and grief of these thoughts would bring it on."[26]

Three decades after Zane's first appeal to the Army, twenty-seven-year-old Minerich approached the military courts with several advantages. For one, he would initiate his appeal during what he called an "era of Japanese American redress and reparations," when the government would admit the calamity of what he labeled "our worst wartime mistake." Instead of looking upon the men "as 'Japs' and 'enemy,'" which Zane had found so abhorrent, judges would rightfully view them, in Zane's hopeful words, "as human beings and American citizens."[27]

In fact, when a 1976 presidential proclamation formally rescinded Executive Order 9066, it also took a major stride in transforming the public persona of Japanese Americans. Recognizing "one of our national mistakes" as a "setback to fundamental American principles," President Gerald Ford called on citizens to affirm the American promise, "that we have learned from the tragedy of that long-ago experience forever to treasure liberty and justice for each individual American, and resolve that this kind of action shall never again be repeated." Four years later, President Jimmy Carter would sign a public law that created the Commission on Wartime Relocation and Internment of Civilians (CWRIC), charged with examining the wartime detention and its impact, reviewing military directives, and recommending "appropriate remedies" to Congress. By then, a change in the Nisei political landscape was also visible. Senators Daniel Inouye of Hawaii, S. I. Hayakawa of California, and Spark Matsunaga of Hawaii cosponsored legislation that was endorsed by Congressmen Norman Mineta and Robert Matsui, both of California, as well as the Japanese American Citizens League.[28]

With a more responsive public that was no longer entrenched in "wartime hysteria," more Nisei in prominent national positions, and a year's experience practicing law, Minerich had advantages that Zane did not. He also had Zane. When he acquired Zane's excruciatingly detailed paperwork in 1979, Minerich astutely and compassionately maintained ties with the "good man who made a Herculean and unselfish effort" and who "could've been Ernest Hemingway" but who had still met with failure. Admittedly, the "completely inexperienced" Minerich, brimming with good intentions, "hadn't the faintest idea" how to undertake the process. The novice attorney began by reviewing Zane's documents and background literature, studying attorney Frank Chuman's *Bamboo People* for the legal history of Nikkei, and contacting a Los Angeles veterans' group for guidance on upgrading discharges. Minerich prepared his first draft for the DB boys to review in January 1980.[29]

On June 3, 1980, a month before the CWRIC was signed into law, Minerich submitted a new brief, with personal statements from the men and a support letter from Zane appended, to the army's Office of the Judge Advocate General. This would lend a "new perspective," he proposed, beginning with the notion that these men actually were not tried for willfully disobeying a superior officer. Instead, he maintained, they were tried for exiting through the left door, a "relatively mild civilly disobedient action" taken against the "utterly repugnant treatment" not only of the men but of all Nikkei during the war. Minerich made no effort to challenge the "legal sufficiency" of the record, which Zane had unsuccessfully attempted in 1949. He centered his case on the men's choice—their moral conviction and right—to "demand an explanation for the unconstitutional and immoral acts of the government at the time."[30]

Laying the historical groundwork in a brief that was more clear and less rambling than Zane's, Minerich described the wartime paranoia against Nikkei "victims of bigotry," quoting historian Roger Daniels's statement that the myth of military necessity was "a fig leaf for a particular variant of American racism." While Minerich acknowledged that resistance was an exception to the more typical submissiveness of Japanese Americans during the war, he identified other ways in which Nikkei demonstrated that "patriotism does not require submission." There were those who had opposed the JACL's stance of cooperation and compliance, answered "no" on the loyalty questionnaire, and refused military induction.[31]

On behalf of the nine applicants from Company B, Minerich debated points from past testimony: Major Aycock did not actually give an initial order for the men to march to the field house; "willfulness" on the part of the men was wholly lacking, for they did not stop with an intent to disobey; and the men never had the chance to resume marching to follow the alleged order. "Unforgivably," the men were not able to "express their disquietude." In his brief, Minerich also defended a man from Company A and another from Company C, each arrested for refusing to fall out after hearing General Philoon's speech informing the soldiers that they could speak to their commanding officers.[32]

All eleven men, Minerich concluded, had the right to request clarification from the government for their unjust military treatment. They needed hope that they could "participate in the same rights and ideals they were willing to fight and die for." No, he continued, we could not expect "blind fidelity" to the mechanism of injustice. Again quoting Daniels, he noted that "there are those . . . who will find more heroism in resistance than in patient resignation," Minerich closed with a concise appeal: "Justice and good conscience demand that these men be given an honorable discharge. A mistake has been made and history is seldom so generous as to allow it to be corrected in enough time to help those originally hurt."[33]

In December, the men were notified of the JAG's decision: honorable discharge certificates would replace their dishonorable discharges. This act of clemency took into account the men's "34 years of demonstrated good conduct and citizenship" despite the handicap of their punitive discharges. "Happy," was the reaction of Hayakawa's wife, Yoshiko. "After all, we live here and our kids are here." Likewise, "as long as you're living here," Sumoge agreed, "that was an accomplishment." Still, he understood that "it's just a paper," noticing that the army's action did not set aside their general court-martial convictions. "We didn't get the back pay. The record wasn't corrected." So Sumoge and Mas Kataoka approached Minerich again: "If you can, please, correct the record, including back pay, mustering out pay (bonuses to help servicemen begin lives as civilians), and everything we should get. Otherwise, being a civilian is really nothing." Minerich, too, admitted in his letter of congratulations to Zane that in declaring the action one of clemency, the army did not acknowledge wrongdoing. "Perhaps that is more than we could possibly hope for," he commented. Still, he would ask the men if they wished to pursue the matter further.[34]

The men agreed, and Minerich plowed ahead. Maneuvering between various departments of the army and the Board of Veterans' Appeals, he gained counsel from a national expert on upgrading military charges. San Francisco attorney Thomas W. Turcotte also offered encouragement, adding that the men's previous victory represented a "tacit admission" by the army that "an incredible injustice occurred." On September 15, 1982, a Mr. Tyler from the Pentagon called Minerich's secretary to set up a hearing, commenting that these "fellows got a real rotten deal."[35]

A HEARING AT THE PENTAGON

Two years after their initial success, on December 8, 1982, the men had their day in court. Their case would appear before the Army Board for

Correction of Military Records at the Pentagon in Washington, D.C. As required by law, the five Army Board members who would try their case were civilian employees of the Department of the Army. Six of the DB boys, including Kenjiro Hayakawa, accompanied Minerich.[36]

The men's request was fourfold, Minerich explained at the hearing: vacate their court-martial convictions, as if they had never existed; change the reason for their army release from general courts-martial to the expiration of their terms of service; change their date of discharge to June 7, when their service would normally have ended; and restore their back pay from March 1944, their date of transfer to Fort McClellan, through June 7, 1946.[37]

The real issue, Minerich maintained from the outset, was the men's decision to exit by the left door. Offering a "historical-moral-constitutional perspective," he justified their actions by arguing that it was unreasonable to expect "blind obedience" to the very government and military that had caused the injustices the men had suffered. Their actions could not be separated from the historical setting. The government's wartime treatment of Japanese Americans was based on false reasons: There was no military necessity. There were no documented acts of sabotage or espionage. Currently there were efforts to recognize and rectify that wartime mistake, Minerich added, citing intentions of the CWRIC, the state of California, and Los Angeles County to compensate wartime victims.[38]

In support of his premise, Minerich invited oral statements from four of the men (and included written statements from Hayakawa and Sumoge in his evidence), clarified questions from Army Board members, and rebutted their queries. Wasn't everybody treated equally in the army and expected to obey orders? the Army Board asked. "There are fundamental principles of our Constitution and the democratic principles upon which the country is based that go beyond having to obey an order," Minerich explained. He quoted statements from government officials supporting the "military necessity" argument that had since been proved "utterly false." These courageous men demonstrated human dignity in their own way. "You have to have a pretty good reason to do something not consistent with what your commander wants you to do," he insisted. And if there was ever such a situation, this was it. How were these men treated differently? the board wanted to know. The difference was the historical context and circumstances of that time, which justified the relatively mild action the men took, Minerich replied. Why didn't they speak out when the relocation started rather than on the eve of combat training? The events "twisted their minds," for they were "good soldiers" until they decided, "Well, this is the last that it can go." Would you have a problem if a Caucasian took the same action? asked the board. This incident "flew in the face so dramatically of basic, fundamental constitutional and human principles that it warranted some type of speaking out," Minerich rejoined.[39]

The Army Board interspersed further questions between the men's testimonies and Minerich's responses: What about the country's security? No legitimate reasons existed for treating Japanese people differently than Germans, Italians, or others. How is this different from Vietnam veterans' protests as a matter of conscience? There was the immediacy of the internment and relocation. Your sense of duty to country could lead you to fight or lead you to uphold the country's fundamental principles. These men chose the latter, and they chose to express their concerns. What constitutional rights were usurped? Due process and equal protection, according to Minerich. While the court-martial did follow due process, court-martial summaries indicated the court's tendency to think that the men were more loyal to Japan than to the United States. Were constitutional rights ever challenged in courts? Yes, but the U.S. Supreme Court upheld decisions in the Hirabayashi, Yasui, and Korematsu cases because it deferred to the military's groundless finding of "military necessity." In the Mitsuye Endo case, Minerich said, the Supreme Court held that the government could not detain loyal citizens (although it did not actually rule on the constitutionality of detention itself). So the men chose not to follow legal procedures in vindicating their constitutional rights? The framework for raising these questions was not in place. The men felt that the court-martial was the only forum in which they could present their feelings, Minerich concluded.[40]

Steering away from factual disparities that Zane had previously argued in vain, Minerich recentered his debate. He firmly placed the incidents within their historical context and founded the men's actions in constitutional principles. Near the hearing's end, his mention of the Supreme Court's Endo decision (that the government could not detain "concededly loyal" persons against their will) became a critical question for the Army Board chairman, Gordon M. Hobbs, especially because it occurred on December 18, 1944, after the men had been confined for six months. Within the last few minutes, Hobbs paraphrased Minerich's statement that the men "didn't or could not have filed suit to vindicate what they felt was a violation of the constitutional rights of their family, relatives and friends." He then affirmed from their testimony the men's decision to "take the court-martial and thereby be given the opportunity to make a statement about what they felt was a violation of their constitutional rights."[41] The hearing was over within four hours.

## AN ANSWER

Their answer came forty days later, on January 17, 1983. The Army Board did not set aside their court-martial convictions, but it did recommend that their military records be corrected and it reinstated their military benefits. By a three-to-two decision, it voted to rescind the men's sentences after two years (the period of their imprisonment), void their dishonorable discharges, and indicate that on May 31, 1946, they were honorably discharged due to the expiration of their terms of service. The Army Board still found no basis for setting aside the men's convictions, though it admitted in its written conclusions that their sentences appeared to be too severe. "Their actions were more in the nature of a protest" rather than an "outright refusal to undergo combat training," it acknowledged. The two dissenting members maintained that the men's refusal to obey orders was a direct attempt to avoid combat duty, that they were aware of conditions in the camps for more than two years, and that their willful disobedience of orders avoided assignment to the high-casualty 442nd Regimental Combat Team.[42]

Still, the eleven DB boys, led by Minerich and Zane, achieved a partial verdict since leaving Leavenworth thirty-six years before. The Army Board's conclusion affirmed what the men had maintained all along: that military actions to confine them for more than two years were "an injustice."[43]

Among the small number of Nisei who spoke out during the war, the DB boys had a distinct podium. Other Japanese American protesters included those who challenged the removal and detention of American citizens (Minoru Yasui, Gordon Hirabayashi, Fred Korematsu, and Mitsuye Endo), those who refused to report for the draft (the Heart Mountain Fair Play Committee and others from the Poston, Tule Lake, Granada, and Minidoka camps), those who answered "no" and "no" to questions 27 and 28 on the loyalty questionnaire, and a Nisei journalist who stood against mass incarceration and defended the Fair Play resisters (James Omura).

After thirty-six years and a hearing at the Pentagon, the DB boys celebrate their honorable discharges from the army. Kenjiro Hayakawa is at the far left in the front row. Fred Sumoge is second from the right in the back, and Charles Zane and Paul Minerich are standing to his left. (Kenjiro Hayakawa, 1982)

All refused to comply with government or military orders, and all believed their rights as citizens were compromised.[44] The DB boys were serving in the U.S. armed forces, where discipline and hierarchy were explicit values, liberties were restricted, and order was expected. Legally and ethically, they still stood their ground.

On the legal issue, the Bill of Rights was on their side eventually. "The guarantees of the Bill of Rights and other constitutional provisions were not abrogated by the existence of the war," declared Judge Louis E. Goodman in 1944, after dismissing charges against twenty-six draft resisters from Tule Lake. The First Amendment guarantees the right "to petition the government for a redress of grievances," and the Fifth Amendment forbids depriving any person of "life, liberty, or property, without due process of law." In the absence of those rights, the men viewed the court-martial as the last resort for expressing their feelings. In fact, criticisms of the inconsistencies in the military justice system, which is different from the civilian system and "so dependent on the will of the commander," were so significant during World War II that the government instigated major changes. After the war, the new Department of Defense created a common code of justice for the military, which was enacted in 1950. The new Uniform Code of Military Justice was dedicated to protecting the "rights of men and women in uniform by providing numerous procedural safeguards for the individual and by ensuring that courts-martial have sufficient independence to enforce those safeguards." The military also included the concept of civilian review, a process followed during the DB boys' successful appeal at the Pentagon.[45]

On the ethical side, Zane had pinpointed situations that "no citizen of the United States and no soldier of the United States should have been expected to take with silence." Minerich, too, criticized the contradictory expectation that the men show "blind obedience" to the government and military that had caused their injustices. "It is shocking to the conscience," Judge Goodman had likewise maintained in his 1944 ruling on the Tule Lake resisters, that "an American citizen be confined on the ground of disloyalty, and then, while so under duress and restraint, be compelled to serve in the armed forces, or be prosecuted for not yielding to such compulsion."[46]

For the DB boys, the 1983 decision was cause for elation, though they remained anonymous. "I think this is possible only in America," enthused Hayakawa. "I was sweating. That was close," Sumoge added happily. During the hearing, their young attorney had stated, "World War II for these men, I think, should be put at an end."[47] Now it was appropriate to do so. The men could get on with their lives, unencumbered.

PART IV

# TODAY

# FIFTEEN

# *"Opening the Closets of History"*

## THE COMMUNITY TODAY

**M**Y dad used to say you could shoot a cannonball down the main drag and never hit anybody," recalled Hood River native Howard Rice. "Now you have to be careful not to hit a 'boardhead,'" he commented, referring to the influx of windsurfers, kiteboarders, and snowboarders. For sure, this tiny farm community in the Cascade foothills is on a fast track toward economic and demographic change that has eclipsed days past. It has, in fact, metamorphosed into what one land use planner has called the "funky capital of a premiere outdoor sports region."[1]

### CHANGES

The wind that old-timers once cussed at, the water, and the mountains attracted 640,000 tourists during 2005 alone and has stimulated a 60 percent population surge in Hood River since the postwar days. In 2009, the percentage of visitors who came to the area for outdoor activities was nearly double the percentage for the rest of the state. Propelled by fifty-mile-per-hour winds during the summer, colorful sailboards and kiteboards now scoot across the waters of the Columbia, while, farther inland, kayakers head upstream and cyclists hit the mountain trails. During winter months, skiers and snowboarders set off for snow-packed runs on the slopes of Mount Hood. The downtown core, bolstered by its reputation as a tourist mecca, has been revitalized with upscale bistros and boutiques, windsurfing shops, galleries, and residential lofts. Businesses manufacture aerospace equipment, sports gear and clothing, liquor, beer, maritime products, and glass.[2] Today a conglomerate of "boardheads" and active professionals rubs shoulders with locals, adding a new cultural and social dimension to this community in transition.

The economic picture has shifted too. Logging and jobs in the wood products industry declined beginning in the 1970s. Pears and cherries have supplanted the once-favored Hood River apples as the area's most lucrative local crops, and the valley leads the world in producing Anjou pears. Its fifteen thousand acres of orchards now produce nearly half the nation's winter pears. Adding to its market appeal, the pear, Oregon's top fruit crop, became the state fruit in 2006. Still, employment in the agriculture industry has dropped 8 percent since 1950, affected by more mechanized production, competition from cheaper foreign fruit, higher costs and lower prices, and a corresponding increase in food manufacturing. Now just one-fifth of valley jobs involve producing and packing crops,[3] which have diversified to include nuts, berries, wine grapes, vegetables, and herbs. Among the local farmers are twenty or so Sansei,[4] who continue the tradition their parents and grandparents began on family orchards. Several have added produce stands, increasingly popular along scenic roadsides. Others join in the community's special events, which attract out-of-towners to such galas as the Hood River Blossom Festival, Harvest Fest, and Heirloom Apple Days.[5]

"Hood River is a microcosm of the state of Oregon," county administrator David Meriwether stated, based on what he had discerned from the community's cultural, philosophical, and political make-up. He noted that the valley's span of rural and urban, agricultural, and forest communities mirrors the spectrum visible in the state. In town, the "more urbane, liberal constituency" contrasts with the "more conservative and agriculturally oriented" residents in the rural areas, he observed. This new range, according to historian and resident Eckard Toy, contributes to a tug-of-war between longtime residents who are mindful of preserving the small town's roots and valley newcomers and their more politically liberal "new age sentiment." As can be expected, those differences emerge in debates on such issues as environmentalism (including complaints about the use of pesticides on farms) as well as property development (from the prospect of subdivisions and businesses on farmland to increased commercialization of the nearby Mount Hood Meadows ski resort).

Adding to the mix is a rise in ethnic diversity, for in 2000, a quarter of Hood River county's populace was Hispanic, a fivefold increase over twenty years.[6] These contract laborers who once returned to Mexico at the end of the seasonal harvest have, like the Issei before them, gradually settled down with their families, some leaving farmwork for steadier, better-paying jobs. Locals see and hear the impact of entwining cultures, from displays of Mexican staples at grocery stores to the cadence of Spanish language at their schools and businesses. A number have made efforts to involve Latino families, such as inviting them to their churches. Others recognize the same community resentment that the Japanese endured: Why don't these newcomers learn our language? Why don't they adopt our culture? Is it possible they will take over and run the country? Some sense an unwelcoming climate, though locals still clearly favor hiring laborers who work for less pay.

In the seven decades since World War II began, dramatic changes are evident in the valley. With Hood River's revitalized physical and cultural landscape and the passage of time, the Nikkei community is much different, as is its relationship with its white neighbors. Out of the wounded past, challenges, lessons, and possibilities are emerging.

## FEWER JAPANESE AMERICANS

While the Latino population is on the increase, the number of Nikkei in the valley is shrinking. In 2000, 238 Japanese American residents accounted for little more than 1 percent of the county's population and were less than two-thirds of their 1950 number. Two factors effected that decline and altered the climate. First, with the death of the last surviving Issei woman in December 2000, the early immigrant Japanese are gone from the valley; even the number of Nisei is dwindling. Succeeding second, third, and fourth generations of Japanese Americans, all U.S. citizens, are less and less familiar with the language and customs of their more tradition-bound ancestors. "We Nisei are more Americanized than our parents were," explained Ruth Akiyama. "There's no language barrier anymore, and Sansei are more educated." Membership in the main Nikkei organization diminished to such an extent that the Mid-Columbia JACL dissolved in 2006.[7]

A second aspect is the growing biracial nature of the Nikkei population, owing to the greater acculturation of succeeding generations and, earlier, the repeal of antimiscegenation laws (in 1959 in Oregon, and in 1967 when the U.S. Supreme Court declared Virginia's antimiscegenation law unconstitutional). "Some old-timers may be turning over in their graves," suggested Mam Noji. "There's a lot of intermarriage. I'm gonna guess that in a few generations there'll be a lot of blondes with Japanese names." Though there was little interracial dating among young Nisei, a marked difference is apparent in the generations that follow. Among the sixteen Nisei veterans whose names were removed from the county honor roll, only one married a non-Japanese. But forty of their forty-one children, members of the Sansei, contributed to Japanese Americans having the highest rate of outmarriage among AsianPacific Islander Americans. Nationally, 31 percent of the Nikkei population identified themselves as multiracial in the 2000 census. In Hood River, 23 percent of Nikkei married outside their race. According to Harry Kitano, key factors in outmarriage were acculturation and generation (related to less family control and the adoption of American ways), as were locales (such as Hood River) with fewer Japanese Americans.[8] "Another generation, I don't think the Japanese will be Japanese anymore," quipped veteran and retired civic leader Jan Kurahara.

CHANGING ATTITUDES

That vision of intermingling cultures contrasts sharply with the community's divisive image during the early twentieth century. The past *was* a horrendous burden to bear. But Nisei today would rather speak of change. "To tell you the truth, the community now is nothing like it was sixty years ago," remarked Kurahara. "I mean, the people are different, the atmosphere is different. . . . I don't know how it all happened, but it did." Then, in a more reflective mode, he added, "A lot of the people didn't really have any prejudice one way or the other. They were just scared to talk up."[9] Mam Noji assented. "Today I cannot think of any one person who is not friendly. I really can't." Offered Shig Imai, "Well, we're a part of the community, just like the rest of them. The kids are all accepted in the high schools and there's no problem there. I mean, they don't discriminate openly." Then, more tentatively, he added, "I don't think they do." In their optimistic view of the present and their ever hopeful outlook on the future, what was left unsaid did signal an undercurrent of insecurity still felt by Nikkei. Psychologist Donna Nagata characterized the wartime consequences for Nisei as "a direct assault on their self-esteem, their expectations, and their identity as Americans."[10]

Hood River natives who lived through the war also prefer to shutter their pain from the past and focus on the present. "The Japanese Americans right now are just part of the community," commented self-described "professional volunteer" Kathleen Nichols. "I don't set them apart." Retired orchardist and volunteer fire fighter Keith Lage agreed, "We don't even think about it now. We're a mixed-up community." Former mayor Bill Pattison reflected, "The situations that took place in '45 and '46 melt away awfully fast. . . . It was there, it was noticed, it was ugly at the time. . . . Those bad times will soon be forgotten. . . . Time has eroded most of the bad thoughts." Jane Rice, local news correspondent and school cook, remarked, "I think that we are living in different times. I don't think that there is anything like that going on. Better not be."

Residents' sentiments changed gradually, Kurahara observed, and in ways unspoken. "Time takes care of everything; then people are saying to themselves that this is natural now. 'We didn't ever treat you unwell.' You kind of grow out of the guilt complex after awhile. And pretty soon," noted Kurahara, "'He's my good friend now.'" Just one person expressed remorse to Kurahara for the way the community treated Nikkei. "I'm sorry the way they treated you so badly," the man apologized, leaving Kurahara to shake his head, since this acquaintance was part of that community. "Maybe it's self-defense," reasoned Kurahara. "You don't want to admit what's bad because otherwise it'd be all bad." Sometimes actions spoke louder than words. After Sab Akiyama began his downtown optometry practice in 1960, he was surprised that one of his new patients was the store owner who had denied him service after the war.

Just as Nikkei dealt with the trauma of their war years through what sociologist Tetsuden Kashima called "social amnesia," it seemed that many of their mainstream neighbors "forgot" as well. Both groups appeared to suppress their feelings and memories of emotionally charged events from the past.[11] Some resorted to denial. One aged local remembered Japanese as "good farmers, good neighbors, good friends." After the war, he maintained, there were few businesses that did not welcome Japanese back to the valley. His memory conflicted, however, with that of several Nisei who remembered this man personally refusing them service. Another resident expressed disdain for citizens who spied on their neighbors before the war. Nonetheless, this person's name appeared on the county registry of deputized spies. Pattison, the former mayor, cited long ago actions that went as far as eliminating physical evidence. "When something was politically or ethnically questioned by those in power, they purged that stuff, they dumped their files. Many files were burned in the late 1930s through 1945."[12]

Within their measured optimism about the present, an edgy self-consciousness about the past and a self-imposed hush on discussing it are still evident among the few remaining Nisei. "It is like an eerie crime scene, which nobody dares discuss," observed Sansei Joan Yasui Emerson.[13] A number of Nisei, in fact, resettled elsewhere after the war or chose not to return to the valley until decades later. Nisei still privately admit to a sense of lingering prejudice, disclosed Connie Nice, coordinator of the History Museum of Hood River. That will likely fade, she believes, only after their generation is gone. Longtime president of the Mid-Columbia JACL Nancy Ritz Tamura noticed that, on the one hand, residents who spoke out against Japanese Americans during the war seem to have reconciled their thinking. On the other hand, among Nikkei, she sees "some residual hanging out," even among Sansei who choose not to join organizations that discriminated against their families.

"It was the most miserable time in my whole life," admitted Mitzi Asai Loftus, one of the few native Hood River Nisei to speak and write candidly about those years. She suffered terrible loneliness after the war, even at church, where parishioners moved out of her pew, classmates in her Sunday school class avoided her, and the minister turned his head when she filed out. Because of the unbearable prejudice, she did not tell her parents she had changed her name from Mitsuko to Mitzi, and she left the valley for good after graduating from college. "I became 200 percent American and 0 percent Japanese," she declared, illustrating Nagata's premise that Nisei after the war tended to minimize their cultural heritage in their push to become "good Americans." Historian David Yoo also posited that "If Nisei chose not to highlight their racial-ethnic difference, they did so because their history offered ample evidence of how such markers could [be] used against them." Others recognized a Nikkei tendency to repress or deny their feelings or to rationalize what they had faced, which Amy Iwasaki Mass likened to their self-defense against pain.[14] "The hurt and pain," admitted a local Sansei, "still persists in all the Nisei I know, despite their words." She went on, "I can only imagine the deep psychological wounds the evacuation must have inflicted. . . . None of them want to cry and show weakness—a typical Japanese response. But their hearts are full of unshed tears. . . . History is determined by what people feel."

Nevertheless, many Nisei express their eagerness, as one described it, to put an impenetrable "happy mask over their wounded humanity" and move on. "War does a lot of strange things to our thinking," conceded Mam Noji. "You have to consider the atmosphere people were living in. You have to be generous about those people who lived under those conditions. They faced a lot of prejudice too. . . . I take my hat off to those people for trying to make right from what wrong they did." Time, of course, has had an effect. "One thing about life," observed Sab Akiyama, "you don't live forever, so most of those folks who were highly prejudiced are gone."

Historian Eckard Toy, an upper valley resident, described a "context of sadness" and a "certain puzzlement" about the differences and causes of racial strain. There was also a lack of awareness. "People don't all know about it," he added. With the passage of time, the demise of dissident community leaders, and the entry of a new generation of locals (including transplants) in the valley, many residents have scant awareness of their community's past.

### LESSONS AND LANDMARKS

That lapse in the community's knowledge of its past prompted various efforts to retell the story. One took place in the valley's classrooms. Nancy Moller, who recalled seeing the "No Japs" signs when she arrived during the war, revised the history curriculum when she taught at Hood River Valley High School four decades later. Her goal was to have students examine how their local community was caught up in racism and seek their own answers to how and why events occurred. For sixteen years, students in Moller's twentieth-century United States history course paired up during the oral history portion of their projects, interviewing valley Nisei who had been incarcerated. This fifteen-day "Japanese Minority" unit extended from 1972 through 1988. Her students, initially anxious, returned from their interviews full of information—as well as reports of tasty refreshments their hosts had served. One of the most interesting outcomes, according to Moller, was learning that Sansei knew little to nothing about what their parents had experienced.

The lessons made racism more palpable. Student Marty C. confessed, "I didn't even know that Japanese Americans were sent away to camps until I took this class. . . . I know that I wouldn't have wanted to be shipped off to some camp, because I've lived in places like that for the summer and it wasn't good." Some felt that open prejudice was almost nonexistent in their community. Students Sid S. and Jerry P. believed that, during the early seventies, Japanese Americans in the valley were accepted just as other law-abiding citizens were, citing the percentage involved in county and school government. They concluded, "If people got to know each other better, we believe prejudice would not exist."

Other students believed that racism was still prevalent. Lark S. broadened her view in 1973 when she polled sixty-five people younger than twenty years old. Among her respondents, 74 percent believed that racism still existed in the valley, although half of those rated it as "little." Still, 12 percent answered that they would oppose a son or daughter becoming engaged to someone outside their race. In her investigation of open prejudice in the valley, Charlene G. interviewed the Exalted Ruler of the local Elks Association. She learned that the Elks' policy still included the "white clause" excluding nonwhites from membership and that the local lodge had voted to remove that clause; the National Convention abolished the clause a month later, in October 1973. Student Peter M. thought that those still in the "silent hating business" might have produced a "hidden effect" that could cause "reluctance by some Japanese Americans to get involved in the community." Had it not been for the "Great American Mistake," he mused, we might even have a Japanese American governor. Val W. concluded, "I feel that the Japanese suffered a lot during this time and in some ways they still do. I personally would like to put the Americans in this same situation and see how they would react."[15] What she forgot was that most "Japanese" were Americans, too.

In 1994, the first local exhibition about the local Nikkei wartime experience was displayed, forty-nine years after Japanese Americans returned to the valley. This traveling exhibition from the Smithsonian National Museum of American History in Washington, D.C., depicted the history of the first Japanese settlers and linked to a parallel exhibition on Issei in Oregon. After showings in Portland, Salem, and eastern and southern Oregon, the show still had openings in its schedule to travel to other communities. Would Hood River be interested? Oregon's exhibit coordinator, George Katagiri, understood the apprehension that Hood River Nikkei might feel. After all, the third and fourth generations felt accepted, and the exhibit "might rock the boat."[16]

Third-generation Finnish American and president of the Mid-Columbia JACL at the time, Maija Annala Yasui saw a chance for healing. "If you aren't sharing that story, you're going to be a part of the same thing happening again," she warned. The Yasui family added a local voice by offering an extensive collection of artifacts and records from their prewar store and farm, and volunteers sifted through fifty years of mice droppings to uncover fifty boxes of belongings in the Yasui packing shed. On May 21, 1994, *In This Great Land of Freedom: The Japanese Pioneers of Oregon* opened in Hood River. Its venue was significant: the Hood River American Legion Hall, home to the organization that had led the campaign against returning Nikkei. Longtime manager Marge Kageyama, married to a Nisei veteran, quickly and decisively agreed, even requesting that Legionnaires repaint the dark entry in order to provide an appropriate frame for local photos. Within less than two weeks, seven hundred visitors viewed the exhibition, and local students composed half that number. Two weeks after it closed, an affirming letter, written by Ruth Ellsworth of Hood River, appeared in the local newspaper: "The doors open where they had been closed, a view for us of democratic principles, the universal rights of humankind being denied, and now there's an awakening worldwide and a chance to participate together in welcoming our neighbors."[17] As Katagiri observed, "This is a way to make amends," though, being practical, he worried about discrimination aimed at other populations, including Iraqi citizens during the Gulf War.[18]

A second exhibition, which opened in March 2006, was also significant. When Connie Nice assumed her coordinator position at the History Museum, there was little outward evidence of the wartime fray. The museum housed several cases of "touristy" Japanese artifacts, and a three-page handout, "Culture of the Japanese in Hood River," passed over the years from 1925 through World War II. After researching a community member's inquiry, she said, she was "kind of shocked" to learn of the community's past. Envisioning an exhibition that would tell the missing history, she quickly sensed resistance from museum volunteers. They were reluctant to "open a can of worms" for fear that it would "offend their neighbors or the guy that sits next to them at church or the person that lives down the road or the guy they shop with at the grocery store." Not one to sweep history under the rug, however, Nice vowed to present the story in a professional, respectful manner and felt that, coming from outside the valley, she could do so objectively, without the "emotional baggage" of a longtime valley resident.[19]

In 2005, Nice convened a brainstorming committee of locals, including Japanese Americans. The group decided on when the story should begin and end and what artifacts and documents should be included. Their exhibition, "A Circle of Freedom: Lost & Restored," had four sections about the local Japanese American wartime experience: "Our Lives Before," "Our Lives Removed," "Our Lives in Camp," and "Our Lives in Service." The concise display would be semipermanent, with a kiosk to augment the story and featuring a DVD produced by Nice's son, Aaron.

David Meriwether, the county administrator who oversaw the museum, clearly saw the merits of the exhibition. "I understand that it can be sensitive information," he maintained, "but it is part of history . . . part of the public record." In fact, he understood more than most the intimidation that could arise from revisiting the past. His own great-grandfather had been a member of the Ku Klux Klan in the South. "That was a different time and a different place. . . . But I should not take that personally now in terms of reflection on me or on my kids," he explained. During the planning stages in 2005, Meriwether discussed the museum project with the County Board of Commissioners, which offered its support. Plans for the exhibition proceeded.

A surprising stash of documents contributed to the exhibit, although its source seemed unlikely. The local American Legion historian, Bud Collins, made the Hood River post's wartime letters and documents available to the local museum and to a Hood River native employed at the state Veterans Affairs office. (During the Legionnaires' move from their downtown quarters, they stored their files in a member's barn. When Collins discovered that mice had eaten through many of the papers, he salvaged two apple boxes full but burned the rest.)[20] "I could get rid of them next week and nobody'd know," he admitted. "I've been saving them for some reason." But he was realistic and honest in his assessment of the situation. "We all want to, you know, quit hashing it over, do away with it. But you can't turn your back on history. . . . These are the facts. This is history. . . . You may disagree with it, but it's too damn late to change it now." But, he concluded, "you can add to it."

The two county administrators closest to the exhibition shared Collins's outlook. "This is a great nation, and we've done many wonderful things," Meriwether declared. "This isn't one of them, and we always need to be mindful of how we treat and how we interact with each other." Nice, the museum coordinator, set personal goals for the exhibition. "I'm hoping that people will just stop and think: Could we do that again? Are we doing that again, with Latinos or Mexicans or Muslims? . . . I'm not saying that that little exhibit's gonna change the world," she admitted, but, she added, "I want people to walk away and say, 'Maybe we didn't do that right,' and I hope then that they're not going to repeat history."

Another community project set a goal of healing at its permanent tribute for Japanese Americans. The Central Gorge Master Gardener Association featured a Japanese memorial garden at its Oregon State University Extension Service learning garden. Members could "teach about art and gardening and peace—all in one place," according to project chair Rita Saling. In a 2006 letter to the *Hood River News*, she explained, "Hopefully, this will be a further step to help all of us heal from the long-time wounds." Designed by Japanese landscape architect Sadafumi Uchiyama and dedicated in 2010, the garden combines stone and water with plants from the town's Japanese sister city, Tsuruta. A one-hundred-year-old spruce tree anchors the Japanese garden, which faces the rolling Cascades and the lands developed by Issei. At the formal groundbreaking in 2007, local Nisei Cliff Nakamura recognized Caucasian friends and "veterans who knew what we went through during the war."[21]

## CONTINUAL CHALLENGES

Across the nation and the state, the wounds from war have been torn open in recent years. The terrorist attacks of September 11, 2001, caused the collective pulse of the entire country to skip a beat and generated fear so intense that an ABC News–Washington Post poll the next day reported that two out of three Americans were willing to surrender their civil rights in order to combat terrorism. The tenor of those discussions heightened as citizens likened the racial profiling that targeted Muslim and Arab Americans to that used against Japanese Americans during World War II.[22]

The following February, concerned citizens in Hood River presented a forum, "Civil Liberties in a Time of War: A Dialogue." Columbia River Fellowship for Peace, a peace and justice non-profit group, addressed current and past injustices, centering on the USA PATRIOT Act (which expanded the government's intelligence-gathering powers six weeks after

9/11), military tribunals, racial profiling, and detention. Speakers included a U.S. attorney, a former president of the ACLU of Oregon, and a Palestinian rights advocate. The audience gave a standing ovation to Dr. Homer Yasui of Portland, who made his first hometown public statement since World War II. Yasui told his family's wartime story, paid tribute to Hood River Nikkei, and read his own "roll of honor," naming local whites who had gone out of their way to support Nikkei during their difficult years.[23]

The Portland Nikkei community reacted even more swiftly, sponsoring its own educational forum just a month after 9/11. Its "Dialogue for Peace and Understanding" was intended to reach out to the Arab American and Muslim American communities, who made up half the audience. The program began with information on the suspension of constitutional rights when Japanese Americans were incarcerated, discussed Arab American stereotypes, related the fears of the Islamic community, and offered ways of dealing with racial prejudice and discrimination. Nikkei, Arab Americans, and Muslim Americans spoke, as did the Portland police chief. "We must stand in solidarity," asserted Scott Sakamoto, Portland JACL president, "with our Middle Eastern, Arab American, Muslim, and Palestinian brothers and sisters as well as all people who are the targets of racial or religious hatred." Later initiatives by the Portland Nikkei community involved speaking out on behalf of an Arab American held without charge in a high-security federal prison, participating in the Portland Joint Terrorism Task Force, and joining an Oregon Muslim community rally to condemn international violence and attacks against non-combatant civilians. In 2007, the program "Fighting for Civil Rights in an Era of Terror" presented information on threats to civil rights, both past and present. Issues ranged from the unsuccessful case *Yasui v. United States* (appealing Hood River native Yasui's conviction for violating the wartime curfew order) to the Foreign Intelligence Surveillance Act to local attorney (and Muslim convert) Brandon Mayfield's account of his wrongful jailing in 2004 as a "material witness" in the Madrid train bombings. Since then, annual programs have featured civil rights programs conducted jointly through coalitions with other communities, including the Latino and lesbian, gay, bisexual, and transgender communities.[24]

Public figures in Oregon and elsewhere have also drawn parallels between events in 1941 and 2001. During a radio broadcast in February 2003, U.S. Representative Howard Coble, a Republican from North Carolina, remarked that the World War II internment of Japanese Americans was justified. "It wasn't safe for them to be on the street," he commented, adding that some "probably were intent on doing harm to us, just as some of these Arab Americans are probably intent on doing harm to us." The JACL and the National Association for the Advancement of Colored People called for Coble's resignation, and the Democratic National Committee called for him to resign as chair of the House judiciary subcommittee on homeland security. Coble retained his post and reneged on his agreement to meet with the JACL.[25]

Two months later, a citizen in the southern Oregon town of Klamath Falls responded to plans for a memorial in nearby Newell, California, the site of the Tule Lake concentration camp by asking, "Can't you realize that the Japanese people were put under guard for their own safety?" If a memorial were built, "it would be a total disgrace and insult to our veterans," she objected. The next year, that same message permeated a book by syndicated columnist Michelle Malkin, who roused military historians, scholars, and bureaucrats alike with her book *In Defense of Internment*. She based her premise on data that the government's Commission on Wartime Relocation and Internment of Civilians had found inconsequential. Malkin's columns, blog, and numerous media appearances reached millions.[26]

Closer to home, another controversy with wartime roots festered in rural Gresham, east of Portland and fifty miles from Hood River. Gresham's city council made plans to quietly approve a monument in honor of a former mayor and doctor who had delivered more than five thousand babies. A city committee investigating Dr. Herbert Hughes's alleged directorship of Oregon Anti-Japanese Inc., a group opposed to the postwar return of Nikkei, concluded that his association with this group had been "temporary." A historical research volunteer commented that the good accomplished by the former mayor tipped the balance in his favor. Members of the Portland and Gresham JACL chapters flooded the city council's office and requested a fuller investigation. As a result, the council decided against erecting the monument and proposed a task force to involve experts in historical research.[27]

## A DAY OF REMEMBRANCE

Back in Hood River, a Sansei cultural and social advocate scored a coup by bringing in internationally acclaimed ukulele musician Jake Shimabu-

Joan Yasui Emerson welcomed more than five hundred guests to Hood River's Day of Remembrance, finally giving local Japanese Americans a "welcome home" party. (Kirby Neumann-Rea, *Hood River News*)

kuro to headline a fund-raiser for Bravissimo! Columbia Gorge Music and Arts Camp. When Joan Yasui Emerson (daughter of community leader Ray Yasui and niece of activist attorney Minoru Yasui) realized the event preceded the anniversary of a significant date in Nikkei history, she broadened the program's scope.

Thus it was that on February 18, 2007, the Hood River community came together to "break the silence" that had hung over the valley for sixty-five years. It did so, as the local newspaper reported, with "tales of fear, hatred, embarrassment, joy, friendship, and heroism" told to a standing-room-only audience of more than five hundred.[28] "We're opening the closets of history, sharing from the past," said Lawson Inada, Oregon's poet laureate and emcee for the event. He invited the audience to "open [y]our hearts, clear the air."

The Day of Remembrance commemorated the anniversary of the day, February 19, 1942, when President Franklin D. Roosevelt signed Executive Order 9066, authorizing the incarceration of Japanese Americans. The official commemoration, unanimously approved by Congress in 2004, had its roots in the Pacific Northwest, first marked in 1978 at the

George Akiyama and other Nisei World War II veterans stood to be recognized at
Hood River's Day of Remembrance. (Kirby Neumann-Rea, *Hood River News*)

Camp Harmony assembly center near Puyallup, Washington.[29]

During planning for the Hood River event, a range of community
members agreed on the purpose: "There are still people in this community
who say: 'But you people were the enemy. We all had to sacrifice during the
war.' And that is the educational job we have to meet for this day. As well,
many young people know nothing of this period of history."[30]

"Nobody ever gave the Nisei and Issei a 'welcome home' party. I guess
this is finally it, sixty-five years later," quipped Emerson. "Nowhere was the
vitriol and the demand for taking away the rights of American citizens of
Japanese ancestry greater than in this valley," she remarked, noting that it
was no wonder then that silence hung over local history "like a shroud."
It was time, she maintained, to address "the shame that has been leveled
at the Japanese people," while those who suffered were still alive. With the
aim of seeking to understand what happens "when rhetoric overpowers
reason, when fear overpowers fairness, when crime and corruption take
the place of compassion and our Constitution," she organized exhibits and
a panel of Japanese Americans and "white folks" to lend their "voices in
this suffocating silence."[31]

"Notice how swiftly children slip into their parents' voices like a mask?" queried Hood River native Virginia Euwer Wolf, award-winning author of young adult fiction. She recalled her curiosity at school after the war when new classmates returned from camp, but how, as youngsters, they had been taught not to ask questions about what mystified them the most. "Simultaneously our community was teaching us one of the most ominous and lasting lessons we would learn, that we must not ask about what was in all those gaping adult silences." Because of that, "we would later pay such penalties for not knowing," she added. Nancy Moller recalled the naïveté of youth from her days as a high school teacher. When she spoke of what had happened to Japanese Americans during the war, her students objected, "That couldn't happen." "Just ask your parents," she told them. "The students did and got silence for an answer," she noted, which motivated her to design her intensive curriculum on Japanese Americans.

"What does it take for good men and women to rise up and bear witness to atrocities against other beings and assaults against our Constitution?" Emerson had asked. Other speakers described their lives after the bombing of Pearl Harbor and upon their return to the valley. They spoke of Hood River native son Minoru Yasui's challenge of the curfew and his appeal to the Supreme Court, and they honored the military service of Nisei GIs. Exhibits further captured the courageous stands of local citizens who were reviled themselves for speaking out in defense of Nikkei, offered literature about significant people and events, and promoted ongoing programs that would continue dialogue about civil liberties.

Still, there were skeptics who discredited any effort to memorialize the past. One resident privately commented to a county administrator, "Are they still complaining about that?" But the following week, two letters in the local newspaper captured the meaning of the event. "After too many years of silence," resident Gale Arnold wrote, "the Day of Remembrance opened the door to healing a giant rift in this beautiful valley. Those who had long endured this injustice were finally acknowledged and appreciated." In her letter of thanks, event coordinator Emerson pointed out that the Day of Remembrance was now a part of the valley's collective, mutual history: "After 65 years of silence, the sunshine seemed to break through the fog, as our history fought to be clothed in more truth and accuracy, and as it found its way into our consciousness. Burdens and pain, borne silently and alone, and years lost from the forced journey from Hood River, were finally mourned with tears, surrounded by the understanding and love of hundreds. . . . Once again, I stand in awe of the power of the people of a loving, hopeful community."[32]

Community members, whether assisting or simply attending this event, took giant steps toward confronting the ghost haunting their valley's past. Nikkei as well as their white neighbors were publicly coming to grips with the trauma that had consumed them. For Nikkei, that involved correcting distortions through community support, as scholar Chalsa Loo theorized. By publicly recognizing evidence of the government's injustice ("system blame," she termed it), Nikkei might move from self-blame and shame to more purposeful behaviors and admission that they were not at fault.[33]

## LOOKING AHEAD

In a candid reflection, containing a dash of futility laced with a touch of hope, veteran Mam Noji predicted, "We Japanese Americans will never become 100 percent acceptable. Why, there's a lot of *hakujin* who can't tolerate each other. This world's not perfect, you know. But it's come a long way." Considering the multiple issues that still plagued the country, the state, and the community, community members offered insights for addressing their future.

Two non-native locals spoke of keeping the dialogue alive. "You can always learn from the past," maintained Nellie Hjaltalin, who returned to her family farm after retiring from Portland's Meier & Frank department store. Lessons emerge from "what has happened and what mistakes you don't want to make again," she offered. Kathy Murray Nishimoto, former JACL president who was raised in Portland and married a Sansei orchard-ist, expanded that thinking. "We need to keep talking about it. I really feel we need to keep it in the public eye since 9/11. We have Arab-descent truck drivers picking up fruit from the packing house, and I have to remind our employees not to stereotype them. This is exactly what happened to the Japanese. . . . We just can't let it repeat itself. Hard, but talking about it all the time keeps it real."

Several residents resolved to address the roots of intolerance. Hood River native Nichols decried put-downs, more recently of the Hispanic population. "When I hear people talk about *them*, you know who they're talking about. 'We don't want *them* to be in our country,'" she added, echo-ing frequently heard comments. And, she admitted, "We have not always been the good guys. We have our dirty little faults." To offset that, Nichols advised, "Don't take anything for face value. Do your own studying about it. Is it fact or perception? Because we're people that are swayed easily." Museum coordinator Nice also addressed some of the reasons for intolerance and divisiveness. "We're all here as immigrants, with the exception of Native Americans . . . I think fear drives most prejudice. . . . We have to get to know who people really are. . . . We're so intolerant of other people's views." She continued, "They say that a community that forgets its roots has nowhere to go. . . . We need to learn from our mistakes and realize that if we become too divided, we will fall." Legionnaire and Meals on Wheels volunteer Bud Collins added simply, "The world is getting smaller and smaller. We've got to live together. . . . People need people."

For others, education was key. "There will always be the 'them' and 'us' as long as humans are going forward," began Pattison, the former mayor and retired insurance agent. From that interplay, he saw a negative force emerging. "Now, the ugliness may be just throwing bad words back and forth without anything, or you can grab an AK-47 and rat-tat-tat." But he offered a solution. "The answer to prevent that is education. If we can get this country more and more educated, the fewer problems we're going to have." Former JACL president Nancy Tamura also saw the need to learn from the past. "We have too many omissions to our history," she explained. "How do we learn from our blights if they are not presented to our students as learning experiences and mistakes that should not be made in their lifetimes?" Resident and historian Eckard Toy underscored this point. "There's no substitute for learning about others. Educators must be a part of the process, and the curriculum in schools should reflect that as well . . . there has to be a consciousness of what went wrong, an understanding of why it went wrong, and why we behaved as we did and how we can change."

Keith Doroski, Legion Post No. 22 commander from 2001 to 2003, recognized citizens' responsibilities to convey the whole history, not just selected portions. "You can't just pick and choose what history you keep or let go. In the past, we tended to downplay the atrocities or mistakes that we've made and raise up and praise the things that went well," the Persian Gulf War veteran elaborated. "To a lot of people, it's a very touchy, sensitive subject. But I don't think it's something that should just lie buried somewhere. . . . Look, this is what we've done, and this was wrong. . . . But still, that doesn't change the fact that it happened. And it shouldn't happen."

Youth advocate, community drug prevention coordinator, third-generation Finnish American, and former JACL president Maija Yasui offered her own antidote in a 1995 essay for the local newspaper. She opened by recognizing the community's past. "We are a community known for its history of prejudice and intolerance, especially towards newcomers of a different race or culture." After making this admission, she expressed her hope. "I believe there is still enough time to prevent injustice, racial tension, and prejudice from escalating to a point of frequent litigation, separation, strikes and violence." Still, she felt, there was cause for concern regarding the treatment of valley newcomers. "This culture of cultural suppression is recurring in Hood River with Hispanic immigrants as its focus. We are still critical, even fearful, of people who look and act differently, who have different customs, and speak a different language. Hispanic labor is vital to our economy, but once again we are trying to exclude these immigrants from our community. . . . The children of these Hispanic immigrants are being forced to cast off their culture and become as 'white' as possible to succeed." She concluded with a challenge. "Imagine how much richer our community would be if we learned from the strengths of each new immigrant."[34]

Offering his own brand of realism and hope, historian David Peterson del Mar concluded in his book *Oregon's Promise: An Interpretive History*: "To come to terms with racism and factionalism we must surrender our pretensions of innocence and exceptionalism. Oregon has been no Eden, welcoming and granting opportunities to all people with a ready mind and willing hands. Its promise remains unfulfilled. But we can change that."[35]

That harks back to the response that Reverend Sherman Burgoyne mailed each letter writer who volunteered to help when he and the valley were under siege in 1945: "The battle for American decency happened to be here this year. We fought it and won. Next year it may be in your part of America and I'm counting on you to stand true."[36] Those words still ring true today, for, unfortunately, there continue to be ample occasions to heed his advice.

# SIXTEEN

# No *"Ordinary Soldiers"*

## THE PATRIOT TEST

I T was almost as if serving their country tested their courage, their resolve, even their Americanism. Pacific war hero Frank Hachiya had written a former teacher, "Although I hate war more than anyone can, I think it is a very good place to test oneself—one is either a man or a mouse—as the saying goes. If I come out of the war, I shall know for sure." For Sagie Nishioka, the determining factor was allegiance to his country. "That's where the test was, I believe, whether we're loyal or not." As a quiet young adult who suffered all his life from a war injury and successfully challenged the state to gain his job, he recalled the words of his Second Battalion officer: "You've got to be a little better than the whites." Nishioka internalized that advice. "We had to do something to turn this notion that we were second-grade citizens. . . . There were no choices but do what we did." Nisei GIs' sense of mission compelled them toward "conspicuous gallantry" that would "counteract conclusively the ridiculous charges" against them, according to sociologist Tamotsu Shibutani. Historian James Hirabayashi, too, affirmed what the veterans were saying, namely, that these Nisei, in their zeal to be accepted, put themselves in the position of proving their right to citizenship. Sadly, of course, that should have been theirs by birthright.[1]

Other Hood River Nisei veterans voiced similar needs to demonstrate their mettle. "It seems silly to say that as American citizens we have to prove ourselves," admitted Sab Akiyama. For him, the turning point in overcoming prejudice was the return of all the wartime GIs. "Caucasian servicemen really respected the 100th and the 442nd and the MIS. That's where most of the hate was melted," he added. Older brother George used his regiment's motto to convey his feelings. "The spirit of the 442nd and the 100th was 'Go for Broke.' We just went up there and did the job." The alternative would have been detrimental. "What if we had refused to go?" he wondered. "Things could have been much worse. . . . The family got put in the camp, and my dad was in prison for being head of the Japanese society. Most of us were mad at the government for doing

Sagie Nishioka
(Linda Tamura, 2002)

that, so we just wanted to prove once and without a doubt that we were good, loyal Americans. Now we could have said 'to heck with that' and just said we're not gonna fight. All the people back here would have been in a lot worse situation, don't you think? The 442nd really helped wipe out discrimination. . . . We changed a lot of people's minds." For Mam Noji, there was no doubt. "This was where we belonged," he affirmed. "We earned our right to stay here."

The "spirit of *seishin*" (overcoming fate), the same resilience that Issei demonstrated during their early days in the United States,[2] propelled Nisei forward. The battlefield became a trial. "Yeah, it was scary," admitted George Akiyama, "but you've still got your group behind you. It was not like you were way out by yourself. . . . It's like this old Chinese proverb: You have a bunch of toothpicks, or chopsticks. It's hard to break. Just one, two, or three of them, you could snap it pretty easily. It was not just a single person being brave. There were a lot of others."

Standing up for their rights counted as another way in which Nisei GIs proved themselves. "We stayed back here and fought for justice," said Fred Sumoge, a discipline barrack boy who was court-martialed and imprisoned for insubordination. "Fighting for justice over here may be harder than going overseas," he continued, reflecting on the thirty-seven-year process that eventually nullified his dishonorable discharge. "I didn't refuse basic training. This all began when they started to discriminate.... If I'd been in the camp, I'd have done the same thing." Fellow DB boy Kenjiro Hayakawa agreed, quietly adding, "You do what you think is right."

General Mark Clark, European theater commander, cut to the core when he addressed challenges in the Nikkei past. "Japanese Americans have triumphed over bigotry and prejudice, eliminated discriminatory legislation and practices, and secured new opportunities and dignity for themselves and their children."[3]

## RECOGNIZING NISEI VETERANS

Those whose consciences had awakened did take measures to recognize Nisei veterans as individuals and as a group, across both the nation and the state. Among those, local veteran Koe Nishimoto served with the Military Intelligence Service during the postwar occupation of Japan. He gained statewide acclaim when he became the first Japanese American to be named state commander of the Oregon Veterans of Foreign Wars, from 1979 to 1980, making him the second Nisei VFW state commander in the country, after the California VFW elected the first Nisei the previous year.[4]

MIS veteran and war hero Frank Hachiya, who was finally honored and buried in his hometown three years after his 1945 death, gained national distinction. In 1963, when Congress honored Nisei service in World War II, Oregon congressman Al Ullman called Hachiya "perhaps the greatest Japanese American war hero of World War II in the South Pacific." The state representative also put to rest the controversy over how the GI died. Mistakenly shot by his own comrades, Ullman revealed, the mortally wounded Hachiya still managed to crawl in front of Japanese lines and lay maps of the enemy's defenses at an American officer's feet. For that, a grateful nation posthumously awarded Hachiya the Distinguished Service Cross, the highest decoration awarded to a Nisei in the Pacific theater at that time. In 1980, the Presidio's Defense Language Institute expressed its gratitude in its own way. The central building at the new Asian-language complex in Monterey, California, was dedicated Hachiya Hall.

Congressman Ullman also lauded local Nisei as a group. "Surely no other group can surpass the record of the Japanese American soldiers for loyalty and patriotism under arduous conditions," he declared. "Their record of outstanding citizenship during wartime is only matched by their record during peacetime." He went on to praise Nisei in his district for their "industriousness and model citizenship," adding, "Most of my Nisei constituents work in farming and related activities in Hood River County, the home area of Sergeant Hachiya, and in Malheur County. The quality of their crops and their general efficiency in both production and marketing is well known."[5]

## UNVEILING THE ENIGMA OF THE MIS

The value of Nisei linguists in the South Pacific still seemed obscure, despite the plaudits they earned from military commanders. "You're damned right, those Nisei boys have got a place in the American heart—now and forever," proclaimed General Joseph W. Stilwell, commander of the Chinese-Burma-India theater. "These Nisei have bought an awful big chunk of America with their own blood." In 1945, incensed at the treatment of Nikkei on the mainland, he threatened to form a "pick-axe club" to protect Nisei veterans. When "any bar-fly commando" picked on any of them, he maintained, "we ought to bang them over the head with a pick-axe, and I'm willing to be the charter member of such a club." Colonel Sidney F. Mashbir disclosed the role of the Allied Translator and Interpreter Section (ATIS) to the press in the fall of 1945 by claiming that no group had as much to lose. "Capture would have meant indescribable horror to them and their relatives in Japan." Had they been captured, Lieutenant Colonel Wallace H. Moore added, in a 1945 speaking tour, "they ran an even greater risk than the rank and file of other American troops." At the 1963 Arlington National Cemetery tribute to Nisei, Judge John F. Aiso, former academic training director for Japanese-language schools at Camps Savage and Snelling, expressed his admiration for the men of the MIS. They demonstrated, he asserted, that "Americans don't hesitate to bear arms against blood relatives when freedom and moral principles are at stake." More than that, however, they fought with skills just as vital as nuclear weapons, proving that "language can be employed not only in waging wars, but also in our quest for world peace."[6]

Colonel Mashbir of ATIS similarly asserted that it would be impossible to determine how many hundreds of American lives and billions of dollars were saved due to intelligence supplied by Nisei. Still, they remained America's "secret weapon." They received few awards, there were minimal official records of their attachments to combat units, and the men themselves continued to be discreet about their intelligence operations. Military records were just as steadfast in keeping their secrets. In 1948, a ten-volume history of military intelligence in the southwestern Pacific did detail the role of Nisei in the MIS. But the military restricted the document and blocked the public from viewing it. Likewise, the MIS Language School staff compiled the school's history, which it ultimately did not publish. World War II military intelligence documents, in fact, were restricted until 1972, when the Freedom of Information Act declassified them, finally making the files accessible to the public. Still, by 1988, official files were "buried, scattered, or scant," according to Don Nakatsu, MIS veteran and author. And the men spoke little about their intelligence operations, owing not only to what MIS veteran Harry Akune called the "regular Nisei self-deprecatory manner" but to the fact that, in Nakatsu's view, Nisei were "neither motivated nor organized to publicize their story."[7]

More activism by veterans finally did result in national recognition. Led by Harry Fukuhara (one of nine Nisei inducted into the Military Intelligence Corps Hall of Fame), who set a goal of achieving official recognition for the MIS, members of the Military Intelligence Service Association of Northern California spent two years researching and collecting data, with support from Senator Daniel Akaka of Hawaii, Secretary of the Army Louis Caldera, and then Army Chief of Staff General Eric Shinseki. Their efforts led to a Presidential Unit Citation, equivalent to a Distinguished Service Cross for an individual. The award, presented on April 3, 2000, recognized the MIS for "extraordinary heroism in military operations against an armed enemy." And though there had been no official publicity about the MIS for sixty-two years, the U.S. Army published an official account in 2007, written by James McNaughton, command historian for the Defense Language Institute Foreign Language Center. "The MIS Nisei," he concluded, "remained true to their wartime pledge of secrecy, their service known to but a few."[8]

## LOCAL TRIBUTES

The year 2001 brought dual tributes to Hood River Nisei veterans. Both honors stemmed from suggestions made by a city employee who was unaware of the local wartime antipathy. That March, City Recorder Anita Smith attended a Seattle ceremony honoring two native sons who had received the Congressional Medal of Honor. The summer before, fifty-five years after the end of the war, President Bill Clinton had bestowed these honors on twenty-two Asian Pacific American veterans of World War II.⁹ Impressed by Seattle's homage, Smith suggested a similar tribute at Hood River's own Fourth of July parade, and the planning commenced.¹⁰

The local newspaper set a far-reaching and sanguine tone for the day, pronouncing, "An honor this Independence Day overshadows the deep mistrust and suspicion faced by two Hood River Valley natives more than fifty years ago." The front page featured a photo of George Akiyama and Mam Noji, publicizing their meritorious wartime service and their selection as grand marshals for the local Fourth of July parade. Baring reminders of the lack of welcome the men received when they returned home—their names removed from the courthouse honor roll and a barbershop's refusal to cut Akiyama's hair—the newspaper also noted that "neither man is bitter or resentful over the hardships they and their families endured." Instead, it projected optimistically, "there is vindication in the belated but warm welcome they will receive."¹¹

On July 4, 2001, Keith Doroski, commander of American Legion Post No. 22, observed from the lead car, just ahead of the Oregon National Guard Humvee carrying the two grand marshals: "The crowd snapped to attention as a wave. People would stand up, they would wave. All the cameras came up. As the procession moved along, people would get to their feet. Some were saluting, some were saying kind words. It was a really, really warm reception. . . . The Nisei veterans had suffered the same atrocities as all the other people in the war. But at the same time, their families were interned and they came back to an uncertain future. This was overdue."

When Doroski introduced the two veterans at a ceremony following the parade, the crowd broke into prolonged applause. Afterward, a soloist, accompanied by a community band, belted out the "Star Spangled Banner." Akiyama and Noji accepted their honor on behalf of all local Nisei veterans. "That was a great honor representing the rest of the veterans," Akiyama declared. "We were saluting the flag, and it just reminded you of how patriotic everybody should be." Noji too was awestruck. "That was a great honor for us Nisei. A lot of people said it was late in coming. Wasn't that a nice thing to say? But where in the world did all those people come from?" As soon as Smith, the city recorder, learned about the wartime discrimination that Nisei had faced, "it made it all the better for

Mam Noji and George Akiyama, with Akiyama's grandchildren, rode in an Oregon National Guard Humvee when they served as grand marshals for Hood River's Fourth of July parade in 2001. (Linda Tamura, 2001)

me," she exclaimed. After the parade, Noji thanked her for her gesture and expressed hope that "this might be the beginning of healing." Not long afterward, Smith acted on another idea. "They need a brick," she declared to city manager Lynn Guenther.

The bricks on Smith's mind composed part of a veterans' memorial garden at the city's downtown Overlook Park. The tiny public plaza's fountain mimics natural waterfalls in the Columbia Gorge, and the basalt column near the base of the fountain highlights the names of local veterans who had given their lives during World War II and the Korean and Vietnam Wars. The city's memorial also features two deep red, hybrid tea rose bushes named Veterans' Honor, introduced at Arlington Cemetery in Washington, D.C., in 1999.[12] Commemorative bricks along the base, sponsored by individuals and businesses, bore the names of local veterans. City manager Guenther, former commander of Fairchild Air Force Base in Washington, agreed with Smith, maintaining, "Anyone who has served this country shouldn't have to carry any of those scars." He proposed Smith's idea to the Post No. 22 Legion board members, who set the plan in motion.

Thus, on a cold and gusty November 10, 2001, about seventy-five citizens gathered at Hood River's Overlook Memorial Park. The annual Veterans Day ceremony began with a flyby by military jets, the pledge of allegiance, and the national anthem. Keith Doroski, Legion post commander, unveiled the newest brick (purchased by the Legion), inscribed "IN HONOR OF ALL NISEI VETERANS." Declared Doroski, "It is high time to pay tribute to these brave men who fought gallantly, many times above and beyond the call of duty." He personalized their experience by adding, "Imagine, if you will, fighting for your adopted country against your country of origin while your family is imprisoned." That statement, quoted in a local news writer's "Round Table" column, "Our Freedom Demands All of Us Be Involved," hit a nerve. Sab Akiyama penned his rebuttal to the *Hood River News*. "We, the Niseis are natural-born citizens of the U.S.A. This is our country—not our 'adopted' country. Our service in the military was to fight against the Axis powers and not the 'country of our origin.'"[13] Good intentions were still blurred by inaccuracies. This time, however, a Nisei spoke out to correct the record.

### SHADES OF THE PAST

Another Nisei veterans' memorial in the state (which also included Hood River names) became mired in controversy. The city of Beaverton, west of Portland, began constructing its own veterans' memorial in 1999, to honor those who had served from the Spanish American War to the Kosovo conflict. Nisei from the area, remembering how they had been denied membership by Legion posts, were reluctant to purchase commemorative bricks. Eventually veteran Art Iwasaki proposed building a separate wall dedicated solely to Japanese Americans.[14]

Three years after planning began, on a very dreary and showery Saturday, a crowd of well over a hundred congregated at Beaverton's Veterans Memorial Park under sagging, rain-drenched tents to dedicate the Nisei Veterans Wall. The outdoor ceremony on February 15, 2003, also commemorated the sixty-first anniversary of Executive Order 9066, which had resulted in the incarceration of those of Japanese ancestry. Nearly three hundred bricks on the wall bore inscriptions with the names of veterans or veterans' organizations, each purchased by a family member or friend.[15]

Dozens of Nisei veterans stood out in the crowd, wearing star-spangled ties and military dress hats. Two Nisei veterans and three Japanese Americans of other generations spoke during the morning program, and it was the comments of Peggy Nagae that created a stir. Nagae, a Sansei attorney, had led the legal campaign to overturn former Hood Riverite Minoru Yasui's wartime curfew conviction and challenge the constitutionality of the evacuation. Early in her remarks that day, she itemized the legal, legislative, and governmental blows that had diminished the rights of Nikkei war heroes. Nagae's first example related to the Hood River American Legion post opposing Japanese landownership and rallying for laws to strip the immigrant Issei of their legal rights to farm. Her second included the Oregon American Legion among groups that had backed legislation to prohibit Issei from owning or leasing land.[16] Local Legion members took issue, insisting that any statements about past actions had no relevance to the commemoration, and they requested that those remarks be cut from a planned broadcast of the event.

Afterward, Nikkei community leaders reviewed Nagae's remarks and agreed that the events she described were well documented. Nagae herself explained that her intention had been to show that "in the face of all that happened, the Nikkei were patriotic, fought for their country and fought at a time when they, themselves, faced true prejudice." A Portland Nisei veteran noted, "To celebrate the dedication of the memorial without reference to earlier events would be a hollow ceremony."[17]

As a result, a group of five Nikkei organizations led by the Oregon Nisei Veterans mailed a letter to the Legion post. They explained that historical accounts of Japanese American veterans and the social and political environment at the time served the purpose of the Day of Remembrance. After expressing regret that some felt offended, their letter continued, "We have determined that the statements were historically accurate and that nothing said was misleading or inappropriate. We feel that the speaker addressed exactly what a Day of Remembrance is supposed to do—for all Americans to remember, and not forget, a very shameful chapter in the history of our country." The Nikkei groups did make a concession. They added a postscript to the videotaped program stating that past actions by Legion posts did not represent the organization's current leaders or membership and that they recognized that posts were making strides to improve relationships with Japanese American veterans and communities. In addition, they included footage of the Hood River post's efforts in 2001 to correct the past: first, the Nisei veteran grand marshals at the Fourth of July parade and, second, the unveiling of the brick for Nisei veterans at the veterans' memorial garden. As Nagae later reflected, the incident, which underscored the sensitivities involved in both reliving and facing the past, was "painful on many different levels."[18] Now, however, Nikkei were more resolute in telling their story, unedited.

## ANTIDOTE

"A war brings out the best and the worst in people," observed Noji. "It's not gonna change," he lamented. "We'll still have our quarrels." Nonetheless, he mustered a trace of optimism: "Somehow we still survive." That resurging hope seemed the antidote for Nisei GIs in the face of wartime trauma. They did their best. They proved themselves. They changed people's minds. They made a difference. Reflecting on the past and preparing for the future, they offered their simple, sage advice.

### UNDERSTANDING DIFFERENCES: INTERMINGLE, MINIMIZE DIFFERENCES, LEARN FROM OTHERS

"We were different. We had the wrong kind of face. We had the wrong names," said Noji. "The frailty of human beings is that we're never the same," he reasoned. "The ability to live with the differences is what we're all shooting for." Being a realist, he added, "It's inherent in people to disagree and fight. That's been ever since man was put on this earth." Noji resolved, "We don't have the understanding of other people as well as we should. We just don't even *learn* from our past mistakes. . . . We've simply got to learn to get along." A world traveler, he perceived a universal commonality. "We are all immigrants or children of immigrants. I think if we could intermingle a lot more, we could minimize our differences. I find that wants and desires of all people are not that much different. We all want the same thing."

Sab Akiyama cautioned, "We were victims of prejudice. But as victims one time, we sure don't want to become perpetrators." Stressing the need for compassion, he observed, "Most of the time if you understand a person, there's probably not that much difference. A lot of Caucasians found out in World War II that out in the battlefield when the blood is flowing, it doesn't make any difference where it came from." Akiyama added his own goal. "I just hope we learn something ourselves about how unjust prejudice can be and free our minds to accept different ethnic groups."

"We don't want any minority group to be treated like that again—or anybody, as far as that goes," maintained George Akiyama. "No ethnic group should be discriminated against. All citizens should be treated alike."

Veteran Min Asai was one of the first three Nikkei to return to the valley after the war. In a speech to local high school students, he charged them with responsibility for their future.

> Let us remember that these things happened in these United States,
> champion of human rights and liberties; and unless we are vigilant it
> can happen again. . . . I think we owe it to ourselves and our nation to be
> ever alert so that some event will not cause the loss of our rights to any
> of our citizens at any time. The national government . . . can never erase
> the shame that America caused by evacuating and placing some of their
> citizens in concentration camps for no other reason than their ancestry.
> Let us be sure that incidents like this do not happen again.[19]

The matter of civil rights took on special meaning for men who had sacrificed two years of freedom for their beliefs. "I can't just stand around when people do something in front of me for no reason," explained Fred Sumoge. Characterized as reticent (by both himself and others), he was nonetheless principled. "I was quiet—until they treat you below 50 percent

George Akiyama.
(Linda Tamura, 2002)

and your life is concerned." Referring to the give-and-take balance in his court-martial for refusing a military order, Sumoge added, "The reason this happened was the discrimination. That's all it was, total discrimination." His stance was clear: he had not resisted the draft; he had accepted it. He had, however, resisted the discrimination. "Somebody fought for all the *nihonjin* over here. There was a wrong. I wanted to make the wrong right." He went on, "You can't just push us around. Just take orders like that? . . . I thought, there's a lot of fighting that has to be done in this country."

Sumoge also believed in disclosure. "People should know what happened in the army. They didn't know we faced the machine gun." And it was especially important to him that people conscientiously consider their own actions. "If you just say 'okay, okay' and simply 'be a sheep and follow the crowd,'" he cautioned, "you don't use your own mind." Kenjiro Hayakawa, also imprisoned for disobeying an officer's order, spoke simply and evenly, "You do what you think is right."

U.S. congressman from Hawaii and veteran Spark M. Matsunaga underscored the need to take action and speak out when he gave his tribute to Nisei at Arlington National Cemetery in 1963: "So long as a single member of our citizenry is denied the use of public facilities and denied the right to earn a decent living because and solely because of the color of his skin, we who 'fought against prejudice and won' ought not sit idly by and tolerate the perpetuation of injustices."[20]

## EDUCATION: LEARN, ASK QUESTIONS, ACT

"I think it's a shame all this isn't written in the history books," lamented George Akiyama about the Japanese American World War II experience. "You know, there's people today . . . who've never heard about it, they say. This should be in the history books so the young people know what's going on." Sagie Nishioka had often spoken at schools as a representative of the Purple Heart Battalion. "Teach what transpired all those years, from World War II to the present time," he agreed heartily.

For DB boy Fred Sumoge, the lesson to be learned was basic: "The lesson, well, is, people should ask—just like you—'Why did you do it?'" Answering his own question, he explained that a person needs a reason to act. Otherwise, "What is life? . . . If there's a fire, I think I'll go in and save somebody, even if I get burned and die, because I have a reason." But while training for combat at Fort McClellan, Sumoge explained, "I had no reason." So learning, asking questions, and acting on one's conscience were imperative to them.

### BREAKING THEIR SILENCE

Not given to lavish exchanges about their accomplishments, Nikkei families fell into their own rhythms. "All the brothers, after dinner, we'd be sitting around and maybe in two hours time, there'd be a hundred words spoken," chuckled Sab Akiyama. Their children even commented, but, Akiyama explained, "It seems like we don't converse much with each other but we still kind of understand . . . what their ideas or thoughts are." That unspoken language transcended their quiet. Referring to his brother George's wartime heroism, Sab continued, "The war experience—he never talked much about it," attributing this behavior to the Issei manner of minimizing accomplishments. George suggested a reason for the lack of discussion about his exploits and medals, saying, "We're pretty modest . . . I don't know, maybe that's the Japanese custom."

In addition to affecting Nikkei adaptive styles, wartime trauma had a multiplying effect on Nisei quietude. Some travails resulted from the battlefield, compelling Mam Noji to omit what he "chose to forget" when sharing recollections of the South Pacific. "War is hell, you know," he confided knowingly to a fellow veteran.[21] "Men don't talk about war experiences to their own families, you know." The stresses of war were just as apparent for those subjected to incarceration. "Why should I bring up all that hardship we went through?" asked Hit Imai, who experienced both camp and military life. For him, the effect of discrimination was potent. "We never mention to our kids about this discrimination. Just like Japanese *ganbatte*, take it to your heart and keep it to yourself. . . . That's why a lot of people don't know what we've gone through."

Speaking about their convictions and imprisonment became an especially personal issue for the DB boys, even with their spouses. "I don't think I even told her," Sumoge said, referring to his late wife. "You don't talk about those things." Sumoge did convey his purpose to her. "I kind of told her I was fighting discrimination. I was fighting for democracy."[22] Hayakawa, too, admitted, "I've never told anybody about the war." But after he was honorably discharged, the outlook was more promising. "If I remained dishonorably discharged, I could not talk forever. . . . Now that I have this paper, I can talk to my sons if I want to." Still, according to eldest son, Ken, Mr. Hayakawa did not divulge his past, though his sons "figured it out" by listening to their mother and their father's friends.

Recognizing the challenges that veterans face on reentering civilian life, social scientists have drawn parallels among war veterans and those who faced political or racial oppression. Scholar Loo noted that many Japanese Americans, like victims of post-traumatic stress disorder, avoided situations tied to their traumas. Sociologist Robert S. Laufer, in his analysis of war trauma, similarly observed a pattern of repressing the war experience.[23] In her study of the impact of internment on Nikkei, Donna K. Nagata likened Nisei silence (denying or repressing unpleasant memories) to a form of post-traumatic stress disorder. Nisei silence could also emanate from shame or guilt, she claimed, as well as from Japanese cultural values that emphasize *shikataganai*, or a sense of fatalism about factors beyond one's control, and *gaman*, or the suppression of emotions, in addition to their manner of conveying emotional topics indirectly or nonverbally and avoiding confrontations, family conflict, and embarrassment. Loo also tied Nisei quietude to relationships with their Sansei children, proposing that Nisei might be protecting the next generation from carrying a burden that they themselves had borne (similar to Holocaust survivors), or, in their sensitivity to others' feelings, they may have perceived that Sansei were not interested in learning about the Nisei's wartime challenges. That duality in others' perceptions created a dilemma, acknowledged Nagata. Some may have viewed the Nisei's public silence as acceptance of their unjust treatment. To the contrary, however, silence could actually communicate the extent of injustice rather than acceptance of it. And while Sansei interpreted their parents' reticence as the result of suffering and injustice, others likely did not. As Nagata explained: "Non-Japanese Americans who were distanced from the internment were more likely to interpret the silence as a sign that either Japanese Americans accepted their fate, were not sufficiently traumatized by the event to voice a concern, or had coped well enough with the trauma such that there was no need to voice a concern about what had happened."[24]

For Nisei in Hood River, there was also the issue of "opening up a can of worms" by awakening any residual animosities among longtime residents and making themselves vulnerable again to the hurt they remembered so well. Through the years, veterans and other Nisei do seem to have become more open to acknowledging their wartime experiences. Spurred not by Nisei but by Sansei and other community members, Hood River's 2007

Day of Remembrance became pivotal for opening the community's eyes—and affirming the Nisei as valid, valued members. "I want to find the voices in this suffocating silence, not just the remaining Japanese voices who can tell me my people's history but the voices of the white folk," Sansei coordinator Joan Emerson had challenged the audience. "What does it take for good men and women to rise up and bear witness to atrocities against other beings and assaults against our Constitution?"[25]

The program, which included a tribute and recognition of thirty-eight local Nisei veterans (both living and deceased), became a "vivid afternoon history lesson," according to the local newspaper. The community's acknowledgment of what Nisei had faced and affirmation of who they were evoked visible, though not always vocalized, responses from Nisei veterans. One who was among those recognized for their sacrifices wept for twenty minutes during the program. A frail Nisei gentleman dabbed at the tears on his face for two hours. Another Nisei confided afterward that he had not shed a tear since leaving the valley, going to camp, and serving in the armed forces. Yet on that day, he admitted, his well of tears just did not run dry. Being surrounded by five hundred citizens mourning the past and attempting to make amends for the future became a cathartic and poignant milestone for the community—and the men.[26]

With time and the passing of so many of their peers, the numbers of Nisei have now dwindled. Gradually, with more community interest as well as stronger activism by succeeding generations, the public is witnessing Nisei evolution toward greater personal reflection and candor. This, noted Nagata, illustrated developmental stages marking their transition toward coping positively with the trauma of their past. First concerned about making waves and calling attention to themselves, Nisei seemed to be moving from self-blame to understanding that the fault lay at the feet of the government (not with themselves) and perhaps finally toward more purposefulness and assertiveness in their actions. Loo cited Alan Nishio, cochair of Southern California's National Coalition for Redress/Reparations (NCRR): "We have come full-circle, from feeling what happened to us was our fault, to understanding that we were victims of racism and war hysteria, and then to fighting for justice as a community."[27]

That transition was just as evident for the DB boys. "I'm a private guy," conceded Fred Sumoge. "I don't want publicity." In fact, when assistant editor of the JACL's *Pacific Citizen* Martha Nakagawa interviewed him and Tim Nomiyama in 1999, he spoke on one condition. The resulting article,

Fred Sumoge and Kenjiro Hayakawa with the author, July 2003.

"'DB Boys,' an Untold WWII Story," simply stated that he "asked to remain anonymous since he has not shared his past with his family yet."[28] Shunning the camera as well, Sumoge agreed to the interview because "I just want the story out. I wanted people to know that Nisei had stood up for their rights." But revealing the past was uncomfortable in both the telling and the asking, he reflected. No, he had not told his family; they didn't ask (except for a nephew, who "knows almost everything" because he asked). "Maybe they're not asking because they thought I was ashamed of what I did . . . they don't ask, I don't say." That admission was tested for this project. "You came here, and you said, 'I'm asking.' I thought, 'I think I said the wrong thing.' So I have to tell the truth." For Kenjiro Hayakawa, finally divulging his story was also a leap, but one that he accepted. "Just write the truth. It's all history. You can't change it," he remarked. On revealing a previously concealed part of his life, he concluded, "I think I told you enough already, and I feel good about that."

In removing the filter from their memories and resurrecting the past, Nisei veterans were stepping away from the "social amnesia" that had corralled them for far too long. Recovering history and recovering *from* it are closely and personally intertwined, author and curator Karen Ishizuka has reminded us. Both involve "private and public mediation between remembering and forgetting, speaking out and being silent." But the struggle to preserve memory and affect our future continues. As noted scholar Gary Y. Okihiro has suggested, it is time for "the silences of meaning [to] be whispered around the campfires of our consciousness"[29]—and those of the veterans.

## "JUST AMERICANS"

"Americanism is a matter of the mind and the heart; Americanism is not, and never was, a matter of race or ancestry. A good American is one who is loyal to this country and to our creed of liberty and democracy. Every loyal American citizen should be given the opportunity to serve this country."[30] Dillon S. Myer, director of the War Relocation Authority, used these words from President Franklin D. Roosevelt's statement approving a Nisei combat team during World War II to introduce a tribute to the World War II military service of Nisei at Arlington National Cemetery in 1963. He also squarely addressed the challenge Japanese Americans had faced: "There were in this country many unscrupulous or misguided self-styled patriots who would accept no other proof of loyalty and Americanism." Citing as an example the removal of Nisei names from Hood River's honor roll, he continued, "It took the kind of heroism and dramatic action displayed by the Nisei in uniform to awaken the American conscience and to stir people of good will everywhere into taking the necessary action to erase the results of the racists' campaigns."[31]

General Mark Clark, who vied successfully to bring the 100th/442nd under his command in Europe, was equally laudatory when he testified in 1981 before the Commission on Wartime Relocation and Internment of Civilians: "The heroic exploits of the Japanese American soldier, especially in World War II, should be an inspiration to all of what courage, loyalty, honesty, and devotion to America and its democratic ideals can achieve."[32]

Those accounts resemble accolades given after the war by Major General Jacob L. Devers, Allied commander in Europe. "There is one supreme, final test of loyalty for one's native land—readiness and willingness to fight for, and if need be, to die for one's country. These Americans pass that test with colors flying. They . . . more than earned the right to be called just Americans, not Japanese Americans. Their Americanism may be described only by degree, and that the highest."[33]

Shig Imai and daughter Sheri Imai-Swiggart (right) with author at the Oregon regional tribute to Congressional Gold Medal recipients (Eric Ballinger, February 26, 2012)

Nearly seven decades after the war's onset, the United States did present its highest civilian honor to all Japanese American World War II veterans. On November 2, 2011, at the U.S. Capitol complex, aged Nisei veterans received a collective Congressional Gold Medal. Public Law 111–254, signed by President Barak Obama on October 5, 2010, commended the 100th Battalion and the 442nd Regimental Combat Team: "The United States remains forever indebted to the bravery, valor, and dedication to country these men faced while fighting a 2-fronted battle of discrimination at home and fascism abroad." The law also honored the Military Intelligence Service, acknowledging not only that its "highly classified intelligence operations" had been vital to military successes in the Pacific Theater but that the MIS was "invaluable to occupation forces as they assisted Japan in a peaceful transition to a new, democratic form of government."[34]

"We did our part, just like the rest of them," allowed Shig Imai, one of the few local, living Nisei veterans able to recognize the national honor bestowed on them. "We all did whatever had to be done." Their mission, George Akiyama had claimed, was clear. "You're doing this for your coun-

Mam Noji and Harry Tamura. (Linda Tamura, 2002)

try. Especially us, we had to prove that we were good soldiers, that we were good citizens and loyal Americans—for the way that people were being treated back at home." Harry Tamura had simply added, "I tried to do my best to serve this country. I think I did the best I can do."

The Nisei veterans were humble indeed about their roles. "Naaw, I'm just an ordinary soldier," insisted George Akiyama, countering the suggestion that he was a hero. "I just did part of my job. If I gave my life, I might have been a hero." A true patriot, concurred Sagie Nishioka, was one who was wounded or killed. "That shows true love of this country." Added Shig Imai, "I just feel I'm among the rest of the Americans, the same as the rest of them." Japanese American soldiers, observed Monroe Sweetland, former Oregon state senator and wartime overseas Red Cross field service representative, "performed in tremendous proportions, far enlarging the significance of any one soldier. They didn't go out demanding attention; there was a unique modesty about their patriotism."

"I guess when you join the forces, you're American by heart to do it," exclaimed Hit Imai. The Hood River Nisei veterans did engage in battles throughout their lives—battles for their country, certainly, but also battles for their civil rights and battles for their dignity. Against all odds, they fought honorably and courageously—through their actions more than their words—with pride surpassing the overwhelming prejudice they faced.

At Hood River's 2007 Day of Remembrance, Joan Emerson had challenged the community: "History needs correction. History needs questioning. History needs first-person voices on record." Though typically keeping their emotions close to their hearts, Nisei veterans have answered by navigating the minefields of their past, reaching into their souls, and disclosing memories that have been, at times, uncomfortable to tell. Local Nikkei have also linked arms with forward-thinking members of their community and started to move ahead. By shedding light on the angst of the past[35] and becoming attuned to opportunities that an increasingly diverse valley population can wield, the Nikkei and their community hold promise for forging new memories in the valley.

"I think we who served made it much easier for the rest of us to live where we are," confided Mam Noji. "We had a lot of doubts in those days. But today I think we could say we're proud to have served—and come home alive." Recalling the aura of respect and pride so evident during the playing of the national anthem at local school sporting events, Noji's reflection struck a chord for the future: "When everybody places their hands over their hearts, seems awfully serene, doesn't it?" That's an apt imperative for the future from one who served honorably—through his actions and now with his timeless words.

# AFTERWORD

O N Memorial Day, May 31, 2011, nearly five hundred gathered at
Hood River's Idlewilde Cemetery to remember, to put the past
behind them, and to move on. The headline in the *Hood River
News* called the event "an acknowledgement of wrongs." Veteran Shig Imai
viewed it simply as "a healing moment."[1]

The seed planted by local Legionnaire Bud Collins years before had
borne fruit—a public acknowledgment of discrimination against Japanese
Americans in the valley and a commitment to repair the unspoken yet
still painful breach. From the initial plan for a bench honoring the sixteen
Nisei whose names had been blotted out on the community honor roll to
a large, marble monument listing *all* Nikkei who had served in the armed
forces, the idea took shape. Ultimately, it prompted a plan to renovate the
cemetery's Walk of Honor for all valley veterans.[2]

Almost sixty-seven years after the deed that the community was no
longer willing to ignore, Idlewilde Cemetery sexton Bob Huskey emceed
a heartfelt program of music, prayer, poetry, and a portrayal of Frank
Hachiya, who had sacrificed his life during World War II. Past commander
Dennis Leonard and Commander Roy Elliott of Legion Post No. 22 joined
U.S. Representative Greg Walden and Huskey in unveiling the monument while the names of the 140 veterans were read. Those men's service
extended from World War II to the Vietnam War.

In his address, Congressman Walden underscored the depth of the injustice and the imperative to recognize it publicly:

It's hard to believe as we gather on this cool Memorial Day morning in the year 2011 that less than 70 years ago our valley was ripped apart by the heat of discriminatory passions of war. As Japanese Americans fought courageously in far-off lands and seas against the gathered forces of oppression, here at home their loved ones were rounded up and sent away to internment camps, their homes destroyed, some of their lands taken away or turned over to property caretakers. Abhorrently, the names of sixteen Japanese Americans who had selflessly served in the cause of freedom were stripped from the sacred wall erected by the American Legion at the courthouse to forever honor their bravery and their service. . . .

This was not a proud chapter in the history of the Hood River valley. I know it's an agonizing chapter that some would just as soon not reopen. But a wound as deep as this one cannot heal if it is not appropriately treated. Today we get about that healing process with the best of our ability. Nothing we say today can right the wrongs of the past. But hopefully our acknowledgement of those wrongs can help us and those to come from allowing such actions to *ever* occur again.

Today all across our great country, Americans are gathered in public spaces just like these to recognize and remember all men and women—all Americans of every size and color and creed who have sacrificed so much for so many. I'm reminded of the poignant words of Gen. John Pershing, the Commander of the American Forces of World War I and the first chairman of the American Battle Monuments Commission. He said of the fallen: "Time will not dim the glory of their deeds." As long as we continue to gather as we are today, we can make sure his words always ring true. . . .

But words alone are not enough of a tribute. That's why we mark off the land so we can walk the hallowed grounds on which they fought and died for us. It's why we mark off the land and build monuments in recognition of their bravery and sacrifice. So, from Arlington National Cemetery to Idlewilde Cemetery and everywhere in between, we build monuments to heal wounds. We build monuments to live up to Gen. Pershing's expectation that time would not dim the glory of their deeds.

The monument we dedicate here today reminds us that in 1941 more than 5,000 Japanese Americans were serving in the United States military.[3] Despite being summarily discharged in the wake of the attack on Pearl Harbor, they convinced the military governor of the islands that they were ready to serve and were eventually redesignated as the 100th Infantry Battalion sent to the European Theatre, where they made a strong and lasting impression on the Italian Front.

Gen. Mark W. Clark, the Allied 5th Army Commander, said this of the Nisei: "Gen. Marshall gave me very strict personnel instructions to report to him immediately the outcome in the Battalion's first baptism of fire. After their first engagement, I said, 'They performed magnificently on the field of battle. I've never had such fine soldiers. Send me all ya got!'" And we did. . . .

It takes a special person to overcome such hostility and still want to serve his country with courage and with conviction. Thank you to each of you and to *all* who have served. And while we pay special attention today to the dedication of *this* monument and all it represents, let us all remember all those who have served and worn our nation's uniform. . . . We may never be able to fully understand all that they endured. But we will always keep bright the glory of their deeds.

The seven-by-ten-foot marble monument, with the names of Nikkei veterans engraved in black,[4] will be placed at the northwest corner of an enlarged, oval-shaped plaza. The walkway, which is to be renamed the Bud Collins Walk of Honor, is dedicated to the Legionnaire and community volunteer who died a year too early to see his community come together.[5]

On Memorial Day 2011, veteran Shig Imai and Bob Huskey, Idlewilde Cemetery sexton, stand by the newly dedicated monument honoring Japanese American veterans. (Adam Lapierre, *Hood River News*)

# NOTES

## INTRODUCTION

1   Frank Davey, *Report on the Japanese Situation in Oregon Investigated for Governor Ben W. Olcott* (Salem, OR: State Printing Department, 1920), 3, 7.

2   For Hood River County population, see U.S. Bureau of the Census, *Thirteenth, Fourteenth, Fifteenth, Sixteenth, Eighteenth Census of the United States*, Vol. 3, Pt. 2 (Washington, DC: Government Printing Office, 1910–50).

3   According to the War Relocation Authority (WRA), 90,491 people were evacuated first to assembly centers and 17,915 joined them at government relocation centers. See U.S. Department of the Interior, *The Evacuated People: A Qualitative Description* (Washington, DC: Government Printing Office, 1946), 8.

4   While the federal government called them "relocation centers," President Roosevelt referred to "concentration camps" in 1942 press conferences. See Roger Daniels, "Words Do Matter: A Note on Inappropriate Terminology and the Incarceration of the Japanese Americans," in *Nikkei in the Pacific Northwest: Japanese Americans and Japanese Canadians in the Twentieth Century*, ed. Louis Fiset and Gail M. Nomura (Seattle: University of Washington Press, 2005), 201. Though usage is still debated, "concentration camp" now more commonly connotes "a barbed-wire enclosure where people are interned or incarcerated under armed guard." See Tetsuden Kashima, *Judgment without Trial: Japanese American Imprisonment during World War II* (Seattle: University of Washington Press, 2001), 8.

5   *Hood River News*, January 26, 1945, 10; Resolution, American Legion, Post 22, January 5, 1943, Kevin Flanagan (assistant librarian, American Legion Library,

Indianapolis), e-mail to the author, June 12, 2002.

6   Linda Tamura, *The Hood River Issei: An Oral History of Japanese Settlers in Oregon's Hood River Valley* (Urbana: University of Illinois Press, 1993), 283.

7   Ibid.

8   Arthur A. Hansen, "Resettlement: A Neglected Link in Japanese America's Narrative Chain," preface to *Regenerations Oral History Project: Rebuilding Japanese American Families, Communities, and Civil Rights in the Resettlement Era*, vol. 1, *Chicago Region* (Los Angeles: Japanese American National Museum, 2000), 1.

9   Brian Niiya, *Japanese American History: An A-to-Z Reference from 1868 to the Present* (Los Angeles: Japanese American National Museum, 1993), 295.

10  Tetsuden Kashima, "Japanese American Internees Return, 1945 to 1955: Readjustment and Social Amnesia," *Phylon* 16 (Summer 1980): 108, 113.

11  U.S. Department of Veterans Affairs, Office of the Actuary, "Projected WWII Veterans & WWII Veteran Deaths," from VetPop2007, table 2L, May 2011; National Center for Veterans Analysis and Statistics, http://www.va.gov/vetdata/Veteran Population.asp, The Veteran Population Model, from VetPop2007, Table 2D: Deaths by State, Period, Age Group, Gender, 2000–2036; 2L: Veterans by State, Period, Age Group, Gender, 2000–2036. June 30, 2011.

CHAPTER 1. "GROWING UP IN TWO WORLDS"

1   Commercial Club, *Hood River* (Hood River, OR: Commercial Club, 1910), 6; S. F. Blythe and E. R. Bradley, *A Pen Picture of Hood River and Hood River Valley* (Hood River, OR: E. R. Bradley, 1900).

2   Donovan and Associates, *City of Hood River Historic Context Statement*, City of Hood River, OR, June 1991, 31–32, History Museum of Hood River files, Hood River, OR [hereafter Hood River Museum files]; Susan Garrett Crowley, ed., *Legacy: A Centennial Celebration of Hood River & the Columbia Gorge* (Hood River, OR: Hood River News, 1995), 74–79; David J. Burkhart, *It All Began with Apple Seeds: Growing Fruit in the Hood River Valley, 1880–1980* (Bend, OR: Maverick Publications, 2007), 36; U.S. Census, *Fourteenth Census*, 1:382.

3   Linda Tamura, *Hood River Issei*, 83.

4   John Bodnar, *The Transplanted: A History of Immigrants in Urban America* (Bloomington: Indiana University Press, 1985), 72–79.

5   Linda Tamura, *Hood River Issei*, 20. Among twenty-three of twenty-four local Nisei whose information was available, fourteen had parents who emigrated from southwestern Japan.

6   Yosaburo Yoshida, "Sources and Causes of Japanese Emigration," *The Annals*

*of the American Academy of Political and Social Science* 34 (September 1909): 379.

7   Linda Tamura, *Hood River Issei*, 1–2, 19–22.

8   Harry H. L. Kitano, *Generations and Identity: The Japanese American* (Needham Heights, MA: Ginn Press, 1993), 85, 117; Eileen Tamura, *Americanization, Acculturation, and Ethnic Identity: The Nisei Generation in Hawaii* (Urbana: University of Illinois Press, 1994), 33; Paul R. Spickard, *Japanese Americans: The Formation and Transformations of an Ethnic Group* (New York: Twayne, 1996), 69–70.

9   Frank S. Miyamoto, "An Immigrant Community in America," in *East across the Pacific: Historical and Sociological Studies of Japanese Immigration and Assimilation*, ed. Hilary Conroy and T. Scott Miyakawa (Santa Barbara, CA: American Bibliographical Center Clio Press, 1972), 241; Kitano, *Generations*, 84–93; Eileen Tamura, *Americanization*, 33–34.

10  Thomas D. Murphy, *Ambassadors in Arms* (Honolulu: University of Hawaii Press, 1954), 11.

11  Roger Daniels, Sandra C. Taylor, and H. L. Kitano, *Japanese Americans: From Relocation to Redress* (Salt Lake City: University of Utah, 1986), 4; Eileen Tamura, *Americanization*, 50.

12  Mitzi Asai Loftus, *Made in Japan and Settled in Oregon* (Coos Bay, OR: Pigeon Point Press, 1990), 57.

13  Ibid., 74.

14  Spickard, *Japanese Americans*, 80.

15  Kitano, *Generations*, 118.

16  Linda Tamura, *Hood River Issei*, 120.

17  Bodnar, *The Transplanted*, 76.

18  Dorothy Swaine Thomas, *The Salvage: Japanese American Evacuation and Resettlement* (Berkeley: University of California Press, 1952), 580.

19  Martha Ferguson McKeown, "Frank Hachiya: He Was an American at Birth— and at Death." *Sunday Oregonian*, May 20, 1945, 3; Harry Takagi, correspondence with author, September 13, 2002; Bessie Asai, conversation with the author, January 7, 2002; Claude Morita, correspondence with author, March 7, 2005.

20  Franklin Odo, *No Sword to Bury: Japanese Americans in Hawai'i during World War II* (Philadelphia: Temple University Press, 2004), 268; Eileen Tamura, *Americanization*, 179.

21  Cited in Spickard, *Japanese Americans*, 78.

22  Kitano, *Generations*, 88, 123; Eileen Tamura, *Americanization*, 34, 179.

23  Linda Tamura, *Hood River Issei*, 257, 114.

24  Eileen Tamura, *Americanization*, 34.

25 U.S. Bureau of the Census, *Fifteenth Census*, vol. 3, pt. 2, table 17.

26 Thomas, *Salvage*, 611, cited in Spickard, *Japanese Americans*, 174, 80.

## CHAPTER 2. "NICE PEOPLE SO LONG AS THEY ARE IN A MINORITY"

1 Linda Tamura, *Hood River Issei*, 20, 63–64. The Immigration Commission reported that before 1911 many Japanese laborers worked for $1.50, $1.60, and $1.75 a day, while others earned $1.75, $2.00, and $2.25 for the same work.

2 Lawson Fusao Inada, Akemi Kikumura, and Mary Worthington, eds., *In This Great Land of Freedom: The Japanese Pioneers of Oregon*, (Los Angeles: Japanese American National Museum, 1993), 8, 14–15, 19.

3 Donovan and Associates, *City of Hood River*, 2–11; Crowley, *Legacy: A Centennial Celebration of Hood River*, 67, 24–28; Hood River County Historical Society, *History of Hood River County: 1852-1982*, vol. 1 (Dallas, TX: Taylor Publishing, 1982), 12–13, 44; Linda Tamura, *Hood River Issei*, 67–68.

4 Linda Tamura, *Hood River Issei*, 68; Hood River County Historical Society, *History of Hood River County*, 2:80; Jason Pierce, "The Winds of Change: The Decline of Extractive Industries and the Rise of Tourism in Hood River County, Oregon," *Oregon Historical Quarterly* 108 (Fall 2007): 416; Burkhart, *It All Began with Apple Seeds*, 39.

5 Commercial Club, *Hood River, Oregon*, 3–8, 12–14, 23–27.

6 Burkhart, *It All Began with Apple Seeds*, 41–42.

7 Linda Tamura, *Hood River Issei*, 75, 68, 87.

8 Inada, Kikumura, and Worthington, *In This Great Land*, 16; U.S. War Relocation Authority, "Prejudice in Hood River Valley: A Case Study in Race Relations," Community Analysis Report no. 13, June 6 (Washington, D.C.: Government Printing Office, 1945), 3.

9 Donovan and Associates, *City of Hood River*, 16.

10 Marvin Gavin Pursinger, "Oregon's Japanese in World War II: A History of Compulsory Relocation," Ph.D. diss., University of Southern California, 1962, 10.

11 Linda Tamura, *Hood River Issei*, 22; Yuji Ichioka, "Amerika Nadeshiko: Japanese Immigrant Women in the United States, 1900-1924," *Pacific Historical Review* 49 (May 1980): 342–43.

12 Roger Daniels, *Asian America: Chinese and Japanese in the United States since 1850* (Seattle: University of Washington Press, 1988), 127; Inada, Kikumura, and Worthington, *In This Great Land*, 20.

13 Tamura, "Grandma Noji," unpublished family book (1984), 40–41.

14 Mid-Columbia Japanese American Citizens League, "Japanese-Americans in Hood River," Hood River, OR, 2 MC/JACL.

15 Linda Tamura, *Hood River Issei*, 83, 117–18, 87–88; Davey, *Japanese Situation in Oregon*, 14; Inada, Kikumura, and Worthington, *In This Great Land*, 16; Pursinger, "Oregon's Japanese," 11; U.S. War Relocation Authority, "Prejudice in Hood River Valley," 3.

16 Linda Tamura, *Hood River Issei*, 83; Pursinger, "Oregon's Japanese," 11; Hood River County Historical Society, *History of Hood River County*, 1:15; Burkhart, *It All Began with Apple Seeds*, 83–85.

17 *Hood River News*, February 2, 1923, 4.

18 Lauren Kessler, *Stubborn Twig* (New York: Random House, 1993), 68–69.

19 Eileen Tamura, *Americanization*, 49.

20 Linda Tamura, *Hood River Issei*, 88.

21 Pursinger, "Oregon's Japanese," 58–59, 54, 60; Daniels, *Asian America*, 144–45, 133.

22 Donovan and Associates, *City of Hood River*, 20–22, 27, 31–33.

23 Linda Tamura, *Hood River Issei*, 89–90.

24 Donovan and Associates, *City of Hood River*, 25–27.

25 Davey, "Report on the Japanese Situation," 8; Linda Tamura, *Hood River Issei*, 89–90; U.S. War Relocation Authority, "Prejudice in Hood River Valley," 6.

26 Davey, "Report on the Japanese Situation," 7, 14–15; Pursinger, "Oregon's Japanese," 27–30.

27 U.S. War Relocation Authority, "Prejudice in Hood River Valley," 6; Linda Tamura, *Hood River Issei*, 92.

28 C. C. Chapman, *Oregon Voter* (Portland), November 1, 1919, 4–5.

29 Linda Tamura, *Hood River Issei*, 91; Inada, Kikumura, and Worthington, *In This Great Land*, 27; Ted W. Cox, *The Toledo Incident of 1925* (Corvallis, OR: Old World Publications, 2005), 32–55; Daniel P. Johnson, "Anti-Japanese Legislation in Oregon, 1917–1923," *Oregon Historical Quarterly* 97:2 (Summer 1996): 176–77.

30 Donovan and Associates, *City of Hood River*, 29–36.

31 Johnson, "Anti-Japanese Legislation," 190–203.

32 U.S. War Relocation Authority, "Prejudice in Hood River Valley," 7–8; Linda Tamura, *Hood River Issei*, 89.

33 Hood River County Historical Society, *History of Hood River County*, 1:15; Donovan and Associates, *City of Hood River*, 21, 31–34.

34 Kashima, *Judgment without Trial*, 16, 21–22, 30–32.

35 In the late 1980s, the local sheriff's office discovered documents that verified information that Kurahara reported in his biography. Janus Y. Kurahara, *Ganbatte: A Nisei's Story* (Bloomington, IN: AuthorHouse, 1999), 241–47; List,

Japanese and Americans of Japanese ancestry living in Hood River Valley with corresponding names of locals deputized to spy on them, Smithsonian Institute Asian Pacific American Collection, Washington, D.C.; Jan Kurahara, correspondence with author, May 15, 2005.

36 U.S. War Relocation Authority, "Prejudice in Hood River Valley," 8; Linda Tamura, *Hood River Issei*, 118.

CHAPTER 3. "WHY DIDN'T YOU TELL US THE WAR WAS COMING?"

1 Walter LaFeber, *The Clash: A History of U.S.-Japan Relations* (New York: W. W. Norton, 1997), 80–82, 84–98,186–209.

2 Linda Tamura, *Hood River Issei*, 145; Loftus, *Made in Japan*, 11.

3 Mary Beth Norton et al., *A People and a Nation: A History of the United States*, vol. 2, *Since 1865* (Boston: Houghton Mifflin, 1998), 772–75.

4 Audrie Girdner and Anne Loftis, *The Great Betrayal: The Evacuation of the Japanese-Americans during World War II* (London: Macmillan, 1969), 2; "Pacific Coast Defense," *Life*, January 12, 1942, 65; *Oregonian*, December 8, 1941; Floyd J. McKay, *An Editor for Oregon: Charles A. Sprague and the Politics of Change* (Corvallis: Oregon State University Press, 1998), 131.

5 The government's report described the "Army losing their heads . . . in the Booneville [*sic*] Dam affair." Commission on Wartime Relocation and Internment of Civilians [hereafter CWRIC], *Personal Justice Denied* (Washington, DC: Government Printing Office, 1982), 65.

6 *Hood River County Sun*, December 12, 1941; *Hood River News*, December 12, 1941.

7 The eight- to twelve-foot-tall watchtowers were located on the heights and downtown, according to Bill Pattison, former mayor.

8 *Hood River County Sun*, December 12, 1941; Mid-Columbia JACL, "Japanese-Americans in Hood River," 5.

9 Linda Tamura, *Hood River Issei*, 283; Odo, *No Sword to Bury*, 70.

10 U.S. Bureau of the Census, *Seventeenth Census of the United States; Eighteenth Census of the United States.*

11 Linda Tamura, *Hood River Issei*, 283.

12 George Akiyama, Tot (Taro) Asai, Sho Endow, Kenjiro Hayakawa, Mam (Mamoru) Noji, and Bill Yamaki were serving in the U.S. Army when World War II began.

13 Tomeseichi Akiyama, Otoichi Nishimoto, Satoru Uyeno, Ryusuke Watanabe, and Masuo Yasui were all initially detained at the Fort Missoula Justice Department Center. Akiyama family story, MC/JACL Notebook; CWRIC, *Personal Justice Denied*, 55.

14  Linda Tamura, *Hood River Issei*, 146, 188; Kashima, *Judgment without Trial*, 47, 109.

15  Linda Tamura, *Hood River Issei*, 148, 153; *Oregonian*, December 10, 1941; *Hood River News*, December 26, 1941, January 2, 1942.

16  CWRIC, *Personal Justice Denied*, 62; Linda Tamura, *Hood River Issei*, 155–56.

17  Linda Tamura, *Hood River Issei*, 156; *News*, February 13, 1942; Kurahara, *Ganbatte*, 244–5; Girdner and Loftis, *The Great Betrayal*, 16; CWRIC, *Personal Justice Denied*, 50; Roger Daniels, correspondence with author, December 24, 2004.

18  Roger Daniels, "Incarcerating Japanese Americans," *Organization of American Historians Magazine of History* 16:3 (2002): 20.

19  Supreme Court justice Owen J. Roberts attracted national attention when a commission he chaired falsely reported in January 1942 that Nikkei spies assisted Japan in attacking Pearl Harbor. The next month, California attorney general Earl Warren (later governor and chief justice of the U.S. Supreme Court) testified about the danger of Japanese sympathizers within the country and predicted fifth-column activities. A week after the bombing of Pearl Harbor, Secretary of the Navy Frank Knox blamed the "treachery" in Hawaii on "the most effective fifth column work that's come out of this war, except in Norway." See CWRIC, *Personal Justice Denied*, 55–57; Greg Robinson, *By Order of the President: FDR and the Internment of Japanese Americans* (Cambridge, MA: Harvard University Press, 2001), 778, 94–96; Roger Daniels, *Prisoners without Trial: Japanese Americans in World War II* (New York: Hill and Wang, 1993), 37.

20  Floyd J. McKay, "Civil Liberties Suspended: Pacific Northwest Editors and the Nikkei," paper presented at Conference on the History of the Nikkei in the Pacific Northwest, University of Washington, Seattle, May 5–7, 2000, 9.

21  Robert C. Sims, "The 'Free Zone' Nikkei: Japanese Americans in Idaho and Eastern Oregon in World War II," in *Nikkei in the Pacific Northwest: Japanese Americans and Japanese Canadians in the Twentieth Century*, ed. Louis Fiset and Gail M. Nomura (Seattle: University of Washington Press, 2005), 240.

22  Timothy Olmstead, "Nikkei Internment: The Perspective of Two Oregon Weekly Newspapers," *Oregon Historical Quarterly* 85 (Spring 1984): 8.

23  *Oregon Journal*, December 9, 1941.

24  *Oregonian*, December 10, 1941.

25  *Life*, December 22, 1941, 81. General Hideki Tojo, who became prime minister of Japan in October 1941, led his country into war with the United States and Great Britain and pushed the Japanese offensive in China, Southeast Asia, and the Pacific.

26  *Oregon Journal*, December 10, 1941; Linda Tamura, *Hood River Issei*, 148; Roger

Daniels, *Concentration Camps North America: Japanese in the United States and Canada during World War II* (Malabar, FL: Robert E. Krieger, 1981), 50.

27  Linda Tamura, *Hood River Issei*, 152.

28  Girdner and Loftis, *The Great Betrayal*, 3–4.

29  Linda Tamura, *Hood River Issei*, 152.

30  Mid-Columbia JACL, "Japanese-Americans in Hood River," 4; Linda Tamura, *Hood River Issei*, 151–52, 306. Governor Sprague's written response on January 19, 1942, expressed "full confidence in the sincerity of your pledge."

31  *Hood River News*, January 16, 1942, December 12,1941; *Oregon Journal*, December 8,1941; *Oregonian*, December 8, 1941; Pursinger, "Oregon's Japanese," 79–80.

32  *Guide* (Hood River High School student newspaper), in *Hood River News*, January 2, 1942.

33  CWRIC, *Personal Justice Denied*, 71–72; Morton Grodzins, *Americans Betrayed: Politics and the Japanese Evacuation* (Chicago: University of Chicago Press, 1949), 387; Robinson, *By Order of the President*, 102.

34  Lloyd Chiasson, "The Japanese-American Encampment: An Editorial Analysis of 27 West Coast Newspapers," *Newspaper Research Journal* (1991): 97–105.

35  McKay, "Civil Liberties Suspended," 1–13.

36  *Oregonian*, December 19, 1941, February 28, 1942; *Oregon Journal*, December 16, 1941, March 24, 1942; *Capital Journal*, December 17, 1941. In the California poll, three-fourths of respondents supported evacuating aliens and one-third supported evacuating Nisei. See McKay, "Civil Liberties Suspended," 7, 24.

37  *Hood River County Sun*, December 12, 1941, February 13, 1942.

38  Olmstead, "Nikkei Internment," 18–20; *Hood River News*, January 9, 1942, December 19, 1941, February 20, 1942.

39  Pursinger, "Oregon's Japanese," 107–15; Grodzins, *Americans Betrayed*, 42; CWRIC, *Personal Justice Denied*, 69.

40  *Hood River News*, March 13, 1942; Linda Tamura, *Hood River Issei*, 161; Board of Director Minutes and Resolution, February 16, 1942, Hood River Chamber of Commerce, Hood River, OR; Dee Lumber and Sawmill Workers' Local Union, letter to Governor Robert Sprague, February 24, 1942, Resolution to Governor Robert Sprague from Hood River B.P.O.E. No. 1507, March 6, 1942, Robert Sprague Mss., Oregon Historical Society, Portland [hereafter Sprague Mss., OHS].

41  Nyssa's Gate City I.O.O.F., Waldport's Townsend Club, Portland's Progressive Business Men's Club and Women's Advertising Club, Polk County's Elkin's Rural Women's Club, Monmouth's Luckimuth Farmers Union, and Klamath County's Pomona Grange all took stands against the Japanese population. See Pursinger, "Oregon's Japanese," 121–24.

42  CWRIC, *Personal Justice Denied*, 69, 113; Pursinger, "Oregon's Japanese," 125.

Clarence E. Oliver was a Portland high school teacher; C. B. Lewis was a Portland nurseryman. The governor concluded that local communities should work out solutions to Japanese problems. See Pursinger, "Oregon's Japanese," 71–75.

43 Don Butzin, "Present Japanese Situation Discussed by Authority," *Hood River County Sun*, December 19, 1941, 1; Ellen Eisenberg, "'As Truly American as Your Son': Voicing Opposition to Internment in Three West Coast Cities," *Oregon Historical Quarterly* 104:4 (Winter 2003): 542–47; Charles Davis and Jeffrey Kovac, "Confrontation at the Locks: A Protest of Japanese Removal and Incarceration during World War II," *Oregon Historical Quarterly* 107:4 (Winter 2006): 486–509.

44 Daniels, *Asian America*, 218; Michi Weglyn, *Years of Infamy: The Untold Story of America's Concentration Camps* (New York: Morrow Quill, 1976), 111; Pursinger, "Oregon's Japanese," 125; Eisenberg, "'As Truly American as Your Son,'" 544–65; McKay, *An Editor for Oregon*, 125.

45 Robinson, *By Order of the President*, 101–2; Governor Robert Sprague, telegram to Att. Gen. Francis Biddle, February 17, 1942, Folder 15, Box 4, Sprague Records, Oregon State Archives [hereafter OSA]; McKay, *An Editor for Oregon*, 126.

46 CWRIC, *Personal Justice Denied*, 82.

47 Ibid., 52–55, 72–83; McNaughton, *Nisei Linguists*, 12.

48 The president's beliefs in evolution influenced his long-standing views that Nikkei, whether aliens or citizens, were inherently "dangerous and foreign." See Robinson, *By Order of the President*, 71, 116–17, 120.

49 Robert Asahina, *Just Americans: How Japanese Americans Won a War at Home and Abroad* (New York: Gotham Books, 2006), 18.

50 CWRIC, *Personal Justice Denied*, 6, 82–85.

51 Linda Tamura, *Hood River Issei*, 160–61; *Hood River News*, March 27, 1942.

52 Mid-Columbia JACL, "Japanese-Americans in Hood River"; Grace Yamaki, telephone conversation with the author, February 18, 2002.

53 CWRIC, *Personal Justice Denied*, 103.

54 Weglyn, 29; Linda Tamura, *Hood River Issei*, 179; U.S. Bureau of the Census, *Seventeenth Census of the United States*.

55 Lieutenant General DeWitt issued Civilian Exclusion Order no. 49, which was posted on May 7, 1942, at noon. Hood River Nikkei left the valley on May 13, 1942. *Hood River News*, May 8, 1942, May 15, 1942; Linda Tamura, *Hood River Issei*, 166–67.


CHAPTER 4. "FIGHTING FOR GOOD UNCLE SAM"

1 Daniels, *Asian America*, 249, 253.

2 Sharon Marick, "Looking Ahead," *Ruralite* 26:10 (October 1979): 16–17.

3   Harry Takagi, letter to the author, August 5, 2002.

4   "Bill Yamaki," by Bill Yamaki, unpublished manuscript, provided by Lily Yamaki, author's files.

5   Bill Yamaki, Sho Endow, and Taro Asai were already serving in the military.

6   McNaughton, *Nisei Linguists*, 6; Frank F. Chuman, *The Bamboo People: The Law and Japanese-Americans* (Del Mar, CA: Publisher's, 1976), 253; Tamotsu Shibutani, *The Derelicts of Company K: A Sociological Study of Demoralization* (Berkeley: University of California Press, 1978), 80.

7   Girdner and Loftis, *The Great Betrayal*, 268; Shibutani, *Derelicts of Company K*, 80.

8   Harry Takagi materials, from Carolyn Brady, author's files.

9   Daniels, *Asian America*, 249.

10  Masayo Umezawa Duus, *Unlikely Liberators: The Men of the 100th and 442nd*, trans. Peter Duus (Honolulu: University of Hawaii Press, 1987), 19, 54.

11  CWRIC, *Personal Justice Denied*, 187; McNaughton, *Nisei Linguists*, 48.

12  Daniels, *Asian America*, 254.

13  McKeown, "Frank Hachiya," 3; *Honolulu Star-Bulletin*, February 15, 1945.

14  CWRIC, *Personal Justice Denied*, 187; Eric L. Muller, *Free to Die for Their Country: The Story of the Japanese American Draft Resisters* (Chicago: University of Chicago Press, 2001), 41.

15  Muller, *Free to Die*, 42–48; CWRIC, *Personal Justice Denied*, 187–89.

16  Duus, *Unlikely Liberators*, 58.

17  Muller, *Free to Die*, 47–50.

18  Asahina, *Just Americans*, 47.

19  Linda Tamura, *Hood River Issei*, 190–92.

20  *Time*, February 2, 1942, 4. Harry O. Takagi acknowledged that the magazine's misprint of his middle initial was "evidence that my handwriting has not improved." Takagi, correspondence, September 13, 2002.

21  Takagi, correspondence, August 5, 2002.

22  McKeown, "Frank Hachiya," 3.

23  Duus, *Unlikely Liberators*, 70; Asahina, *Just Americans*, 51.

24  U.S. Department of the Interior, *People in Motion: The Postwar Adjustment of the Evacuated Japanese-Americans* (Washington, DC: U.S. Government Printing Office, 1947), 11.

25  Chester Tanaka, *Go for Broke: A Pictorial History of the Japanese American 100th Infantry Battalion and the 442d Regimental Combat Team* (Richmond, CA: Go for Broke, 1982), 17–18; Sho Endow, interview by the author, July 12, 1999, transcript; Harry Tamura, interview by the author, March 7, 2004.

26  Duus, *Unlikely Liberators*, 62.

27  Tanaka, *Go for Broke*, 1–2.

28 Ibid., 2; Lyn Crost, *Honor by Fire: Japanese Americans at War in Europe and the Pacific* (Novato, CA: Presidio Press, 1994), 183–84.

29 Tanaka, *Go for Broke*, 13, 17, 23; Crost, *Honor by Fire*, 15–16, 60.

30 Duus, *Unlikely Liberators*, 63–66; Thelma Chang, *"I Can Never Forget": Men of the 100th/442nd* (Honolulu: Sigi Productions, 1991), 112–16; James P. Dale, "Memo on Japanese- American Soldiers at Camp Shelby, Mississippi: General Resume of Racial, Social and Subversive Situation," July 8, 1943, Assistant Secretary of War McCloy files, RG 107, Entry 180, U.S. National Archives and Records Administration, College Park, MD (hereafter McCloy files), 2, 4; William P. Scobey, letter to Col. C. W. Pence, August 29, 1943, McCloy files.

31 Military Intelligence Service, Counter Intelligence Group, Censorship Branch, "Morale of Japanese-Hawaiian Soldiers at Camp Shelby, Mississippi," August 12, 1943, McCloy files; Dale, "Memo on Japanese-American Soldiers"; Col. Joseph S. Dougherty, "Special Inspections Relative to American-Japanese Soldiers," Memo to Inspector General, June 19, 1943, McCloy files, 4.

32 Gen. John J. McCloy, letter to Gen. McNair, September 23, 1943, McCloy files.

33 After graduating from Fort Snelling in 1945, Harry Takagi was assigned to the Pentagon's Allied Air Force Intelligence unit in Washington, D.C. Once the war ended, he transferred to the U.S. Strategic Bombing Survey Team and served as a translator in Japan. Brady, Takagi family history; Harry Takagi, letters to Vienna Annala, February 26, 1942, May 28, 1942, MC/ JACL files.

34 Takagi, letter to Vienna Annala (former teacher), from Camp Grant, MC/ JACL.

35 Duus, *Unlikely Liberators*, 58. An intelligence report of June 19, 1943, confirmed that "American-Japanese officers and enlisted personnel of the [442nd] combat team were excluded from service schools," but it recommended that they be allowed to attend. Dougherty, "Special Inspections," 4, 6. Claude Morita, a Hood River Nisei formerly employed in the Specialist Force Protection of Navy Intelligence Operations, notes that the military conducted service schools for nearly all occupations, including officers, cooks, yeomen, pilots, crane operators, and "nearly any occupation you can think of to keep ships, airplanes, and tanks running." Morita, correspondence, August 5, 2007.

36 Bill Hosokawa, *Nisei: The Quiet Americans* (New York: William Morrow, 1969), 403; Duus, *Unlikely Liberators*, 58, 227.

37 Muller, *Free to Die*, 64.

38 Ibid., 64.

39 Weglyn, *Years of Infamy*, 48.

40 Noji, letter to Mrs. Rumbaugh, December 28, 1941, Rumbaugh letters, The History Museum, Hood River, Oregon, files.

1   *Hood River News*, April 24, 1942.

2   Linda Tamura, *Hood River Issei*, 162.

3   Hackett Furniture Company advertised a new four-piece bedroom set for $89 in the *Hood River News*, April 5, 1942.

4   Min Asai, notes from speech to local school students, n.d., Minoru Asai family files, Hood River, OR.

5   Linda Tamura, *Hood River Issei*, 162.

6   *Hood River News*, April 10, 1942.

7   Linda Tamura, *Hood River Issei*, 164.

8   Chiz Tamura, interview by the author, November 29, 2001, transcript; Linda Tamura, *Hood River Issei*, 166.

9   Linda Tamura, *Hood River Issei*, 166–67.

10  Ibid., 167.

11  Teunis J. Wyers, letter to Governor Charles Sprague, May 27, 1942, Folder 12, Box 4, Sprague Records, OSA.

12  Linda Tamura, *Hood River Issei*, 167–68.

13  Kiyo Akiyama, letter to Vienna Annala, 1942, notebook, MC/JACL. Annala taught and served as principal at Oak Grove School from 1936 until 1943. She corresponded with many Japanese American children and servicemen during the war. After her death in June 1984, niece Maija Yasui retained her letters. Copies are part of the notebook, MC/JACL.

14  Henry Akiyama, letter to Vienna Annala, May 1942, notebook, MC/JACL.

15  Linda Tamura, *Hood River Issei*, 170.

16  Akiyama, letter to Annala, notebook, MC/JACL.

17  Tommy Wakamatsu, letter to Vienna Annala, May 14, 1942, Florence Takagi to Annala, n.d., notebook, MC/JACL.

18  Linda Tamura, *Hood River Issei*, 173–74; Loftus, *Made in Japan*, 103.

19  Henry Akiyama, letter to Vienna Annala, May 22, May 29, 1942, notebook, MC/JACL.

20  Kiyo Akiyama, letter to Vienna Annala, May 18, May 25, June 6, 1942, notebook, MC/JACL.

21  President Roosevelt used the term "concentration camps" in early press conferences but later avoided any association with Nazi extermination camps. Scholar Roger Daniels, among others, denounced the use of euphemisms to soften the effects of Executive Order 9066. Aliens and citizens alike were detained in American concentration camps, he admonishes. Not only were all deemed guilty without due process, they were deprived of real property and incarcerated merely because of their ancestry. See Daniels, *Asian America*, 228.

22 Ibid., 225. The sites were on federal land so that improvements would benefit the public. CWRIC, *Personal Justice Denied*, 156.

23 Edward Miyakawa, *Tule Lake* (Waldport, OR: House by the Sea Publishing, 1979), 88.

24 Henry Akiyama, letter to Annala, July 9, July 18, 1943.

25 Mid-Columbia JACL, "Japanese-Americans in Hood River," 5.

26 CWRIC, *Personal Justice Denied*, 163.

27 Linda Tamura, *Hood River Issei*, 190–98. Among Tule Lake residents, one-third were considered "disloyals," one-third were their family members, and the remainder simply chose not to move. More than seven thousand eventually applied to repatriate or expatriate to Japan; two-thirds of them were Nisei who renounced their citizenship. Altogether, twenty thousand Japanese Americans filed applications by the end of 1945. Daniels, *Asian Americans*, 262–65; CWRIC, *Personal Justice Denied*, 251.

28 The words "detention" (the term the CWRIC uses in its report) and "internment" are common terms for the Japanese exclusion. According to Tetsuden Kashima, "internment" refers to the imprisonment of civilian enemy nationals, while "incarceration" is appropriate for those imprisoned in the War Department's assembly centers and the War Relocation Authority's camps. The word "imprisonment," he maintains, encompasses both terms, defining the process of arresting individuals without criminal charge, detaining them without trial, and placing them inside primitive prisons. Kashima, *Judgment without Trial*, 8–9.

29 McKeown, "Frank Hachiya," 3.

30 Daisuke Kitagawa, in Linda Tamura, *Hood River Issei*, 207.

31 Ibid.; Kitano, *Generations and Identity*, 122.

32 Hugh G. Ball (editor, *Hood River News*), letter to Governor Robert Sprague, October 19, 1942, Folder 7, Box 2, Sprague Records, OSA.

33 Ibid.

34 Min Asai, notes from speech, Minoru Asai family files.

35 U.S. Department of the Interior, *People in Motion*, 11; Weglyn, 29.

36 Japanese American Citizens League, National Education Committee, *A Lesson in American History: The Japanese American Experience*, Curriculum and Resource Guide (San Francisco: JACL, 1996), 13–14.

37 Minoru Yasui had resigned his position at the Japanese consulate general in Chicago after the bombing of Pearl Harbor before defying the curfew in Portland, Oregon. In 1983, he filed a *coram nobis* petition challenging his conviction, based on newly discovered documents revealing that the Justice Department did not regard Japanese Americans as security threats during

the war. Before the case was decided in the Ninth Circuit Court of Appeals, Yasui died of cancer, on November 12, 1986. Although his family moved for a Supreme Court review, the court dismissed his petition in 1987, and his case died, too. See Robert S. Yasui, *The Yasui Family of Hood River, Oregon* (Hood River, OR: Holly Yasui, Desktop Publishing, 1987), 58–61; John Tateishi, *And Justice for All: An Oral History of the Japanese American Detention Camps* (New York: Random House, 1984), 71–82; Peter Irons, ed., *Justice Delayed: The Record of the Japanese American Internment Cases* (Middletown, CT: Wesleyan University Press, 1989), 29–30.

38  Wallace Turner, "Bitter Memories of World War II Detention," *New York Times Daily Magazine*, August 10, 1981, 18.


CHAPTER 6. "GETTING SHOT FROM AHEAD OF US AND BEHIND US"

1  G-2 is headquarters for the U.S. Army's Office of the Deputy Chief of Staff for Intelligence, responsible for information that helps commanders accomplish combat missions.

2  Joseph D. Harrington, *Yankee Samurai* (Detroit: Pettigrew Enterprises, 1979), 8.

3  Crost, *Honor by Fire*, 21, 32.

4  Brigadier General John Weckerling, "Nisei Language Experts: Japanese Americans Play Vital Role in U.S. Intelligence Service in WWII," in *John Aiso and the M.I.S.: Japanese-American Soldiers in the Military Intelligence Service, World War II*, by Tad Ichinokuchi (Los Angeles: The Military Intelligence Service Club of Southern California, 1988), 187–88; Crost, *Honor by Fire*, 21–22; McNaughton, *Nisei Linguists*, 20–21.

5  Masaharu Ano, "Loyal Linguists: Nisei of World War II Learned Japanese in Minnesota," *Minnesota History* 45 (1977): 276.

6  Military Intelligence Service Association (MISA) of Northern California and the National Japanese American Historical Society (hereafter MISA of Northern California and the NJAHS), *The Pacific War and Peace: Americans of Japanese Ancestry in Military Intelligence Service, 1941 to 1952* (San Francisco: Military Intelligence Service Association of Northern California and the National Japanese American Historical Society, 1991), 16; Military Intelligence School Language Service *MISLS Album, 1946* (Nashville, TN: Battery Press, 1990), 8.

7  Ano, "Loyal Linguists," 274.

8  McKeown, "Frank Hachiya," 3; Morita, correspondence. Social scientist Alexander H. Leighton addresses the situation in *The Governing of Men: General*

*Principles and Recommendations Based on Experience at a Japanese Relocation Camp* (Princeton, NJ: Princeton University Press, 1945), 80.

9 Daniels, *Asian America*, 247–48; Military Intelligence Service Association of Northern California and the National Japanese American Historical Society, *Pacific War and Peace*, 18.

10 Crost, *Honor by Fire*, 22–24; McNaughton, *Nisei Linguists*, 49–54.

11 Ano, "Loyal Linguists," 278.

12 Ibid., 78–79; Mamoru Noji, interview by the author, July 5, 1999, transcript.

13 Hosokawa, *Nisei*, 397; Harrington, *Yankee Samurai*, 89; Ano, "Loyal Linguists," 280; Weckerling, "Nisei Language Experts," 191–92; MIS Historical Committee, *MIS Veterans*, 3; McNaughton, *Nisei Linguists*, 108–10.

14 MISA of Northern California and the NJAHS, *Pacific War and Peace*, 18.

15 Kiyoshi Yano, "Participating in the Mainstream of American Life amidst Drawback of Racial Prejudice and Discrimination," in *John Aiso and the M.I.S.*, by Ichinokuchi, 17; McNaughton, *Nisei Linguists*, 131. Judge John F. Aiso of California (the first commissioned Nisei in the MIS and former director of academic training at the MIS language schools in Minnesota) stated that the War Department deemed Nisei too valuable for noncommissioned officer status but also banned commissions because of their race. Judge Aiso's tribute to Nisei in G-2 at Arlington National Cemetery, June 2, 1963, cited by Representative Edward R. Roybal of California in the *Congressional Record*, 88th Cong., 1st Sess. (1963), 10663. McNaughton's book cites surveillance of Nisei at Camp Savage, where up to three informants per barrack kept an eye on Nisei. McNaughton, *Nisei Linguists*, 114–15.

16 Japanese American Veterans Association, "American Courage Award Presented to WWII Army Military Intelligence Service, Akaka and Shinseki Praise MIS," *MIS Northwest Association Newsletter*, November 2004, 2–3; CWRIC, *Personal Justice Denied*, 254; Crost, *Honor by Fire*, 21.

17 CWRIC, *Personal Justice Denied*, 254.

18 Mamoru Noji, "This I Remember," unpublished manuscript, December 1994, author's files.

19 U.S. Army Center of Military History, "Named Campaigns—World War II: Asiatic-Pacific Theater," http://www.army.mil/cmh.

20 Crost, *Honor by Fire*, 35, 45–47.

21 U.S. Army Center of Military History, "Named Campaigns," 5; Patrick K. O'Donnell, *Into the Rising Sun* (New York: Simon & Schuster, 2002), 5, 17, 63, 66.

22 U.S. Army Center of Military History, "Named Campaigns," 4, www.army.mil/cmh.

23 Noji, "This I Remember," 2–3.

24 Ibid., 2.

25 Ibid., 3; Noji, interview, July 5, 1999.

26 O'Donnell, *Into the Rising Sun*, 66; U.S. Army Center of Military History, "Named Campaigns," 6.

27 Noji, "This I Remember," 3; Mamoru Noji, interview by the author, January 8, 2002, transcript.

28 Crost, *Honor by Fire*, 54.

29 Ibid., 33, 35–36, 51; MIS Historical Committee, *MIS Veterans*, 10–11.

30 McNaughton, *Nisei Linguists*, 165, 189.

31 Noji, "This I Remember," 4.

32 Noji, interview, July 5, 1999, January 8, 2002; Noji, correspondence with the author, January 9, 2004; Weckerling, "Nisei Language Experts," 193; Military Intelligence Service Northwest Association, "The Unprecedented Story of the Military Intelligence Service," commemorating the fiftieth anniversary of the end of World War II, September 7–9, 1995. Kibei composed 12.5 percent of Nisei evacuated to the camps, or nine thousand of the seventy-two thousand Nisei, according to Ano, "Loyal Linguists," 274.

33 Noji, "This I Remember," 4.

34 Crost, *Honor by Fire*, 52, 54–55, 161, 204; MIS Historical Committee, *MIS Veterans*, 8, 11; Ted Tsukiyama, "Deciphering the Z Plan," in *Secret Valor: M.I.S. Personnel, World War II Pacific Theater*, by Military Intelligence Service Veterans Club of Hawaii (Honolulu: Military Intelligence Service Veterans Club of Hawaii, 1993), 55–57.

35 O'Donnell, *Into the Rising Sun*, 119, 149–53; U.S. Army Center of Military History, "Named Campaigns," 11; Crost, *Honor by Fire*, 204; Harrington, *Yankee Samurai*, 246–47; *MIS Northwest Association Newsletter*, November 2004, 3; McNaughton, *Nisei Linguists*, 296.

36 Harrington, *Yankee Samurai*, 247; Crost, *Honor by Fire*, 205; McNaughton, *Nisei Linguists*, 296.

37 *Honolulu Star-Bulletin*, February 15, 1945.

38 *Hood River News*, April 27, 1945.

39 Hosokawa, *Nisei*, 414–15.

40 Fukei, *Japanese American Story*, 69.

41 *New York Times*, December 7, 1991, 4; MIS Historical Committee, *MIS Veterans*, 12; Charles Hillinger, "Secret Weapon: Japanese-American Soldiers Saved Time and Lives in World War II," in *John Aiso and the M.I.S.*, by Ichinokuchi, 177.

42 *Congressional Record*, 88th Congress, 10667.

43 The National Personnel Records Center states that a major portion of army military personnel records from 1912 through 1959 was destroyed by a fire and

that records regarding Private Hachiya's death were not in their files. NPRC letter, February 13, 2004; Harrington, *Yankee Samurai*, 248; *Honolulu Star-Bulletin*, February 15, 1945; Crost, *Honor by Fire*, 205; McNaughton, *Nisei Linguists*, 296–97.

44 Richard Sakakida miraculously escaped after being imprisoned by the Japanese for nine months. "American Courage Award Presented to WWII Army MIS; Akaka and Shinseki Praise MIS," *MIS Northwest Association Newsletter*, November 2004, 5; Richard B. Oguro, *Sen Pai Gumi* (Honolulu: Hochi Press, 1980), 18; Harrington, *Yankee Samurai*, 66–69, 132–33, 351.

45 O'Donnell, *Into the Rising Sun*, 153, 175–78; Crost, *Honor by Fire*, 208–9.

46 Howitzers lobbed shells, unlike long-barreled artillery and naval guns that propelled ammunition long distances, often many miles. Noji speculated that howitzers contributed to his hearing loss.

47 During the battle of Iwo Jima, 6,140 Americans and almost 20,000 Japanese died. Attacks on Okinawa resulted in 12,500 Americans killed or missing in action, as well as the deaths of 110,000 Japanese and 159,000 Okinawan civilians. O'Donnell, *Into the Rising Sun*, 226–27, 261–62.

48 Crost, *Honor by Fire*, 32, referenced Colonel Sidney F. Mashbir of ATIS in Brisbane, Australia, and an October 29, 1945, report of General Willoughby.

49 Military Intelligence Service Veterans Club of Hawaii, *Secret Valor*, 17; Dan Nakatsu, "The Nisei Soldiers of U.S. Military Intelligence: America's Superb Secret Weapon of World War II," in *John Aiso and the M.I.S.*, by Ichinokuchi, 47, cited in "MISLS Graduates in Combat Zone," in *Secret Valor*, by Military Intelligence Service Veterans Club of Hawaii, 43.

50 Harrington, *Yankee Samurai*, 88; Ano, "Loyal Linguists," 284; Crost, *Honor by Fire*, 33; McNaughton, *Nisei Linguists*, 52, 123, 130, 294. Grades are administrative classifications for pay.

51 Crost, *Honor by Fire*, 33; McNaughton, *Nisei Linguists*, 257, 384; Harrington, *Yankee Samurai*, 87–88. Bill Yamaki, the first Nisei enlistee from Hood River, was an exception. He served with ATIS in Brisbane, Australia, then became an aide-de-camp to Major General William F. Marquat, who carried out Japanese economic policies for General McArthur, commanding general of the Headquarters Fourteenth AA Command.

52 Ano, "Loyal Linguists," 287.

53 CWRIC, *Personal Justice Denied*, 256; Daniels, *Asian America*, 247; Crost, *Honor by Fire*, 54; Ano, "Loyal Linguists," 73; Military Intelligence Service Veterans Club of Hawaii, *Secret Valor*, 2. After V-J Day, August 15, 1945, Nisei linguists were instrumental in promoting peaceful relations between the Occupation forces and Japanese citizens. Nisei participated in surrender ceremonies, helped frame Japan's post–World War II constitution, served

as translators during war crimes trials, and gathered vital statistics for an atomic bomb survey. Military Intelligence Service Northwest Association, "Unprecedented Story," 36; Military Intelligence School Language School, "History of MISLS," in *MISLS Album*, 15; MIS Historical Committee, *MIS Veterans*, 20.


## CHAPTER 7. "FROM SOMEWHERE IN EUROPE"

1 Tanaka, *Go for Broke*, 1.
2 Ibid., 50.
3 Duus, *Unlikely Liberators*, 89–90.
4 Members of the 442nd Combat Team, *The Story of the 442nd Combat Team*, Information-Education Section, Mediterranean Theater of Operations, United States Army (San Francisco: Company K Club, 1979), 3; Tanaka, *Go for Broke*, 23.
5 Duus, *Unlikely Liberators*, 100–101, 118; Tanaka, *Go for Broke*, 24–38.
6 Duus, *Unlikely Liberators*, 128–29, 135–37; Crost, *Honor by Fire*, 137–38; Tanaka, *Go for Broke*, 44–47.
7 Asahina, *Just Americans*, 32. The new regiment included, among others, three battalions of infantrymen; an antitank company, a cannon company, and an engineering company; and the 522nd Field Artillery Battalion.
8 Crost, *Honor by Fire*, 147.
9 Duus, *Unlikely Liberators*, 156–57; Crost, *Honor by Fire*, 150–51.
10 Tanaka, *Go for Broke*, 58.
11 Ibid., 73; Chang, *"I Can Never Forget,"* 148.
12 Crost, *Honor by Fire*, 158–59; Duus, *Unlikely Liberators*, 159–60; Tanaka, *Go for Broke*, 74.
13 Battle conditions made soldiers susceptible to trench foot, caused by long exposure to moisture and cold. Untreated, it could require amputation. Asahina, *Just Americans*, 151.
14 Crost, *Honor by Fire*, 175.
15 Duus, *Unlikely Liberators*, 161–62; Tanaka, *Go for Broke*, 75–71; Crost, *Honor by Fire*, 174.
16 Crost, *Honor by Fire*, 175–76.
17 Duus, *Unlikely Liberators*, 164–65.
18 Ibid.
19 Tanaka, *Go for Broke*, 50; Crost, *Honor by Fire*, 79.
20 Tanaka, *Go for Broke*, 62.
21 Ibid., 81–82; Members of the 442nd Combat Team, *Story of the 442nd*, 26–27.
22 Tanaka, *Go for Broke*, 75–88; Crost, *Honor by Fire*, 179–82.

23  For references on other troops, see Crost, *Honor by Fire*, 184; Tanaka, *Go for Broke*, 92; Duus, *Unlikely Liberators*, 201.

24  Crost, *Honor by Fire*, 185.

25  Tanaka, *Go for Broke*, 92; Asahina, *Just Americans*, 164; Duus, *Unlikely Liberators*, 202.

26  *Hood River News*, January 5, 1945; Headquarters 92d Infantry Division Citation to Staff Sgt. George Akiyama, October 3, 1945.

27  Crost, *Honor by Fire*, 197; Duus, *Unlikely Liberators*, 216. See also Duus, *Unlikely Liberators*, 211–16; Tanaka, *Go for Broke*, 102–3.

28  Crost, *Honor by Fire*, 199; Duus, *Unlikely Liberators*, 217; "Rescue of the Lost Battalion," Go for Broke Educational Foundation, http://www.goforbroke.org/history/history_historical_campaigns_rescue.asp.

29  Crost, *Honor by Fire*, 249–50.

30  Tanaka, *Go for Broke*, 119; Crost, *Honor by Fire*, 251.

31  Tanaka, *Go for Broke*, 120–22.

32  Ibid., 122; Crost, *Honor by Fire*, 253.

33  *Hood River News*, December 14, 1945.

34  Tanaka, *Go for Broke*, 119–25, 128–30.

35  Ibid., 129–30.

36  Sho Endow explained that K rations included a separate meal for breakfast, lunch, and supper. "You'd get a fruit bar, three cigarettes, matches, toilet paper. . . . They give you a can of DDT, so you just sprinkle that DDT around a canvas . . . to keep the bugs out of your system."

37  Tanaka, *Go for Broke*, 130–40; Crost, *Honor by Fire*, 263–64.

38  CWRIC, *Personal Justice Denied*, 258; Tanaka, *Go for Broke*, 143.

39  Tanaka, *Go for Broke*, 66.

40  CWRIC, *Personal Justice Denied*, 258.

CHAPTER 8. "I'VE GOT A LOT OF FIGHTING TO DO RIGHT HERE"

1  Harry Takagi, correspondence with author, September 13, 2002.

2  Fred Sumoge, interview by the author, August 31, 2003, transcript; LaFeber, *Clash*, 200.

3  Tow Hori, interview by the author, August 14, 2005, transcript; Paul Tsuneishi (MIS veteran and former Pacific Southwest JACL governor), interview by the author, September 5, 2001. Hori, who volunteered for the military service after World War II began, was stationed at Fort Riley, Kansas, and Fort McClellan, Alabama, and was sent to the newly formed 1800th Infantry Battalion, where the army kept alleged troublemakers of German, Italian, and Japanese descent under surveillance.

4   *Discipline Barrack Boys*, videotape, Paul Minerich Collection, Hirasaki National Resource Center, Japanese American National Museum, Los Angeles, September 9, 1984, author transcript, 2.

5   The army did not want to send "troublemakers" to Camp Shelby, so potential "agitators" remained at Fort Riley, according to Hori. GIs suspected *inu* ("dogs" in Japanese) of acting as informants for military officials. Tow Hori, interview by the author, August 3, 2003, transcript; Hori, interview, July 1, 2004, August 21, 2005; Dougherty, "Special Inspections," 1; Brookhart, "Investigation Relative to Japanese American Soldiers," 8–9, McCloy files.

6   Travel log, mileage page, April 14–29, 1943, Franklin Delano Roosevelt, Franklin Delano Roosevelt Library, Hyde Park, New York [hereafter FDR travel log]; Hori, interview, August 3, 2003; Capt. Smith W. Brookhart Jr., "Investigation Relative to Japanese American Soldiers," War Department, July 28, 1943, 1–16, McCloy files.

7   Brookhart, "Investigation Relative to Japanese American Soldiers," 3, 5; Tow Hori, interview by the author, August 27, 2003, transcript; *Discipline Barrack Boys*; Mas Kataoka statement, Army Board for Correction of Military Records [hereafter ABCMR], transcript of hearing, December 8, 1982, 86, copy in Fred Sumoge files.

8   Hori, interview, August 3, 2003, July 1, 2004; Tow Hori, interview by the author, September 5, 2001, transcript; Capt. Harold J. Crase, testimony to Col. Dougherty, June 4, 1943, Maj. Crase testimony to Capt. Brookhart, Jr., Inspector General's Department, July 11, 1943, 127, McCloy files.

9   FDR travel log, 41–44.

10  Army inspectors sent to investigate Hakuban Nozawa's complaint interviewed Nisei from Fort Riley's motor pool, but according to Mas Ogawa, one of the Fort Riley GIs, the nervous men were noncommittal. See *Discipline Barrack Boys*. Nozawa "received no satisfaction or explanation," according to the 1948 brief filed by Zane to appeal the men's convictions. Charles Edmund Zane, brief in support of Discipline Barrack Boys, 1948, Tow Hori files, Los Angeles.

11  Inagaki had joined the JACL's national secretary Mike Masaoka for the announcement of the all-volunteer Nisei combat team at the Pentagon, where he met Colonel Scobey and eventually became the second, after Masaoka, to volunteer. In his May 11, 1943, letter voicing disappointment at Nisei reactions to the combat team and vowing to "straighten the perverted perspective of the Nisei in the centers," he attached a Nisei GI's letter and asked for clarification. Inagaki, letter to Col. Scobey, with attachment, May 11, 1943, Morale of Japanese-Americans file, McCloy files.

12  Col. Scobey to Inagaki, May 14, 1943, Morale of Japanese-Americans file, McCloy files.

13  Assistant Secretary of War McCloy, memo to the Inspector General, May 21, 1943, enclosing extract from letter, McCloy files.

14  Dougherty, "Special Inspections Relative to American-Japanese Soldiers," June 19, 1943, McCloy files.

15  Scobey, memo to McCloy, June 28, 1943, McCloy files.

16  Brookhart, "Investigation Relative to Japanese American Soldiers," July 28, 1943, 6–12, Capt. Crase testimony, July 11, 1943, 128–29, McCloy Files.

17  Brookhart, "Investigation Relative to Japanese American Soldiers," 15, 9, McCloy files.

18  Ibid., 15.

19  Scobey, "Memorandum for Mr. McCloy: Confinement of Japanese American soldiers at Fort Riley," September 23, 1943, 5, McCloy files.

20  McCloy, memo to Brig. Gen. Porter, Asst. Chief of Staff, G-3, Sept. 24, 1943, McCloy files.

21  Maj. Gen. Ray E. Porter, Asst. Chief of Staff, G-3, "Memorandum for the Asst. Sec. of War," November 15, 1943, McCloy files.

22  Tow Hori, correspondence with the author, January 6, 2004; Zane, brief.

23  The Anniston Public Library's search of *Anniston Star* issues did not reveal that headline. The material may have come from *McClellan News*, the Fort McClellan newspaper.

24  See Ichioka, *Issei*, 13–14.

25  Kenjiro Hayakawa general court-martial records, U.S. Army Judiciary, Department of the Army, Arlington, VA, copies in author's files; Hayakawa background statement, 1, Hayakawa files, U.S. Army, copies in author's files.

26  The number of men varies in different records. Fred Sumoge recalled that there were more than 100. Castelnuovo's account in *Soldiers of Conscience* (41) states that 103 Japanese Americans were "milling around and engaging in heated conversation." Court-martial records for Sumoge and Hayakawa report 43 men. Staff Judge Adv.'s Review, Maj. Ronald D. Miller, May 23, 1944, 1, Sumoge court-martial records; memorandum for the Secretary of the Army, T. Wade Markley, Chairman, Clemency and Parole Board No. 1, 17 February 1949, 3, Hayakawa files; Zane, brief, 4.

27  Sumoge court-martial records, 41; McDonald, statement, 24; Hayakawa court-martial records, 30; Zane, brief, 4.

28  Maj. Aycock, testimony, April 1944, Hayakawa court-martial records, 29–31, 35; Maj. Aycock, testimony, April 12–13, 1944, Sumoge court-martial records, 8, 41; Cpl. Ballinger statements, April 1944, Hayakawa court-martial records; Lt. Lawson statement, Hayakawa, court-martial records, Apr. 1944; Hayakawa court-martial records, 30, 35; Sumoge court-martial records, 8, 10, 14, 41, 49; Fred Sumoge, interview by the author, June 30, 2004, transcript; Zane, brief, 4–7.

29  Tow Hori, interview by the author, January 6, 2004, transcript; Hori, interview, July 1, 2004, April 29, 2007; Sumoge, interview, June 30, 2004, July 13, 2003, October 18, 2009; Zane, brief, 1.

30  Fred Sumoge, interview by the author, July 13, 2003, transcript; Zane, brief, 1; Paul Minerich, brief, 3; Shigeo Hamai, statement, ABCMR transcript of hearing, December 8, 1982, 79, Pentagon.

31  Memorandum for The Sec. of the Army, T. Wade Markley, Chairman, Clemency Parole Board No. 1, February 17, 1949, 4. Castelnuovo (*Soldiers of Conscience*, 46), states that seventy-five exited to the right.

32  Californian Tow Hori rejoined his unit, thinking "there might be a chance" of working toward a solution. Three days later, in a "secret memo" dated March 23, 1944, forty-three men who had exited to the right requested an audience with the commanding general. These men's reasons included a lack of understanding of how to present their problems to the proper authority; a strong desire to correct problems caused by the mass evacuation; a belief that the evacuation of Nikkei was "unjust, undemocratic and un-American" and based on insufficient grounds; a desire to fight the wrongs of evacuation; and their decision to resort to drastic measures in order to attract attention. The memo maintained that the men were "100% loyal to the country of our birth" and that they would perform in a superior manner if they were confident the government would rectify injustices caused by the evacuation. Finally, it referred to those in the stockade as "martyrs for the cause" who were "bull-headed" but not disloyal, simply "doing their part . . . to correct the wrongs and injustices caused by Evacuation." See "Reasons for Recent Kibei Activities," March 23, 1944, Paul Minerich Collection, Hirasaki National Resource Center, Japanese American National Museum, Los Angeles. Within a month, all who signed the secret memo were called for court-martial. Once their training ended, all seventy-eight who exited to the right were transferred to the 1800th Battalion at Lebanon, Tennessee, where the army was keeping German, Italian, and Japanese alleged to be troublemakers under surveillance. The men repaired roads, bridges, and fences damaged by combat troop and tank maneuvers in the southern states. See Cedric Shimo, "The 1800th Engineering General Service Battalion," speech delivered at the Life Interrupted Conference: The Japanese American Experience in World War II, Little Rock, Arkansas, September 25, 2004, 8.

33  Zane, brief, 1.

34  Hayakawa, statement, Hayakawa court-martial files, 2.

35  *Pacific Citizen*, March 25, April 1, April 15, April 22, April 29, 1944.

36  Sumoge court-martial records, 26.

37  Sumoge statement, Sumoge investigation transcript, April 1944, 4–6.

38 Hayakawa, investigation transcript, 1–5.

39 Court-martial records for both Sumoge and Hayakawa included recommendations for a general court-martial from three investigating officers. Sumoge and Hayakawa court-martial records. A brief of Charles Edmund Zane's appeal states that eight of the twenty-eight from Company A were acquitted, but Technician Fifth Grade Harold S. Murata and Technician Fifth Grade Samuel S. Tsuruta returned later, on other specifications of the same charge, bringing the total to thirty. The discrepancy in the final number is not explained. Zane, brief, 2. Sumoge remembered that of the twenty-eight in the stockade, eight were released, but that Murata and Tsuruta voluntarily returned after others outside gave them "a rough time." That brought the number to twenty-two. Then, before trial, one was given a medical discharge. Zane, brief, 2; Sumoge, interview, July 13, 2003, 4; Fred Sumoge, interview by the author, August 29, 2007, October 18, 2009, transcript.

40 Proceedings of a General Court-Martial, April 3, 1994, Detail for the Court, Sumoge court-martial records, 6a.

41 William Winthrop, *Military Law and Precedents*, 2d ed. (reprint; Boston: Little, Brown, 1920); Sumoge court-martial records, 7–39.

42 During Sumoge's two-day court-martial, his defense objected five times to prosecutors admitting evidence beyond the specific charge: failure to march. Members of the court overruled each objection. Sumoge court-martial records, 40–69.

43 Sumoge statement, Sumoge files.

44 Sumoge court-martial records, 7–67.

45 Hayakawa court-martial records, 1–25.

46 Ibid., 28–29, 31–37.

47 Ibid., 38–56.

48 Sumoge statement, Sumoge files.

CHAPTER 9. "DISCARD MY UNIFORM FOR GOOD"

1 Norton et al., *People and a Nation*, 808, 780–87; LaFeber, *Clash*, 225–36, 247–48.

2 Noji, "This I Remember," 7; Noji, interview, January 8, 2002.

3 William E. Reid, 1st Lieut., QMC, letter to Mr. Junkichi Hachiya, July 19, 1946, FH IDPF, U.S. Army Human Resources Command.

4 Monroe Mark Sweetland to Hugh Ball, February 20, 1945, Sweetland family files, Anchorage, AK.

5 Claude Morita, a friend of the Hachiyas, surmises that the family was Konkokyo. One could be Buddhist, Christian, and Konkokyo at the same time, he

added. This outgrowth of the Shinto sect, with more than 430,000 believers around the world, had its headquarters in Okayama, where the Hachiya family lived in Japan. Followers of Kami (the deity), they sought to work together to live lives based on unconditional love and to resolve world problems peacefully. Claude Morita, letters to the author, April 21, 2005, March 17, 2007. Katashi and Hiroko Kobayashi, Tora Ooga, Masako Yoshida, and Kayano Ishii, interview by the author of members of Okayama Konkokyo and friends of Frank Hachiya's mother, Okayama, Japan, November 1, 2010, http://www.konkokyo.or.jp/eng/index.html.

6  McKeown, "Frank Hachiya," 3.

7  Eric Saul, "Something about Japanese Americans and Their Values," speech at Nakamura/Okubo Medal of Honor Commemorative Program, Seattle, March 25, 2001, 3; Crost, *Honor by Fire*, 305; U.S. Department of the Interior, *People in Motion*, 19.

8  Crost, *Honor by Fire*, 306. No other unit of the 442nd's size and length of service had won seven Presidential Unit Citations. Saul, "Something about Japanese Americans," 4; Tanaka, *Go for Broke*, 146.

9  Crost, *Honor by Fire*, 265.

10  Military Intelligence Service Veterans Club of Hawaii, *Secret Valor*, 17; McNaughton, *Nisei Linguists*, 460.

11  Nakatsu, "Nisei Soldiers," 77; MIS Association of Northern California, *Pacific War and Peace*, 34.

12  Commanding officers issued daily morning reports to their superiors, which detailed personnel changes, thus providing a record for the unit.

13  Linda Tamura, "Ironic Heroes: 'The Enemy's Our Cousin: Pacific Northwest Nisei in the United States Military Service,'" *Columbia* (Spring 2006): 15; Harry Fukuhara, interview by the author, September 28, 2005, transcript.

14  Harrington, *Yankee Samurai*, 87–88; Crost, *Honor by Fire*, 33. See also chapter 6.

15  Asahina explained that decisions about individual awards could be influenced by numerous factors, including the number of approvals required by those removed from the action, eyewitness credibility, and the quality of writing. He added that in relation to the size of units, only the Ninth Division earned more Distinguished Unit Citations, though it was in combat half again as long as the 100th/442nd. Before an upgrade in 2000, the proportion of Medals of Honor to Distinguished Service Crosses (one to forty-seven) was five times lower than that of general U.S. forces during World War II. Asahina, *Just Americans*, 199, 201, 259–60.

16  Hosokawa, *Nisei*, 411–12; Crost, *Honor by Fire*, 179, 254.

17  Crost, *Honor by Fire*, 262–63.

18  Crost relates that the roadside delay was due to an officers' meeting where they

considered linking the 100th Battalion of the Thirty-fourth Division with the 442nd Regimental Combat Team and that General Clark's high regard for the unit made racial bias unlikely. Nevertheless, the snubs were disheartening to the men. Ibid., 145–46; Duus, *Unlikely Liberators*, 136–37; Tanaka, *Go for Broke*, 47.

19  Crost, *Honor by Fire*, 178–79; Asahina, *Just Americans*, 51.

20  Asahina, *Just Americans*, 144; Crost, *Honor by Fire*, 189, 191.

21  Duus, *Unlikely Liberators*, 179, 204, 211; Crost, *Honor by Fire*, 176, 179, 182, 187–89, 197, 303.

22  Crost, *Honor by Fire*, 202; "100th Bn. Losses," *Hawaii Herald*, July 16, 1982.

23  Shibutani, *Derelicts of Company K*, 420–21, 435.

24  Robert Rhodes, "Prisoners of Conscience: Closing Fort Leavenworth," *Mennonite Weekly Review*, December 6, 2002, 6–10.

25  Adj. Gen. memo to Judge Adv. Gen., April 17, November 23, 1945, Sumoge court-martial records; Adj. Gen. memo to Judge Adv. Gen., April 11, November 24, 1945, Hayakawa court-martial records.

26  Military awards are for the sixteen Hood River Nisei whose names were removed from the honor roll plus seven who registered outside the valley and whose names were not listed.

27  Crost, *Honor by Fire*, 268.


CHAPTER 10. "NO JAPES WANTED IN HOOD RIVER"

1  *Hood River News*, November 10, 1944, November 17, 1944, November 29,1944; *Hood River County Sun*, November 10, 1944, 1; Burkhart, *It All Began with Apple Seeds*, 123, 129.

2  *Hood River News*, October 8, 1943; "Lets [*sic*] Get This Straight," December 19, 1944, Post 22.

3  Linda Tamura, "Wrong Face, Wrong Name: The Return of Japanese American Veterans to Hood River, Oregon, after World War II," in *Remapping Asian American History*, ed. Sucheng Chan (Walnut Creek, CA: AltaMira Press, 2003), 113.

4  Akiyama did not keep those letters nor did a survey of *Life* issues uncover his letter. The Captain Belvedere Brooks Post in New York did charge Post No. 22 with delivering a "black eye" to the entire American Legion and publicly offered membership to all sixteen Nisei. Linda Tamura, "Wrong Face, Wrong Name,"112; *San Francisco Chronicle*, December 14, 1944.

5  *Hood River News*, January 5, 1945.

6  Private Eichi Wakamatsu, a member of the 442nd Regimental Combat Team, was wounded in France on October 30, 1944. *Hood River News*, December 22, 1944; *Colorado Times*, March 1, 1945; Johnny Wakamatsu, letter to Post 22, January 6, 1945, Post 22.

7 *Hood River County Sun*, May 22, 1942. The Naturalization Act of 1790 restricted naturalization to "free white persons," although those of African, Filipino, and Chinese descent subsequently became eligible. It was not until 1952, 162 years later, that Japanese and Koreans gained the same privileges. Chuman, *Bamboo People*, 65–67.

8 Hood River's poll results were harsher than those of Gallup polls conducted in California, Washington, Nevada, Arizona, and elsewhere in Oregon, where, according to the *Hood River County Sun*, 31 percent would not permit Japanese to return, 24 percent would allow only citizens to return, 29 percent would allow all to return, and 16 percent were undecided. Linda Tamura, *Hood River Issei*, 216.

9 In its April 2, 1943, editorial, the *Hood River County Sun* complained that the competing *Hood River News* explained away the "dastardliness of the Pearl Harbor attack" and was now preparing residents for the return of the Japanese. The derided *Hood River News*, addressing "our Japanese problem" in its 1943 New Year's Day editorial, owned up to the "hatred of Japanese" that lingered in the valley before the war. Issei could justifiably be deported, it admitted, but Nisei citizens presented a constitutional "headache." Still, it pleaded for a solution to the race problem. *Hood River County Sun*, April 2, 1943; Linda Tamura, *Hood River Issei*, 215.

10 "Letter to All," American Legion Post 22 Archives, reprinted in *Hood River County Sun*, January 26, 1945; Shoemaker to Edward F. Scheiberling, National Commander, American Legion, January 26, 1945, Post 22; "Open letter to Burgoyne," *Hood River County Sun*, January 26, 1945.

11 Linda Tamura, "Wrong Face, Wrong Name," 112; "The Bull," *Hood River Post 22 Newsletter*, n.d.

12 U.S. War Relocation Authority, "Prejudice in Hood River Valley," 4; Commander Jess B. Edington to Edward N. Scheiberling, National Commander), American Legion Hdqts., December 15, 1944, Post 22; Minutes, Hood River Chamber of Commerce, January 7, 1943; *Hood River News*, January 29, June 25, 1943.

13 *Hood River News*, editorial, April 2, 1943.

14 Wendell Webb (Associated Press reporter), quoted in "An Accurate Reporter," *Hood River News*, editorial, May 28, 1943.

15 Edington to Scheiberling; *Hood River News*, December 15, 1944.

16 *Hood River News*, November 24, 1944.

17 Linda Tamura, "Wrong Face, Wrong Name," 112; H. H. to J. Howard Haley (chief, Real Estate Section, Office of Alien Property, NY), December 13, 1944, Post 22.

18 "Statement on Japanese," n.d., 3–8, Post 22.

19 Resolution, November 4, 1944, Post 22; "Statement on Japanese," Post 22.

20 Chuman, *Bamboo People*, 167–68; Eileen Tamura, *Americanization*, 85; Yamato Ichihashi, *Japanese in the United States* (Stanford, CA: Stanford University Press, 1932), 323.

21 Kevin Flanagan, assistant librarian, American Legion National Headquarters, Indianapolis, confirmed the sixteen Hood River Nisei names through local Selective Service Board records mailed to the Legion's national commander during the investigation. This list corrects that of Kazuo Ito in his book, *Issei*, which relied on the memory of a local Issei and which was the source for Linda Tamura's *Hood River Issei*. Moore to Howard D. Samuel, April 15, 1947; Kevin Flanagan, correspondence with the author, June 12, 2002; Ito, *Issei*, 692; *Hood River News*, December 15, 1944, April 13, 1945.

22 *New York Herald Tribune*, December 3, 1944; *St. Louis Post-Dispatch*, December 6, 1944; *New York Times*, December 9, 1944; *PM*, December 14, 1944; *Detroit Free Press*, December 22, 1944; *Salt Lake Tribune*, in *Hood River News*, December 28, 1944; *Chicago Sun* in *Hood River News*, January 5, 1945; *Des Moines Register*, January 15, 1945; *Colliers*, January 20, 1945.

23 *New York Herald Tribune*, December 3, 1944; Royce Brier, "This World Today," *San Francisco Chronicle*, December 14, 1944; *PM*, December 14, 1944; *New York Daily News*, December 13, 1944; Burno Shaw (Blue Network radio station commentator), telegram, December 5, 1944; *New York Times*, December 9, 1944; *Salt Lake Tribune*, December 28, 1944; *America* December 30, 1944; *Des Moines Register*, January 15, 1945.

24 McKay, *Editor for Oregon*, 184; *Eastern Oregon Review*, January 19, 1945; *Bellevue Herald* (IA), January 18, 1945.

25 V. J. A. Martenel (?), New York City, NY, February 18, 1945, Post 22. Martenel sent a copy of the *New York Times* editorial with "Shame" written across it. Three students from Philips-Exeter Academy (Exeter, N.H.), letter to Hood River Legion, December 5, 1944, Post 22. Twenty-three of their classmates signed another letter mailed the same day. Mrs. W. C. Collins, Kissimmee, FL, letter to the editor, *Hood River News*, December 22, 1944; C. Carlos, Hood River, OR, letter to the editor, *Hood River News*, January 19, 1945; H. Tabor, Glenrock, WY, December 15, 1944, letter, Post 22; W. L. Phillips, Chesterton, IN, letter, n.d., Post 22; W. C. Weber, Bridgeport, CT, letter, February 18, 1945, Post 22; R. Turbish, Ellenville, NY, postcard, February 2, 1945, Post 22; Selena M. Holden, Pawtucket, RI, letter to the editor, *Hood River News*, December 22, 1944.

26 Lt. B. B. Moyer Jr., Pratt, KS, letter, December 24, 1944, Post 22; Ralph G. Martin, "Legion Post Arouses Ire," 2; Clinton B. Conger, "GIs Indignant," *San Francisco Chronicle*, December 31, 1944.

27  G. S. Norman Jr., 1st Lt. Infantry, letter, December 30, 1944, Post 22; Pfc R. C. Brantly, letter, January 1, 1945, Post 22; Martin, "Legion Post Arouses Ire," 2; "Rescue of Lost Battalion," Go for Broke Educational Foundation, http://www.goforbroke.org, 2–3; J. W. Parks, 2nd Lt. Infantry, and four others, letter, January 7, 1945, Post 22.

28  F. D. Chinnock, Staff Sgt., letter, January 28, 1945, Post 22; C. W. Reed, Redding, CA, letter to the editor, *Hood River News*, January 12, 1945; Beatrice Stevens, "Free and Equal? The Japanese-Americans in Oregon," prepared for the Workshop on Intercultural Education, Summer 1945, Oregon Historical Society, Portland, 16.

29  Sgt. J. Lill (in the military, overseas), letter to the editor, *Hood River News*, January 12, 1945; K. Butzin, letter, December 5, 1945; D. Butzin, San Francisco, CA, letter, December 26, 1944; H. E. Lyon, Pacific Area, letter, April 5, 1945, Post 22; M. C. Wells, U.S. Maritime Service Officers School, Neptune Beach, Alameda, CA, letter to the editor, *Hood River News*, January 12, 1945. Lieutenant Swanson named Reverend Isaac Inouye and Isao Namba among local Nisei who were teaching Japanese language to white American officers and soldiers. *Hood River News*, January 19, 1945.

30  H. J. Merrill, U.S. Coast Guard, San Francisco, CA, letter to the editor, *Hood River News*, December 29, 1944; J. P. Thomsen, letter to the editor, *Hood River News*, January 5, 1945.

31  William L. Worden, "The Hate That Failed," *Saturday Evening Post*, May 4, 1946, 22–23, 137–38; "An Un-American Act?" *Detroit Free Press*, reprinted in *Hood River News*, December 22, 1944; "Hood River Post Receives Rebuke," *Hood River County Sun*, December 22, 1944; "Hood River Legionnaires Blotting a Glorious Escutcheon," *Salt Lake Tribune*, December 28, 1944; "Hood River Unabashed by Its Anti-Nisei Action," *PM*, February 24, 1944; Linda Tamura, *Hood River Issei*, 217.

32  The author organized, sorted, and counted letters in the Hood River American Legion Post files.

33  L.L.S., Portland, OR, December 15, 1944; G.G.M., Gresham, OR, December 20, 1944; Capt. F.A.K., Lomita, CA, February 25, 1945, Post 22. Earl E. Fisher, State Senator from Beaverton, OR, letter, December 16, 1944, Post 22. H.S., San Pedro, CA, December 15, 1944; S.H.D., El Paso, TX, January 3, 1945; J.L.T., Portland, OR, December 21, 1944; F.E.K., Dallas, TX, February 7, 1945; J.M., Portland, OR, December 16, 1944; R.H., Zillah, WA, December 24, 1944; A.F.G., West Lake, OR, December 1944; N.H., Howard, CO, December 8, 1944, all letters to Post 22, Post 22. J.G., South Pacific, letter to his mother, excerpted in *Hood River News*, December 29, 1944; Z.W., Vancouver, WA, letter to Post 22, December 19, 1944, Post 22.

34 Roger N. Baldwin, director of the American Civil Liberties Union (ACLU), condemned the Hood River post's action in a speech at the Portland City Club. *Oregonian*, December 2, 1944; *Hood River News*, December 8, 1944; *PM*, December 24, 1944; Galen M. Fisher, Pacific Coast, Committee on American Principles and Fair Play, San Francisco, CA, letter to Post 22, December 15, 1944, Post 22; Afton Dill Nance, letter to Hood River Legion, March 3, 17, 1945, Post 22. Martha McKeown, Laca Fletcher, and C. R. Masiker represented the Odell Methodist Church, which unanimously resolved to restore Japanese American names on the county honor roll. If the names were not restored, they requested a county listing of all names. *Hood River News*, January 12, 1945, January 19, 1945; G.L.K., Pasadena Ban the Japs Committee, telegram to Post 22, December 16, 1944, Post 22; *Oregonian*, January 9, 1945.

35 E.G., *Hood River News*, January 12, 1945, 9; *Hood River County Sun*, January 19, 1945; Hazel V. Smith (Mrs. Carl L. Smith), *Hood River News*, December 8, 1944; Esther Kesti, *Hood River News*, December 15, 1944; Jack Hanser, *Hood River News*, December 29, 1944.

36 W. Sherman Burgoyne, letter to the editor, *Hood River News*, January 5, 1945; letter to Post 22, January 11, 1945, Post 22; Frank H. Smith, letter to the editor, *Hood River News*, January 5, 1945.

37 Post 22's official reply to the criticism appeared in the *Hood River News*, December 22, 1944; *Oregonian*, December 20, 1944; and *Oregon Legionnaire*, January 1945, 11.

38 Agricultural Adjustment Administration data, U.S. War Relocation Authority, "Prejudice in Hood River Valley," 8, 11. In 1942, 77 of the 1,142 Hood River valley farm operators were Japanese who worked ninety-eight tracts of farmland, according to the *Hood River County Sun*, March 6, 1942. They accounted for 2,898.4 acres of the 36,881 total acreage. This figure differs from the sixty-eight farms cited by the War Relocation Authority in "Prejudice in Hood River Valley" (8) and the eighty-four cited by the *Pacific Citizen*, February 10, 1945.

39 U.S. War Relocation Authority, "Prejudice in Hood River Valley," 5, 11; *Hood River News*, January 12, 1945.

40 U.S. War Relocation Authority, "Prejudice in Hood River Valley," 5, 11; *Hood River News*, January 12, 1945, January 26, 1945, February 9, 1945.

41 *Hood River News*, January 26, 1945; *Hood River County Sun*, January 26, 1945; Linda Tamura, *Hood River Issei*, 314.

42 *Hood River News*, February 2, 1945; *Hood River County Sun*, February 2, 1945.

43 *Hood River News*, February 9, 1945; *Hood River County Sun*, February 9, 1945.

44 *Hood River News*, February 16, 1945; *Hood River County Sun*, February 16, 1945; *Hood River News*, February 23, 1945; *Hood River County Sun*, February 23, 1945. T. S. Van Vleet was a retired school principal living in Los Angeles.

45 *National Legionnaire*, February 1945; J. E. Edington, letter to National Commander Edward N. Scheiberling, December 15, 1944, Post 22; *National Legionnaire*, February 1945, 1, 4. Kenjiro Hayakawa's name was not replaced because of his dishonorable discharge; Fred Sumoge's name was never included because he registered for the draft in Portland.

46 Kent Shoemaker informed Commander Scheiberling that the Legion's Japanese Committee and Executive Committee had recommended replacing the names, but that he "led the opposition." Viewing the telegram from Scheiberling merely as a recommendation, he held out for circulating petitions to "get an honest to God true picture of the continent." Of Post 22's membership, he explained, "Some wanted to replace the names. Some wanted to take the board down and have a bond [sic] fire. Others said they would take their son's name off if the Jap names were put back, and now some are saying they will tear the board down if the names are put back." Kent Shoemaker, letter to Commander Scheiberling, January 26, 1945, Post 22. *Pacific Citizen*, February 10, 1945, 3127. *Oregon Journal*, March 7, 1945; Bud Collins (Hood River Legion historian), interview by the author, July 13, 2006.

47 *Hood River News*, April 13, 1945; Loftus, *Made in Japan*, 132; Commander Edward N. Scheiberling, telegram to Hood River Legion, March 8, 1945, Post 22; *Survey Midmonthly*, April 1945; *Hood River News*, March 9, 1945; *Oregon Journal*, March 8, 1945.

48 *Hood River News*, March 9, 1945; Loftus, *Made in Japan*, 131; Kessler, *Stubborn Twig*, 242; Daniels, *Concentration Camps*, 150–51; *Hood River News*, March 23, 1945; *Hood River County Sun*, March 23, 1945.

49 *Hood River News*, December 22, 1944, February 23, 1945, February 2, 1945, March 16, 1945.

50 Ibid., February 23, 1945; *Honolulu Star-Bulletin*, February 15, 1945; *New York Times*, February 17, 1945; *Hood River News*, February 23 1945.

51 J. P. Harrison, Cleveland, OH, letter to Post 22, February 22, 1945; M.P.T., New York, February 18, 1945; W. Marconi, Camp Blanding, FL, letter to Post 22, February 24, 1945; Afton Dill Nance for the Committee, Pasadena, CA, letter to Post 22, March 3, 1945, Post 22.

52 *Hood River News*, December 22, 1944, February 16, 1945; *Detroit Free Press*, in *Hood River News*, February 22, 1944; *The Dalles Optimist*, in *Hood River News*, December 29, 1944; *San Francisco Chronicle*, in *Hood River News*, January 5, 1945; *Chicago Sun*, in *Hood River News*, January 5, 1945.

53 *Hood River News*, January 19, 1945; Dan M. McDade, *Oregon Journal*, in *Hood River News*, January 26, 1945; *Hood River News*, March 16, 1945.

54 *Hood River County Sun*, April 2, 1943, January 5, 1945; *PM*, December 24, 1944; *Oregonian*, June 16, 1946; H.F.M., *Hood River County Sun*, January 19, 1945.

55 U.S. Representatives Lowell Stockman (March 30, 1944), Homer D. Angell (February 10, 1944), and James W. Mott (February 15, 1944) and U.S. Senator Rufus C. Holman (February 18, 1944) all supported measures barring Japanese, though Representative Mott made an exception for native-born Japanese in the armed services. U.S. Representative Harris Ellsworth (February 11, 1944) gave assurance of his "deep concern and interest in our Japanese problem." C. D. Nickelsen, County Judge, letter to Mr. Jack Eccles, Commander American Legion, Hood River, Oregon, April 8, 1944. Letters to Post 22, Post 22.

56 Linda Tamura, *Hood River Issei*, 223, 314; Inada, Kikumura, and Worthington, *In This Great Land of Freedom*, 43. In 1947, the Multnomah County Circuit Court declared the 1945 Alien Land Law unconstitutional. Acting on a suit filed by Etsuo Namba and his Nisei son Kenjin, it ruled that the law infringed on the Fourteenth Amendment's equal protection provision.

## CHAPTER 11. "NINETY PERCENT ARE AGAINST THE JAPS!"

1 CWRIC, *Personal Justice Denied*, 231.

2 Myer, *Uprooted Americans*, 198; Worden, "Hate That Failed," 137; Linda Tamura, *Hood River Issei*, 224; Linda Tamura, "Wrong Face, Wrong Name," 115; *Oregonian*, March 13, 1945.

3 Charles A. Michie, "Three Plague Spots within a Democracy," *PM*, February 25, 1945, 11.

4 U.S. Bureau of the Census, *Oregon Population of Counties by Decennial Census: 1900 to 1990*, http://www.census.gov/population/cencounts/or190090.txt, 1; Michie, "Three Plague Spots," 11; *Pacific Citizen*, February 10, 1945; Richard L. Neuberger, "All Quiet on Hood River as Japs Return to Valley," *Sunday Oregonian*, June 16, 1946, 28; Neuberger, "Their Brothers' Keepers," *Saturday Review of Literature* 29 (August 10, 1946): 5–6, 27–28; Arline Winchell Moore, "Hood River Redeems Itself," *Asia and the Americas* 6 (July 1946): 316–17.

5 Worden, "Hate That Failed," 137.

6 Stevens, "Free and Equal?" 35; Neuberger, "Their Brothers' Keepers," 6; Linda Tamura, "Wrong Face, Wrong Name," 116; *Hood River News*, January 12, 1945; Neuberger, "Their Brothers' Keepers," 28; Neuberger, "All Quiet on Hood River," 28.

7 Neuberger, "Their Brothers' Keepers," 6; *Hood River News*, April 16, 1943; Linda Tamura, "Wrong Face, Wrong Name," 114.

8 Moore to Howard D. Samuel (editor in chief), *Dartmouth* (Hanover, NH), April 15, 1947; *Hood River News*, January 12, 1945, 1; Linda Tamura, *Hood River Issei*, 225. In compiling its report summarizing prominent valley citizens'

views about the return of valley Japanese, the Oregon State Police consulted an attorney, a druggist, and a newspaper editor as well as the chief of police, the superintendent of the irrigation district, the district attorney, a justice of the peace, the sheriff, and a county judge.

9   Michie, "Three Plague Spots," 11; *Hood River County Sun*, August 6, 1943.

10  U.S. War Relocation Authority, "Prejudice in Hood River," 12.

11  *Hood River News*, January 5, January 12, January 19, 1945; *Hood River County Sun*, January 5, 1945; *Oregonian*, January 13, 1945; *Oregon Journal*, January 13, 1945; *Pacific Citizen*, January 20, 1945.

12  "Min Asai's Story," Minoru Asai family files, 1–2; Linda Tamura, *Hood River Issei*, 226; Ray Sato, letter to the author, January 17, 1984; Turner, "Bitter Memories," 18.

13  Linda Tamura, "Grandma Noji," 114; *Oregonian*, April 5, 1945; Linda Tamura, *Hood River Issei*, 226–7; Chiz Tamura, interview by the author, December 21, 2001, transcript; Noji, interview, January 8, 2002; Tamura, "Grandma Noji," 116–18.

14  Linda Tamura, "Wrong Face, Wrong Name," 116.

15  Kurahara, *Ganbatte*, 131; Jan Kurahara, interview by the author, August 31, 2001, transcript; Linda Tamura, "Wrong Face, Wrong Name," 107; *Oregonian*, December 23, 1945.

16  Linda Tamura, "Wrong Face, Wrong Name," 116; *Hood River County Sun*, January 19, 1945; *Pacific Citizen*, January 16, 1945; Moore, "Hood River Redeems Itself," 316; Tamura, "Wrong Face, Wrong Name," 117; Victor McLaughlin, interview by Judith Austin, Idaho Oral History Center, May 29, 1984, Idaho Historical Society, Boise.

17  Kurahara, *Ganbatte*, 125; Moore, "Hood River Redeems Itself," 316.

18  Turner, "Bitter Memories," 8; Loftus, *Made in Japan*, 137; *37th Division Veteran News*, 37th Division Veterans' Association, Columbus, OH, February 1947, 15:2, 1, 11; Linda Tamura, "Wrong Face, Wrong Name," 117; Girdner, *Great Betrayal*, 398; Kessler, *Stubborn Twig*, 241.

19  "Min Asai's Story"; Loftus, *Made in Japan*, 95.

20  Moore, "Hood River Redeems Itself," 317; Sato, letter; Neuberger, "Their Brothers' Keepers," 27; Worden, " Hate That Failed," 138; Moore, "Hood River Redeems Itself," 317; Dillon S. Myer, *Uprooted Americans: The Japanese Americans and the War Relocation Authority during World War II* (Tucson: University of Arizona Press, 1971), 156.

21  *Hood River News*, January 12, 1945, December 29, 1944; June Haviland to Hood River Legion, December 30, 1944, Post 22.

22  Linda Tamura, *Hood River Issei*, 241; Stevens, "Free and Equal?" 36; Loftus, *Made in Japan*, 135; Tamura, *Hood River Issei*, 242.

23 Neuberger, "Their Brothers' Keepers," 6, 27; *Pacific Citizen*, May 3, 1947.

24 Officers of the League for Liberty and Justice were Avon Sutton, president; Wallace J. Miller, vice president; Mrs. Carl Smith, secretary-treasurer; and Mrs. Max Moore and Reverend Sherman Burgoyne, central committee. Linda Tamura, *Hood River Issei*, 237–38, 316; Stevens, "Free and Equal?" 36; *Hood River News*, June 8, 1945; Neuberger, "Their Brothers' Keepers, 6; *Hood River News*, June 8, 1945; Crost, *Honor by Fire*, 117–31.

25 *Hood River News*, May 4, 25, 1945; Moore, "Hood River Redeems Itself," 317.

26 *Pacific Citizen*, May 3, 1947; U.S. War Relocation Authority, "Prejudice in Hood River Valley," 13, 16; *Hood River News*, December 22, 1944, March 2, 1923; *PM*, December 29, 1945; U.S. War Relocation Authority, "Prejudice in Hood River Valley," 13; Min Asai, "Civil Rights," notes from speech to local high school students, Minoru Asai family files.

27 Neuberger, "All Quiet on Hood River," 28; *The Bull* (Post 22 newsletter), n.d., Post 22; *Hood River News*, December 22, 1944.

28 Jess Edington to National Commander Scheiberling, December 15, 1944, Decatur Baldwin to National Commander Scheiberling, December 12, 1944, Kent Shoemaker to National Commander Scheiberling, January 26, 1945, Post 22.

29 Ralph G. Martin, "Hood River Odyssey," *New Republic* 115 (December 16, 1946): 815; *Hood River News*, December 22, 1944, January 26, 1945; Stevens, "Free and Equal?" 36.

30 U.S. Department of the Interior, *People in Motion*, 52.

31 Kent Shoemaker to National Commander Scheiberling, January 26, 1945, Post 22.

32 U.S. Department of the Interior, *People in Motion*, 58; Girdner and Loftis, *Great Betrayal*, 396; *Pacific Citizen*, February 10, 1945; Pierce, "Winds of Change," 410; Sato, letter.

33 Anna Reeploeg Fisher, *Exile of a Race* (Sidney, BC: Peninsula Printing, 1965), 198–99; *PM*, December 29, 1945; U.S. War Relocation Authority, "Prejudice in Hood River Valley," 16, 9.

34 John Kitasako, "Methodist Minister Led Fight for Freedom in Hood River," *Pacific Citizen* (May 3, 1947), 1.

35 Kent Shoemaker to National Commander Scheiberling, January 26, 1945, Post 22.

36 Moore to Howard D. Samuel, April 15, 1947; Loftus, *Made in Japan*, 102; Kurahara, *Ganbatte*, 132; Shig Imai, interview by the author, November 13, 2001, transcript; George Tamura, interview by the author, November 20, 2001, transcript; Kitasako, "Methodist Minister," 1.

37 In his letter to the American Legion's national commander, Kent Shoemaker

sought to convince him that local farmers were "well read and clear thinkers." He declared, "We are not a Hill Billy farming community," claiming that "we have been rated the highest cultured farming community in the world by the National Electric Light Association." Shoemaker to Scheiberling, January 26, 1945.

38 Arline Moore to Howard D. Samuel, April 15, 1947, in author's files. Wallace Miller sent George Tamura a copy of his February 18, 1945, letter to Kent Shoemaker with an appended note.

39 The author wishes to thank Willamette University alumni Kristi Murphy, Lindsey Young, and Anne Coleman for their data analyses.

40 Noji, interview by the author, January 8, 2002, transcript; Linda Tamura, *Hood River Issei*, 239; Kitasako, "Methodist Minister," 1.

41 *Hood River County Sun*, March 14, 1945; *Hood River News*, January 5, 1945; Kitasako, "Methodist Minister," 1.

42 "Min Asai's Story," Minoru Asai family files.

43 Arline Moore to Mam Noji, April 23, 1947, in author's files.

44 Myer, *Uprooted Americans*, 155; Moore, "Hood River Redeems Itself," 317; *Oregon Journal*, April 24, 1945; *Hood River News*, April 27, 1945; *Hood River County Sun*, March 23, 1945; *Hood River News*, May 4, 1945. Two of the seven war bond ads in the May 4, 1945, issue of the *Hood River News* refer to the Japanese enemy.

45 Moore, "Hood River Redeems Itself," 317; U.S. War Relocation Authority, "Prejudice in Hood River Valley," 14. While 40.3 percent of the Nikkei population returned to Hood River, 68.9 percent returned to Oregon, 51.9 percent returned to California, and 40.2 percent returned to Washington. Linda Tamura, *Hood River Issei*, 226, 283.

46 U.S. War Relocation Authority, "Prejudice in Hood River Valley," 17.


CHAPTER 12. "YOU COULD FEEL IT"

1 *Hood River News*, January 3, 1947; Mid-Columbia Veterans and Servicemen Testimonial Banquet program, December 28, 1946, author's files.

2 Mid-Columbia Veterans and Servicemen Testimonial Banquet program, Minoru Asai family files.

3 Noji, "This I Remember," 5, author's files.

4 Ralph G. Martin, "Hood River Odyssey," *New Republic* 115 (December 16, 1946): 814; Linda Tamura, "Wrong Face, Wrong Name," 117; Henry Akiyama, interview, *Conversations*, KTOO TV (Juneau, AK), October 1989.

5 Linda Tamura, *Hood River Issei*, 229.

6 U.S. Department of the Interior, *People in Motion*, 47, 57–58, 62.

7 Nikkei were permitted to apply for leaves from camp in order to fill the demand for seasonal farm labor. See Linda Tamura, *Hood River Issei*, 201–3; CWRIC, *Personal Justice Denied*, 165–69; Kashima, "Japanese American Internees Return," 109.

8 Garrett, *Coming Plague*, 47.

9 Laufer, "Serial Self," 43–46; Chalsa M. Loo, "An Integrative-Sequential Treatment Model for Posttraumatic Stress Disorder: A Case Study of the Japanese American Internment and Redress," *Clinical Psychology Review* 13 (1993): 90.

10 Sato, letter.

11 Kitano, *Generations and Identity*, 63, 85, 95; Loo, "An Integrative-Sequential Treatment Model," 103; James Hirabayashi, "Nisei: The Quiet American? A Re-evaluation," *Amerasia Journal* 3:1 (1975): 118–19.

12 Kurahara, *Ganbatte*, 133; Togo W. Tanaka, "How to Survive Racism in America's Free Society," in *Voices Long Silent: An Oral Inquiry into the Japanese American Evacuation*, ed. Arthur A. Hansen and Betty E. Mitson (Fullerton: Japanese American Project, California State University), 88, 212.

13 Weglyn, *Years of Infamy*, 273; Amy Iwasaki Mass, "Psychological Effects of the Camps on Japanese Americans," in *Japanese Americans: From Relocation to Redress*, by Roger Daniels, Sandra C. Taylor, and H. L. Kitano (Salt Lake City: University of Utah Press, 1986), 160. See also Donna K. Nagata, "The Japanese American Internment: Exploring the Transgenerational Consequences of Traumatic Stress," *Journal of Traumatic Stress* 3:1 (1990): 47–69.

14 Kashima, "Japanese American Internees Return," 113; Kashima, Civil Liberties Symposium, Twin Falls, ID, June 21, 2007; Sumoge's actions constitute a face-saving technique, as defined by Kitano (*Generations and Identity*, 88–90).

15 S. Frank Miyamoto, "Problems of Interpersonal Style among the Nisei," *Amerasia Journal* 13:2 (1986–87): 32–39; Hirabayashi, "Nisei," 116–24.

16 David Burkhart (former Hood River County agricultural extension agent), letter to the author, April 24, 2007; Burkhart, *It All Began with Apple Seeds*, 123, 129.

17 Linda Tamura, *Hood River Issei*, 247–49. The Evacuation Claims Act, signed by President Harry S. Truman, resulted from a bill drafted by the WRA and lengthy lobbying by JACL executive secretary Mike Masaoka and his wife, Etsu. Chuman, *Bamboo People*, 240–45.

18 Inada, Kikumura, and Worthington, *In This Great Land of Freedom*, 43–44; Johnson, "Anti-Japanese Legislation," 204–5.

19 Weglyn, *Years of Infamy*, 273; Minako Maykovich, cited in Nagata, *Legacy of Injustice*, 33; Kitano, *Generations and Identity*, 63.

20 Hansen, "Resettlement, 1, 7.

21 Daniels, *Concentration Camps*, 166; Tamura, *Hood River Issei*, 283. Hood Riv-

er's figures are consistent with WRA figures, which show that, among West
Coast Nikkei farmers, only one-fourth returned. U.S. Department of the Interior, *People in Motion*, 47.

22  Neuberger, "All Quiet on Hood River," 28.

23  Moore, "Hood River Redeems Itself," 317; Arline Moore to Howard D. Samuel,
3, author's files.

## CHAPTER 13. "TIME IS A GOOD HEALER"

1   Toru Noji, letter to the author, June 18, 2002.

2   In his article analyzing the return of Japanese to coastal areas, Mervin G.
Shoemaker reported, "Individual Japanese have proven their good citizenship qualities time and again. . . . Peace officers say that members of this
group are among those causing officers the least trouble." *Oregonian*, May
27, 1945.

3   Moore, "Hood River Redeems Itself," 317; Linda Tamura, *Hood River Issei*, 241;
*Pacific Citizen*, April 19, 1947, May 3, 1947.

4   Richard L. Neuberger, "Hood River's Fighting Minister: No Reward for Valor,"
*Pacific Citizen*, October 18, 1947, 1, 5.

5   Miyamoto, "Problems of Interpersonal Style," 38.

6   Martin, "Hood River Odyssey," 815.

7   Kurahara, *Ganbatte*, 138.

8   Stephen S. Fugita and Marilyn Fernandez, *Altered Lives, Enduring Com-
munity: Japanese Americans Remember Their World War II Incarceration*
(Seattle: University of Washington Press, 2004), 108; Loo, "An Integrative-
Sequential Treatment Model," 102; U.S. Department of the Interior, *People in
Motion*, 237, 246; Ruth Akiyama, interview by the author, January 22, 2002,
transcript.

9   Arline Winchell Moore, "The Happy Ending: Return to Hood River," *Pacific
Citizen*, December 22, 1951, 26, 31; Neuberger, "Their Brothers' Keepers," 27;
Martin, "Hood River Odyssey," 814–16.

10  Moore, "Hood River Redeems Itself," 317; U.S. War Relocation Authority,
"Prejudice in Hood River Valley," 13.

11  George Hara, Mid-Columbia JACL, Chronology; Moore, "Happy Ending," 31;
Mits Takasumi, "Mid-Columbia Japanese-American Citizens League (1931 to
1988)" (unpublished manuscript), MC/JACL.

12  Monroe Sweetland, interview by the author, May 21, 2005, transcript.

13  *Oregonian*, September 12, 1948. Oregon's Charles Sprague (1939–43), the only
West Coast governor to boycott Congress's Tolan Committee hearings, which
investigated evacuating Japanese Americans, later regretted his "silent inac-

tivity" and became the state's leading editorial voice on behalf of Japanese American civil rights. E. B. MacNaughton, president of the First National Bank in Portland and later president of Reed College, actively opposed anti-Japanese sentiment and a constitutional amendment to exclude Japanese from the country. Attorney and president of the Multnomah County Bar Association in Portland, Verne Dusenberry was co-counsel in the Namba family's suit, which, in 1949, succeeded in reversing the ban on Issei leasing land. Linda Tamura, *Hood River Issei*, 307; Mervin G. Shoemaker, "Japanese Evacuees: Where Do They Belong, *Oregonian*, 6–7; McKay, *Editor for Oregon*, 180–87; Inada, *In This Great Land*, 43–44.

14 A Hood River resident, educator, historian, and author, McKeown taught Hachiya at Multnomah College in Portland. Sweetland, interview, May 21, 2005; Loni Ding, *The Color of Honor*, videotape (Harriman, NY: CET Productions, 1989); *Oregonian*, May 20, 1945, September 12, 1948; Homer Hachiya, interview by the author, July 30, 2006, transcript; *Oregonian*, September 12, 1948.

15 Billie Lee, "Celebrating a Nikkei Cultural Institution," *Nichi Bei Times*, 1999, from Japanese American Bowling Association, http://www. janba.com. The first five local Nisei to enjoy after-hours bowling were World War II veterans Toru Hasegawa, Hit (Hitoshi) Imai, Harry Inukai, Ted Kawachi, and Taylor Tomita.

16 The Veterans of Foreign Wars also sponsored a bowling team.

17 U.S. War Relocation Authority, "Prejudice in Hood River Valley," 13.

18 David Loftus, letter to the author, April 23, 2000. Price's first name is unknown.

19 *Scene* was published by the Chicago Publishing Corporation from 1949 to 1954, the last two years with the subtitle *International East-West Magazine*. *Scene: The Pictorial Magazine* 4:3 (July 1952): 3.

20 At the time, Sho Endow's name was thought to have been removed from the local honor roll. Later records show that his name was not listed because he did not register for the draft in Hood River.

21 "Post 1479 VFW Japanese-America Members," Shig Imai, Hood River VFW historian, February 18, 2007.

22 An East Coast news editorial also observed that the "blood transfusion" from new members brought "new vigor and new appreciation of American principles." "Hood River Legionnaires Admit a Mistake," *Norfolk Virginia-Pilot*, March 15, 1945; Myer, *Uprooted Americans*, 338.

23 Bud Collins, interview by the author, July 26, 2006; U.S. Department of the Interior, *People in Motion*, 216.

24 *Oregon Journal*, March 28, 1952; *Oregonian*, March 28, 1952; *Oregon Statesman*, March 29, 1952.

25 *Oregonian*, March 28, 1952. The National Conference for Community and Justice, originally the National Conference of Christians and Jews, initiated National Brotherhood Week.

26 *Oregon Journal*, March 31, 1952; *Oregonian*, March 28, 1952.

27 *Oregon Journal*, March 28, 1952; *Oregonian*, March 29, 1952.

28 Telegram to Governor McKay, March 28, 1952, McKay Administration Correspondence; telegrams to Governor McKay from Bob Friedman, March 30, 1952, Mr. and Mrs. Carl Smith, March 30, 1952, Marcia Yuck, March 29, 1952, George Dysart, Chairman (Oregon State Council, American Veterans Committee), March 28, 1952, Mrs. C. H. P., March 30, 1952, Mrs. E. W. P., April 3, 1952, Box 26, Sagie Nishioka Tax Commission File, OSA [hereafter Nishioka Tax File].

29 Rev. and Mrs. Sherman Burgoyne, letter to Sagie Nishioka, March 29, 1952, Sagie Nishioka family files, Hood River, OR; State Rep. Robert Y. Thornton, March 31, 1952, Nishioka Tax File.

30 Gov. Douglas McKay to Rev. S. Darlow Johnson, March 28, 1952, Nishioka Tax File; *Oregon Journal*, March 31, 1952.

31 Ray Smith, letter to Sagie Nishioka, March 31, 1952, Sagie Nishioka family files; Gov. McKay, statement, March 31, 1952, Sagie Nishioka family files; *Oregon Journal*, April 1, 1952; *Oregonian*, March 29, 1952; *Oregon Journal*, March 28, 1952; Ray Smith, letter to Sagie Nishioka, April 7, 1952, Sagie Nishioka family files.

32 Takasumi, "Mid-Columbia Japanese-American Citizens League," 2, MC/JACL; Moore, "Happy Ending," 26.

33 Moore, "Happy Ending," 31.

34 Reverend Collins had lived in Japan for fifteen years and was fluent in Japanese. Katsusaburo Tamura and Kenichi Hasegawa, who both spoke English, assisted him in teaching citizenship classes. Linda Tamura, *Hood River Issei*, 249–52; J. Patricia Krussow, ed., *Aakki-Daakki to Zoomorphic: An Encyclopedia about Hood River County* (Hood River, OR: Friends of the Hood River Library, 1994), 81.

35 Eileen Tamura defines acculturation as adapting to American middle-class life while also retaining one's ethnic identity. This contrasts with assimilation, which is absorbing white middle-class norms while losing traces of one's own cultural heritage. Eileen Tamura, *Americanization*, 237, 49, 52.

36 U.S. Department of the Interior, *People in Motion*, 31; Linda Tamura, *Hood River Issei*, 125–29, 304. This followed a general postwar trend away from segregated churches among Nikkei. U.S. Department of the Interior, *People in Motion*, 233.

37 Takasumi, "Mid-Columbia Japanese-American Citizens League," 3, MC/JACL.

38  U.S. Department of the Interior, *People in Motion*, 249, 195, 245; Eileen Tamura, *Americanization*, 236–37.

39  Takasumi, "Mid-Columbia Japanese-American Citizens League," MC/JACL. Some Nikkei rejected redress because it attached a meaningless, monetary sum to their hardships; others viewed it as a form of welfare that would revive bad memories. S. I. Hayakawa, elected to the U.S. Senate from California, labeled the request for compensation "ridiculous," claiming that the wartime relocation "opened up possibilities" for West Coast Japanese Americans, forcing them to "discover the rest of America" beyond their farms and fishing boats. A splinter group, the National Council for Japanese American Redress, initiated lawsuits against the government. Eventually, the JACL supported appointing a commission to "determine whether a wrong was committed . . . and to recommend appropriate remedies." Daniels, *Asian America*, 333–35.

40  Daniels, *Asian America*, 331. Peter Irons led a team of Sansei lawyers to overturn the convictions of Fred Korematsu, Min Yasui, and Gordon Hirabayashi in 1983, 1985, and 1986, respectively. Peter Irons, *Justice at War: The Story of the Japanese American Internment Cases* (New York: Oxford University Press, 1983), 186–218; Irons, *Justice Delayed*; Niiya, *Japanese American History*, 123–24.

41  Daniels, *Asian America*, 338. See John Tateishi and William Yoshino, "The Japanese American Incarceration: The Journey to Redress," *Human Rights Magazine* (Spring 2000); Daniels, *Asian America*, 330–41; Daniels, Taylor, and Kitano, *Japanese Americans*, 188–223; Niiya, *Japanese American History*, 289–91.

42  Moore, "Hood River Redeems Itself," 317.

43  Martin, *Hood River Odyssey*, 815. Other prominent Nisei veteran community leaders included Min Asai, chair of the county school board and gubernatorial appointee to the Columbia Gorge Commission; Jan Kurahara, county commissioner, county school board chair, and president of the local Rotary Club; and Hugo Shibahara, Chamber of Commerce board member. Ray Yasui was an active Nisei who served as chair of the Apple Growers Association board, a member of the board of the American Automobile Association of Oregon, and the governor's appointee to the Oregon State Board of Higher Education.

44  *Sunday Oregonian*, June 21, 1959.

45  Kurahara, *Ganbatte*, 145. Hood River Orchardists of the Year included Ray Sato (1965), Mamoru Noji (1969), Shig Yamaki (1974), and Toru Omori (1975). Hood River Chamber of Commerce Archives. Linda Tamura, "The Making of an American: A Woman Ahead of Her Time," *Oregon Historical Quarterly* 103:4 (Winter 2002): 511–29; Krussow, *Aakki-Daakki to Zoomorphic*, 138; *Hood River News*, April 7, 2007.

46 Kashima, "Japanese American Internees Return," 114; Hansen, "Resettlement," 1.

47 Joan Yasui Emerson, e-mail to author, October 3, 2001; O'Brien and Fugita, "Generational Difference," 236–38.

## CHAPTER 14. "GUILTY OF COURAGE"

1 Fred Sumoge, interview by the author, September 11, 2005, transcript, 2; Fred Sumoge, memo to Paul Minerich, n.d., Paul Minerich Collection, Hirasaki National Resource Center, Japanese American National Museum, Los Angeles [hereafter Minerich Collection].

2 Fred Sumoge, memo to Charles Edmund Zane, October 4 [no year], Minerich Collection; C. Craig Cannon (aide to Gen. Dwight D. Eisenhower), letter to Hakuban Nozawa, October 15, 1946, Minerich Collection; Justin N. Feldman (director, Veterans Affairs, NY), letter to Hakuban Nozawa, February 12, 1947, Sumoge files; David Avstreih (attorney, Mt. Vernon, NY), letter to Hakuban Nozawa, December 31, 1946, Sumoge files.

3 Charles D. Carle (Office of the Adjutant General), letter to Hakuban Nozawa, February 16, 1948, Minerich Collection; Nozawa, letter to Charles Ross (president's secretary), November 27, 1948, Minerich Collection; Nozawa, letter to Louis Johnson (secretary of defense), April 16, 1949, Minerich Collection; Nozawa, letter to Maj. Gen. Harry Vaughan (presidential military aide), September 6, 1949, Sumoge files; Nozawa, letter to Charles Edmond Zane, September 19, 1948, Minerich Collection.

4 George A. Spiegelberg, letter to Hakuban Nozawa, September 23, 1949, Minerich Collection; Drew Pearson, letter to Nozawa, July 13, 1950, Sumoge files; Nozawa, letter to Pearson, July 14, June 15, 1950, Minerich Collection; Fred Sumoge, interview by the author, September 18, 2005, transcript; Nozawa, letter to Pearson, July 15, 1950, Minerich Collection.

5 Gus Solomon, letter to Fred Sumoge, August 9, 1947, Sumoge files.

6 Charles Edmond Zane, letter to Paul Minerich, May 6, 1980, Minerich Collection; Kenjiro Hayakawa, interview by the author, July 1, 2004, transcript; Martha (Fusako) Kataoka, interview by the author, October 2, 2005.

7 *Discipline Barrack Boys*, videotape, Minerich Collection.

8 Ibid.

9 Fred Sumoge, handwritten answers to Charles Zane's questions, May 17, 1948, Zane, memo to Discipline Barrack Boys, July 6, 1948, Zane, letter to Discipline Barrack Boys, August 30, 1948, Minerich Collection.

10 Charles Zane, letter to Army Board, September 1948, Zane, brief, 1–3, 6, 12, 18, Tow Hori files. In his 1948 brief, Zane accused the court of forming preju-

dicial conclusions based on statements not previously made. For example, a court member asked Sumoge whether he understood Aycock's order to give his name to Corporal Ballinger, even though neither Aycock nor Ballinger made that claim. The use of biased terminology became an issue when the court asked Sergeant McDonald whether he had had "trouble" with the men at an earlier time and when Wiseman asked Sumoge whether he was "asked to do things the American soldier was not asked to do." To that, Zane erupted in his brief, "What in hell did Wiseman think Sumoge was, if not an American soldier?"

11  Zane, brief, 7–63.

12  John L. Cronkrite (executive secretary, Army Board), letter to Sumoge, November 3, 1948, Sumoge files; Gerald C. Cowden, letter for Cronkrite to Zane, May 13, 1949, Hori files; T. Wade Markley (chair, Clemency and Parole Board No. 1), memo to Secretary of the Army, February 17, 1949, Hayakawa and Sumoge court-martial records, U.S. Army Judiciary, Department of the Army, Arlington, VA.

13  Charles Zane to Congressman Gordon L. McDonough, May 24, 1949, Minerich Collection. Congressman McDonough's communication to Zane (June 10, 1949) included a letter from O. A. Scott, Lt. Col., General Staff Corps Liaison, who was "of the opinion that these cases can be satisfactorily resolved by petitioning the Judge Advocate General (JAG) for a new trial." The Articles of War, amended by Title II, Public Law 759, 80th Congress, and effective February 1, 1949, authorized the JAG, upon application of an accused person, and upon good cause, to grant a new trial, or to vacate a sentence, and grant other appropriate relief. Correspondence between McDonough and Zane, Hori files.

14  Charles Zane, letter to Army Board, June 17, 1949, Zane, letter to President Harry S. Truman, June 17, 1949, Hori files.

15  G. K. Heiss (colonel, General Staff Corps, special assistant, Office of the Secretary of the Army), letter to Charles Zane, June 30, 1949, Hori files.

16  Charles Zane, letter to Discipline Barrack Boys, July 29, 1949, Minerich Collection.

17  Zane, brief submitted to G. K. Heiss (colonel, General Staff Corps, special assistant, Office of the Secretary of the Army), September 14, 1949, Minerich Collection; Zane, to President Harry S. Truman, September 28, 1949, Hori files.

18  George A. Spiegelberg, letter to Maj. Gen. Harry H. Vaughan, September 26, 1949, Hori files; Charles Zane, letter to Maj. Gen. Vaughan, January 1, 1949, responding to Judge Advocate General's October 13, 1949, letter, Minerich Collection; Zane to President Harry S. Truman, November 2, 1949, Hori files.

19  Charles Zane, letter to fifty-five people, organizations, and publications, November 1, 1949, Minerich Collection.

20 Charles Zane, letter to congressmen, May 24, 1949, Minerich Collection.

21 G. K. Heiss, letter to Charles Zane, November 4, 1949, John L. Cronkite, letter to Zane, December 8, 1949, Hori files.

22 Hakuban Nozawa, letter to Drew Pearson, July 15, 1950, Nozawa, letter to Fred Sumoge, July 15, 1950, Sumoge files.

23 Charles Zane, brief, February 1952, 4–5, 7–12, 14, Minerich Collection.

24 Ibid., 13–14, 18, 21, 29.

25 Charles Zane, letter to General Dwight D. Eisenhower, May 29, 1954, Zane, letter to Tats Kushida (JACL), November 27, 1951, William E. Kent (insurance agent), letter to Mike Masaoka (JACL), October 10, 1951, Minerich Collection. Article of War 53, to which petitions refer, was repealed by section 12 of an act of May 5, 1950 (U.S. Code, Title 50, Section 740), which also set a deadline of May 31, 1952, for submitting petitions. A. G. Eger, letter to Zane, Hayakawa and Sumoge court-martial records.

26 Charles Zane, letter to Paul Minerich, May 6, 1980, Minerich Collection.

27 Paul Minerich, brief in Support of Application for Secretarial Review of Punitive Discharge Pursuant to 10 U.S.C. Sec. 874 (b), March 1980, Charles Zane, letter to Minerich, May 6, 1980, Minerich Collection.

28 Proclamation No. 4417, Federal Register Number 35, p. 7741, February 20, 1976; Irons, *Justice Delayed*, 103–4, 223; John Tateishi, "The Japanese American Citizens League and the Struggle for Redress," in *Japanese Americans: from Relocation to Redress*, ed. Roger Daniels, Sandra C. Taylor, and H. L. Kitano (Salt Lake City: University of Utah Press, 1986), 191–93.

29 Minerich, brief, 5, Minerich Collection. Minerich, interview, November 16, 2005; correspondence with author, November 12, 2005; letter to men, January 31, 1980, Sumoge files.

30 Minerich to Col. Donald W. Hansen, JAG, June 3, 1980, Hayakawa and Sumoge court-martial records; Minerich, brief, 3–5, 31–33, Minerich Collection.

31 Minerich, brief, 5–14, Minerich Collection. See Muller, *Free to Die for Their Country*.

32 Minerich, brief, 5–14, Minerich Collection.

33 Ibid., 31–33.

34 Paul Minerich, letter to Charles Zane, December 9, 1980, Minerich Collection.

35 Thomas W. Turcotte, letter to Paul Minerich, March 1, 1982; Minerich's secretary, memo, September 15, 1982, Sumoge files.

36 Army Board for Correction of Military Records, transcript 39092951/531–12–4951, December 8,1982 [hereafter Army Board 1982 transcript], 5, Sumoge files. A uniform code of military justice for all branches of the military, developed after World War II, included safeguards for individuals as well as civilian review. Frederick Bernays Wiener, *The Uniform Code of Military Justice:*

*Explanation, Comparative Text, and Commentary* (Washington, D.C.: Combat Forces Press, 1950), preface. DB boys Shigeo Hamai, Tim Nomiyama, Masuo Morita, Masao Kataoka, Kenjiro Hayakawa, and Harold Tsunehara, as well as Gary Itano (son of Henry Masami Itano), joined Minerich at the hearing.

37 Since the men's releases occurred on different dates in May and June 1946 and Hakuban Nozawa was the only one who was sure of his date, June 7 was suggested. See Army Board 1982 transcript, 12–14.

38 Minerich, brief, 8–9; Army Board 1982 transcript, 8–9, 20–22. The *Los Angeles Times* reported that the congressional commission to study wartime internment had reached a consensus on compensating survivors, Paul Minerich explained to the board. The state of California and the Los Angeles County Board of Supervisors also approved payments to Nikkei state and county employees who lost their jobs.

39 Ibid., 50, 52, 55, 63, 66, 69.

40 Ibid., 71–75, 99–100, 110, 114–17, 120–24. The Supreme Court did not rule on the constitutionality of the Endo case, although Justice William O. Douglas claimed that detaining Japanese Americans met constitutional standards. The impact of the court's ruling was to end the wartime detention of Japanese Americans, as Paul Minerich stated in his 1980 brief. Irons, *Justice at War*, 341–44.

41 Irons, *Justice Delayed*, 403; Army Board 1982 transcript, 118–19, 122–23.

42 Department of the Army, Office of the Assistant Secretary, letter to Paul Minerich, January 17, 1983, Sumoge files; Minerich, April 14, 2007, telephone interview by the author; U.S. Army Board, Proceedings, AC82–10429, 105.01, December 8, 1982, Sumoge files.

43 Department of the Army, Office of the Assistant Secretary, letter to Paul Minerich, January 17, 1983, Sumoge files; U.S. Army Board, Proceedings, AC82–10429, 105.01, December 8, 1982, 6, Sumoge files. Hayakawa and Sumoge both received back pay of less than $1,500 and mustering-out pay of $200. USAFAC Computation of Settlement Amount Due Under 10 U.S.: C. 1552, Minerich Collection.

44 Eric L. Muller, "The Japanese American Cases: A Bigger Disaster Than We Realized," *Howard Law Journal 50th Anniversary Edition: Loyalty and Criminal Justice; A Mini-Symposium* (Winter 2006): 437. Four landmark World War II cases challenged the forced removal and detention of West Coast Nikkei. First, native Hood River son Minoru Yasui challenged his conviction for violating the curfew at the Court of Appeals and the Supreme Court. In 1983, he filed a *coram nobis* petition challenging his conviction after legal scholar Peter Irons discovered that the government had suppressed evidence in the Korematsu, Hirabayashi, and Yasui cases. The U.S. District Court in Portland granted the government's motion to vacate Yasui's conviction and dismiss his

petition. Though he appealed, Yasui died before a decision was made, and his case, too, was over. Niiya, *Japanese American History*, 123–24. Second, Gordon Hirabayashi was found guilty of violating both curfew and exclusion orders. While the Supreme Court upheld his curfew conviction in 1943, his *coram nobis* case in Seattle in 1988 eventually resulted in both convictions being vacated. Niiya, *Japanese American History*, 163–65, 124. Third, Fred Korematsu unsuccessfully challenged the mass evacuation of Nikkei during World War II. In 1944, the Supreme Court upheld his conviction, which was vacated by a San Francisco district court judge in Korematsu's *coram nobis* case. Niiya, *Japanese American History*, 163–65,123. Fourth, based on Mitsuye Endo's case, in 1944 the Supreme Court unanimously ruled that the government had no authority to detain loyal citizens. That decision propelled the War Department to announce that loyal citizens would be released from the camps beginning in January 1945. Niiya, *Japanese American History*, 134–35.

There were other prominent wartime resisters. The Heart Mountain Fair Play Committee in Wyoming represented the only organized draft resisters in the camps. Sixty-three men declined to report for their physicals, and each spent three years in prison. In 1946, the seven leaders' convictions were overturned, and the following year, President Truman pardoned all draft resisters. Niiya, *Japanese American History*, 162. The so-called no-no boys were Nikkei who replied in the negative to or refused to complete two questions in the camp loyalty questionnaires. Intended to gauge their loyalty, questions 27 and 28 referred to their willingness to serve in the military and their allegiance to the United States. Many renounced their U.S. citizenship and expatriated to Japan; others chose to reinstate their citizenship. Niiya, *Japanese American History*, 270–71. Journalist James Omura spoke against mass incarceration of Nikkei at the 1942 Tolan Committee hearings and, as editor of the Japanese American newspaper *Rocky Shimpo*, defended the Fair Play Committee and Nisei draft resistance. He was tried in 1944, along with leaders of the Fair Play Committee. Arthur A. Hansen, "Peculiar Odyssey: Newsman Jimmie Omura's Removal from and Regeneration within Nikkei Society, History, and Memory," in *Nikkei in the Pacific Northwest*, ed. Fiset and Nomura, 278–307.

45 Chuman, *Bamboo People*, 254; U.S. Navy, Office of Judge Adv. Gen., *Index and Legislative History*, unpaginated.

46 *Discipline Barrack Boys*; Army Board 1982 transcript, 8–9; Chuman, *Bamboo People*, 255.

47 The eleven men's names were deleted from public records in order to protect their privacy, and Minerich declined an interview with the army press. Tom Philpott, "11 Japanese-Americans cleared in WWII Protest," *Army Times*, August 2, 1983, 114.

1  Brian Litt, "A Place to Call Home," *Gorge Guide* 24 (2006): 34.

2  Bud Collins, interview by the author, July 13, 2006, transcript; Genevieve Scholl-Erdmann (marketing director, Hood River Chamber of Commerce), e-mail to the author, January 11, 2007; Longwoods International, 2009 Longwoods Visitor Profile: Mt. Hood Columbia River Gorge Regional Visitor Profile Data, 2009, Kerry Cobb, Executive Director, Hood River County Chamber of Commerce; Linda Tamura, "Wrong Face, Wrong Name," 118; *Hood River News*, May 18, 2005; Janet Cook, "The Changing Face of Hood River," *Hood River News*, May 18, 2005; Stu Watson, "Arts, Recreation Meet at Vibrant City in Columbia Gorge, *Sunday Oregonian*, April 8, 2007.

3  Pierce, "Winds of Change," 412–15; *Hood River News*, August 26, October 18, 2006; Hood River Chamber of Commerce, *Hood River Business Directory*, April 20, 2005, 4; Linda Tamura, "Wrong Face, Wrong Name,"119; Lee Foster, January 12, 2002; Dallas Fridley, e-mail to the author, January 17, 2007; Dallas Fridley, "2005 Job Growth in Region 9," Oregon Labor Market Information System, Oregon Employment Department, http://www.Oregon.gov, April 4, 2006; Fridley, "Food Manufacturing Main Course in Columbia Gorge and Basin," Oregon Employment Department, http://www.Oregon.gov, November 28, 2005.

4  Author's calculations.

5  Davinne McKeown-Ellis, "Got Fruit?" *Gorge Guide* 24 (2006): 50–51.

6  "Persons of Spanish Language," 1990 Census, pt. 39, Oregon, Characteristics of Population, vol. 1, table 119, 33–246; 1980 Census, information provided by Ford Schmidt (Mark O. Hatfield Library, Willamette University), e-mail to the author, August 11, 2004.

7  Linda Tamura, "Wrong Face, Wrong Name," 91, 93. Membership in the Mid-Columbia JACL chapter dwindled to forty by 2005 and dissolved in 2006, seventy-five years after its formation in 1931. Cliff Nakamura, letter to *Pacific Citizen*, November 3, 2006.

8  Chuman, *Bamboo People*, 335; Tamura, Linda "Wrong Face, Wrong Name," 119. Four of the forty Sansei who intermarried wed other Asian Americans. Tamura, "Wrong Face, Wrong Name," 97, 98; Kitano, *Generations*, 129–30.

9  A Hood River resident since 1946, Jan Kurahara eventually became the county's civil defense director, then served as a municipal court judge in The Dalles, Oregon, and worked for the U.S. Army Corps of Engineers. Kurahara, *Ganbatte*, 123–229.

10  Nagata, *Legacy of Injustice*, 30.

11  Kashima, "Japanese American Internees Return," 112–13.

12  Former Hood River mayor Bill Pattison explained that because of the govern-

ment executive order, files gathered on individuals and groups of families were purged, presumably to avoid litigation.

13 "Day of Remembrance," *Hood River News*, February 14, 2007.

14 Day of Remembrance, Hood River, OR, February 18, 2007, transcription of program by the author; Nagata, *Legacy of Injustice*, 33; David K. Yoo, *Growing Up Nisei: Race, Generation, and Culture among Japanese Americans of California, 1924–49* (Urbana: University of Illinois Press, 2000), 174; Mass, "Psychological Effects,"160; CWRIC, *Personal Justice Denied*, 299.

15 Student papers by Mary C., n.d.; Sid S. and Jerry P., n.d., 1972–74; Lark S., September 25, 1973; Charlene G., September 5, 1973; Peter M., September 25, 1973; Val W., November 2, 1978, made available by Nancy Moller, Hood River, OR, author's files.

16 *Gorge Weekly*, December 17, 1993. Portland's Multnomah County Library was one of twenty libraries selected to host the Smithsonian traveling exhibition, sponsored in cooperation with the Japanese American National Museum in Los Angeles and the Oregon Nikkei Legacy Center in Portland. The exhibition also appeared in Portland, Klamath Falls, Ontario, and Salem, Oregon.

17 *Hood River News*, June 22, 1994.

18 *Gorge Weekly*, December 17, 1993.

19 Connie Nice, interview by the author, July 13, 2006, transcript.

20 From 2001 to 2002, the Hood River Post's commander, Keith Doroski, and the author discovered letters and files in the bottom of the local Legion post's file cabinet. They organized and made copies of many of those documents.

21 *Hood River News*, October 6, 2007, December 16, 2006; "Home and Garden Gorge Style," *News*, July 28, 2007.

22 *Forbes*, October 15, 2001, 56; *Oregonian*, July 15, 2005.

23 "Forum in Hood River: Varied Voices Speak," *Portland Chapter JACL Newsletter* 7:2 (March 2002): 2.

24 "Dialogue for Peace and Understanding," *Portland Chapter JACL Newsletter* 6:10 (November 2001): 1; "A Day of Terror: A Need for Tolerance," *Portland Chapter JACL Newsletter* 6:9 (October 2001): 1; "Liberty and Justice for All . . . ," *Portland Chapter JACL Newsletter* 8:4 (May 2003): 1; "JACL/Portland Chapter 2004 Annual Report: Highlights," *Portland Chapter JACL Newsletter* 9:11 (January 2005): 2; "Warrantless Spying of Americans," *Portland Chapter JACL Newsletter* 10:11 (February 2006): 1; John Kodachi, "President's Message," *Portland Chapter JACL Newsletter* 12:8 (January 2007): 1; "Day of Remembrance 2007," *Portland Chapter JACL Newsletter* 12:10 (March 2007): 1; "200% American," *Portland Chapter JACL Newsletter* 14:9 (March 2009): 1; "Strength through Coalitions," *Portland Chapter JACL Newsletter* 15:7 (February 2010): 1; "Day of Remembrance 2011," *Portland Chapter JACL Newsletter* 16:8 (March 2011): 1.

25 *Pacific Citizen*, July 18, 2003, 20.

26 Peggy Birch, "If You're Going to Teach History, You Should Get It Right," *Klamath Falls Herald and News*, April 28, 2003, reprinted in *Portland JACL Newsletter* 8:1 (June 2003): 5–7; Tom Ikeda (Densho, Japanese American Legacy Project), letter to members, July 5, 2005.

27 *Oregonian*, March 7, 2006, March 12, 2006, March 17, 2006; *Portland JACL Newsletter* (April 2006), 11.

28 *Hood River News*, February 24, 2007.

29 *Pacific Citizen*, March 19, 2004; "Geppo," *Epworth United Methodist Church Newsletter*, 108:2 (February 2007).

30 Minutes, Planning Committee, Hood River Day of Remembrance, October 4, 2006, author's files.

31 *Hood River News*, February 14, 2007; Day of Remembrance, February 18, 2007, transcript.

32 *Hood River News*, February 24, 2007.

33 Loo, "An Integrative-Sequential Treatment Model," 106–8.

34 Maija Yasui, "Learn from Past Mistakes So They Are Not Repeated," *Panorama, Hood River News*, April 19,1995, 10.

35 David Peterson del Mar, *Oregon's Promise: An Interpretive History* (Corvallis: Oregon State University Press, 2003), 281.

36 Martin, "Hood River Odyssey," 815.

## CHAPTER 16. NO "ORDINARY SOLDIERS"

1 McKeown, "Frank Hachiya," 3; Shibutani, *Derelicts of Company K*, 100; Hirabayashi, "Nisei," 124.

2 Mid-Columbia JACL, notes about family and events in Hood River, MC/JACL.

3 Gen. Mark Clark, statement to the Commission on Wartime Relocation and Internment of Civilians, Washington, D.C., July 14, 1981, 4, author's files.

4 Before serving as Oregon's state commander of the VFW, Koe Nishimoto completed one-year terms as state junior vice commander and state senior vice commander. Lil Nishimoto, telephone conversation with the author, February 18, 2002; Patrick Jordan (VFW Post 4248 and former VFW state commander, Oregon), telephone conversation with the author, March 10, 2007; Oregon Department of Veterans Affairs, *150 Years of Oregon Veterans* (Salem: Oregon Department of Veterans Affairs, 2010), 99.

5 Congressman Al Ullman, Cong. Rec., 88th Cong., 1st sess., 1963, 10667; *Oregonian*, May 5, 1980.

6 McNaughton, *Nisei Linguists*, 369, 458, 460; Military Intelligence Service Vet-

erans Club of Hawaii, *Secret Valor*, 17; Cong. Rec., 88th Cong., 1st sess., 1963, 10663.

7   McNaughton, *Nisei Linguists*, 458–60; Nakatsu, "Nisei Soldiers," 77. Harry Akune was inducted into the Military Intelligence Corps Hall of Fame in 1996. Akune, telephone interview by the author, July 3, 2004, transcript.

8   Linda Tamura, "Ironic Heroes: 'The Enemy's Our Cousin: Pacific Northwest Nisei in the United States Military Service,'" *Columbia* (Spring 2006): 19; MIS NORCAL, "Background of President Unit Citation," 5–7; *MIS-Northwest Association Newsletter*, Seattle, November 2004, 3; McNaughton, *Nisei Linguists*, 462.

9   The Medal of Honor is normally granted within three years of service, but in 1996 Congress allowed the army to review the records of 104 Asian Pacific Americans for possible upgrade. All of these men had received the Distinguished Service Cross, the second-highest military award, but there were concerns that a climate of racial prejudice during World War II had prevented their receiving the military's highest individual award. As a result, twenty Nisei, a Chinese American, and a Filipino American were upgraded to the Medal of Honor. *Pacific Citizen*, June 30, 2000.

10  Tom Yates, manager of Hood River's Fourth of July parade, and Linda Adams of the county veterans' office carried out Anita Smith's recommendation to honor local Nisei veterans.

11  *Hood River News*, June 30, 2001.

12  Jackson and Perkins rose breeders in Medford, Oregon, developed the roses; 10 percent of sales supported veterans' medical research. Office of Public Affairs, Department of Veterans Affairs, *Vanguard* 15 (May 1999): 9.

13  Jim Semlor, "Round Table," *Hood River News*, November 14, 2001; Sab Akiyama, letter to editor, *Hood River News*, December 5, 2001.

14  Beaverton City Council, Beaverton Veterans Memorial Donation Request, Bill no. 00–16, January 10, 2000. Art Iwasaki of Hillsboro, Oregon, served with the 442nd Regimental Combat Team in I Company and was injured in Carrara, Italy, where Sagie Nishioka was also wounded. Clarence E. Mershon, *Along the Sandy: Our Nikkei Neighbors* (Portland, OR: Guardian Peaks Enterprises, 2006), 171–75.

15  "We Remember . . . ," *Portland JACL Newsletter* 8 (February 2003): 11; *Portland JACL Newsletter* 8 (March 2003): 2; Janie Har, "A Memorial Day," *Oregonian*, February 15, 2003.

16  Yasui, *Yasui Family of Hood River*, 71–73; Peggy Nagae, speech, Oregon Nikkei Veterans' ceremony, Beaverton Veterans Memorial Park, Beaverton, OR, February 15, 2003.

17  Nagae, e-mail to several participants, February 25, 2003; George Katagiri, e-mail to several participants, February 25, 2003.

18 Oregon Nisei Veterans, Oregon Nikkei Legacy Center, Japanese Ancestral Society, JACL (Portland chapter), and JACL (Gresham/Troutdale chapter), letter to American Legion, Beaverton Post No. 124, March 7, 2003; Tim Rooney, e-mail to several participants, February 24, 2003; Nagae, e-mail to several participants, March 1, 2003.

19 Minoru Asai, speech to Wy'east High School students, n.d., 5, Minoru Asai family files.

20 Congressman Spark M. Matsunaga, Arlington National Cemetery, June 2, 1963, in Cong. Rec., 88th Cong., 1st sess., 1963, 10666.

21 Mam Noji, letter to Hiro Nishimura, July 12,1998, author's files.

22 Sumoge, in *Discipline Barrack Boys*.

23 Loo, "An Integrative-Sequential Treatment Model," 102; Robert S. Laufer, "The Serial Self: War Trauma, Identity, and Adult Development," in *Human Adaptation to Extreme Stress: From the Holocaust to Vietnam*, ed. John P. Wilson, Zev Harel, and Boaz Kahana (New York: Plenum Press, 1988), 45.

24 Donna K. Nagata, *Legacy of Injustice: Exploring the Cross-Generational Impact of the Japanese American Internment* (New York: Plenum Press, 1993), 100–101, 215.

25 Ibid., 213; George Akiyama, interview by the author, February 25, 2007, transcript; Joan Emerson, statement, Hood River Day of Remembrance, Hood River, OR, February 18, 2007, transcript.

26 *Hood River News*, February 28, 2007; Emerson, conversation with the author, February 21, 2007.

27 Nagata, *Legacy of Injustice*, 213; Evelyn Yoshimura, "Reparations at Last: NCRR Leaders Look to Past and Future," League of Revolutionary Struggle, Unity/Unidad, 3–4, cited in Loo, "An Integrative-Sequential Treatment Model," 108.

28 Martha Nakagawa, "'DB Boys,' an Untold WWII Story," *Pacific Citizen*, November 12–18, 1999, 1, 5.

29 Kashima, *Judgment without Trial*, 216–19; Karen L. Ishizuka, *Lost and Found: Reclaiming the Japanese American Incarceration* (Urbana: University of Illinois Press, 2006), 184, 191; Gary Y. Okihiro and Joan Myers, *Whispered Silences: Japanese Americans and World War II* (Seattle: University of Washington Press, 1996), 244.

30 CWRIC, *Personal Justice Denied*, 191.

31 Arlington National Cemetery commemoration of the twentieth anniversary of the rescinding of restrictions on military service by American citizens of Japanese ancestry, June 2, 1963; Cong. Rec., 88th Cong., 1st Sess., 1963, 10660.

32 Gen. Mark Clark, statement to the Commission on Wartime Relocation and Internment of Civilians, Washington, D.C., July 14, 1981, author's files.

33 Crost, *Honor by Fire*, 304.

34 The Congressional Gold Medal will be displayed at the Smithsonian Institution. Shaun Tandon, "US Honors Japanese Americans for Two-Front Fight," *American Foreign Press*, November 2, 2011, http://www.google.com/hosted-news/afp/article/ALeqM5gyjmibqwpS9eLZveGO3OL5be26lQ?docId=CNG.b1ecd2f45c2af3823a72fc1471df02dc.761; Jordan Steffen, *Chicago Tribune*, October 6, 2010, chicagotribune.com/news/nationworld/la-na-veterans-medal; Public Law 111–254, 111th Cong., 2nd Sess., 2010, author's files.

35 Acknowledging the deafening silence about the war years, Joan Emerson spoke of the "need to open some doors and windows to let in some light." Emerson, e-mail to several recipients, February 13, 2007. At the 2007 Day of Remembrance, Lawson Inada, Oregon's fifth poet laureate, similarly urged the crowd to "take this dark chapter of American history and bring it to light."

AFTERWORD

1 *Hood River News*, June 1, 2011.

2 Dennis Leonard, June 4, 2011; Bob Huskey, June 6, 2011.

3 This figure is likely the total of 3,000 volunteers from Hawaii and 2,355 volunteers from the mainland who formed the combined 100th Battalion and 442nd Regimental Combat Team in 1943.

4 Donations for the monument came from the Hood River County Historical Society, twenty-three members of the Nikkei community, and Idlewilde Cemetery. *Hood River News*, June 22, 2011.

5 Charles "Bud" Collins died on February 4, 2010, in Hood River.

# SELECTED BIBLIOGRAPHY

## INTERVIEWS

(Interviews conducted by the author in Hood River, Oregon, unless otherwise indicated)

*Hood River Nisei Veterans*
George Akiyama, Sab Akiyama, Sho Endow, Kenjiro Hayakawa (Los Angeles), Hit Imai, Shig Imai, Jan Kurahara, Sagie Nishioka (Salem), Mamoru Noji, Fred Sumoge (Los Angeles), Harry Takagi (phone and e-mail, Tokyo), Harry Tamura, Johnny Wakamatsu (Lindon, UT)

*Nisei Veteran Family and Community Members, Other Veterans, and Resource People*
Ruth Akiyama, Harry Akune (phone, Gardena, CA), Ada May Arens,* Bessie Asai, Marie Asai, Ed Bartlien (phone), Bonnie and Ray Calmettes, Bud Collins, Keith Doroski, Frank Emi (phone, San Gabriel, CA), Lee and Naomi Foster,* Harry Fukuhara (phone, San Jose, CA), Hugh Garrabrant (phone), Howard Getchell, Mildred Goe, Lynn Guenther, Homer Hachiya (phone, Anaheim, CA), George Hara (phone, Portland, OR), Ken Hayakawa (phone, Montebello, CA), Yoshiko Hayakawa (in-person and phone, Montebello, CA), Doris Hill, Nellie Hjaltalin, Tow Hori (Los Angeles), Bob Huskey, Ayako (Koke) Iwatsuki, Gladys Jacobson, Martha (Fusako) Kataoka (phone, Los Angeles), Ralph Kirby,* Suma Kobayashi, Athalie Lage,* Keith Lage, Dennis Leonard, Ned Marshall, Harold McIsaac, David Meriwether, Paul Minerich (phone, Santa Ana, CA), Nancy

Moller, Claude Morita (e-mail, Kyushu, Japan), Connie Nastasi, Connie Nice, Kathleen Nichols, Kathy Nishimoto, Toru Noji (interview, Portland, OR; e-mail, Parkville, MD), Tim Nomiyama (phone, Westminster, CA), Robert Nunamaker,* Clarence Olmstead, Bill Pattison, Howard and Jane Franz Rice,* Ellouise Robison (phone), Paul Sanstrum, Cedric Shimo (Los Angeles), Ed Shoemaker, Anita Smith, Floyd Stifel, Monroe Sweetland (Milwaukie, OR), Chiz Tamura (Portland, OR), George Tamura, Nancy Tamura, Eckard Toy, Gowlan and Jeannette Wells,* Dr. Stanley Wells, Lucile Bachman Wyers,* Maija Yasui

* interviewed by Joan Yasui Emerson

OTHER SOURCES

American Legion, Post No. 22. General files, 1942. Hood River, OR.

Ano, Masaharu. "Loyal Linguists: Nisei of World War II Learned Japanese in Minnesota." *Minnesota History* 45 (1977): 273–87.

Asahina, Robert. *Just Americans: How Japanese Americans Won a War at Home and Abroad.* New York: Gotham Books, 2006.

Bell, Reginald. *Public School Education of Second-Generation Japanese in California.* Stanford, CA: Stanford University Press, 1935.

Blythe, S. F., and E. R. Bradley. *A Pen Picture of Hood River and Hood River Valley.* Hood River, OR: E. R. Bradley, 1900.

Bodnar, John. *The Transplanted: A History of Immigrants in Urban America.* Bloomington: Indiana University Press, 1985.

Burkhart, David J. *It All Began with Apple Seeds: Growing Fruit in the Hood River Valley, 1880–1980.* Bend, OR: Maverick Publications, 2007.

Castelnuovo, Shirley. *Soldiers of Conscience: Japanese American Military Resisters in World War II.* Westport, CT: Praeger, 2008.

Chang, Thelma. *"I Can Never Forget": Men of the 100th/442nd.* Honolulu: Sigi Productions, 1991.

Chiasson, Lloyd. "The Japanese-American Encampment: An Editorial Analysis of 27 West Coast Newspapers." *Newspaper Research Journal* (1991): 97–105.

Chuman, Frank F. *The Bamboo People: The Law and Japanese-Americans.* Del Mar, CA: Publisher's, 1976.

Columbia Gorge Economic Development Association (CGEDA). "County Employment." The Dalles, OR: CGEDA. www.cgeda.com/wrcoempl.htm. August 2001.

———. "Statistics by Economic Sector, 1997 Population," Table 1., 1997 Economic Census. The Dalles, OR: CGEDA. www.cgeda.com/depophr.htm. August 2001.

Commercial Club. *Hood River, Oregon.* Hood River, OR: Commercial Club, 1910.

Commission on Wartime Relocation and Internment of Civilians. *Personal Justice Denied.* Washington, DC: Government Printing Office, 1982.

Conroy, Hilary, and T. Scott Miyakawa, eds. *East across the Pacific: Historical and Sociological Studies of Immigration and Assimilation.* Santa Barbara, CA: ABC-Clio Press, 1972.

Cox, Ted W. *The Toledo Incident of 1925.* Corvallis, OR: Old World Publications, 2005.

Crost, Lyn. *Honor by Fire: Japanese Americans at War in Europe and the Pacific.* Novato, CA: Presidio Press, 1994.

Crowley, Susan Garrett, ed. *Legacy: A Centennial Celebration of Hood River & the Columbia Gorge.* Hood River, OR: Hood River News, 1995.

CWRIC. *See* Commission on Wartime Relocation and Internment of Civilians.

Daniels, Roger. *Asian America: Chinese and Japanese in the United States since 1850.* Seattle: University of Washington Press, 1988.

———. *Concentration Camps North America: Japanese in the United States and Canada during World War II.* Malabar, FL: Robert E. Krieger, 1981.

———. "Incarcerating Japanese Americans." *Organization of American Historians Magazine of History* 16:3 (2002).

———. *The Politics of Prejudice.* Berkeley: University of California Press, 1962.

———. *Prisoners without Trial: Japanese Americans in World War II.* New York: Hill and Wang, 1993.

———. "Words Do Matter: A Note on Inappropriate Terminology and the Incarceration of the Japanese Americans." In *Nikkei in the Pacific Northwest: Japanese Americans and Japanese Canadians in the Twentieth Century,* edited by Louis Fiset and Gail M. Nomura. Seattle: University of Washington Press, 2005.

Daniels, Roger, Sandra C. Taylor, and H. L. Kitano. *Japanese Americans: From Relocation to Redress.* Salt Lake City: University of Utah Press, 1986.

Davey, Frank. *Report on the Japanese Situation in Oregon Investigated for Governor Ben W. Olcott.* Salem, OR: State Printing Department, 1920.

Davis, Charles. "Attorney for the Betrayed." *Oregon State Bar Bulletin* (June 1999): 15–18.

———. "Land of the Free?" *Oregon State Bar Bulletin* (July 1999): 19–24.

Davis, Charles, and Jeffrey Kovac. "Confrontation at the Locks: A Protest of Japanese Removal and Incarceration during World War II." *Oregon Historical Quarterly* 107:4 (Winter 2006): 486–509.

Ding, Loni. *The Color of Honor.* Videotape. Harriman, NY: CET Productions, 1989.

*Discipline Barrack Boys,* videotape. Paul Minerich Collection, Hirasaki National

Resource Center, Japanese American National Museum, Los Angeles. September 9, 1984.

Donovan and Associates. *City of Hood River Historic Context Statement*. City of Hood River, OR, June 1991, 31–32, History Museum of Hood River files, Hood River, OR.

Duus, Masayo Umezawa. *Unlikely Liberators: The Men of the 100th and 442nd*. Translated by Peter Duus. Honolulu: University of Hawaii Press, 1987.

Eisenberg, Ellen. "'As Truly American as Your Son': Voicing Opposition to Internment in Three West Coast Cities." *Oregon Historical Quarterly* 104:4 (Winter 2003): 542–65.

Falk, Stanley L., and Warren M. Tsuneishi. *MIS in the War against Japan*. Vienna, VA: Japanese American Veterans Association of Washington, D.C., 1995.

Fiset, Louis, and Gail M. Nomura, eds. *Nikkei in the Pacific Northwest: Japanese Americans and Japanese Canadians in the Twentieth Century*. Seattle: University of Washington Press, 2005.

Fisher, Anna Reeploeg. *Exile of a Race*. Sidney, BC: Peninsula Printing, 1965.

Fridley, Dallas. "Food Manufacturing Main Course in Columbia Gorge and Basin." Oregon Labor Market Information System. Oregon Employment Department. http://www.oregon.gov. November 28, 2005.

———. "2005 Job Growth in Region 9." Oregon Labor Market Information System. Oregon Employment Department. http://www.Oregon.gov. April 4, 2006.

Fugita, Stephen S., and Marilyn Fernandez. *Altered Lives, Enduring Community: Japanese Americans Remember Their World War II Incarceration*. Seattle: University of Washington Press, 2004.

Fukei, Budd. *The Japanese American Story*. Minneapolis, MN: Dillon Press, 1976.

Garrett, Laurie. *The Coming Plague: Newly Emerging Diseases in a World Out of Balance*. New York: Farrar, Straus & Giroux, 1994.

Girdner, Audrie, and Anne Loftis. *The Great Betrayal: The Evacuation of the Japanese-Americans during World War II*. London: Macmillan Company, 1969.

Grodzins, Morton. *Americans Betrayed: Politics and the Japanese Evacuation*. Chicago: University of Chicago Press, 1949.

Hansen, Arthur A. "Resettlement: A Neglected Link in Japanese America's Narrative Chain." In *Regenerations Oral History Project: Rebuilding Japanese American Families, Communities, and Civil Rights in the Resettlement Era*. Vol. 1, *Chicago Region*. Los Angeles: Japanese American National Museum, 2000.

Hansen, Arthur A., and Betty E. Mitson, eds. *Voices Long Silent: An Oral Inquiry into the Japanese American Evacuation.* Fullerton: Japanese American Project, California State University, 1974.

Harrington, Joseph D. *Yankee Samurai.* Detroit: Pettigrew Enterprises, 1979.

Higashi, Roy. *Japanese-Americans of the Mid-Columbia Area and Their Relatives.* Hood River, OR: Higashi Printing Company, 1994.

Hillinger, Charles. "Secret Weapon: Japanese-American Soldiers Saved Time and Lives in World War II." In *John Aiso and the M.I.S.,* by Tad Ichinokuchi, 176–78. Los Angeles: The Military Intelligence Service, 1988.

Hirabayashi, James. "'Concentration Camp' or 'Relocation Center': What's in a Name?" *Japanese American National Museum Quarterly* 9:3 (October 1994): 5–10.

———. "Nisei: The Quiet American? A Re-evaluation." *Amerasia Journal* 3:1 (1975): 114–29.

Honda, Harry K. "The MIS Story." *Pacific Citizen* 117, November 1993.

Hood River County Historical Society. *History of Hood River County: 1852–1982.* Vol. 1. Dallas, TX: Taylor Publishing, 1982.

———. *History of Hood River County: 1852–1987.* Vol. 2. Dallas, TX: Taylor Publishing, 1987.

Hosokawa, Bill. *Nisei: The Quiet Americans.* New York: William Morrow, 1969.

Ichihashi, Yamato. *Japanese in the United States.* Stanford, CA: Stanford University Press, 1932.

Ichinokuchi, Tad. *John Aiso and the M.I.S.: Japanese-American Soldiers in the Military Intelligence Service, World War II.* Los Angeles: The Military Intelligence Service Club of Southern California, 1988.

Ichioka, Yuji. "Amerika Nadeshiko: Japanese Immigrant Women in the United States, 1900- 1924." *Pacific Historical Review* 49 (May 1980): 339–57.

———. *The Issei: The World of the First Generation Japanese Immigrants, 1885–1924.* New York: Free Press, 1988.

Inada, Lawson Fusao, Akemi Kikumura, and Mary Worthington, eds. *In This Great Land of Freedom: The Japanese Pioneers of Oregon.* Los Angeles: Japanese American National Museum, 1993.

Inukai, H. *Tule Lake Directory and Camp News.* Hood River, OR: Inukai Publishing, 1988.

Irons, Peter. *Justice at War: The Story of the Japanese American Internment Cases.* New York: Oxford University Press, 1983.

———, ed. *Justice Delayed: The Record of the Japanese American Internment Cases.* Middletown, CT: Wesleyan University Press, 1989.

Ishizuka, Karen L. *Lost and Found: Reclaiming the Japanese American Incarceration.* Urbana: University of Illinois Press, 2006.

Ito, Kazuo. *Issei: A History of Japanese Immigrants in North America.* Translated by Shinichiro Nakamura and Jean S. Gerard. Seattle: Executive Committee for Publication of *Issei*, 1973.

Japanese American Citizens League, National Education Committee. *A Lesson in American History: The Japanese American Experience.* Curriculum and Resource Guide. San Francisco: JACL, 1996.

Japanese American Veterans Association. "American Courage Award Presented to WWII Army Military Intelligence Service, Akaka and Shinseki Praise MIS." *MIS Northwest Association Newsletter,* November 2004, 2–3

Johnson, Daniel P. "Anti-Japanese Legislation in Oregon, 1917–1923." *Oregon Historical Quarterly* 97:2 (Summer 1996): 176–210.

Kashima, Tetsuden. "Japanese American Internees Return, 1945 to 1955: Readjustment and Social Amnesia." *Phylon* 16 (Summer 1980): 107–15.

———. *Judgment without Trial: Japanese American Imprisonment during World War II.* Seattle: University of Washington Press, 2001.

Kessler, Lauren. *Stubborn Twig.* New York: Random House, 1993.

Kitano, Harry H. L. *Generations and Identity: The Japanese American.* Needham Heights, MA: Ginn Press, 1993.

———. *Japanese Americans: The Evolution of a Subculture.* Englewood Cliffs, NJ: Prentice- Hall, 1976.

Kitano, Harry H. L., and Roger Daniels. *Asian Americans: Emerging Minorities.* Englewood Cliffs, NJ: Prentice-Hall, 1998.

Kitasako, John. "Methodist Minister Led Fight for Freedom in Hood River." *Pacific Citizen,* May 3, 1947, 1.

Krussow, J. Patricia, ed. *Aakki-Daakki to Zoomorphic: An Encyclopedia about Hood River County.* Hood River, OR: Friends of the Hood River Library, 1994.

Kurahara, Jan Y. *Ganbatte: A Nisei's Story.* Hood River, OR: AuthorHouse, 1999.

LaFeber, Walter. *The Clash: A History of U.S.-Japan Relations.* New York: W. W. Norton, 1997.

Leighton, Alexander H. *The Governing of Men: General Principles and Recommendations Based on Experience at a Japanese Relocation Camp.* Princeton, NJ: Princeton University Press, 1945.

Linehan, Thomas M. "Japanese American Resettlement in Cleveland during and after World War II. *Journal of Urban History* 20 (November 1993): 54–80.

Litt, Brian. "A Place to Call Home." *Gorge Guide* 24, no. 34 (2006): 34.

Loftus, Mitzi Asai. *Made in Japan and Settled in Oregon.* Coos Bay, OR: Pigeon Point Press, 1990.

Loo, Chalsa M. "An Integrative-Sequential Treatment Model for Posttraumatic Stress Disorder: A Case Study of the Japanese American Internment and Redress." *Clinical Psychology Review* 13 (1993): 89–117.

Marick, Sharon. "Looking Ahead." *Ruralite* 26:10 (October 1979): 16–17.

Martin, Ralph G. "Hood River Odyssey." *New Republic* 115 (December 16, 1946): 814–15.

———. "Legion Post Arouses Ire of 7th's GIs." *Stars and Stripes*, January 5, 1945, 2.

McCloy, John J., Collection. Record Group 107, Entry 180, National Archives and Records Administration, College Park, MD.

McKay, Floyd J. "Civil Liberties Suspended: Pacific Northwest Editors and the Nikkei." Paper presented at the Conference on the History of the Nikkei in the Pacific Northwest, University of Washington, Seattle, May 5–7, 2000.

———. *An Editor for Oregon: Charles A. Sprague and the Politics of Change.* Corvallis: Oregon State University Press, 1998.

McKeown, Martha Ferguson. "Frank Hachiya: He Was an American at Birth— and at Death." *Sunday Oregonian*, May 20, 1945, 3.

McKeown-Ellis, Davinne. "Got Fruit?" *Gorge Guide* 24 (2006): 50–51.

McNaughton, James C. *Nisei Linguists: Japanese Americans in the Military Intelligence Service during World War II.* Washington, DC: Department of the Army, 2006.

Members of the 442nd Combat Team. *The Story of the 442nd Combat Team.* Information- Education Section, Mediterranean Theater of Operations, United States Army. Reprinted by Company K Club, San Francisco, 1979.

Merrill, Zed. "America's Secret WWII Weapon." *Northwest Senior Life* (Portland/Vancouver edition) 2:10 (August 2002): 30, 35.

Mershon, Clarence E. *Along the Sandy: Our Nikkei Neighbors.* Portland, OR: Guardian Peaks Enterprises, 2006.

Michie, Charles A. "Three Plague Spots within a Democracy." *PM*, February 25, 1945, 11.

Mid-Columbia Japanese American Citizens League. "Japanese-Americans in Hood River." Hood River, OR: MC/JACL, Marie Asai files, n.d.

———. "Mid-Columbia Japanese-American Citizens League." Notebook. Hood River, OR: MC/JACL, Marie Asai files, n.d.

Military Intelligence School Language Service. *MISLS Album, 1946.* Nashville, TN: Battery Press, 1990.

Military Intelligence Service Association of Northern California. "Background of the Presidential Unit Citation for MIS." Walnut Creek, CA, 2004.

Military Intelligence Service Association of Northern California and the National Japanese American Historical Society. *The Pacific War and Peace: Americans of Japanese Ancestry in Military Intelligence Service, 1941 to 1952.* San Francisco: Military Intelligence Service Association of Northern California and the National Japanese American Historical Society, 1991.

Military Intelligence Service Northwest Association. "The Unprecedented Story of the Military Intelligence Service." Commemorating the 50th anniversary of the end of World War II. September 7–9, 1995.

Military Intelligence Service Veterans Club of Hawaii. *Secret Valor: M.I.S. Personnel, World War II Pacific Theater*. 50th Anniversary Reunion, July 8–10. Honolulu: Military Intelligence Service Veterans Club of Hawaii, 1993.

Minerich, Paul, Collection. Hirasaki National Resource Center, Japanese American National Museum, Los Angeles, CA.

MIS Historical Committee. *MIS Veterans: The Nisei Intelligence War against Japan*. Honolulu: MIS Historical Committee, n.d.

MISA of Northern California and the NJAHC. *See* Military Intelligence Service Association of Northern California and the National Japanese American Historical Society.

Miyakawa, Edward. *Tule Lake*. Waldport, OR: House by the Sea Publishing, 1979.

Miyamoto, S. Frank. "Problems of Interpersonal Style among the Nisei." *Amerasia Journal* 13:2 (1986–87): 29–45.

Moore, Arline Winchell. "The Happy Ending: Return to Hood River." *Pacific Citizen*, December 22, 1951, 26, 31.

———. "Hood River Redeems Itself." *Asia and the Americas* 6 (July 1946): 316–17.

Morison, Samuel Eliot. *The Oxford History of the American People*. Vol. 3, *1869 through the Death of John F. Kennedy*. Cambridge: Oxford University Press, 1972.

Muller, Eric L. *Free to Die for Their Country: The Story of the Japanese American Draft Resisters*. Chicago: University of Chicago Press, 2001.

———. "The Japanese American Cases: A Bigger Disaster Than We Realized." *Howard Law Journal 50th Anniversary Edition: Loyalty and Criminal Justice* (Winter 2006): 417–74.

Murphy, Thomas D. *Ambassadors in Arms*. Honolulu: University of Hawaii Press, 1954.

Myer, Dillon S. *Uprooted Americans: The Japanese Americans and the War Relocation Authority during World War II*. Tucson: University of Arizona Press, 1971.

Nagata, Donna K. "The Japanese American Internment: Exploring the Transgenerational Consequences of Traumatic Stress." *Journal of Traumatic Stress* 3:1 (1990): 47–69.

———. *Legacy of Injustice: Exploring the Cross-Generational Impact of the Japanese American Internment*. New York: Plenum Press, 1993.

Nakagawa, Martha. "'DB Boys,' an Untold WWII Story." *Pacific Citizen*, November 12–18, 1999, 1, 5.

Nakano, Mei. *Japanese American Women: Three Generations, 1890–1990.* Berkeley, CA: Mina Press Publishing and National Japanese American Historical Society, 1990.

Nakatsu, Don. "The Nisei Soldiers of U.S. Military Intelligence: America's Superb Secret Weapon of World War II." In *John Aiso and the M.I.S.,* by Tad Ichinokuchi, 176–78. Los Angeles: The Military Intelligence Service, 1988.

Neuberger, Richard L. "All Quiet on Hood River as Japs Return to Valley." *Sunday Oregonian,* June 16, 1946, 28.

———. "Hood River's Fighting Minister: No Reward for Valor." *Pacific Citizen,* October 18, 1947, 1, 5. Reprinted from the *Progressive,* Madison, WI.

———. "The Nisei Come Back to Hood River." *Reader's Digest* 49 (November 1946): 102–4.

———. "Their Brothers' Keepers." *Saturday Review of Literature* 29 (August 10, 1946): 5–6, 27–28.

Ng, Wendy Lee. "Collective Memory, Social Networks, and Generations: The Japanese American Community in Hood River, Oregon." Ph.D. diss., University of Oregon, August 1989.

Niiya, Brian. *Japanese American History: An A-to-Z Reference from 1868 to the Present.* Los Angeles: Japanese American National Museum, 1993.

Noji, Mamoru. "This I Remember." Manuscript, December 1994.

Norton, Mary Beth, David M. Katzman, Paul D. Escott, Howard P. Chudacoff, Thomas G. Paterson, and William M. Tuttle, Jr. *A People and a Nation: A History of the United States.* Vol. 2, *Since 1865.* Boston: Houghton Mifflin, 1998.

O'Brien, David J., and Stephen S. Fugita. "Generational Differences in Japanese Americans' Perceptions and Feelings about Social Relationships between Themselves and Caucasian Americans." In *Culture, Ethnicity, and Identity: Current Issues in Research,* edited by William C. McCready, 223–40. New York: Academic Press, 1983.

Odo, Franklin. "In the Nation's Wartime Service: The Japanese American Story." *JANM Quarterly* 10:3 (Winter 1995): 15–26.

———. *No Sword to Bury: Japanese Americans in Hawai'i during World War II.* Philadelphia: Temple University Press, 2004.

O'Donnell, Patrick K. *Into the Rising Sun.* New York: Simon & Schuster, 2002.

Oguro, Richard B. *Sen Pai Gumi.* Honolulu: Hochi Press, 1980.

Okihiro, Gary Y., and Joan Myers. *Whispered Silences: Japanese Americans and World War II.* Seattle: University of Washington Press, 1996.

Olmstead, Timothy. "Nikkei Internment: The Perspective of Two Oregon Weekly Newspapers." *Oregon Historical Quarterly* 85 (Spring 1984): 5–32.

Oregon, State of. *Report on the Japanese Situation in Oregon.* Salem: State Printing Department, 1920.

Oregon American Legion Department Headquarters. *Oregon Legionnaire* 27 (February 1945).

Oregon Bureau of Labor. *Census: Japanese Population in Oregon.* Salem: State Printing Department, 1929.

Oregon Department of Veterans Affairs. *150 Years of Oregon Veterans.* Salem: Oregon Department of Veterans Affairs, 2010.

Oregon State Archives. *Life on the Home Front: Oregon Responds to World War II.* Exhibit. http://arcweb.sos.state.or.us/exhibits/ww2/index.htm. May 2007.

Peterson del Mar, David. *Oregon's Promise: An Interpretive History.* Corvallis: Oregon State University Press, 2003.

Philpott, Tom. "11 Japanese-Americans cleared in WWII Protest." *Army Times,* August 2, 1983.

Pierce, Jason. "The Winds of Change: The Decline of Extractive Industries and the Rise of Tourism in Hood River County, Oregon." *Oregon Historical Quarterly* 108 (Fall 2007): 410–31.

Pursinger, Marvin Gavin. "Oregon's Japanese in World War II: A History of Compulsory Relocation." Ph.D. diss., University of Southern California, 1962.

Rhodes, Robert. "Prisoners of Conscience: Closing Fort Leavenworth." *Mennonite Weekly Review,* December 6, 2002, 6–10.

Robinson, Greg. *By Order of the President: FDR and the Internment of Japanese Americans.* Cambridge, MA: Harvard University Press, 2001.

Santayana, George. *The Life of Reason or the Phases of Human Progress.* New York: Charles Scribner's Sons, 1906.

Saul, Eric. "Something about Japanese Americans and Their Values." Speech at Nakamura/Okubo Medal of Honor Commemorative Program, Seattle, March 25, 2001.

Shibutani, Tamotsu. *The Derelicts of Company K: A Sociological Study of Demoralization.* Berkeley: University of California Press, 1978.

Shimo, Cedric. "Military Experience in Different Forms: The 1800th Engineering General Service Battalion." Speech at Life Interrupted Conference: The Japanese American Experience in World War II. Little Rock, Arkansas, September 25, 2004.

Spickard, Paul R. *Japanese Americans: The Formation and Transformations of an Ethnic Group.* New York: Twayne, 1996.

Sprague, Charles. Manuscript Collection. Oregon Historical Society, Portland.
———. Records. Oregon State Archives, Salem.

Stearns, Marjorie R. "The History of the Japanese People in Oregon." Master's thesis, University of Oregon, 1937.

Stevens, Beatrice. "Free and Equal? The Japanese-Americans in Oregon." Prepared for the Workshop on Intercultural Education, Portland, summer 1945. Oregon Historical Society, Portland.

Tamura, Eileen. *Americanization, Acculturation, and Ethnic Identity: The Nisei Generation in Hawaii*. Urbana: University of Illinois Press, 1994.

Tamura, Linda. "Grandma Noji." Unpublished family book. 1984.

———. *The Hood River Issei: An Oral History of Japanese Settlers in Oregon's Hood River Valley*. Urbana: University of Illinois Press, 1993.

———. "Ironic Heroes: 'The Enemy's Our Cousin: Pacific Northwest Nisei in the United States Military Service.'" *Columbia* (Spring 2006): 12–19.

———. "The Making of an American: A Woman Ahead of Her Time." *Oregon Historical Quarterly* 103:4 (Winter 2002): 510–29.

———. "Wrong Face, Wrong Name: The Return of Japanese American Veterans to Hood River, Oregon, after World War II." In *Remapping Asian American History*, edited by Sucheng Chan. Walnut Creek, CA: AltaMira Press, 2003.

Tanaka, Chester. *Go for Broke: A Pictorial History of the Japanese American 100th Infantry Battalion and the 442d Regimental Combat Team*. Richmond, CA: Go for Broke, 1982.

Tateishi, John. *And Justice for All: An Oral History of the Japanese American Detention Camps*. New York: Random House, 1984.

———. "The Japanese American Citizens League and the Struggle for Redress." In *Japanese Americans: from Relocation to Redress*, edited by Roger Daniels, Sandra C. Taylor, and H. L. Kitano. Salt Lake City: University of Utah Press, 1986.

Tateishi, John, and William Yoshino. "The Japanese American Incarceration: The Journey to Redress." *Human Rights Magazine* (Spring 2000).

tenBroek, Jacobus, Edward N. Barnhart, and Floyd W. Matson. *Prejudice, War and the Constitution*. Berkeley: University of California Press, 1954.

Thomas, Dorothy Swaine. *The Salvage: Japanese American Evacuation and Resettlement*. Berkeley: University of California Press, 1952.

Thomas, Dorothy Swaine, and Richard S. Nishimoto. *The Spoilage: Japanese American Evacuation*. Berkeley: University of California Press, 1946.

Tsukiyama, Ted. "Deciphering the Z Plan." In *Secret Valor*, by Military Intelligence Service Veterans Club of Hawaii, 55–57. Honolulu: Military Intelligence Service Veterans Club of Hawaii, 1993.

Turner, Wallace. "Bitter Memories of World War II Detention." *New York Times Daily Magazine*, August 10, 1981, 18.

Uchida, Yoshiko. *The Invisible Thread*. New York: Julian Messner, 1991.

U.S. Bureau of the Census. "The Asian and Pacific Islander Population in the United States: March 2002." May 2003.

———. "Census 2000 Redistricting Data (Public Law 94–171) Summary File, Matrices PL1 and PL2." March 2004.

———. Thirteenth, Fourteenth, Fifteenth, Sixteenth, Seventeenth, Eighteenth Census of the United States. Washington, DC: Government Printing Office, 1910–60.

U.S. Department of the Army, Board for Correction of Military Records. Case of Shigeo Hamai et al. Transcript. Case no. 39092951/531–12–4951, December 8, 1982, Washington, DC.

———. Center of Military History. "Named CampaignsWorld War II: Asiatic-Pacific Theater." http://www.army.mil/cmh.

———. Defense Commands. World War II. Record Group 499. National Archives and Records Administration, College Park, MD.

———. Judiciary. Kenjiro Hayakawa and Fred Sumoge general court-martial records. Arlington, VA.

U.S. Department of the Interior. The Evacuated People: A Qualitative Description. Washington, DC: Government Printing Office, 1946.

———. People in Motion: The Postwar Adjustment of the Evacuated Japanese-Americans. Washington, DC: Government Printing Office, 1947.

U.S. Department of the Navy, Office of the Judge Advocate General. Index and Legislative History: Uniform Code of Military Justice. Buffalo, NY: William S. Hein and Co., 2000.

U.S. Department of Veterans Affairs, National Center for Veterans Analysis and Statistics, http://www.va.gov/vetdata/Veteran_Population.asp, The Veteran Population Model, from VetPop2007, Table 2D: Deaths by State, Period, Age Group, Gender, 2000–2036; 2L: Veterans by State, Period, Age Group, Gender, 2000–2036. June 30, 2011.

U.S. Department of Veterans Affairs, Office of the Actuary. "Projected World War II Veterans and World War II Veteran Deaths." VetPop2007, Table 2L. May 2011.

U.S. Department of Veterans Affairs, Office of Public Affairs. Vanguard 15 (May 1999): 9.

U.S. War Relocation Authority. "Prejudice in Hood River Valley: A Case Study in Race Relations." Community Analysis Report no. 13, June 6. Washington, DC: Government Printing Office, 1945.

Uyeda, Clifford, and Barry Saiki. The Pacific War and Peace: Americans of Japanese Ancestry in Military Intelligence Service, 1941 to 1952. San Francisco: Military Intelligence Service Association of Northern California and the National Japanese American Historical Society, 1991.

Weglyn, Michi. Years of Infamy: The Untold Story of America's Concentration Camps. New York: Morrow Quill, 1976.

Wiener, Frederick Bernays. The Uniform Code of Military Justice: Explanation, Comparative Text, and Commentary. Washington, DC: Combat Forces Press, 1950.

Wilson, John P., Zev Harel, and Boaz Kahana, eds. *Human Adaptation to Extreme Stress: From the Holocaust to Vietnam.* New York: Plenum Press, 1988.

Wilson, Robert A., and Bill Hosokawa. *East to America.* New York: William Morrow, 1980.

Winthrop, William. *Military Law and Precedents.* 2d ed. Reprint. Boston: Little, Brown, and Company, 1920.

Worden, William L. "The Hate That Failed." *Saturday Evening Post,* May 4, 1946, 22–23, 137–38.

Yasui, Maija. "Learn from Past Mistakes So They Are Not Repeated." *Hood River News Panorama,* April 19, 1995, 10.

Yasui, Robert S. *The Yasui Family of Hood River, Oregon.* Hood River, OR: Holly Yasui, Desktop Publishing, 1987.

Yoo, David K. *Growing Up Nisei: Race, Generation, and Culture among Japanese Americans of California, 1924-49.* Urbana: University of Illinois Press, 2000.

Yoshida, Yosaburo. "Sources and Causes of Japanese Emigration." *The Annals of the American Academy of Political and Social Science* 34 (September 1909): 377–87.

Yoshimura, Evelyn. "Reparations at Last: NCRR Leaders Look to Past and Future." League of Revolutionary Struggle, Unity/Unidad, October 15, 1990, 3–4.

Zane, David. *Oh! Downtrodden.* Roslyn Heights, NY: Libra Publishers, 1976.

# INDEX